Real-Time Optimization

Special Issue Editor
Dominique Bonvin

MDPI • Basel • Beijing • Wuhan • Barcelona • Belgrade

Special Issue Editor
Dominique Bonvin
Ecole Polytechnique Fédérale de Lausanne
Switzerland

Editorial Office
MDPI AG
St. Alban-Anlage 66
Basel, Switzerland

This edition is a reprint of the Special Issue published online in the open access journal *Processes* (ISSN 2227-9717) from 2016–2017 (available at: http://www.mdpi.com/journal/processes/special_issues/real_time_optimization).

For citation purposes, cite each article independently as indicated on the article page online and as indicated below:

Author 1; Author 2. Article title. *Journal Name* **Year**, *Article number*, page range.

First Edition 2017

ISBN 978-3-03842-448-2 (Pbk)
ISBN 978-3-03842-449-9 (PDF)

Photo courtesy of Prof. Dr. Dominique Bonvin

Table of Contents

About the Special Issue Editor

Dominique Bonvin, Ph.D., is Director of the Automatic Control Laboratory of EPFL in Lausanne, Switzerland. He received his Diploma in Chemical Engineering from ETH Zürich and his Ph.D. degree from the University of California, Santa Barbara. He served as Dean of Bachelor and Master studies at EPFL between 2004 and 2011. His research interests include modeling, identification and optimization of dynamical systems.

Preface to "Real-Time Optimization"

Process optimization is the method of choice for improving the performance of industrial processes, while enforcing the satisfaction of safety and quality constraints. Long considered as an appealing tool but only applicable to academic problems, optimization has now become a viable technology. Still, one of the strengths of optimization, namely, its inherent mathematical rigor, can also be perceived as a weakness, since engineers might sometimes find it difficult to obtain an appropriate mathematical formulation to solve their practical problems. Furthermore, even when process models are available, the presence of plant-model mismatch and process disturbances makes the direct use of model-based optimal inputs hazardous.

In the last 30 years, the field of real-time optimization (RTO) has emerged to help overcome the aforementioned modeling difficulties. RTO integrates process measurements into the optimization framework. This way, process optimization does not rely exclusively on a (possibly inaccurate) process model but also on process information stemming from measurements. Various RTO techniques are available in the literature and can be classified in two broad families depending on whether a process model is used (explicit optimization) or not (implicit optimization or self-optimizing control).

This Special Issue on Real-Time Optimization includes both methodological and practical contributions. All seven methodological contributions deal with explicit RTO schemes that repeat the optimization when new measurements become available. The methods covered include modifier adaptation, economic MPC and the two-step approach of parameter identification and numerical optimization. The six contributions that deal with applications cover various fields including refineries, well networks, combustion and membrane filtration.

This Special Issue has shown that RTO is a very active area of research with excellent opportunities for applications. The Guest Editor would like to thank all authors for their timely collaboration with this project and excellent scientific contributions.

Dominique Bonvin
Special Issue Editor

Review

Modifier Adaptation for Real-Time Optimization—Methods and Applications

Alejandro G. Marchetti [1,4], **Grégory François** [2], **Timm Faulwasser** [1,3] and **Dominique Bonvin** [1,*]

1   Laboratoire d'Automatique, Ecole Polytechnique Fédérale de Lausanne, CH-1015 Lausanne, Switzerland;
    alejandro.marchetti@epfl.ch (A.G.M.); timm.faulwasser@epfl.ch (T.F.)
2   Institute for Materials and Processes, School of Engineering, The University of Edinburgh,
    Edinburgh EH9 3BE, UK; gregory.francois@ed.ac.uk
3   Institute for Applied Computer Science, Karlsruhe Institute of Technology,
    76344 Eggenstein-Leopoldshafen, Germany; timm.faulwasser@kit.edu
4   French-Argentine International Center for Information and Systems Sciences (CIFASIS),
    CONICET-Universidad Nacional de Rosario (UNR), S2000EZP Rosario, Argentina;
    marchetti@cifasis-conicet.gov.ar
*   Correspondence: dominique.bonvin@epfl.ch; Tel.: +41-21-693-3843

Academic Editor: Michael Henson
Received: 22 November 2016; Accepted: 12 December 2016; Published: 20 December 2016

Abstract: This paper presents an overview of the recent developments of modifier-adaptation schemes for real-time optimization of uncertain processes. These schemes have the ability to reach plant optimality upon convergence despite the presence of structural plant-model mismatch. Modifier Adaptation has its origins in the technique of Integrated System Optimization and Parameter Estimation, but differs in the definition of the modifiers and in the fact that no parameter estimation is required. This paper reviews the fundamentals of Modifier Adaptation and provides an overview of several variants and extensions. Furthermore, the paper discusses different methods for estimating the required gradients (or modifiers) from noisy measurements. We also give an overview of the application studies available in the literature. Finally, the paper briefly discusses open issues so as to promote future research in this area.

Keywords: real-time optimization; modifier adaptation; plant-model mismatch

---

1. Introduction

This article presents a comprehensive overview of the modifier-adaptation strategy for real-time optimization. Real-time optimization (RTO) encompasses a family of optimization methods that incorporate process measurements in the optimization framework to drive a real process (or plant) to optimal performance, while guaranteeing constraint satisfaction. The typical sequence of steps for process optimization includes (i) process modeling; (ii) numerical optimization using the process model; and (iii) application of the model-based optimal inputs to the plant. In practice, this last step is quite hazardous—in the absence of additional safeguards—as the model-based inputs are indeed optimal for the model, but not for the plant unless the model is a perfect representation of the plant. This often results in suboptimal plant operation and in constraint violation, for instance when optimal operation implies operating close to a constraint and the model under- or overestimates the value of that particular constraint.

RTO has emerged over the past forty years to overcome the difficulties associated with plant-model mismatch. Uncertainty can have three main sources, namely, (i) parametric uncertainty when the values of the model parameters do not correspond to the reality of the process at hand; (ii) structural plant-model mismatch when the structure of the model is not perfect, for example in the case of unknown phenomena or neglected dynamics; and (iii) process disturbances. Of course these three sources are not mutually exclusive.

RTO incorporates process measurements in the optimization framework to combat the detrimental effect of uncertainty. RTO methods can be classified depending on how the available measurements are used. There are basically three possibilities, namely, at the level of the process model, at the level of the cost and constraint functions, and at the level of the inputs [1].

1. The most intuitive strategy is to use process measurements to improve the model. This is the main idea behind the "two-step" approach [2–5]. Here, deviations between predicted and measured outputs are used to update the model parameters, and new inputs are computed on the basis of the updated model. The whole procedure is repeated until convergence is reached, whereby it is hoped that the computed model-based optimal inputs will be optimal for the plant. The requirements for this to happen are referred to as the *model-adequacy conditions* [6]. Unfortunately, the model-adequacy conditions are difficult to both achieve and verify.

2. This difficulty of converging to the plant optimum motivated the development of a modified two-step approach, referred to as Integrated System Optimization and Parameter Estimation (ISOPE) [7–10]. ISOPE requires both output measurements and estimates of the gradients of the plant outputs with respect to the inputs. These gradients allow computing the plant cost gradient that is used to modify the cost function of the optimization problem. The use of gradients is justified by the nature of the necessary conditions of optimality (NCO) that include both constraints and sensitivity conditions [11]. By incorporating estimates of the plant gradients in the model, the goal is to enforce NCO matching between the model and the plant, thereby making the modified model a likely candidate to solve the plant optimization problem. With ISOPE, process measurements are incorporated at two levels, namely, the model parameters are updated on the basis of output measurements, and the cost function is modified by the addition of an input-affine term that is based on estimated plant gradients.

    Note that RTO can rely on a *fixed* process model if measurement-based adaptation of the cost *and* constraint functions is implemented. For instance, this is the philosophy of Constraint Adaptation (CA), wherein the measured plant constraints are used to shift the predicted constraints in the model-based optimization problem, without any modification of the model parameters [12,13]. This is also the main idea in Modifier Adaptation (MA) that uses measurements of the plant constraints and estimates of plant gradients to modify the cost and constraint functions in the model-based optimization problem without updating the model parameters [14,15]. Input-affine corrections allow matching the first-order NCO upon convergence. The advantage of MA, which is the focus of this article, lies in its proven ability to converge to the plant optimum despite structural plant-model mismatch.

3. Finally, the third way of incorporating process measurements in the optimization framework consists in directly updating the inputs in a control-inspired manner. There are various ways of doing this. With Extremum-Seeking Control (ESC), dither signals are added to the inputs such that an estimate of the plant cost gradient is obtained online using output measurements [16]. In the unconstrained case, gradient control is directly applied to drive the plant cost gradient to zero. Similarly, NCO tracking uses output measurements to estimate the plant NCO, which are then enforced via dedicated control algorithms [17,18]. Furthermore, Neighboring-Extremal Control (NEC) combines a variational analysis of the model at hand with output measurements to enforce the plant NCO [19]. Finally, Self-Optimizing Control (SOC) uses the sensitivity between the uncertain model parameters and the measured outputs to generate linear combinations of the outputs that are locally insensitive to the model parameters, and which can thus be kept constant at their nominal values to reject the effect of uncertainty [20].

The choice of a specific RTO method will depend on the situation at hand. However, it is highly desirable for RTO approaches to have certain properties such as (i) guaranteed plant optimality upon convergence; (ii) fast convergence; and (iii) feasible-side convergence. MA satisfies the first requirement since the model-adequacy conditions for MA are much easier to satisfy than those of the two-step approach. These conditions are enforced quite easily if convex model approximations are used instead of the model at hand as shown in [21]. The rate of convergence and feasible-side convergence are also critical requirements, which however are highly case dependent. Note that these two requirements often oppose each other since fast convergence calls for large steps, while feasible-side convergence often requires small and cautious steps. It is the intrinsic capability of MA to converge to the plant optimum despite structural plant-model mismatch that makes it a very valuable tool for optimizing the operation of chemical processes in the absence of accurate models.

This overview article is structured as follows. Section 2 formulates the static real-time optimization problem. Section 3 briefly revisits ISOPE, while Section 4 discusses MA, its properties and several MA variants. Implementation aspects are investigated in Section 5, while Section 6 provides an overview of MA case studies. Finally, Section 7 concludes the paper with a discussion of open issues.

2. Problem Formulation

2.1. Steady-State Optimization Problem

The optimization of process operation consists in minimizing operating costs, or maximizing economic profit, in the presence of constraints. Mathematically, this problem can be formulated as follows:

$$\mathbf{u}_p^{\star} = \arg\min_{\mathbf{u}} \quad \Phi_p(\mathbf{u}) := \phi(\mathbf{u}, \mathbf{y}_p(\mathbf{u})) \tag{1}$$

$$\text{s.t.} \quad G_{p,i}(\mathbf{u}) := g_i(\mathbf{u}, \mathbf{y}_p(\mathbf{u})) \leq 0, \quad i = 1, \ldots, n_g,$$

where $\mathbf{u} \in \mathbf{R}^{n_u}$ denotes the decision (or input) variables; $\mathbf{y}_p \in \mathbf{R}^{n_y}$ are the measured output variables; $\phi : \mathbf{R}^{n_u} \times \mathbf{R}^{n_y} \to \mathbf{R}$ is the cost function to be minimized; and $g_i : \mathbf{R}^{n_u} \times \mathbf{R}^{n_y} \to \mathbf{R}, i = 1, \ldots, n_g$, is the set of inequality constraints on the input and output variables.

This formulation assumes that ϕ and g_i are known functions of $\mathbf{u}$ and $\mathbf{y}_p$, i.e., they can be directly evaluated from the knowledge of $\mathbf{u}$ and the measurement of $\mathbf{y}_p$. However, in any practical application, the steady-state input-output mapping of the plant $\mathbf{y}_p(\mathbf{u})$ is typically unknown, and only an approximate nonlinear steady-state model is available:

$$\mathbf{F}(\mathbf{x}, \mathbf{u}) = \mathbf{0}, \tag{2a}$$

$$\mathbf{y} = \mathbf{H}(\mathbf{x}, \mathbf{u}), \tag{2b}$$

where $\mathbf{x} \in \mathbf{R}^{n_x}$ are the state variables and $\mathbf{y} \in \mathbf{R}^{n_y}$ the output variables predicted by the model. For given $\mathbf{u}$, the solution to (2a) can be written as

$$\mathbf{x} = \boldsymbol{\xi}(\mathbf{u}), \tag{3}$$

where $\boldsymbol{\xi}$ is an operator expressing the steady-state mapping between $\mathbf{u}$ and $\mathbf{x}$. The input-output mapping predicted by the model can be expressed as

$$\mathbf{y}(\mathbf{u}) := \mathbf{H}(\boldsymbol{\xi}(\mathbf{u}), \mathbf{u}). \tag{4}$$

Using this notation, the model-based optimization problem becomes

3

$$\mathbf{u}^\star = \arg\min_{\mathbf{u}} \Phi(\mathbf{u}) := \phi(\mathbf{u}, \mathbf{y}(\mathbf{u})) \tag{5}$$

$$\text{s.t.} \quad G_i(\mathbf{u}) := g_i(\mathbf{u}, \mathbf{y}(\mathbf{u})) \leq 0, \quad i = 1, \ldots, n_g.$$

However, in the presence of plant-model mismatch, the model solution $\mathbf{u}^\star$ does not generally coincide with the plant optimum $\mathbf{u}_p^\star$.

2.2. Necessary Conditions of Optimality

Local minima of Problem (5) can be characterized via the NCO [11]. To this end, let us denote the set of active constraints at some point $\mathbf{u}$ by

$$\mathcal{A}(\mathbf{u}) = \left\{ i \in \{1, \ldots, n_g\} \mid G_i(\mathbf{u}) = 0 \right\}. \tag{6}$$

The Linear Independence Constraint Qualification (LICQ) requires that the gradients of the active constraints, $\frac{\partial G_i}{\partial \mathbf{u}}(\mathbf{u})$ for $i \in \mathcal{A}(\mathbf{u})$, be linearly independent. Provided that a constraint qualification such as LICQ holds at the solution $\mathbf{u}^\star$ and the functions Φ and G_i are differentiable at $\mathbf{u}^\star$, there exist unique Lagrange multipliers $\boldsymbol{\mu}^\star \in \mathbb{R}^{n_g}$ such that the following Karush-Kuhn-Tucker (KKT) conditions hold at $\mathbf{u}^\star$ [11]

$$\mathbf{G} \leq \mathbf{0}, \quad \boldsymbol{\mu}^\mathsf{T}\mathbf{G} = 0, \quad \boldsymbol{\mu} \geq \mathbf{0}, \tag{7}$$

$$\frac{\partial \mathcal{L}}{\partial \mathbf{u}} = \frac{\partial \Phi}{\partial \mathbf{u}} + \boldsymbol{\mu}^\mathsf{T}\frac{\partial \mathbf{G}}{\partial \mathbf{u}} = \mathbf{0},$$

where $\mathbf{G} \in \mathbb{R}^{n_g}$ is the vector of constraint functions G_i, and $\mathcal{L}(\mathbf{u}, \boldsymbol{\mu}) := \Phi(\mathbf{u}) + \boldsymbol{\mu}^\mathsf{T}\mathbf{G}(\mathbf{u})$ is the Lagrangian function. A solution $\mathbf{u}^\star$ satisfying these conditions is called a KKT point.

The vector of active constraints at $\mathbf{u}^\star$ is denoted by $\mathbf{G}^a(\mathbf{u}^\star) \in \mathbb{R}^{n_g^a}$, where n_g^a is the cardinality of $\mathcal{A}(\mathbf{u}^\star)$. Assuming that LICQ holds at $\mathbf{u}^\star$, one can write:

$$\frac{\partial \mathbf{G}^a}{\partial \mathbf{u}}(\mathbf{u}^\star)\mathbf{Z} = \mathbf{0},$$

where $\mathbf{Z} \in \mathbb{R}^{n_u \times (n_u - n_g^a)}$ is a null-space matrix. The reduced Hessian of the Lagrangian on this null space, $\nabla_r^2 \mathcal{L}(\mathbf{u}^\star) \in \mathbb{R}^{(n_u - n_g^a) \times (n_u - n_g^a)}$, is given by [22]

$$\nabla_r^2 \mathcal{L}(\mathbf{u}^\star) := \mathbf{Z}^\mathsf{T} \left[\frac{\partial^2 \mathcal{L}}{\partial \mathbf{u}^2}(\mathbf{u}^\star, \boldsymbol{\mu}^\star) \right] \mathbf{Z}.$$

In addition to the first-order KKT conditions, a second-order necessary condition for a local minimum is the requirement that $\nabla_r^2 \mathcal{L}(\mathbf{u}^\star)$ be positive semi-definite at $\mathbf{u}^\star$. On the other hand, $\nabla_r^2 \mathcal{L}(\mathbf{u}^\star)$ being positive definite is sufficient for a strict local minimum [22].

3. ISOPE: Two Decades of New Ideas

In response to the inability of the classical two-step approach to enforce plant optimality, a modified two-step approach was proposed by Roberts [8] in 1979. The approach became known under the acronym ISOPE, which stands for Integrated System Optimization and Parameter Estimation [9,10]. Since then, several extensions and variants of ISOPE have been proposed, with the bulk of the research taking place between 1980 and 2002. ISOPE algorithms combine the use of a parameter estimation problem and the definition of a modified optimization problem in such a way that, upon convergence, the KKT conditions of the plant are enforced. The key idea in ISOPE is to incorporate plant gradient information into a gradient correction term that is added to the cost function. Throughout the ISOPE literature, an important distinction is made between optimization problems that include process-dependent constraints of the form $\mathbf{g}(\mathbf{u}, \mathbf{y}) \leq \mathbf{0}$ and problems that do not include them [7,9]. Process-dependent constraints depend on the outputs $\mathbf{y}$, and not only on the inputs $\mathbf{u}$. In this section, we briefly describe the ISOPE formulations that we consider to be most relevant for contextualizing the MA schemes that will be presented in Section 4. Since ISOPE includes a parameter estimation problem, the steady-state outputs predicted by the model will be written in this section as $\mathbf{y}(\mathbf{u}, \boldsymbol{\theta})$ in order to emphasize their dependency on the (adjustable) model parameters $\boldsymbol{\theta} \in \mathbb{R}^{n_\theta}$.

3.1. ISOPE Algorithm

The original ISOPE algorithm does not consider process-dependent constraints in the optimization problem, but only input bounds. At the kth RTO iteration, with the inputs $\mathbf{u}_k$ and the plant outputs $\mathbf{y}_p(\mathbf{u}_k)$, a parameter estimation problem is solved, yielding the updated parameter values $\boldsymbol{\theta}_k$. This problem is solved under the output-matching condition

$$\mathbf{y}(\mathbf{u}_k, \boldsymbol{\theta}_k) = \mathbf{y}_p(\mathbf{u}_k). \tag{8}$$

Then, assuming that the output plant gradient $\frac{\partial \mathbf{y}_p}{\partial \mathbf{u}}(\mathbf{u}_k)$ is available, the ISOPE modifier $\lambda_k \in \mathbb{R}^{n_u}$ for the gradient of the cost function is calculated as

$$\lambda_k^\mathsf{T} = \frac{\partial \phi}{\partial \mathbf{y}}(\mathbf{u}_k, \mathbf{y}(\mathbf{u}_k, \boldsymbol{\theta}_k)) \left[\frac{\partial \mathbf{y}_p}{\partial \mathbf{u}}(\mathbf{u}_k) - \frac{\partial \mathbf{y}}{\partial \mathbf{u}}(\mathbf{u}_k, \boldsymbol{\theta}_k) \right]. \tag{9}$$

Based on the parameter estimates $\boldsymbol{\theta}_k$ and the updated modifier λ_k, the next optimal RTO inputs are computed by solving the following *modified* optimization problem:

$$\mathbf{u}_{k+1}^\star = \arg\min_{\mathbf{u}} \ \phi(\mathbf{u}, \mathbf{y}(\mathbf{u}, \boldsymbol{\theta}_k)) + \lambda_k^\mathsf{T} \mathbf{u} \tag{10}$$
$$\text{s.t.} \quad \mathbf{u}^\mathrm{L} \leq \mathbf{u} \leq \mathbf{u}^\mathrm{U}.$$

The new operating point is determined by filtering the inputs using a first-order exponential filter:

$$\mathbf{u}_{k+1} = \mathbf{u}_k + \mathsf{K}(\mathbf{u}_{k+1}^\star - \mathbf{u}_k). \tag{11}$$

The output-matching condition (8) is required in order for the gradient of the modified cost function to match the plant gradient at $\mathbf{u}_k$. This condition represents a model-qualification condition that is present throughout the ISOPE literature [7,10,23,24].

3.2. Dealing with Process-Dependent Constraints

In order to deal with process-dependent constraints, Brdyś et al. [25] proposed to use a modifier for the gradient of the Lagrangian function. The parameter estimation problem is solved under the output-matching condition (8) and the updated parameters are used in the following modified optimization problem:

$$\mathbf{u}_{k+1}^\star = \arg\min_{\mathbf{u}} \ \phi(\mathbf{u}, \mathbf{y}(\mathbf{u}, \boldsymbol{\theta}_k)) + \lambda_k^\mathsf{T} \mathbf{u} \tag{12}$$
$$\text{s.t.} \quad g_i(\mathbf{u}, \mathbf{y}(\mathbf{u}, \boldsymbol{\theta}_k)) \leq 0, \quad i = 1, \dots, n_g,$$

where the gradient modifier is computed as follows:

$$\lambda_k^{\mathsf{T}} = \left[\frac{\partial \phi}{\partial \mathbf{y}}\left(\mathbf{u}_k, \mathbf{y}(\mathbf{u}_k, \boldsymbol{\theta}_k)\right) + \mu_k^{\mathsf{T}}\frac{\partial \mathbf{g}}{\partial \mathbf{y}}\left(\mathbf{u}_k, \mathbf{y}(\mathbf{u}_k, \boldsymbol{\theta}_k)\right)\right]\left[\frac{\partial \mathbf{y}_p}{\partial \mathbf{u}}(\mathbf{u}_k) - \frac{\partial \mathbf{y}}{\partial \mathbf{u}}(\mathbf{u}_k, \boldsymbol{\theta}_k)\right]. \tag{13}$$

The next inputs applied to the plant are obtained by applying the first-order filter (11), and the next values of the Lagrange multipliers to be used in (13) are adjusted as

$$\mu_{i,k+1} = \max\{0, \ \mu_{i,k} + b_i(\mu_{i,k+1}^\star - \mu_{i,k})\}, \quad i = 1, \ldots, n_g, \tag{14}$$

where $\mu_{k+1}^\star$ are the optimal values of the Lagrange multipliers of Problem (12) [7]. This particular ISOPE scheme is guaranteed to reach a KKT point of the plant upon convergence, and the process-dependent constraints are guaranteed to be respected upon convergence. However, the constraints might be violated during the RTO iterations leading to convergence, which calls for the inclusion of conservative constraint backoffs [7].

3.3. ISOPE with Model Shift

Later on, Tatjewski [26] argued that the output-matching condition (8) can be satisfied without the need to adjust the model parameters $\boldsymbol{\theta}$. This can be done by adding the bias correction term $\mathbf{a}_k$ to the outputs predicted by the model,

$$\mathbf{a}_k := \mathbf{y}_p(\mathbf{u}_k) - \mathbf{y}(\mathbf{u}_k, \boldsymbol{\theta}). \tag{15}$$

This way, the ISOPE Problem (10) becomes:

$$\mathbf{u}_{k+1}^\star \in \arg\min_{\mathbf{u}} \phi(\mathbf{u}, \mathbf{y}(\mathbf{u}, \boldsymbol{\theta}) + \mathbf{a}_k) + \lambda_k^{\mathsf{T}}\mathbf{u} \tag{16}$$

$$\text{s.t.} \quad \mathbf{u}^L \le \mathbf{u} \le \mathbf{u}^U,$$

with

$$\lambda_k^{\mathsf{T}} := \frac{\partial \phi}{\partial \mathbf{y}}(\mathbf{u}_k, \mathbf{y}(\mathbf{u}_k, \boldsymbol{\theta}) + \mathbf{a}_k)\left[\frac{\partial \mathbf{y}_p}{\partial \mathbf{u}}(\mathbf{u}_k) - \frac{\partial \mathbf{y}}{\partial \mathbf{u}}(\mathbf{u}_k, \boldsymbol{\theta})\right]. \tag{17}$$

This approach can also be applied to the ISOPE scheme (12) and (13) and to all ISOPE algorithms that require meeting Condition (8). As noted in [26], the name ISOPE is no longer adequate since, in this variant, there is no need for estimating the model parameters. The name *Modifier Adaptation* becomes more appropriate. As will be seen in the next section, MA schemes re-interpret the role of the modifiers and the way they are defined.

4. Modifier Adaptation: Enforcing Plant Optimality

The idea behind MA is to introduce correction terms for the cost and constraint functions such that, upon convergence, the modified model-based optimization problem matches the plant NCO. In contrast to two-step RTO schemes such as the classical two-step approach and ISOPE, MA schemes do not rely on estimating the parameters of a first-principles model by solving a parameter estimation problem. Instead, the correction terms introduce a new parameterization that is specially tailored to matching the plant NCO. This parameterization consists of modifiers that are updated based on measurements collected at the successive RTO iterates.

4.1. Basic MA Scheme

4.1.1. Modification of Cost and Constraint Functions

In basic MA, first-order correction terms are added to the cost and constraint functions of the optimization problem [14,15]. At the kth iteration with the inputs $\mathbf{u}_k$, the modified cost and constraint functions are constructed as follows:

$$\Phi_{m,k}(\mathbf{u}) := \Phi(\mathbf{u}) + \varepsilon_k^{\Phi} + (\lambda_k^{\Phi})^{\mathsf{T}}(\mathbf{u} - \mathbf{u}_k) \tag{18}$$

$$G_{m,i,k}(\mathbf{u}) := G_i(\mathbf{u}) + \varepsilon_k^{G_i} + (\lambda_k^{G_i})^{\mathsf{T}}(\mathbf{u} - \mathbf{u}_k) \leq 0, \quad i = 1, \dots, n_g, \tag{19}$$

with the modifiers $\varepsilon_k^{\Phi} \in \mathbb{R}$, $\varepsilon_k^{G_i} \in \mathbb{R}$, $\lambda_k^{\Phi} \in \mathbb{R}^{n_u}$, and $\lambda_k^{G_i} \in \mathbb{R}^{n_u}$ given by

$$\varepsilon_k^{\Phi} = \Phi_p(\mathbf{u}_k) - \Phi(\mathbf{u}_k), \tag{20a}$$

$$\varepsilon_k^{G_i} = G_{p,i}(\mathbf{u}_k) - G_i(\mathbf{u}_k), \quad i = 1, \dots, n_g, \tag{20b}$$

$$(\lambda_k^{\Phi})^{\mathsf{T}} = \frac{\partial \Phi_p}{\partial \mathbf{u}}(\mathbf{u}_k) - \frac{\partial \Phi}{\partial \mathbf{u}}(\mathbf{u}_k), \tag{20c}$$

$$(\lambda_k^{G_i})^{\mathsf{T}} = \frac{\partial G_{p,i}}{\partial \mathbf{u}}(\mathbf{u}_k) - \frac{\partial G_i}{\partial \mathbf{u}}(\mathbf{u}_k), \quad i = 1, \dots, n_g. \tag{20d}$$

The zeroth-order modifiers ε_k^{Φ} and $\varepsilon_k^{G_i}$ correspond to bias terms representing the differences between the plant values and the predicted values at $\mathbf{u}_k$, whereas the first-order modifiers λ_k^{Φ} and $\lambda_k^{G_i}$ represent the differences between the plant gradients and the gradients predicted by the model at $\mathbf{u}_k$. The plant gradients $\frac{\partial \Phi_p}{\partial \mathbf{u}}(\mathbf{u}_k)$ and $\frac{\partial G_{p,i}}{\partial \mathbf{u}}(\mathbf{u}_k)$ are assumed to be available at $\mathbf{u}_k$. A graphical interpretation of the first-order correction for the constraint G_i is depicted in Figure 1. Note that, if the cost and/or constraints are perfectly known functions of the inputs $\mathbf{u}$, then the corresponding modifiers are equal to zero, and no model correction is necessary. For example, the upper and lower bounds on the input variables are constraints that are perfectly known, and thus do not require modification.

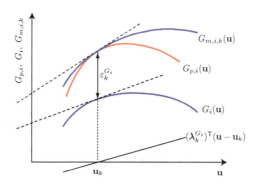

Figure 1. First-order modification of the constraint G_i at $\mathbf{u}_k$.

At the kth RTO iteration, the next optimal inputs $\mathbf{u}_{k+1}^{\star}$ are computed by solving the following *modified* optimization problem:

$$\mathbf{u}_{k+1}^{\star} = \arg\min_{\mathbf{u}} \Phi_{m,k}(\mathbf{u}) := \Phi(\mathbf{u}) + (\lambda_k^{\Phi})^{\mathsf{T}}\mathbf{u} \tag{21a}$$

$$\text{s.t.} \quad G_{m,i,k}(\mathbf{u}) := G_i(\mathbf{u}) + \varepsilon_k^{G_i} + (\lambda_k^{G_i})^{\mathsf{T}}(\mathbf{u} - \mathbf{u}_k) \leq 0, \quad i = 1, \dots, n_g. \tag{21b}$$

Note that the addition of the constant term $\varepsilon_k^\Phi - (\lambda_k^\Phi)^\mathsf{T} \mathbf{u}_k$ to the cost function does not affect the solution $\mathbf{u}_{k+1}^\star$. Hence, the cost modification is often defined by including only the linear term in $\mathbf{u}$, that is, $\Phi_{m,k}(\mathbf{u}) := \Phi(\mathbf{u}) + (\lambda_k^\Phi)^\mathsf{T} \mathbf{u}$.

The optimal inputs can then be applied directly to the plant:

$$\mathbf{u}_{k+1} = \mathbf{u}_{k+1}^\star. \tag{22}$$

However, such an adaptation strategy may result in excessive correction and, in addition, be sensitive to process noise. Both phenomena can compromise the convergence of the algorithm. Hence, one usually relies on first-order filters that are applied to either the modifiers or the inputs. In the former case, one updates the modifiers using the following first-order filter equations [15]:

$$\varepsilon_k^G = (\mathbf{I}_{n_g} - \mathbf{K}^\varepsilon)\varepsilon_{k-1}^G + \mathbf{K}^\varepsilon \left(\mathbf{G}_p(\mathbf{u}_k) - \mathbf{G}(\mathbf{u}_k) \right), \tag{23a}$$

$$\lambda_k^\Phi = (\mathbf{I}_{n_u} - \mathbf{K}^\Phi)\lambda_{k-1}^\Phi + \mathbf{K}^\Phi \left(\frac{\partial \Phi_p}{\partial \mathbf{u}}(\mathbf{u}_k) - \frac{\partial \Phi}{\partial \mathbf{u}}(\mathbf{u}_k) \right)^\mathsf{T}, \tag{23b}$$

$$\lambda_k^{G_i} = (\mathbf{I}_{n_u} - \mathbf{K}^{G_i})\lambda_{k-1}^{G_i} + \mathbf{K}^{G_i} \left(\frac{\partial G_{p,i}}{\partial \mathbf{u}}(\mathbf{u}_k) - \frac{\partial G_i}{\partial \mathbf{u}}(\mathbf{u}_k) \right)^\mathsf{T}, \quad i = 1, \dots, n_g, \tag{23c}$$

where the filter matrices $\mathbf{K}^\varepsilon$, $\mathbf{K}^\Phi$, and $\mathbf{K}^{G_i}$ are typically selected as diagonal matrices with eigenvalues in the interval $(0, 1]$. In the latter case, one filters the optimal RTO inputs $\mathbf{u}_{k+1}^\star$ with $\mathbf{K} = \mathrm{diag}(k_1, \dots, k_{n_u})$, $k_i \in (0, 1]$:

$$\mathbf{u}_{k+1} = \mathbf{u}_k + \mathbf{K}(\mathbf{u}_{k+1}^\star - \mathbf{u}_k). \tag{24}$$

4.1.2. KKT Matching Upon Convergence

The appeal of MA lies in its ability to reach a KKT point of the plant upon convergence, as made explicit in the following theorem.

Theorem 1 (MA convergence $\Rightarrow$ KKT matching [15]). *Consider MA with filters on either the modifiers or the inputs. Let $\mathbf{u}_\infty = \lim_{k \to \infty} \mathbf{u}_k$ be a fixed point of the iterative scheme and a KKT point of the modified optimization Problem (21). Then, $\mathbf{u}_\infty$ is also a KKT point of the plant Problem (1).*

4.1.3. Model Adequacy

The question of whether a model is adequate for use in an RTO scheme was addressed by Forbes and Marlin [27], who proposed the following model-adequacy criterion.

Definition 1 (Model-adequacy criterion [27]). *A process model is said to be adequate for use in an RTO scheme if it is capable of producing a fixed point that is a local minimum for the RTO problem at the plant optimum $\mathbf{u}_p^\star$.*

In other words, $\mathbf{u}_p^\star$ must be a local minimum when the RTO algorithm is applied at $\mathbf{u}_p^\star$. The plant optimum $\mathbf{u}_p^\star$ satisfies the first- and second-order NCO of the plant optimization Problem (1). The adequacy criterion requires that $\mathbf{u}_p^\star$ must also satisfy the first- and second-order NCO for the modified optimization Problem (21), with the modifiers (20) evaluated at $\mathbf{u}_p^\star$. As MA matches the first-order KKT elements of the plant, only the second-order NCO remain to be satisfied. That is, the reduced Hessian of the Lagrangian must be positive semi-definite at $\mathbf{u}_p^\star$. The following proposition characterizes model adequacy based on second-order conditions. Again, it applies to MA with filters on either the modifiers or the inputs.

Proposition 1 (Model-adequacy conditions for MA [15]). *Let $\mathbf{u}_p^\star$ be a regular point for the constraints and the unique plant optimum. Let $\nabla_r^2 \mathcal{L}(\mathbf{u}_p^\star)$ denote the reduced Hessian of the Lagrangian of Problem (21) at $\mathbf{u}_p^\star$. Then, the following statements hold:*

   i *If $\nabla_r^2 \mathcal{L}(\mathbf{u}_p^\star)$ is positive definite, then the process model is adequate for use in the MA scheme.*
   ii *If $\nabla_r^2 \mathcal{L}(\mathbf{u}_p^\star)$ is not positive semi-definite, then the process model is inadequate for use in the MA scheme.*
   iii *If $\nabla_r^2 \mathcal{L}(\mathbf{u}_p^\star)$ is positive semi-definite and singular, then the second-order conditions are not conclusive with respect to model adequacy.*

Example 1 (Model adequacy). *Consider the problem $\min_u \Phi_p(u) = u_1^2 + u_2^2$, for which $\mathbf{u}_p^\star = [0, \ 0]^\mathsf{T}$. The models $\Phi_1(\mathbf{u}) = u_1^2 + u_2^4$ and $\Phi_2(\mathbf{u}) = u_1^2 - u_2^4$ both have their gradients equal to zero at $\mathbf{u}_p^\star$, and their Hessian matrices both have eigenvalues $\{2, 0\}$ at $\mathbf{u}_p^\star$, that is, they are both positive semi-definite and singular. However, Φ_1 is adequate since $\mathbf{u}_p^\star$ is a minimizer of Φ_1, while Φ_2 is inadequate since $\mathbf{u}_p^\star$ is a saddle point of Φ_2.*

4.1.4. Similarity with ISOPE

The key feature of MA schemes is that updating the parameters of a first-principles model is not required to match the plant NCO upon convergence. In addition, compared to ISOPE, the gradient modifiers have been redefined. The cost gradient modifier (20c) can be expressed in terms of the gradients of the output variables as follows:

$$
\begin{aligned}
(\lambda_k^\Phi)^\mathsf{T} &= \frac{\partial \Phi_p}{\partial \mathbf{u}}(\mathbf{u}_k) - \frac{\partial \Phi}{\partial \mathbf{u}}(\mathbf{u}_k), \\
&= \frac{\partial \phi}{\partial \mathbf{u}}(\mathbf{u}_k, \mathbf{y}_p(\mathbf{u}_k)) + \frac{\partial \phi}{\partial \mathbf{y}}(\mathbf{u}_k, \mathbf{y}_p(\mathbf{u}_k)) \frac{\partial \mathbf{y}_p}{\partial \mathbf{u}}(\mathbf{u}_k) \\
&\quad - \frac{\partial \phi}{\partial \mathbf{u}}(\mathbf{u}_k, \mathbf{y}(\mathbf{u}_k, \theta)) - \frac{\partial \phi}{\partial \mathbf{y}}(\mathbf{u}_k, \mathbf{y}(\mathbf{u}_k, \theta)) \frac{\partial \mathbf{y}}{\partial \mathbf{u}}(\mathbf{u}_k, \theta).
\end{aligned} \tag{25}
$$

Notice that, if Condition (8) is satisfied, the gradient modifier λ_k^Φ in (25) reduces to the ISOPE modifier (9). In fact, Condition (8) is required in ISOPE in order for the gradient modifier (9) to represent the difference between the plant and model gradients. Put differently, output matching is a prerequisite for the gradient of the modified cost function to match the plant gradient. This requirement can be removed by directly defining the gradient modifiers as the differences between the plant and model gradients, as given in (25).

4.2. Alternative Modifications

4.2.1. Modification of Output Variables

Instead of modifying the cost and constraint functions as in (18) and (19) , it is also possible to place the first-order correction terms directly on the output variables [15]. At the operating point $\mathbf{u}_k$, the modified outputs read:

$$
\mathbf{y}_{m,k}(\mathbf{u}) := \mathbf{y}(\mathbf{u}) + \varepsilon_k^{\mathbf{y}} + (\lambda_k^{\mathbf{y}})^\mathsf{T}(\mathbf{u} - \mathbf{u}_k), \tag{26}
$$

with the modifiers $\varepsilon_k^{\mathbf{y}} \in \mathbb{R}^{n_y}$ and $\lambda_k^{\mathbf{y}} \in \mathbb{R}^{n_u \times n_y}$ given by:

$$
\varepsilon_k^{\mathbf{y}} = \mathbf{y}_p(\mathbf{u}_k) - \mathbf{y}(\mathbf{u}_k), \tag{27a}
$$

$$
(\lambda_k^{\mathbf{y}})^\mathsf{T} = \frac{\partial \mathbf{y}_p}{\partial \mathbf{u}}(\mathbf{u}_k) - \frac{\partial \mathbf{y}}{\partial \mathbf{u}}(\mathbf{u}_k). \tag{27b}
$$

In this MA variant, the next RTO inputs are computed by solving

$$\mathbf{u}_{k+1}^{\star} = \arg\min_{\mathbf{u}} \phi(\mathbf{u}, \mathbf{y}_{m,k}(\mathbf{u})) \tag{28}$$

$$\text{s.t.} \quad \mathbf{y}_{m,k}(\mathbf{u}) = \mathbf{y}(\mathbf{u}) + \varepsilon_k^{\mathbf{y}} + (\lambda_k^{\mathbf{y}})^{\mathsf{T}}(\mathbf{u} - \mathbf{u}_k)$$

$$g_i(\mathbf{u}, \mathbf{y}_{m,k}(\mathbf{u})) \leq 0, \quad i = 1, \ldots, n_g.$$

Interestingly, the output bias $\varepsilon_k^{\mathbf{y}}$ is the same as the model shift term (15) introduced by Tatjewski [26] in the context of ISOPE. The MA scheme (28) also reaches a KKT point of the plant upon convergence and, again, one can choose to place a filter on either the modifiers or the inputs [15].

4.2.2. Modification of Lagrangian Gradients

Section 3.2 introduced the algorithmic approach used in ISOPE for dealing with process-dependent constraints, which consists in correcting the gradient of the Lagrangian function. An equivalent approach can be implemented in the context of MA by defining the modified optimization problem as follows:

$$\mathbf{u}_{k+1}^{\star} = \arg\min_{\mathbf{u}} \Phi_{m,k}(\mathbf{u}) := \Phi(\mathbf{u}) + (\lambda_k^{\mathcal{L}})^{\mathsf{T}}\mathbf{u} \tag{29a}$$

$$\text{s.t.} \quad G_{m,i,k}(\mathbf{u}) := G_i(\mathbf{u}) + \varepsilon_k^{G_i} \leq 0, \quad i = 1, \ldots, n_g, \tag{29b}$$

where $\varepsilon_k^{G_i}$ are the zeroth-order constraint modifiers, and the Lagrangian gradient modifier $\lambda_k^{\mathcal{L}}$ represents the difference between the Lagrangian gradients of the plant and the model,

$$(\lambda_k^{\mathcal{L}})^{\mathsf{T}} = \frac{\partial \mathcal{L}_p}{\partial \mathbf{u}}(\mathbf{u}_k, \mu_k) - \frac{\partial \mathcal{L}}{\partial \mathbf{u}}(\mathbf{u}_k, \mu_k). \tag{30}$$

This approach has the advantage of requiring a single gradient modifier $\lambda_k^{\mathcal{L}}$, but the disadvantage that the modified cost and constraint functions do not provide first-order approximations to the plant cost and constraint functions at each RTO iteration. This increased plant-model mismatch may result in slower convergence to the plant optimum and larger constraint violations prior to convergence.

4.2.3. Directional MA

MA schemes require the plant gradients to be estimated at each RTO iteration. Gradient estimation is experimentally expensive and represents the main bottleneck for MA implementation (see Section 5 for an overview of gradient estimation methods). The number of experiments required to estimate the plant gradients increases linearly with the number of inputs, which tends to make MA intractable for processes with many inputs. Directional Modifier Adaptation (D-MA) overcomes this limitation by estimating the gradients only in $n_r < n_u$ privileged input directions [28,29]. This way, convergence can be accelerated since fewer experiments are required for gradient estimation at each RTO iteration. D-MA defines a $(n_u \times n_r)$-dimensional matrix of privileged directions, $\mathbf{U}_r = [\delta\mathbf{u}_1 \ldots \delta\mathbf{u}_r]$, the columns of which contain the n_r privileged directions in the input space. Note that these directions are typically selected as orthonormal vectors that span a linear subspace of dimension n_r.

At the operating point $\mathbf{u}_k$, the directional derivatives of the plant cost and constraints that need to be estimated are defined as follows:

$$\nabla_{\mathbf{U}_r} j_p := \left.\frac{\partial j_p(\mathbf{u}_k + \mathbf{U}_r\mathbf{r})}{\partial \mathbf{r}}\right|_{\mathbf{r}=0}, \quad j_p \in \{\Phi_p, G_{p,1}, G_{p,2}, \ldots, G_{p,n_g}\}, \tag{31}$$

where $\mathbf{r} \in \mathbf{R}^{n_r}$. Approximations of the full plant gradients are given by

$$\widehat{\nabla\Phi}_k = \frac{\partial\Phi}{\partial\mathbf{u}}(\mathbf{u}_k)(\mathbf{I}_{n_u} - \mathbf{U_r U_r^+}) + \nabla_{\mathbf{U_r}}\Phi_p\mathbf{U_r^+}, \tag{32}$$

$$\widehat{\nabla G}_{i,k} = \frac{\partial G_i}{\partial\mathbf{u}}(\mathbf{u}_k)(\mathbf{I}_{n_u} - \mathbf{U_r U_r^+}) + \nabla_{\mathbf{U_r}}G_{p,i}\mathbf{U_r^+}, \quad i = 1,\ldots,n_g, \tag{33}$$

where the superscript $(\cdot)^+$ denotes the Moore-Penrose pseudo-inverse, and $\mathbf{I}_{n_u}$ is the n_u-dimensional identity matrix. In D-MA, the gradients of the plant cost and constraints used in (20c) and (20d) are replaced by the estimates (32) and (33). Hence, the gradients of the modified cost and constraint functions match the estimated gradients at $\mathbf{u}_k$, that is, $\frac{\partial\Phi_m}{\partial\mathbf{u}}(\mathbf{u}_k) = \widehat{\nabla\Phi}_k$ and $\frac{\partial G_{m,i}}{\partial\mathbf{u}}(\mathbf{u}_k) = \widehat{\nabla G}_{i,k}$.

Figure 2 illustrates the fact that the gradient of the modified cost function $\frac{\partial\Phi_m}{\partial\mathbf{u}}(\mathbf{u}_k)$ and the plant cost gradient $\frac{\partial\Phi_p}{\partial\mathbf{u}}(\mathbf{u}_k)$ share the same projected gradient in the privileged direction $\delta\mathbf{u}$, while $\frac{\partial\Phi_m}{\partial\mathbf{u}}(\mathbf{u}_k)$ matches the projection of the model gradient $\frac{\partial\Phi}{\partial\mathbf{u}}(\mathbf{u}_k)$ in the direction orthogonal to $\delta\mathbf{u}$.

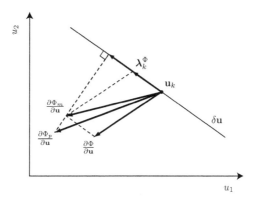

Figure 2. Matching the projected gradient of the plant using D-MA.

In general, D-MA does not converge to a KKT point of the plant. However, upon convergence, D-MA reaches a point for which the cost function cannot be improved in any of the privileged directions. This is formally stated in the following theorem.

Theorem 2 (Plant optimality in privileged directions [29]). *Consider D-MA with the gradient estimates (32) and (33) in the absence of measurement noise and with perfect estimates of the directional derivatives (31). Let $\mathbf{u}_\infty = \lim_{k\to\infty}\mathbf{u}_k$ be a fixed point of that scheme and a KKT point of the modified optimization Problem (21). Then, $\mathbf{u}_\infty$ is optimal for the plant in the n_r privileged directions.*

The major advantage of D-MA is that, if the selected number of privileged directions is much lower than the number of inputs, the task of gradient estimation is greatly simplified. An important issue is the selection of the privileged directions.

Remark 1 (Choice of privileged directions). *Costello et al. [29] addressed the selection of privileged input directions for the case of parametric plant-model mismatch. They proposed to perform a sensitivity analysis of the gradient of the Lagrangian function with respect to the uncertain model parameters $\boldsymbol{\theta}$. The underlying idea is that, if the likely parameter variations affect the Lagrangian gradient significantly only in a few input directions, it will be sufficient to estimate the plant gradients in these directions. The matrix of privileged directions $\mathbf{U_r}$ is obtained by performing singular value decomposition of the normalized (by means of the expected largest variations of the uncertain model parameters $\boldsymbol{\theta}$) sensitivity matrix $\frac{\delta\mathcal{L}^2}{\delta\mathbf{u}\delta\boldsymbol{\theta}}$ evaluated for the optimal inputs corresponding to the nominal parameter values. Only the directions in which the gradient of the Lagrangian is significantly* *affected by parameter variations are retained. Other choices of* $\mathbf{U}_r$ *are currently under research. For example, it is proposed in [30] to adapt* $\mathbf{U}_r$ *at each RTO iteration and considering large parametric perturbations.*

D-MA is particularly well suited for the run-to-run optimization of repetitive dynamical systems, for which a piecewise-polynomial parameterization of the input profiles typically results in a large number of RTO inputs, thus making the estimation of full gradients prohibitive. For instance, Costello et al. [29] applied D-MA very successfully to a flying power-generating kite.

4.2.4. Second-Order MA

Faulwasser and Bonvin [31] proposed the use of second-order modifiers in the context of MA. The use of second-order correction terms allows assessing whether the scheme has converged to a point satisfying the plant second-order optimality conditions. Note that, already in 1989, Golden and Ydstie [32] investigated second-order modification terms for single-input problems.

Consider the second-order modifiers

$$\Theta_k^j := \frac{\partial^2 j_p}{\partial \mathbf{u}^2}(\mathbf{u}_k) - \frac{\partial^2 j}{\partial \mathbf{u}^2}(\mathbf{u}_k), \qquad j \in \{\Phi, G_1, G_2, \ldots, G_{n_g}\}, \tag{34}$$

with $\Theta_k^j \in \mathbb{R}^{n_u \times n_u}$. These modifiers describe the difference in the Hessians of the plant and model costs ($j = \Phi$) and constraints ($j = G_i$), respectively. Second-order MA reads:

$$\mathbf{u}_{k+1}^\star = \underset{\mathbf{u}}{\arg\min} \quad \underbrace{\Phi(\mathbf{u}) + \varepsilon_k^\Phi + (\lambda_k^\Phi)^\mathsf{T}(\mathbf{u} - \mathbf{u}_k) + \tfrac{1}{2}(\mathbf{u} - \mathbf{u}_k)^\mathsf{T}\Theta_k^\Phi(\mathbf{u} - \mathbf{u}_k)}_{=: \, \Phi_{m,k}(\mathbf{u})} \tag{35a}$$

$$\text{s.t.} \quad \underbrace{G_i(\mathbf{u}) + \varepsilon_k^{G_i} + (\lambda_k^{G_i})^\mathsf{T}(\mathbf{u} - \mathbf{u}_k) + \tfrac{1}{2}(\mathbf{u} - \mathbf{u}_k)^\mathsf{T}\Theta_k^{G_i}(\mathbf{u} - \mathbf{u}_k)}_{=: \, G_{m,i,k}(\mathbf{u})} \leq 0, \tag{35b}$$

$$i = 1, \ldots, n_g,$$

$$\mathbf{u} \in \mathcal{C}, \tag{35c}$$

with

$$\mathbf{u}_{k+1} = \mathbf{u}_k + K(\mathbf{u}_{k+1}^\star - \mathbf{u}_k). \tag{36}$$

Note that, in contrast to the first-order formulation (21), we explicitly add the additional constraint $\mathbf{u} \in \mathcal{C}$ in (35c), where $\mathcal{C}$ denotes a known nonempty convex subset of $\mathbb{R}^{n_u}$. This additional constraint, which is not subject to plant-model mismatch, will simplify the convergence analysis.

Next, we present an extension to Theorem 1 that shows the potential advantages of second-order MA. To this end, we make the following assumptions:

A1 Numerical feasibility: For all $k \in \mathbb{N}$, Problem (35) is feasible and has a unique minimizer.
A2 Plant and model functions: The plant and model cost and constraint functions are all twice continuously differentiable on $\mathcal{C} \subset \mathbb{R}^{n_u}$.

Proposition 2 (Properties of second-order MA [31]). *Assume that the second-order MA scheme ((35) and (36)) has converged with* $\mathbf{u}_\infty = \lim_{k \to \infty} \mathbf{u}_k$. *Let Assumptions A1 and A2 hold, and let a linear independence constraint qualification hold at* $\mathbf{u}_\infty$. *Then, the following properties hold:*

i $\mathbf{u}_\infty$ *satisfies the KKT conditions of the plant, and*
ii   *the cost and constraint gradients and Hessians of the modified Problem (35) match those of the plant at* $\mathbf{u}_\infty$.

In addition, if (35) has a strict local minimum at $\mathbf{u}_\infty$ *such that, for all* $d \in \mathbb{R}^{n_d}$,

$$d^T \nabla_r^2 \mathcal{L}(\mathbf{u}_\infty) d > 0, \tag{37}$$

then

iii $\Phi_p(\mathbf{u}_\infty)$ *is a strict local minimum of* $\Phi_p(\mathbf{u})$.

Proposition 2 shows that, if second-order information can be reconstructed from measurements, then the RTO scheme ((35) and (36)) allows assessing, upon convergence, that a local minimum of the modified Problem (35) is also a local minimum of the plant.

Remark 2 (Hessian approximation). *So far, we have tacitly assumed that the plant gradients and Hessians are known. However, these quantities are difficult to estimate accurately in practice. Various approaches to compute plant gradients from measurements will be described in Section 5.1. To obtain Hessian estimates, one can rely on well-known approximation formulas such as BFGS or SR1 update rules [33]. While BFGS-approximated Hessians can be enforced to be positive definite, the convergence of the SR1 Hessian estimates to the true Hessian can be guaranteed under certain conditions ([33] Chap. 6). However, the issue of computing Hessian approximations that can work in a RTO context (with a low number of data points and a fair amount of noise) is not solved yet!*

Remark 3 (From MA to RTO based on surrogate models). *It is fair to ask whether second-order corrections allow implementing model-free RTO schemes. Upon considering the trivial models* $\Phi(u) = 0$ *and* $G_i(u) = 0$, $i = 1, \ldots, n_g$, *that is, in the case of no model, the modifiers are*

$$\varepsilon_k^j = j_p(\mathbf{u}_k), \quad (\lambda_k^j)^\mathsf{T} = \frac{\partial j_p}{\partial \mathbf{u}}(\mathbf{u}_k), \quad \Theta_k^j = \frac{\partial^2 j_p}{\partial \mathbf{u}^2}(\mathbf{u}_k), \quad j \in \{\Phi, G_1, G_2, \ldots, G_{n_g}\},$$

and the second-order MA Problem (35) reduces to a Quadratically Constrained Quadratic Program:

$$\mathbf{u}_{k+1}^\star = \arg\min_{\mathbf{u}} \; \Phi_p(\mathbf{u}_k) + \frac{\partial \Phi_p}{\partial \mathbf{u}}(\mathbf{u}_k)(\mathbf{u} - \mathbf{u}_k) + \tfrac{1}{2}(\mathbf{u} - \mathbf{u}_k)^\mathsf{T} \frac{\partial^2 \Phi_p}{\partial \mathbf{u}^2}(\mathbf{u}_k)(\mathbf{u} - \mathbf{u}_k)$$

$$\text{s.t.} \quad G_{p,i}(\mathbf{u}_k) + \frac{\partial G_{p,i}}{\partial \mathbf{u}}(\mathbf{u}_k)(\mathbf{u} - \mathbf{u}_k) + \tfrac{1}{2}(\mathbf{u} - \mathbf{u}_k)^\mathsf{T} \frac{\partial^2 G_{p,i}}{\partial \mathbf{u}^2}(\mathbf{u}_k)(\mathbf{u} - \mathbf{u}_k) \leq 0, \tag{38}$$

$$i = 1, \ldots, n_g,$$

$$\mathbf{u} \in \mathcal{C},$$

where $\mathcal{C}$ *is determined by lower and upper bounds on the input variables,* $\mathcal{C} = \{\mathbf{u} \in \mathbf{R}^{n_u} : \mathbf{u}^L \leq \mathbf{u} \leq \mathbf{u}^U\}$. *Note that the results of Proposition 2 also hold for RTO Problem(38). Alternatively, the same information can be used to construct the QP approximations used in Successive Quadratic Programming (SQP) approaches for solving NLP problems [33]. The SQP approximation at the kth RTO iteration is given by,*

$$\mathbf{u}_{k+1}^\star = \arg\min_{\mathbf{u}} \; \Phi_p(\mathbf{u}_k) + \frac{\partial \Phi_p}{\partial \mathbf{u}}(\mathbf{u}_k)(\mathbf{u} - \mathbf{u}_k) + \tfrac{1}{2}(\mathbf{u} - \mathbf{u}_k)^\mathsf{T} \frac{\partial^2 \mathcal{L}_p}{\partial \mathbf{u}^2}(\mathbf{u}_k)(\mathbf{u} - \mathbf{u}_k)$$

$$\text{s.t.} \quad G_{p,i}(\mathbf{u}_k) + \frac{\partial G_{p,i}}{\partial \mathbf{u}}(\mathbf{u}_k)(\mathbf{u} - \mathbf{u}_k) \leq 0, \quad i = 1, \ldots, n_g, \tag{39}$$

$$\mathbf{u} \in \mathcal{C},$$

where the constraints are linearized at $\mathbf{u}_k$, *and the Hessian of the Lagrangian function is used in the quadratic term of the cost function. Properties (i) and (iii) of Proposition 2 also hold for RTO Problem (39), and the Hessian of the Lagrangian function of Problem (39) matches the Hessian of the plant upon convergence. As the approximations of the cost and constraints are of local nature, a trust-region constraint may be added [33,34]. Obviously, such an approach leads to a SQP-like RTO scheme based on a surrogate model.*

A thorough investigation of RTO based on surrogate models is beyond the scope of this paper. Instead, we refer the reader to the recent progress made in this direction [35–38].

4.3. Convergence Conditions

Arguably, the biggest advantage of the MA schemes presented so far lies in the fact that any fixed point turns out to be a KKT point of the plant according to Theorem 1. Yet, Theorem 1 is somewhat limited in value, as it indicates *properties upon convergence* rather than stating *sufficient conditions for convergence*. Note that properties-upon-convergence results appear frequently in numerical optimization and nonlinear programming, see for example methods employing augmented Lagrangians with quadratic penalty on constraint violation ([39] Prop. 4.2.1). Hence, we now turn toward sufficient convergence conditions.

4.3.1. RTO Considered as Fixed-Point Iterations

In principle, one may regard any RTO scheme as a discrete-time dynamical system. In the case of MA, it is evident that the values of the modifiers at the kth RTO iteration implicitly determine the values of the inputs at iteration $k + 1$.

We consider here the second-order MA scheme with input filtering from the previous section. Let $\text{vec}(\mathbf{A}) \in \mathbb{R}^{n(n+1)/2}$ be the vectorization of the symmetric matrix $\mathbf{A} \in \mathbb{R}^{n \times n}$. Using this short hand notation, we collect all modifiers in the vector $\Lambda \in \mathbb{R}^{n_\Lambda}$, $n_\Lambda = (n_g + 1)\left(n_u + \frac{n_u(n_u+1)}{2}\right) + n_g + 1$,

$$\Lambda_k := \left(\varepsilon_k^\Phi, (\lambda_k^\Phi)^\mathsf{T}, \text{vec}(\Theta_k^\Phi), \varepsilon_k^{G_1}, (\lambda_k^{G_1})^\mathsf{T}, \text{vec}(\Theta_k^{G_1}), \ \dots \ , \varepsilon_k^{G_{n_g}}, (\lambda_k^{G_{n_g}})^\mathsf{T}, \text{vec}(\Theta_k^{G_{n_g}})\right)^\mathsf{T}. \tag{40}$$

As the minimizer in the optimization problem (35) depends on Λ_k, we can formally state Algorithm (35 and 36) as

$$\mathbf{u}_{k+1} = (1 - \alpha)\mathbf{u}_k + \alpha \mathbf{u}^\star(\mathbf{u}_k, \Lambda_k), \tag{41}$$

whereby $\mathbf{u}^\star(\mathbf{u}_k, \Lambda_k)$ is the minimizer of (35), and, for sake of simplicity, the filter is chosen as the scalar $\alpha \in (0, 1)$. Clearly, the above shorthand notation can be applied to any MA scheme with input filtering. Before stating the result, we recall the notion of a nonexpansive map.

Definition 2 (Nonexpansive map). *The map* $\Gamma : \mathcal{C} \to \mathcal{C}$ *is called nonexpansive, if*

$$\forall x, y \in \mathcal{C}: \quad \|\Gamma(x) - \Gamma(y)\| \leq \|x - y\|.$$

Theorem 3 (Convergence of MA [31]). *Consider the RTO scheme* (41). *Let Assumptions A1 and A2 hold and let* $\alpha \in (0, 1)$. *If the map* $u^\star : u \mapsto u^\star(u, \Lambda(u))$ *is nonexpansive in the sense of Definition 2 and has at least one fixed point on* $\mathcal{C}$, *then the sequence* $(u_k)_{k \in \mathbb{N}}$ *of RTO iterates defined by* (41) *converges to a fixed point, that is,*

$$\lim_{k \to \infty} \|u^\star(u_k, \Lambda(u_k)) - u_k\| = 0.$$

Remark 4 (Reasons for filtering). *Filtering can be understood as a way to increase the domain of attraction of MA schemes. This comes in addition to dealing with noisy measurements and the fact that large correction steps based on local information should be avoided.*

4.3.2. Similarity with Trust-Region Methods

The previous section has investigated global convergence of MA schemes. However, the analysis requires the characterization of properties of the *argmin* operator of the modified optimization problem, which is in general challenging. Next, we recall a result given in [40] showing that one can exploit the similarity between MA and trust-region methods. This similarity has also been observed in [41].

To this end, we consider the following variant of (21)

$$\mathbf{u}_{k+1}^{\star} = \arg\min_{\mathbf{u}} \ \Phi_{m,k}(\mathbf{u}) := \Phi(\mathbf{u}) + (\lambda_k^{\Phi})^{\top} \mathbf{u} \tag{42a}$$

$$\text{s.t.} \quad G_{m,i,k}(\mathbf{u}) := G_i(\mathbf{u}) + \varepsilon_k^{G_i} + (\lambda_k^{G_i})^{\top}(\mathbf{u} - \mathbf{u}_k) \le 0, \quad i = 1, \ldots, n_g, \tag{42b}$$

$$\mathbf{u} \in \mathcal{B}(\mathbf{u}_k, \rho_k). \tag{42c}$$

The only difference between this optimization problem and (21) is the *trust-region constraint* (42c), where $\mathcal{B}(\mathbf{u}_k, \rho_k)$ denotes a closed ball in $\mathbf{R}^{n_u}$ with radius ρ_k centered at $\mathbf{u}_k$.

Consider

$$\omega_k := \frac{\Phi_p(\mathbf{u}_k) - \Phi_p(\mathbf{u}_{k+1}^{\star})}{\Phi_{m,k}(\mathbf{u}_k) - \Phi_{m,k}(\mathbf{u}_{k+1}^{\star})}$$

If $\omega_k \gg 1$, then, at $\mathbf{u}_{k+1}^{\star}$, the plant performs significantly better than predicted by the modified model. Likewise, if $\omega_k \ll 1$, the plant performs significantly worse than predicted by the modified model. In other words, ω_k is a local criterion for the quality of the modified model. In trust-region methods, one replaces (input) filtering with acceptance rules for candidate points. In [40], it is suggested to apply the following rule:

$$\mathbf{u}_{k+1} := \begin{cases} \mathbf{u}_{k+1}^{\star} & \text{if } \omega_k \ge \eta_1 \\ \mathbf{u}_k & \text{otherwise} \end{cases} \tag{43}$$

Note that this acceptance rule requires application of $\mathbf{u}_{k+1}^{\star}$ to the plant.

Another typical ingredient of trust-region methods is an update rule for the radius ρ_k. Consider the constant scalars $0 < \eta_1 \le \eta_2 < 1$, $0 < \gamma_1 \le \gamma_2 < 1$, and assume that the update satisfies the following conditions:

$$\rho_{k+1} \in \begin{cases} [\rho_k, \infty) & \text{if } \omega_k \ge \eta_2 \\ [\gamma_2 \rho_k, \rho_k] & \text{if } \omega_k \in [\eta_1, \eta_2) \\ [\gamma_1 \rho_k, \gamma_2 \rho_k] & \text{if } \omega_k \le \eta_1 \end{cases} \tag{44}$$

As in the previous section, we assume that Assumptions A1 and A2 hold. In addition, we require the following:

A3 Plant boundedness: The plant objective Φ_p is lower-bounded on $\mathbf{R}^{n_u}$. Furthermore, its Hessian is bounded from above on $\mathbf{R}^{n_u}$.

A4 Model decrease: For all $k \in \mathbb{N}$, there exists a constant $\kappa \in (0, 1]$ and a sequence $(\beta_k)_{k \in \mathbb{N}} > 1$ such that

$$\Phi_{m,k}(\mathbf{u}_k^{\star}) - \Phi_{m,k}(\mathbf{u}_{k+1}^{\star}) \ge \kappa \|\nabla \Phi_{m,k}(\mathbf{u}_k)\| \cdot \min \left\{ \rho_k, \frac{\|\nabla \Phi_{m,k}(\mathbf{u}_k)\|}{\beta_k} \right\}.$$

Now, we are ready to state convergence conditions for the trust-region-inspired MA scheme given by (42)–(44).

Theorem 4 (Convergence with trust-region constraints [40]). *Consider the RTO scheme (42)–(44) and let Assumptions A1–A4 hold, then*

$$\lim_{k \to \infty} \|\nabla \Phi_p(\mathbf{u}_k)\| = 0.$$

The formal proof of this result is based on a result on convergence of trust-region methods given in [34]. For details, we refer to [40].

Remark 5 (Comparison of Theorems 3 and 4). *A few remarks on the convergence results given by Theorems 3 and 4 are in order. While Theorem 3 is applicable to schemes with first- and second-order correction terms, the convergence result is based on the nonexpansiveness of the argmin operator, which is difficult to verify in practice. However, Theorem 3 provides a good motivation for input filtering as the convergence result is based on* averaged *iterations of a nonexpansive operator. In contrast, Theorem 4 relies on Assumption A4, which ensures sufficient model decrease ([34] Thm. 6.3.4, p. 131). However, this assumption is in general not easy to verify.*

There is another crucial difference between MA with and without trust-region constraints. The input update (43) is based on ω_k, which requires application of $\mathbf{u}_{k+1}^\star$ to the plant. Note that, if at the kth RTO iteration the trust region is chosen too large, then first $\mathbf{u}_{k+1}^\star$ is applied to the plant, resulting in $\omega_k < \eta_1$ and thus to immediate (re-)application of $\mathbf{u}_k$. In other words, a trust region that is chosen too large can result in successive experiments that do not guarantee plant cost improvement. In a nominal setting with perfect gradient information, this is clearly a severe limitation. However, in any real world application, where plant gradients need to be estimated, the plant information obtained from rejected steps may be utilized for gradient estimation.

4.3.3. Use of Convex Models and Convex Upper Bounds

Next, we turn to the issue of convexity in MA. As already mentioned in Proposition 1, for a model to be *adequate* in MA, it needs to be able to admit, after the usual first-order correction, a strict local minimum at the generally unkown plant optimum $\mathbf{u}_p^\star$. At the same time, it is worth noting that the model is simply a tool in the design of MA schemes. In Remark 3, for instance, we pointed toward second-order MA with no model functions. Yet, this is not the only possible choice. It has been observed in [21] that the adequacy issue is eliminated if one relies on strictly convex models and first-order correction terms. The next proposition summarizes these results.

Proposition 3 (Use of convex models in MA [21]). *Consider the MA Problem (21). Let the model cost and constraint functions Φ and G_i, $i = 1, \ldots, n_g$, be strictly convex functions. Then, (i) Problem (21) is a strictly convex program; and (ii) the model satisfies the adequacy condition of Definition 1.*

Remark 6 (Advantages of convex models). *The most important advantage of convex models in MA is that model adequacy is guaranteed without prior knowledge of the plant optimum. Furthermore, it is well known that convex programs are, in general, easier to solve than non-convex ones. Note that one can relax the strict convexity requirement to either the cost being strictly convex or at least one of the active constraints being strictly convex at the plant optimum [21].*

4.4. Extensions

Several extensions and variants of MA have recently been developed to account for specific problem configurations and needs.

4.4.1. MA Applied to Controlled Plants

MA guarantees plant feasibility upon convergence, but the RTO iterates prior to convergence might violate the plant constraints. For continuous processes, it is possible to generate *feasible* steady-state operating points by implementing the RTO results via a feedback control layer that tracks the constrained variables that are active at the RTO solution [42]. This requires the constrained quantities in the optimization problem to be measured online at sufficiently high frequency. Navia et al. [43] recently proposed an approach to prevent infeasibilities in MA implementation by including PI controllers that become activated only when the measurements show violation of the constraints. In industry, model predictive control (MPC) is used widely due to its ability to handle large multivariable systems with constraints [44]. Recently, Marchetti et al. [45] proposed an approach for integrating MA with MPC, wherein MPC is used to enforce the equality and active inequality constraints of the modified optimization problem. The remaining degrees of freedom are controlled to their optimal values along selected input directions. In order to implement MA on a controlled plant, the gradients are corrected on the tangent space of the equality constraints.

The approach used in industry to combine RTO with MPC consists in including a target optimization stage at the MPC layer [44]. Since the nonlinear steady-state model used at the RTO layer is not in general consistent with the linear dynamic model used by the MPC regulator, the optimal setpoints given by the RTO solution are often not reachable by the MPC regulator. The target optimization problem uses a (linear) steady-state model that is consistent with the MPC dynamic model. Its purpose is to correct the RTO setpoints by computing steady-state targets that are reachable by the MPC regulator [46,47]. The target optimization problem executes at the same frequency as the MPC regulator and uses the same type of feedback. Three different designs of the target optimization problem have been analyzed in [48], each of which guarantees attaining only feasible points for the plant at steady state, and reaching the RTO optimal inputs upon convergence.

Another difficulty arises when the inputs of the model-based optimization problem are not the same as the plant inputs. This happens, for instance, when the plant is operated in closed loop, but only a model of the *open-loop* system is available [49]. In this case, the plant inputs are the controller setpoints r, while the model inputs are the manipulated variables u. Three alternative MA extensions have recently been proposed to optimize a controlled plant using a model of the open-loop plant [50]. The three extensions use the cost and constraint gradients of the plant with respect to the setpoints r:

1. The first approach, labeled "Method UR", suggests solving the optimization problem for u, but computes the modifiers in the space of the setpoints r.
2. The second approach, labelled "Method UU", solves the optimization problem for u, and computes the modifiers in the space of u.
3. The third approach, labelled "Method RR", solves the optimization problem for r, and computes the modifiers in the space of r. It relies on the construction of model approximations for the controlled plant that are obtained from the model of the open-loop plant.

As shown in [50], the three extensions preserve the MA property of reaching a KKT point of the plant upon convergence.

4.4.2. MA Applied to Dynamic Optimization Problems

There have been some attempts to extend the applicability of MA to the dynamic run-to-run optimization of batch processes [51,52]. The idea therein is to build on the repetitive nature of batch processes and perform run-to-run iterations to progressively improve the performance of the batches.

The approach used in [51] takes advantage of the fact that dynamic optimization problems can be reformulated as static optimization problems upon discretization of the inputs, constraints and the dynamic model [17]. This allows the direct use of MA, the price to pay being that the number of decision variables increases linearly with the number of discretization points, as shown in [51]. Note that, if the active path constraints are known in the various intervals of the solution, a much more parsimonious input parameterization can be implemented, as illustrated in ([17] Appendix).

The approach proposed in [52] uses CA (that is, MA with only zeroth-order modifiers) for the run-to-run optimization of batch processes. Dynamic optimization problems are characterized by the presence of both path and terminal constraints. Because of uncertainty and plant-model mismatch, the measured values of both path and terminal constraints will differ from their model predictions. Hence, for each run, one can offset the values of the terminal constraints in the dynamic optimization problem with biases corresponding to the differences between the predicted and measured terminal constraints of the previous batch. Path constraints are modified similarly, by adding to the path constraints a time-dependent function corresponding to the differences between the measured and predicted path constraints during the previous batch. An additional difficulty arises when the final time of the batch is also a decision variable. Upon convergence, the CA approach [52] only guarantees constraint satisfaction, while the full MA approach [51] preserves the KKT matching property of standard MA.

4.4.3. Use of Transient Measurements for MA

MA is by nature a steady-state to steady-state RTO methodology for the optimization of uncertain processes. This means that several iterations to steady state are generally needed before convergence. However, there are cases where transient measurements can be used as well. Furthermore, it would be advantageous to be able to use transient measurements in a systematic way to speed up the steady-state optimization of dynamic processes.

The concept of fast RTO via CA was introduced and applied to an experimental solid oxide fuel-cell stack in the presence of operating constraints and plant-model mismatch [53]. Solid oxide fuel-cell stacks are, roughly speaking, electrochemical reactors embedded in a furnace. The electrochemical reaction between hydrogen and oxygen is almost instantaneous and results in the production of electrical power and water. On the other hand, thermal equilibration is much slower. The fast RTO approach in [53] is very simple and uses CA. The RTO period is set somewhere between the time scale of the electrochemical reaction and the time scale of the thermal process. This way, the chemical reaction has time to settle, and the thermal effects are treated as slow process drifts that are accounted for like any other source of plant-model mismatch. This shows that it is possible to use RTO before steady state has been reached, at least when a time-scale separation exists between fast optimization-relevant dynamics and slow dynamics that do not affect much the cost and constraints of the optimization problem.

In [54], a framework has been proposed to apply MA during transient operation to steady state for the case of parametric plant-model mismatch, thereby allowing the plant to converge to optimal operating conditions in a single transient operation to steady state. The basic idea is simply to implement standard MA during the transient "as if the process were at steady state". Optimal inputs are computed and applied until the next RTO execution during transient. Hence, the time between two consecutive RTO executions becomes a tuning parameter just as the filter gains. Transient measurements obtained at the RTO sampling period are treated as if they were steady-state measurements and are therefore directly used for computing the zeroth-order modifiers and estimating the plant gradients at "steady state". There are two main advantages of this approach: (i) standard MA can be applied; and (ii) the assumption that transient measurements can play the role of steady-state measurements becomes more and more valid as the system approaches steady state. Simulation results in [54] are very encouraging, but they also highlight some of the difficulties, in particular when the dynamics exhibit non-standard behaviors such as inverse response. A way to circumvent these difficulties consists in reducing the RTO frequency. Ultimately, this frequency could be reduced to the point that MA is only solved at steady state, when the process dynamics have disappeared. Research is ongoing to improve the use of transient measurements and characterize the types of dynamic systems for which this approach is likely to reduce the time needed for convergence [55].

4.4.4. MA when Part of the Plant is Perfectly Modeled

As mentioned above, MA is capable of driving a plant toward a KKT point even though the model is structurally incorrect. The only requirement for the model is that it satisfies the model-adequacy conditions, a property that can be enforced if convex model approximations are used [54]. In addition, plant measurements that allow good estimation of the plant constraints and gradients are required. The fact that MA can be efficient without an accurate model does not mean that it cannot benefit from the availability of a good model. For instance, in [56] the authors acknowledge that, for most energy systems, the model incorporates basic mass and energy balances that can often be very rigorously modeled and, thus, there is no need to include any structural or parametric plant-model mismatch. The authors suggest separating the process model equations into two sets of equations. The set of rigorous model equations is denoted the "process model", while the second set of equations is referred to as the "approximate model" and describes performance and efficiency factors, which are much harder to model and therefore susceptible to carry plant-model mismatch. Hence, modifiers are used only for this second set of equations by directly modifying the corresponding model equations. Key to the approach in [56] is data reconciliation, which makes explicit use of the knowledge of the set of "perfect model equations". One of the advantages of not modifying the well-known subparts of the model is that it may reduce the number of plant gradients that need to be estimated, without much loss in performance.

5. Implementation Aspects

The need to estimate plant gradients represents the main implementation difficulty. This is a challenging problem since the gradients cannot be measured directly and, in addition, measurement noise is almost invariably present. This section discusses different ways of estimating gradients, of computing modifiers, and of combining gradient estimation and optimization.

5.1. Gradient Estimation

Several methods are available for estimating plant gradients [57–60]. These methods can be classified as *steady-state perturbation methods* that use only steady-state data, and *dynamic perturbation methods* that use transient data.

5.1.1. Steady-State Perturbation Methods

Steady-state perturbation methods rely on steady-state data for gradient estimation. For each change in the input variables, one must wait until the plant has reached steady state before taking measurements, which can make these methods particularly slow. Furthermore, to obtain reliable gradient estimates, it is important to avoid (i) amplifying the noise present in experimental data [61,62]; and (ii) using past data that correspond to different conditions (for example, different qualities of raw materials, or different disturbance values).

Finite-difference approximation (FDA). The most common approach is to use FDA techniques that require at least $n_u + 1$ steady-state operating points to estimate the gradients. Several alternatives can be envisioned for choosing these points:

- *FDA by perturbing the current RTO point:* A straightforward approach consists in perturbing each input individually around the current operating point to get an estimate of the corresponding gradient element. For example, in the forward-finite-differencing (FFD) approach, an estimator of the partial derivative $\frac{\partial \Phi_p}{\partial u_j}(\mathbf{u}_k)$, $j = 1, \ldots, n_u$, at the kth RTO iteration is obtained as

$$(\widehat{\nabla \Phi_{p,k}})_j = \left[\widehat{\Phi}_p(\mathbf{u}_k + h\mathbf{e}_j) - \widehat{\Phi}_p(\mathbf{u}_k) \right] / h, \qquad h > 0, \tag{45}$$

  where h is the step size, $\mathbf{e}_j$ is the jth unit vector, and the superscript $(\hat{\cdot})$ denotes a noisy measurement. This approach requires n_u perturbations to be carried out at each RTO iteration, and for each perturbation a new steady state must be attained. Alternatively, the central-finite-differencing (CFD) approach can be used, which is more accurate but requires $2n_u$ perturbations at each RTO iteration [61]. Since perturbing each input individually may lead to constraint violations when the current operating point is close to a constraint, an approach has been proposed for generating n_u perturbed points that take into account the constraints and avoid ill-conditioned points for gradient estimation [45].
- *FDA using past RTO points:* The gradients can be estimated by FDA based on the measurements obtained at the current and past RTO points $\{\mathbf{u}_k, \mathbf{u}_{k-1}, \ldots, \mathbf{u}_{k-n_u}\}$. This approach is used in dual ISOPE and dual MA methods [7,63–65]—the latter methods being discussed in Section 5.3. At the kth RTO iteration, the following matrix can be constructed:

$$\mathsf{U}_k := [\ \mathbf{u}_k - \mathbf{u}_{k-1}, \ \ \mathbf{u}_k - \mathbf{u}_{k-2}, \ \ \dots, \ \ \mathbf{u}_k - \mathbf{u}_{k-n_u} \ ] \in \mathbf{R}^{n_u \times n_u}. \tag{46}$$

Assuming that measurements of the cost Φ_p and constraints $G_{p,i}$ are available at each iteration, we construct the following vectors:

$$\delta\tilde{\Phi}_{p,k} := [\ \tilde{\Phi}_{p,k} - \tilde{\Phi}_{p,k-1}, \ \ \tilde{\Phi}_{p,k} - \tilde{\Phi}_{p,k-2}, \ \ \dots, \ \ \tilde{\Phi}_{p,k} - \tilde{\Phi}_{p,k-n_u} \ ]^{\mathsf{T}} \in \mathbf{R}^{n_u}, \tag{47}$$

$$\delta\tilde{G}_{p,i,k} := [\ \tilde{G}_{p,i,k} - \tilde{G}_{p,i,k-1}, \ \ \tilde{G}_{p,i,k} - \tilde{G}_{p,i,k-2}, \ \ \dots, \ \ \tilde{G}_{p,i,k} - \tilde{G}_{p,i,k-n_u} \ ]^{\mathsf{T}} \in \mathbf{R}^{n_u}, \tag{48}$$

$$i = 1, \dots, n_g.$$

The measured cost has measurement noise v_k:

$$\tilde{\Phi}_{p,k} = \Phi_p(\mathbf{u}_k) + v_k. \tag{49}$$

If U_k is nonsingular, then the set of $n_u + 1$ points $\{\mathbf{u}_{k-j}\}_{j=0}^{n_u}$ is said to be poised for linear interpolation in $\mathbf{R}^{n_u}$, and U_k is called a matrix of simplex directions [34]. The cost gradient at $\mathbf{u}_k$ can then be estimated by FDA as follows:

$$\widehat{\nabla\Phi}_{p,k} = (\delta\tilde{\Phi}_{p,k})^{\mathsf{T}}(\mathsf{U}_k)^{-1}, \tag{50}$$

which is known as the *simplex gradient* [34]. The constraint gradients can be computed in a similar way.

Broyden's method. The gradients are estimated from the past RTO points using the following recursive updating scheme:

$$\widehat{\nabla\Phi}_{p,k} = \widehat{\nabla\Phi}_{p,k-1} + \frac{(\tilde{\Phi}_{p,k} - \tilde{\Phi}_{p,k-1}) - \widehat{\nabla\Phi}_{p,k-1}(\mathbf{u}_k - \mathbf{u}_{k-1})}{(\mathbf{u}_k - \mathbf{u}_{k-1})^{\mathsf{T}}(\mathbf{u}_k - \mathbf{u}_{k-1})}(\mathbf{u}_k - \mathbf{u}_{k-1})^{\mathsf{T}}. \tag{51}$$

The use of Broyden's method was investigated for ISOPE in [66] and for MA in [67]. Comparative studies including this gradient estimation method can be found in [58,68].

Gradients from fitted surfaces. A widely used strategy for extracting gradient information from (noisy) experimental data consists in fitting polynomial or spline curves to the data and evaluating the gradients analytically by differentiating the fitted curves [69]. In the context of MA, Gao et al. [36] recently proposed to use least-square regression to obtain local quadratic approximations of the cost and constraint functions using selected data, and to evaluate the gradients by differentiating these quadratic approximations.

5.1.2. Dynamic Perturbation Methods

In dynamic perturbation methods, the steady-state gradients are estimated based on the transient response of the plant. Three classes of methods are described next.

Dynamic model identification. These methods rely on the online identification of simple dynamic input-output models based on the plant transient response. Once a dynamic model is identified, the steady-state gradients can be obtained by application of the final-value theorem. Indeed, the static gain of a transfer function represents the sensitivity (or gradient) of the output with respect to the input. McFarlane and Bacon [70] proposed to identify a linear ARX model and used the estimated static gradient for online optimizing control. A pseudo-random binary sequence (PRBS) was superimposed on each of the inputs to identify the ARX model. In the context of ISOPE, Becerra et al. [71] considered the identification of a linear ARMAX model using PRBS signals. Bamberger and Isermann [72] identified online a parametric second-order Hammerstein model by adding a pseudo-random ternary sequence to each input. The gradient estimates were used for online optimizing control. Garcia and Morari [73] used a similar approach, wherein the dynamic identification was performed in a decentralized fashion. The same approach was also used by Golden and Ydstie [32] for estimating the first- and second-order derivatives of a SISO plant. Zhang and Forbes [60] compared the optimizing controllers proposed in [70] and [32] with ISOPE and the two-step approach.

Extremum-seeking control. The plant gradients can also be obtained using data-driven methods as discussed in [74]. Among the most established techniques, ESC [16] suggests adding a dither signal (e.g., a sine wave) to each of the inputs during transient operation. High-pass filtering of the outputs removes the biases, while using low-pass filters together with correlation let you compute the gradients of the outputs with respect to the inputs. The main limitation of this approach is the speed of convergence as it requires two time-scale separations, the first one between the filters and the periodic excitation, and the second one between the periodic excitation and the controlled plant. Since all inputs have to be perturbed independently, convergence to the plant gradients can be prohibitively slow in the MIMO case. Recent efforts in the extremum-seeking community have led to a more efficient framework, referred to as "estimation-based ESC" (by opposition to the previously described perturbation-based ESC), which seems to be more efficient in terms of convergence speed [75].

Multiple units. Another dynamic perturbation approach relies on the availability of several identical units operated in parallel [76]. The minimal number of required units is $n_u + 1$, since one unit operates with the inputs computed by the RTO algorithm, while a single input is perturbed in each of the remaining n_u units in parallel. The gradients can be computed online by *finite differences between units*. Convergence time does not increase with the number of inputs. Obviously, this approach relies heavily on the availability of several identical units, which occurs for instance when several units, such as fuel-cell stacks, are arranged in parallel. Note that these units must be identical, although some progress has been made to encompass cases where this is not the case [77].

5.1.3. Bounds on Gradient Uncertainty

As discussed in [78], obtaining bounds on gradient estimates is often more challenging than obtaining the estimates themselves. The bounds on gradient estimates should be linked with the specific approach used to estimate the gradients. For the case of gradient estimates obtained by FFD, CFD, and two design-of-experiment schemes, Brekelmans et al. [61] proposed a deterministic quantification of the gradient error due to the finite-difference approximation (truncation error) and a stochastic characterization due to measurement noise. The expressions obtained for the total gradient error are convex functions of the step size, for which it is easy to compute for each scheme the step size that minimizes the total gradient error. Following a similar approach, the gradient error associated with the simplex gradient (50) was analyzed by Marchetti et al. [64].

The gradient estimation error is defined as the difference between the estimated gradient and the true plant gradient:

$$\epsilon_k^{\mathsf{T}} = \widehat{\nabla \Phi}_{p,k} - \frac{\partial \Phi_p}{\partial \mathbf{u}}(\mathbf{u}_k).$$ (52)

From (49) and (50), this error can be split into the truncation error ϵ^t and the measurement noise error ϵ^n,

$$\epsilon_k = \epsilon_k^t + \epsilon_k^n,$$ (53)

with

$$(\epsilon_k^t)^\mathsf{T} = [\Phi_p(\mathbf{u}_k) - \Phi_p(\mathbf{u}_{k-1}), \ \ldots, \ \Phi_p(\mathbf{u}_k) - \Phi_p(\mathbf{u}_{k-n_u})](\mathsf{U}_k)^{-1} - \frac{\partial\Phi_p}{\partial\mathbf{u}}(\mathbf{u}_k), \tag{54a}$$

$$(\epsilon_k^n)^\mathsf{T} = [v_k - v_{k-1}, \ \ldots, \ v_k - v_{k-n_u}](\mathsf{U}_k)^{-1}. \tag{54b}$$

Assuming that Φ_p is twice continuously differentiable with respect to $\mathbf{u}$, the norm of the gradient error due to truncation can be bounded from above by

$$\|\epsilon_k^t\| \leq \mathsf{d}^\Phi r_k, \tag{55}$$

where d^Φ is an upper bound on the spectral radius of the Hessian of Φ_p for $\mathbf{u} \in \mathcal{C}$, and r_k is the radius of the unique n-sphere that can be generated from the points $\mathbf{u}_k, \mathbf{u}_{k-1}, \ldots, \mathbf{u}_{k-n_u}$:

$$r_k = r(\mathbf{u}_k, \mathbf{u}_{k-1}, \ldots, \mathbf{u}_{k-n_u}) = \tag{56}$$
$$\frac{1}{2}\left\| \left[(\mathbf{u}_k - \mathbf{u}_{k-1})^\mathsf{T}(\mathbf{u}_k - \mathbf{u}_{k-1}), \ldots, (\mathbf{u}_k - \mathbf{u}_{k-n_u})^\mathsf{T}(\mathbf{u}_k - \mathbf{u}_{k-n_u}) \right] (\mathsf{U}_k)^{-1} \right\|.$$

In turn, assuming that the noisy measurements $\hat{\Phi}_p$ remain within the interval δ^Φ at steady state, the norm of the gradient error due to measurement noise can be bounded from above:

$$\|\epsilon_k^n\| \leq \frac{\delta^\Phi}{l_{\min,k}}, \tag{57}$$
$$l_{\min,k} = l_{\min}(\mathbf{u}_k, \mathbf{u}_{k-1}, \ldots, \mathbf{u}_{k-n_u}),$$

where $l_{\min,k}$ is the minimal distance between all possible pairs of complement affine subspaces that can be generated from the set of points $\mathcal{S}_k = \{\mathbf{u}_k, \mathbf{u}_{k-1}, \ldots, \mathbf{u}_{k-n_u}\}$. Using (55) and (57), the gradient-error norm can be bounded from above by

$$\|\epsilon_k\| \leq \|\epsilon_k^t\| + \|\epsilon_k^n\| \leq E_k^\Phi := \mathsf{d}^\Phi r_k + \frac{\delta^\Phi}{l_{\min,k}}. \tag{58}$$

5.2. Computation of Gradient Modifiers

5.2.1. Modifiers from Estimated Gradients

The most straightforward way of computing the gradient modifiers is to evaluate them directly from the estimated gradients, according to their definition (20):

$$(\lambda_k^\Phi)^\mathsf{T} = \widehat{\nabla\Phi}_{p,k} - \frac{\partial\Phi}{\partial\mathbf{u}}(\mathbf{u}_k), \tag{59a}$$

$$(\lambda_k^{G_i})^\mathsf{T} = \widehat{\nabla G}_{p,i,k} - \frac{\partial G_i}{\partial\mathbf{u}}(\mathbf{u}_k), \quad i = 1, \ldots, n_g, \tag{59b}$$

where, in principle, any of the methods described in Section 5.1 can be used to obtain the gradient estimates $\widehat{\nabla\Phi}_{p,k}$ and $\widehat{\nabla G}_{p,i,k}$.

5.2.2. Modifiers from Linear Interpolation or Linear Regression

Instead of using a sample set of steady-state operating points to estimate the gradients, it is possible to use the same set to directly compute the gradient modifiers by linear interpolation or linear regression. For instance, Marchetti [65] proposed to estimate the gradient modifiers by linear interpolation using the set of $n_u + 1$ RTO points $\{u_{k-j}\}_{j=0}^{n_u}$. In addition to the plant vectors $\delta\tilde{\Phi}_{p,k}$ and $\delta\tilde{G}_{p,i,k}$ given in (47) and (48), their model counterparts can be constructed at the kth RTO iteration:

$$\delta\Phi_k := [\ \Phi(u_k) - \Phi(u_{k-1}), \quad \dots, \quad \Phi(u_k) - \Phi(u_{k-n_u})\ ]^\mathsf{T} \in \mathbf{R}^{n_u}, \tag{60}$$

$$\delta G_{i,k} := [\ G_i(u_k) - G_i(u_{k-1}), \quad \dots, \quad G_i(u_k) - G_i(u_{k-n_u})\ ]^\mathsf{T} \in \mathbf{R}^{n_u}, \quad i = 1, \dots, n_g. \tag{61}$$

The interpolation conditions for the modified cost function read:

$$\Phi_{m,k}(u_{k-j}) = \Phi(u_{k-j}) + \varepsilon_k^\Phi + (\lambda_k^\Phi)^\mathsf{T}(u_{k-j} - u_k) = \tilde{\Phi}_{p,k-j}, \quad j = 1, \dots, n_u, \tag{62}$$

with $\varepsilon_k^\Phi = \tilde{\Phi}_{p,k} - \Phi(u_k)$. Equation (62) forms a linear system in terms of the gradient modifier and can be written in matrix form as

$$(U_k)^\mathsf{T} \lambda_k^\Phi = \delta\tilde{\Phi}_{p,k} - \delta\Phi_k, \tag{63}$$

where U_k and $\delta\tilde{\Phi}_{p,k}$ are the quantities defined in (46) and (47), respectively. This system of equations has a unique solution if the matrix U_k is nonsingular. The constraint gradient modifiers can be computed in a similar way, which leads to the following expressions for the gradient modifiers [65]:

$$(\lambda_k^\Phi)^\mathsf{T} = (\delta\tilde{\Phi}_{p,k} - \delta\Phi_k)^\mathsf{T}(U_k)^{-1}, \tag{64a}$$

$$(\lambda_k^{G_i})^\mathsf{T} = (\delta\tilde{G}_{p,i,k} - \delta G_{i,k})^\mathsf{T}(U_k)^{-1}, \quad i = 1, \dots, n_g. \tag{64b}$$

Here, the sample points consist of the current and n_u most recent RTO points. However, it is also possible to include designed perturbations in the sample set.

Figure 3 shows how the modified cost function approximates the plant cost function using MA when (i) the points $\{u_k, u_{k-1}\}$ are used to obtain the simplex gradient estimate (50), which is then used in (59a) to compute the gradient modifier, and (ii) the same points are used to compute the linear interpolation gradient modifier (64a). It can be seen that the linear interpolation approach gives a better approximation of the plant cost function, especially if the points are distant from each other.

Remark 7 (Linear regression). *If there are more than $n_u + 1$ sample points, it might not be possible to interpolate all the points. In this case, it is possible to evaluate the gradient modifiers by linear least-square regression.*

Remark 8 (Quadratic interpolation). *In case of second-order MA, it is possible to compute the gradient and Hessian modifiers by quadratic interpolation or quadratic least-squares regression. In this case, the number of well-poised points required for complete quadratic interpolation is $(n_u + 1)(n_u + 2)/2$ (see [34] for different measures of well poisedness that can be used to select or design the points included in the sample set).*

5.2.3. Nested MA

A radically different approach for determining the gradient modifiers has been proposed recently [79]. Rather than trying to estimate the plant gradients, it has been proposed to identify the gradient modifiers directly via derivative-free optimization. More specifically, the RTO problem is reformulated as two nested optimization problems, with the outer optimization computing the gradient modifiers at low frequency and the inner optimization computing the inputs more frequently. We shall use the indices j and k to denote the iterations of the outer and inner optimizations, respectively.

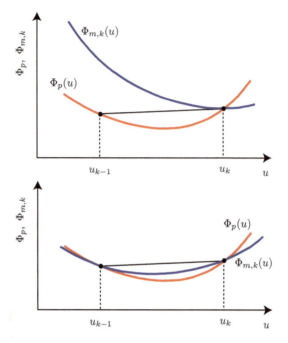

Figure 3. Approximation of the plant cost function. **Top plot:** Modified cost using gradient from FDA; **Bottom plot:** Modified cost using linear interpolation.

The inner optimization problem (for j fixed) is formulated as follows:

$$\mathbf{u}_{k+1}^{\star} = \arg\min_{\mathbf{u}} \Phi_{m,k}(\mathbf{u}) := \Phi(\mathbf{u}) + (\lambda_j^{\Phi})^{\mathsf{T}}\mathbf{u} \tag{65a}$$

$$\text{s.t.} \quad G_{m,i,k}(\mathbf{u}) := G_i(\mathbf{u}) + \varepsilon_k^{G_i} + (\lambda_j^{G_i})^{\mathsf{T}}(\mathbf{u} - \mathbf{u}_k) \leq 0 \qquad i = 1,\ldots,n_g. \tag{65b}$$

Note the difference with (21a): for the inner optimization, the gradient modifiers are considered as constant parameters that are updated by the outer optimization. The values of the converged inputs, $\mathbf{u}_{\infty}^{\star}$, and of the converged Lagrange multipliers associated with the constraints, $\mu_{\infty}^{\star}$, depend on the choice of the modifiers λ_j^{Φ} and $\lambda_j^{G_i}$. For the sake of notation, let us group these modifiers in the matrix $\Lambda_j := \begin{bmatrix} \lambda_j^{\Phi} & \lambda_j^{G_1} & \ldots & \lambda_j^{G_{ng}} \end{bmatrix}$.

Once the inner optimization has converged, the following *unconstrained* outer optimization problem is solved:

$$\Lambda_{j+1}^{\star} = \arg\min_{\Lambda} \quad \left\{ \Phi_p\left(\mathbf{u}_{\infty}^{\star}\left(\Lambda_j\right)\right) + \left(\mu_{\infty}^{\star}\left(\Lambda_j\right)\right)^{\mathsf{T}} \mathbf{G}_p(\mathbf{u}_{\infty}^{\star}) \right\}, \tag{66}$$

and the inner optimization problem is repeated for the modifiers Λ_{j+1}. Note that, since the functions Φ_p and $\mathbf{G}_p$ are unknown, Problem (66) is conveniently solved using derivative-free optimization techniques such as the Nelder-Mead simplex method [79]. Furthermore, it has been shown that separating the MA problem into two nested optimization problems preserves the ability to reach a KKT point of the plant [79]. However, since Nested MA often requires many iterations (for both the j and k indices), it is characterized by potentially slow convergence.

5.3. Dual MA Schemes

Following the idea of the dual ISOPE algorithm [7,63], dual MA schemes estimate the gradients based on the measurements obtained at the current and past operating points by adding a *duality constraint* in the modified optimization problem. This constraint is used to ensure sufficient variability in the data for estimating the gradients reliably. Several dual MA schemes have been proposed that differ in the model modification introduced, the approach used for estimating the gradients, and the choice of the duality constraint.

The following duality constraint is used to position the next RTO point with respect to the n_u most recent points $\{\mathbf{u}_k, \mathbf{u}_{k-1}, \ldots, \mathbf{u}_{k-n_u+1}\}$:

$$\mathcal{D}_k(\mathbf{u}) := \mathcal{D}(\mathbf{u}, \mathbf{u}_k, \mathbf{u}_{k-1}, \ldots, \mathbf{u}_{k-n_u+1}) \leq 0. \tag{67}$$

To compute the simplex gradient (50), or the interpolation modifiers (64) at the next RTO point $\mathbf{u}_{k+1}$, we require the matrix U_{k+1} defined in (46) to be nonsingular. Assuming that the last $n_u - 1$ columns of U_{k+1} are linearly independent, they constitute a basis for the unique hyperplane $\mathcal{H}_k = \{\mathbf{u} \in \mathbf{R}^{n_u} : \mathbf{n}_k^\top \mathbf{u} = b_k, \text{ with } b_k = \mathbf{n}_k^\top \mathbf{u}_k\}$ that contains the points $\{\mathbf{u}_k, \mathbf{u}_{k-1}, \ldots, \mathbf{u}_{k-n_u+1}\}$. Here, $\mathbf{n}_k$ is a vector that is orthogonal to the hyperplane. Hence, the matrix U_{k+1} will be nonsingular if $\mathbf{u}_{k+1}$ does not belong to $\mathcal{H}_k$ [65]. For this reason, duality constraints produce two disjoint feasible regions, one on each side of the hyperplane $\mathcal{H}_k$.

Dual MA schemes typically solve two modified optimization problems that include the duality constraint, one for each side of the hyperplane $\mathcal{H}_k$. For the half space $\mathbf{n}_k^\top \mathbf{u} > b_k$, we solve:

$$\mathbf{u}_{k+1}^+ = \arg\min_{\mathbf{u}} \Phi_{m,k}(\mathbf{u}) = \Phi(\mathbf{u}) + \varepsilon_k^\Phi + (\lambda_k^\Phi)^\top (\mathbf{u} - \mathbf{u}_k) \tag{68}$$
$$\text{s.t.} \quad G_{m,i,k}(\mathbf{u}) = G_i(\mathbf{u}) + \varepsilon_k^{G_i} + (\lambda_k^{G_i})^\top (\mathbf{u} - \mathbf{u}_k) \leq 0, \quad i = 1, \ldots, n_g,$$
$$\mathcal{D}_k(\mathbf{u}) \leq 0, \qquad \mathbf{n}_k^\top \mathbf{u} \geq b_k,$$

while for the half space $\mathbf{n}_k^\top \mathbf{u} < b_k$, we solve:

$$\mathbf{u}_{k+1}^- = \arg\min_{\mathbf{u}} \Phi_{m,k}(\mathbf{u}) = \Phi(\mathbf{u}) + \varepsilon_k^\Phi + (\lambda_k^\Phi)^\top (\mathbf{u} - \mathbf{u}_k) \tag{69}$$
$$\text{s.t.} \quad G_{m,i,k}(\mathbf{u}) = G_i(\mathbf{u}) + \varepsilon_k^{G_i} + (\lambda_k^{G_i})^\top (\mathbf{u} - \mathbf{u}_k) \leq 0, \quad i = 1, \ldots, n_g,$$
$$\mathcal{D}_k(\mathbf{u}) \leq 0, \qquad \mathbf{n}_k^\top \mathbf{u} \leq b_k,$$

The next operating point $\mathbf{u}_{k+1}$ is chosen as the solution that minimizes $\Phi_{m,k}(\mathbf{u})$:

$$\mathbf{u}_{k+1} = \arg\min_{\mathbf{u}} \Phi_{m,k}(\mathbf{u}), \quad \text{s.t.} \quad \mathbf{u} \in \{\mathbf{u}_{k+1}^+, \mathbf{u}_{k+1}^-\}.$$

Several alternative dual MA algorithms have been proposed in the literature, which we briefly describe next:

(a)   The original dual ISOPE algorithm [7,63] estimates the gradients by FDA according to (50) and introduces a constraint that prevents ill-conditioning in the gradient estimation. At the kth RTO iteration, the matrix

$$\bar{U}_k(\mathbf{u}) := [\ \mathbf{u} - \mathbf{u}_k, \quad \mathbf{u} - \mathbf{u}_{k-1}, \quad \ldots, \quad \mathbf{u} - \mathbf{u}_{k-n_u+1}\ ] \in \mathbf{R}^{n_u \times n_u} \tag{70}$$

is constructed. Good conditioning is achieved by adding the lower bound φ on the inverse of the condition number of $\bar{U}_k(\mathbf{u})$:

$$\frac{1}{\kappa_k(\mathbf{u})} = \frac{\sigma_{\min}(\bar{U}_k(\mathbf{u}))}{\sigma_{\max}(\bar{U}_k(\mathbf{u}))} \geq \varphi, \tag{71}$$

where σ_{min} and σ_{max} denote the smallest and largest singular values, respectively. This bound is enforced by defining the duality constraint

$$\mathcal{D}_k(\mathbf{u}) = \varphi\kappa_k(\mathbf{u}) - 1 \leq 0, \tag{72}$$

which is used in (68) and (69).

(b) Gao and Engell [14] proposed a MA scheme that (i) estimates the gradients from the current and past operating points according to (50), and (ii) enforces the ill-conditioning duality constraint (72). However, instead of including the duality constraint in the optimization problem, it is used to decide whether an additional input perturbation is needed. This perturbation is obtained by minimizing the condition number $\kappa_k(\mathbf{u})$ subject to the modified constraints. The approach was labeled Iterative Gradient-Modification Optimization (IGMO) [80].

(c) Marchetti et al. [64] considered the dual MA scheme that estimates the gradients from the current and past operating points according to (50). The authors showed that the ill-conditioning bound (71) has no direct relationship with the accuracy of the gradient estimates, and proposed to upper bound the gradient-error norm of the Lagrangian function:

$$\|e^L(\mathbf{u})\| \leq E^U, \tag{73}$$

where e^L is the Lagrangian gradient error. In order to compute the upper bound as a function of $\mathbf{u}$, we proceed as in (56)–(58) and define the radius $r_k(\mathbf{u}) = r(\mathbf{u}, \mathbf{u}_k, \ldots, \mathbf{u}_{k-n_u+1})$ and the minimal distance $l_{min,k}(\mathbf{u}) = l_{min}(\mathbf{u}, \mathbf{u}_k, \ldots, \mathbf{u}_{k-n_u+1})$. This allows enforcing (73) by selecting $\mathbf{u}$ such that,

$$E_k^L(\mathbf{u}) := d^L r_k(\mathbf{u}) + \frac{\delta^L}{l_{min,k}(\mathbf{u})} \leq E^U, \tag{74}$$

where d^L is an upper bound on the spectral radius of the Hessian of the Lagrangian function, and δ^L is the range of measurement error in the Lagrangian function resulting from measurement noise in the cost and constraints [64]. This bound is enforced by defining the duality constraint used in (68) and (69) as

$$\mathcal{D}_k(\mathbf{u}) = E_k^L(\mathbf{u}) - E^U \leq 0. \tag{75}$$

(d) Rodger and Chachuat [67] proposed a dual MA scheme based on modifying the output variables as in Section 4.2.1. The gradients of the output variables are estimated using Broyden's formula (51). The authors show that, with Broyden's approach, the MA scheme (28) may fail to reach a plant KKT point upon convergence due to inaccurate gradient estimates and measurement noise. This may happen if the gradient estimates are not updated repeatedly in all input directions and if the step $\|\mathbf{u}_{k+1} - \mathbf{u}_k\|$ is too small. A duality constraint is proposed for improving the gradient estimates obtained by Broyden's approach.

(e) Marchetti [65] proposed another dual MA scheme, wherein the gradient modifiers are obtained by linear interpolation according to (64). Using this approach, the modified cost and constraint functions approximate the plant in a larger region. In order to limit the approximation error in the presence of noisy measurements, a duality constraint was introduced that limits the Lagrangian gradient error for at least one point belonging to the simplex with the extreme points $\{\mathbf{u}, \mathbf{u}_k, \ldots, \mathbf{u}_{k-n_u+1}\}$. This duality constraint produces larger feasible regions than (75) for the same upper bound E^U, and therefore allows larger input moves and faster convergence.

6. Applications

As MA has many useful features, it is of interest to investigate its potential for application. Table 1 lists several case studies available in the literature and compares them in terms of the MA variant that is used, the way the gradients are estimated and the number of input variables. Although this list is not exhaustive, it provides an overview of the current situation and gives a glimpse of the potential ahead. From this table, several interesting conclusions can be drawn:

- About half of the available studies deal with chemical reactors, both continuous and discontinuous. In the case of discontinuous reactors, the decision variables are input *profiles*, that can be parameterized to generate a larger set of *constant* input parameters. The optimization is then performed on a run-to-run basis, with each iteration hopefully resulting in improved operation.
- One sees from the list of problems in Table 1 that the Williams-Otto reactor seems to be *the benchmark problem* for testing MA schemes. The problem is quite challenging due to the presence of significant structural plant model-mismatch. Indeed, the plant is simulated as a 3-reaction system, while the model includes only two reactions with adjustable kinetic parameters. Despite very good model fit (prediction of the simulated concentrations), the RTO techniques that cannot handle structural uncertainty, such as the two-step approach, fail to reach the plant optimum. In contrast, all 6 MA variants converge to the plant optimum. The differentiation factor is then the convergence rate, which is often related to the estimation of plant gradients.
- Most MA schemes use FDA to estimate gradients. In the case of FFD, one needs to perturb each input successively; this is a time-consuming operation since, at the current operating point, the system must be perturbed n_u times, each time waiting for the plant to reach steady state. Hence, FDA based on past and current operating points is clearly the preferred option. However, to ensure that sufficient excitation is present to compute accurate gradients, the addition of a duality constraint is often necessary. Furthermore, both linear and nonlinear function approximations have been proposed with promising results. An alternative is to use the concept of neighboring extremals (NE), which works well when the uncertainty is of parametric nature (because the NE-based gradient law assumes that the variations are due to parametric uncertainties). Note that two approaches do not use an estimate of the plant gradient: CA uses only zeroth-order modifiers to drive the plant to the active constraints, while nested MA circumvents the computation of plant gradients by solving an additional optimization problem. Note also that IGMO can be classified as dual MA, with the peculiarity that the gradients are estimated via FDA with added perturbations when necessary.
- The typical number of input variables is small ($n_u < 5$), which seems to be related to the difficulties of gradient estimation. When the number of inputs is much larger, it might be useful to investigate whether it is important to correct the model in all input directions, which is nicely solved using D-MA.
- Two applications, namely, the path-following robot and the power kite, deal with the optimization of dynamic periodic processes. Each period (or multiple periods) is considered as a run, the input profiles are parameterized, and the operation is optimized on a run-to-run basis.
- Five of these case studies have dealt with experimental implementation, four on lab-scale setups and one at the industrial level. There is clearly room for more experimental implementations and, hopefully, also significant potential for improvements ahead!

Table 1. Overview of MA case studies (*FFD*: forward finite difference with input perturbation; *FDA*: finite-difference approximation based on past and current operating points; *NE*: neighboring extremals; *CA*: Constraint Adaptation; *MAWQA*: MA with quadratic approximation; *IGMO*: iterative gradient-modification optimization, where gradients are estimated via FDA with added perturbation when necessary; in bold: **experimental implementation**).

Problems	MA Variant	Ref.	Gradient Est.	# of Inputs	Remarks
Williams–Otto CSTR (*benchmark for MA*)	MA	[64]	FFD	2	basic MA algorithm
	dual MA	[64,65]	FDA, lin. approx.	2	addition of a constraint on gradient accuracy
	2nd-order MA	[31]	FFD	2	addition of second-order correction terms
	MAWQA	[36,81]	quad. approx.	2	gradient computed via quadratic approximation
	nested MA	[82]	—	2	additional optimization to by-pass gradient calculation
	various MA	[80]	various	2	IGMO, dual MA, nested MA and MAWQA
CSTR (*with pyrrole reaction*)	convex MA	[21]	perfect	2	use of convex model
	transient MA	[54]	NE-based	2	use of transient measurements for static optimization
	MAWQA	[83]	quad. approx.	2	gradient computed via quadratic approximation
Semi-batch reactors	dual, nested MA	[79]	FDA, —	3	4 reactions, *run-to-run scheme*
	MA	[84]	FDA	11	1 reaction, *run-to-run scheme*
Distillation column	various MA	[85,86]	various	2	controlled column, dual, nested, transient measurements
Batch chromatography	various MA	[14,87]	various	2	IGMO, dual MA and MAWQA, *run-to-run schemes*
Electro-chromatography	dual MA	[88]	IGMO	2	Continuous process
Chromatographic separation	dual MA	[89]	IGMO	3	Continuous multi-column solvent gradient purification
Sugar and ethanol plant	MA	[56]	FDA	6	heat and power system
Leaching process	MA	[90]	FDA	4	4 CSTR in series, **industrial implementation**
Hydroformylation process	MAWQA	[91]	quad. approx.	4	reactor and decanter with recycle
Flotation column	various MA	[92]	FFD, FDA, —	3	**implemented on lab-scale column**
Three-tank system	MA	[15]; [79]	**FFP**; FDA, —	2	**implemented on lab-scale setup**
Solid-oxide fuel cell	CA	[93]; [53]	—	3; 2	**implemented on lab fuel-cell stack**
Parallel compressors	MA	[94]	FFP	2 & 6	parallel structure exploited for gradient estimation
Path-following robot	CA	[95]	—	700	*periodic operation, enforcing minimum-time motion*
Power kite	D-MA	[28], [96]	FDA	40 → 2	*periodic operation,* **implemented on small-scale kite**

7. Conclusions

This section concludes the paper with a brief discussion of open issues and a few final words.

7.1. Open Issues

As illustrated in this paper, significant progress has been made recently on various aspects of MA. Yet, there are still unresolved issues with respect to both the methodology and applications. In particular, it is desirable for RTO schemes to exhibit the following features [38]:

i   plant optimality and feasibility upon convergence,
ii   acceptable number of RTO iterations, and
iii   plant feasibility throughout the optimization process.

These features and related properties are briefly discussed next.

Feasibility of all RTO iterates. By construction, MA satisfies Feature (i), cf. Theorem 1. However, Theorem 1 does not guarantee feasibility of the successive RTO iterates, nor does it imply anything regarding convergence speed. The Sufficient Conditions for Feasibility and Optimality (SCFO) presented in [35,97] can, in principle, be combined with any RTO scheme and enforce Feature (iii). However, SCFO often fails to enforce sufficiently fast convergence (cf. the examples provided in [35], Section 4.4) because of the necessity to upper bound uncertain plant constraints using Lipschitz constants. Hence, it is fair to search for other approaches that can ensure plant feasibility of the successive RTO iterates. One intuitive way is to replace the first-order (Lipschitz) upper bounds in [35] by second-order upper-bounding functions. For purely data-driven RTO, it has been shown numerically that this outperforms Lipschitz bounds [38]. Furthermore, the handling of plant infeasibility in dual MA has been discussed in [43]. New results given in [98] demonstrate that the combination of convex upper-bounding functions with the usual first-order MA corrections terms implies optimality upon convergence (Feature (i)) and feasibility for all iterates (Feature (iii)). However, a conclusive analysis of the trade-off between convergence speed and the issue of plant feasibility has not been conducted yet. Using the numerical optimization terminology, one could say that it remains open how one chooses the step length in RTO, when plant feasibility and fast convergence are both important.

Robustness to gradient uncertainty. The implementation of MA calls for the estimation of plant gradients. At the same time, as estimated gradients are prone to errors, it is not clear to which extent MA is robust to this kind of uncertainty. Simulation studies such as [15,64] indicate that MA is reasonably robust with respect to gradient uncertainty. For data-driven RTO schemes inspired by SCFO [35], robustness to multiplicative cost gradient uncertainty has been shown [37]. However, the assumption of purely multiplicative gradient uncertainty is hard to justify in practice, as this would imply exact gradient information at any unconstrained local optimum of the plant.

Realistically, one has to assume that gradient uncertainty is additive and bounded. First steps towards a strictly feasible MA scheme can be found in [99], wherein convex upper-bounding functions similar to [98] are combined with dual constraints from Section 5.3 [64].

Exploitation of plant structure for gradient estimation. In the presentation of the different MA variants, it is apparent that the physical structure of the plant (parallel or serial connections, recycles, weak and strong couplings) has not been the focus of investigation. At the same time, since many real-world RTO applications possess a specific structure, it is fair to ask whether one can exploit the physical interconnection structure to facilitate and possibly improve gradient estimation.

Parallel structures with identical units may be well suited for gradient estimation [76]. Recently, it has been observed that, under certain assumptions, parallel structures of heterogeneous units can also be exploited for gradient estimation [94]. A formal and general investigation of the interplay between plant structure and gradient estimation remains open.

RTO of interconnected processes. There is an evident similarity between many RTO schemes and numerical optimization algorithms. For example, one might regard MA adaptation in its simplest form of Section 4.1 as an *experimental gradient descent* method, likewise the scheme of Section 4.3.2 is linked to trust-region algorithms, and Remark 3 has pointed toward a SQP-like scheme. Hence, one might wonder whether the exploitation of structures in the spirit of distributed NLP algorithms will yield benefits to RTO and MA schemes. The early works on distributed ISOPE methods [7,100,101] point into such a direction. Furthermore, a recent paper by Wenzel et al. [102] argues for distributed plant optimization for the sake of confidentiality. In the context of MA, it is interesting to note that different distributed MA algorithms have recently been proposed [103,104]. Yet, there is no common consensus on the pros and cons of distributed RTO schemes.

Integration with advanced process control. Section 4.4.1 discussed the application of MA to controlled plants, and highlighted that the implementation of RTO results by means of MPC can be used to prevent constraint violations. Section 4.4.3 reported on the use of transient data for the purpose of gradient estimation for static MA. In general, it seems that the use of transient measurements in RTO either requires specific dynamic properties of the underlying closed-loop system or a tight integration of RTO and advanced process control. As many industrial multivariable process control tasks are nowadays solved via MPC, this can be narrowed down to the integration of MA and MPC. Yet, there remain important questions: (i) How to exploit the properties of MPC for RTO or MA? (ii) Can one use the gradient information obtained for MA in the MPC layer? While there are answers to Question (i) [45,105]; Question (ii) remains largely unexplored. This also raises the research question of how to design (static) MA and (dynamic) process control in a combined fashion or, expressed differently, how to extend the MA framework toward dynamic RTO problems. The D-MA approach sketched in Section 4.2.3 represents a first promising step for periodic and batch dynamic processes. Yet, the close coupling between MA and economic MPC schemes might bring about interesting new research and implementation directions [106–108].

Model-based or data-driven RTO? The fact that all MA properties also hold for the trivial case of no model gives rise to the fundamental question regarding the role of models in RTO. As shown in Section 4, models are not needed in order to enforce plant optimality upon convergence in MA. Furthermore, models bring about the model-adequacy issue discussed in Section 4.1.3. At the same time, industrial practitioners often spend a considerable amount of time on model building, parameter estimation and model validation. Hence, from the industrial perspective, there is an evident expectation that the use of models should pay off in RTO. From the research perspective, this gives rise to the following question: How much should we rely on uncertain model and how much on available plant data? In other words, what is a good tuning knob between model-based and data-driven RTO?

7.2. Final Words

This overview paper has discussed real-time optimization of uncertain plants using Modifier Adaptation. It has attempted to present the main developments in a comprehensive and unified way that highlights the main differences between the schemes. Yet, as in any review, the present one is also a mere snapshot taken at a given time. As we tried to sketch it, there remain several open issues, some of which will be crucial for the success of modifier-adaptation schemes in industrial practice.

Author Contributions: All authors have worked on all parts of the paper.

Conflicts of Interest: The authors declare no conflict of interest.

References

1. Chachuat, B.; Srinivasan, B.; Bonvin, D. Adaptation strategies for real-time optimization. *Comput. Chem. Eng.* **2009**, *33*, 1557–1567.
2. Chen, C.Y.; Joseph, B. On-line optimization using a two-phase approach: An application study. *Ind. Eng. Chem. Res.* **1987**, *26*, 1924–1930.
3. Darby, M.L.; Nikolaou, M.; Jones, J.; Nicholson, D. RTO: An overview and assessment of current practice. *J. Process Control* **2011**, *21*, 874–884.
4. Jang, S.-S.; Joseph, B.; Mukai, H. On-line optimization of constrained multivariable chemical processes. *AIChE J.* **1987**, *33*, 26–35.
5. Marlin, T.E.; Hrymak, A.N. Real-Time Operations Optimization of Continuous Processes. *AIChE Symp. Ser.—CPC-V* **1997**, *93*, 156–164.
6. Forbes, J.F.; Marlin, T.E.; MacGregor, J.F. Model adequacy requirements for optimizing plant operations. *Comput. Chem. Eng.* **1994**, *18*, 497–510.
7. Brdyś, M.; Tatjewski, P. *Iterative Algorithms for Multilayer Optimizing Control*; Imperial College Press: London UK, 2005.
8. Roberts, P.D. An algorithm for steady-state system optimization and parameter estimation. *J. Syst. Sci.* **1979**, *10*, 719–734.
9. Roberts, P.D. Coping with model-reality differences in industrial process optimisation—A review of integrated system optimisation and parameter estimation (ISOPE). *Comput. Ind.* **1995**, *26*, 281–290.
10. Roberts, P.D.; Williams, T.W. On an algorithm for combined system optimisation and parameter estimation. *Automatica* **1981**, *17*, 199–209.
11. Bazaraa, M.S.; Sherali, H.D.; Shetty, C.M. *Nonlinear Programming: Theory and Algorithms*, 3rd ed.; John Wiley and Sons: Hoboken, NJ, USA, 2006.
12. Chachuat, B.; Marchetti, A.; Bonvin, D. Process optimization via constraints adaptation. *J. Process Control* **2008**, *18*, 244–257.
13. Forbes, J.F.; Marlin, T.E. Model accuracy for economic optimizing controllers: The bias update case. *Ind. Eng. Chem. Res.* **1994**, *33*, 1919–1929.
14. Gao, W.; Engell, S. Iterative set-point optimization of batch chromatography. *Comput. Chem. Eng.* **2005**, *29*, 1401–1409.
15. Marchetti, A.; Chachuat, B.; Bonvin, D. Modifier-adaptation methodology for real-time optimization. *Ind. Eng. Chem. Res.* **2009**, *48*, 6022–6033.
16. Krstic, M.; Wang, H.-H. Stability of extremum seeking feedback for general nonlinear dynamic systems. *Automatica* **2000**, *36*, 595–601.
17. François, G.; Srinivasan, B.; Bonvin, D. Use of measurements for enforcing the necessary conditions of optimality in the presence of constraints and uncertainty. *J. Process Control* **2005**, *15*, 701–712.
18. Srinivasan, B.; Biegler, L.T.; Bonvin, D. Tracking the necessary conditions of optimality with changing set of active constraints using a barrier-penalty function. *Comput. Chem. Eng.* **2008**, *32*, 572–579.
19. Gros, S.; Srinivasan, B.; Bonvin, D. Optimizing control based on output feedback. *Comput. Chem. Eng.* **2009**, *33*, 191–198.
20. Skogestad, S. Self-optimizing control: The missing link between steady-state optimization and control. *Comput. Chem. Eng.* **2000**, *24*, 569–575.
21. François, G.; Bonvin, D. Use of convex model approximations for real-time optimization via modifier adaptation. *Ind. Eng. Chem. Res.* **2013**, *52*, 11614–11625.
22. Gill, P.E.; Murray, W.; Wright, M.H. *Practical Optimization*; Academic Press: London, UK, 2003.
23. Brdyś, M.; Roberts, P.D. Convergence and optimality of modified two-step algorithm for integrated system optimisation and parameter estimation. *Int. J. Syst. Sci.* **1987**, *18*, 1305–1322.
24. Zhang, H.; Roberts, P.D. Integrated system optimization and parameter estimation using a general form of steady-state model. *Int. J. Syst. Sci.* **1991**, *22*, 1679–1693.
25. Brdyś, M.; Chen, S.; Roberts, P.D. An extension to the modified two-step algorithm for steady-state system optimization and parameter estimation. *Int. J. Syst. Sci.* **1986**, *17*, 1229–1243.
26. Tatjewski, P. Iterative Optimizing Set-Point Control—The Basic Principle Redesigned. In Proceedings of the 15th IFAC World Congress, Barcelona, Spain, 21–26 July 2002.

27. Forbes, J.F.; Marlin, T.E. Design cost: A systematic approach to technology selection for model-based real-time optimization systems. *Comput. Chem. Eng.* **1996**, *20*, 717–734.

28. Costello, S.; François, G.; Bonvin, D. Directional Real-Time Optimization Applied to a Kite-Control Simulation Benchmark. In Proceedings of the European Control Conference, Linz, Austria, 15–17 July 2015; pp. 1594–1601.

29. Costello, S.; François, G.; Bonvin, D. A directional modifier-adaptation algorithm for real-time optimization. *J. Process Control* **2016**, *39*, 64–76.

30. Singhal, M.; Marchetti, A.; Faulwasser, T.; Bonvin, D. Improved Directional Derivatives for Modifier-Adaptation Schemes. In Proceedings of the 20th IFAC World Congress, Toulouse, France, 2017, submitted.

31. Faulwasser, T.; Bonvin, D. On the Use of Second-Order Modifiers for Real-Time Optimization. In Proceedings of the 19th IFAC World Congress, Cape Town, South Africa, 24–29 August 2014.

32. Golden, M.P.; Ydstie, B.E. Adaptive extremum control using approximate process models. *AIChE J.* **1989**, *35*, 1157–1169.

33. Nocedal, J.; Wright, S.J. *Numerical Optimization*; Springer: New York, NY, USA, 1999.

34. Conn, A.R.; Scheinberg, K.; Vicente, L.N. *Introduction to Derivative-Free Optimization*; Cambridge University Press: Cambridge, UK, 2009.

35. Bunin, G.A.; François, G.; Bonvin, D. Sufficient Conditions for Feasibility and Optimality of Real-Time Optimization Schemes—I. Theoretical Foundations, 2013; ArXiv:1308.2620 [math.oc].

36. Gao, W.; Wenzel, S.; Engell, S. A reliable modifier-adaptation strategy for real-time optimization. *Comput. Chem. Eng.* **2016**, *91*, 318–328.

37. Singhal, M.; Faulwasser, T.; Bonvin, D. On handling cost gradient uncertainty in real-time optimization. IFAC-PapersOnLine. *IFAC Symp. Adchem.* **2015**, *48*, 176–181.

38. Singhal, M.; Marchetti, A.G.; Faulwasser, T.; Bonvin, D. Real-Time Optimization Based on Adaptation of Surrogate Models. In Proceedings of the IFAC Symposium on DYCOPS, Trondheim, Norway, 6–8 June 2016; pp. 412–417.

39. Bertsekas, D. *Nonlinear Programming*, 2nd ed.; Athena Scientific: Belmont, MA, USA, 1999.

40. Bunin, G.A. On the equivalence between the modifier-adaptation and trust-region frameworks. *Comput. Chem. Eng.* **2014**, *71*, 154–157.

41. Biegler, L.T.; Lang, Y.; Lin, W. Multi-scale optimization for process systems engineering. *Comput. Chem. Eng.* **2014**, *60*, 17–30.

42. Tatjewski, P.; Brdyś, M.A.; Duda, J. Optimizing control of uncertain plants with constrained feedback controlled outputs. *Int. J. Control* **2001**, *74*, 1510–1526.

43. Navia, D.; Martí, R.; Sarabia, D.; Gutiérrez, G.; de Prada, C. Handling Infeasibilities in Dual Modifier-Adaptation Methodology for Real-Time Optimization. In Proceedings of the IFAC Symposium ADCHEM, Singapore, Singapore, 10–13 July 2012; pp. 537–542.

44. Qin, S.J.; Badgwell, T.A. A survey of industrial model predictive control technology. *Control Eng. Pract.* **2003**, *11*, 733–764.

45. Marchetti, A.; Luppi, P.; Basualdo, M. Real-Time Optimization via Modifier Adaptation Integrated with Model Predictive Control. In Proceedings of the 18th IFAC World Congress, Milan, Italy, 28 August–2 September 2011.

46. Muske, K.R.; Rawlings, J.B. Model predictive control with linear models. *AIChE J.* **1993**, *39*, 262–287.

47. Ying, C.-M.; Joseph, B. Performance and stability analysis of LP-MPC and QP-MPC cascade control systems. *AIChE J.* **1999**, *45*, 1521–1534.

48. Marchetti, A.G.; Ferramosca, A.; González, A.H. Steady-state target optimization designs for integrating real-time optimization and model predictive control. *J. Process Control* **2014**, *24*, 129–145.

49. Costello, S.; François, G.; Bonvin, D.; Marchetti, A. Modifier Adaptation for Constrained Closed-Loop Systems. In Proceedings of the 19th IFAC World Congress, Cape Town, South Africa, 24–29 August 2014; pp. 11080–11086.

50. François, G.; Costello, S.; Marchetti, A.G.; Bonvin, D. Extension of modifier adaptation for controlled plants using static open-loop models. *Comput. Chem. Eng.* **2016**, *93*, 361–371.

51. Costello, S.; François, G.; Srinivasan, B.; Bonvin, D. Modifier Adaptation for Run-to-Run Optimization of Transient Processes. In Proceedings of the 18th IFAC World Congress, Milan, Italy, 28 August–2 September 2011.
52. Marchetti, A.; Chachuat, B.; Bonvin, D. Batch Process Optimization via Run-to-Run Constraints Adaptation. In Proceedings of the European Control Conference, Kos, Greece, 2–5 July 2007.
53. Bunin, G.A.; Vuillemin, Z.; François, G.; Nakato, A.; Tsikonis, L.; Bonvin, D. Experimental real-time optimization of a solid fuel cell stack via constraint adaptation. *Energy* **2012**, *39*, 54–62.
54. François, G.; Bonvin, D. Use of transient measurements for the optimization of steady-state performance via modifier adaptation. *Ind. Eng. Chem. Res.* **2014**, *53*, 5148–5159.
55. de Avila Ferreira, T.; François, G.; Marchetti, A.G.; Bonvin, D. Use of Transient Measurements for Static Real-Time Optimization via Modifier Adaptation. In Proceedings of the 20th IFAC World Congress, Toulouse, France, 2017, submitted.
56. Serralunga, F.J.; Mussati, M.C.; Aguirre, P.A. Model adaptation for real-time optimization in energy systems. *Ind. Eng. Chem. Res.* **2013**, *52*, 16795–16810.
57. Bunin, G.A.; François, G.; Bonvin, D. Exploiting Local Quasiconvexity for Gradient Estimation in Modifier-Adaptation Schemes. In Proceedings of the American Control Conference, Montréal, QC, Canada, 27–29 June 2012; pp. 2806–2811.
58. Mansour, M.; Ellis, J.E. Comparison of methods for estimating real process derivatives in on-line optimization. *App. Math. Model.* **2003**, *27*, 275–291.
59. Srinivasan, B.; François, G.; Bonvin, D. Comparison of gradient estimation methods for real-time optimization. *Comput. Aided Chem. Eng.* **2011**, *29*, 607–611.
60. Zhang, Y.; Forbes, J.F. Performance analysis of perturbation-based methods for real-time optimization. *Can. J. Chem. Eng.* **2006**, *84*, 209–218.
61. Brekelmans, R.C.M.; Driessen, L.T.; Hamers, H.L.M.; den Hertog, D. Gradient estimation schemes for noisy functions. *J. Optim. Theory Appl.* **2005**, *126*, 529–551.
62. Engl, H.W.; Hanke, M.; Neubauer, A. *Regularization of Inverse Problems*; Kluwer Academic Publishers: Dordrecht, The Netherlands, 2000.
63. Brdyś, M.; Tatjewski, P. An Algorithm for Steady-State Optimizing Dual Control of Uncertain Plants. In Proceedings of the 1st IFAC Workshop on New Trends in Design of Control Systems, Smolenice, Slovakia, 7–10 September 1994; pp. 249–254.
64. Marchetti, A.; Chachuat, B.; Bonvin, D. A dual modifier-adaptation approach for real-time optimization. *J. Process Control* **2010**, *20*, 1027–1037.
65. Marchetti, A.G. A new dual modifier-adaptation approach for iterative process optimization with inaccurate models. *Comput. Chem. Eng.* **2013**, *59*, 89–100.
66. Roberts, P.D. Broyden Derivative Approximation in ISOPE Optimising and Optimal Control Algorithms. In Proceedings of the 11th IFAC Workshop on Control Applications of Optimisation, St Petersburg, Russia, 3–6 July 2000; pp. 283–288.
67. Rodger, E.A.; Chachuat, B. Design Methodology of Modifier Adaptation for On-Line Optimization of Uncertain Processes. In Proceedings of the IFAC World Congress, Milano, Italy, 28 August–2 September 2011; pp. 4113–4118.
68. Mendoza, D.F.; Alves Graciano, J.E.; dos Santos Liporace, F.; Carrillo Le Roux, G.A. Assessing the reliability of different real-time optimization methodologies. *Can. J. Chem. Eng.* **2016**, *94*, 485–497.
69. Savitzky, A.; Golay, M.J.E. Smoothing and differentiation of data by simplified least squares procedures. *Anal. Chem.* **1964**, *36*, 1627–1639.
70. McFarlane, R.C.; Bacon, D.W. Empirical strategies for open-loop on-line optimization. *Can. J. Chem. Eng.* **1989**, *84*, 209–218.
71. Becerra, V.M.; Roberts, P.D.; Griffiths, G.W. Novel developments in process optimisation using predictive control. *J. Process Control* **1998**, *8*, 117–138.
72. Bamberger, W.; Isermann, R. Adaptive on-line steady state optimization of slow dynamic processes. *Automatica* **1978**, *14*, 223–230.
73. Garcia, C.E.; Morari, M. Optimal operation of integrated processing systems. Part I: Open-loop on-line optimizing control. *AIChE J.* **1981**, *27*, 960–968.

74. François, G.; Srinivasan, B.; Bonvin, D. Comparison of six implicit real-time optimization schemes. *J. Eur. Syst. Autom.* **2012**, *46*, 291–305.

75. Guay, M.; Burns, D.J. A Comparison of Extremum Seeking Algorithms Applied to Vapor Compression System Optimization. In Proceedings of the American Control Conference, Portland, OR, USA, 4–6 June 2014; pp. 1076–1081.

76. Srinivasan, B. Real-time optimization of dynamic systems using multiple units. *Int. J. Robust Nonlinear Control* **2007**, *17*, 1183–1193.

77. Woodward, L.; Perrier, M.; Srinivasan, B. Improved performance in the multi-unit optimization method with non-identical units. *J. Process Control* **2009**, *19*, 205–215.

78. Bunin, G.A.; François, G.; Bonvin, D. From discrete measurements to bounded gradient estimates: A look at some regularizing structures. *Ind. Eng. Chem. Res.* **2013**, *52*, 12500–12513.

79. Navia, D.; Briceño, L.; Gutiérrez, G.; de Prada, C. Modifier-adaptation methodology for real-time optimization reformulated as a nested optimization problem. *Ind. Eng. Chem. Res.* **2015**, *54*, 12054–12071.

80. Gao, W.; Wenzel, S.; Engell, S. Comparison of Modifier Adaptation Schemes in Real-Time Optimization. In Proceedings of the IFAC Symposium on ADCHEM, Whistler, BC, Canada, 7–10 June 2015; pp. 182–187.

81. Wenzel, S.; Gao, W.; Engell, S. Handling Disturbances in Modifier Adaptation with Quadratic Approximation. In Proceedings of the 16th IFAC Workshop on Control Applications of Optimization, Garmisch-Partenkirchen, Germany, 6–9 October 2015.

82. Navia, D.; Gutiérrez, G.; de Prada, C. Nested Modifier-Adaptation for RTO in the Otto-Williams Reactor. In Proceedings of the IFAC Symposium DYCOPS, Mumbai, India, 18–20 December 2013.

83. Gao, W.; Engell, S. Using Transient Measurements in Iterative Steady-State Optimizing Control. In Proceedings of the ESCAPE-26, Portorož, Slovenia, 12–15 June 2016.

84. Jia, R.; Mao, Z.; Wang, F. Self-correcting modifier-adaptation strategy for batch-to-batch optimization based on batch-wise unfolded PLS model. *Can. J. Chem. Eng.* **2016**, *94*, 1770–1782.

85. Rodriguez-Blanco, T.; Sarabia, D.; Navia, D.; de Prada, C. Modifier-Adaptation Methodology for RTO Applied to Distillation Columns. In Proceedings of the IFAC Symposium on ADCHEM, Whistler, BC, Canada, 7–10 June 2015; pp. 223–228.

86. Rodriguez-Blanco, T.; Sarabia, D.; de Prada, C. Modifier-Adaptation Approach to Deal with Structural and Parametric Uncertainty. In Proceedings of the IFAC Symposium on DYCOPS, Trondheim, Norway, 6–8 June 2016; pp. 851–856.

87. Gao, W.; Wenzel, S.; Engell, S. Integration of Gradient Adaptation and Quadratic Approximation in Real-Time Optimization. In Proceedings of the 34th Chinese Control Conference, Hangzhou, China, 28–30 July 2015; pp. 2780–2785.

88. Behrens, M.; Engell, S. Iterative Set-Point Optimization of Continuous Annular Electro-Chromatography. In Proceedings of the 18th IFAC World Congress, Milan, Italy, 28 August–2 September 2011; pp. 3665–3671.

89. Behrens, M.; Khobkhun, P.; Potschka, A.; Engell, S. Optimizing Set Point Control of the MCSGP Process. In Proceedings of the European Control Conference, Strasbourg, France, 24–27 June 2014; pp. 1139–1144.

90. Zhang, J.; Mao, Z.; Jia, R.; He, D. Real-time optimization based on a serial hybrid model for gold cyanidation leaching process. *Miner. Eng.* **2015**, *70*, 250–263.

91. Hernandez, R.; Engell, S. Iterative Real-Time Optimization of a Homogeneously Catalyzed Hydroformylation Process. In Proceedings of the ESCAPE-26, Portorož, Slovenia, 12–15 June 2016.

92. Navia, D.; Villegas, D.; Cornejo, I.; de Prada, C. Real-time optimization for a laboratory-scale flotation column. *Comput. Chem. Eng.* **2016**, *86*, 62–74.

93. Marchetti, A.; Gopalakrishnan, A.; Tsikonis, L.; Nakajo, A.; Wuillemin, Z.; Chachuat, B.; Van herle, J.; Bonvin, D. Robust real-time optimization of a solid oxide fuel cell stack. *J. Fuel Cell Sci. Technol.* **2011**, *8*, 051001.

94. Milosavljevic, P.; Cortinovis, A.; Marchetti, A.G.; Faulwasser, T.; Mercangöz, M.; Bonvin, D. Optimal Load Sharing of Parallel Compressors via Modifier Adaptation. In Proceedings of the IEEE Multi-Conference on Systems and Control, Buenos Aires, Argentina, 19–22 September 2016.

95. Milosavljevic, P.; Faulwasser, T.; Marchetti, A.; Bonvin, D. Time-Optimal Path-Following Operation in the Presence of Uncertainty. In Proceedings of the European Control Conference, Aalborg, Denmark, 29 June–1 July 2016.

96. Costello, S.; François, G.; Bonvin, D. Real-time optimizing control of an experimental crosswind power kite. *IEEE Trans. Control Syst. Technol.* 2016, submitted.

97. Bunin, G.A.; François, G.; Bonvin, D. *Sufficient Conditions for Feasibility and Optimality of Real-Time Optimization Schemes—II. Implementation Issues*, 2013; ArXiv:1308.2625 [math.oc].

98. Marchetti, A.G.; Faulwasser, T.; Bonvin, D. A feasible-side globally convergent modifier-adaptation scheme. *J. Process Control*, 2016, submitted.

99. Marchetti, A.G.; Singhal, M.; Faulwasser, T.; Bonvin, D. Modifier adaptation with guaranteed feasibility in the presence of gradient uncertainty. *Comput. Chem. Eng.* **2016**, doi:10.1016/j.compchemeng.2016.11.027.

100. Brdyś, M.; Roberts, P.D.; Badi, M.M.; Kokkinos, I.C.; Abdullah, N. Double loop iterative strategies for hierarchical control of industrial processes. *Automatica* **1989**, *25*, 743–751.

101. Brdyś, M.; Abdullah, N.; Roberts, P.D. Hierarchical adaptive techniques for optimizing control of large-scale steady-state systems: optimality, iterative strategies, and their convergence. *IMA J. Math. Control Inf.* **1990**, *7*, 199–233.

102. Wenzel, S.; Paulen, R.; Stojanovski, G.; Krämer, S.; Beisheim, B.; Engell, S. Optimal resource allocation in industrial complexes by distributed optimization and dynamic pricing. *at-Automatisierungstechnik* **2016**, *64*, 428–442.

103. Milosavljevic, P.; Schneider, R.; Faulwasser, T.; Bonvin, D. Distributed Modifier Adaptation Using a Coordinator and Input-Output Data. In Proceedings of the 20th IFAC World Congress, Toulouse, France, 2017, submitted.

104. Schneider, R.; Milosavljevic, P.; Bonvin, D. Distributed modifier-adaptation schemes for real-time optimization of uncertain interconnected systems. *SIAM J. Control Optim.* 2016, submitted.

105. Alvarez, L.A.; Odloak, D. Optimization and control of a continuous polymerization reactor. *Braz. J. Chem. Eng.* **2012**, *29*, 807–820.

106. Diehl, M.; Amrit, R.; Rawlings, J.B. A Lyapunov function for economic optimizing model predictive control. *IEEE Trans. Automat. Control* **2011**, *56*, 703–707.

107. Ellis, M.; Durand, H.; Christofides, P.D. A tutorial review of economic model predictive control methods. *J. Process Control* **2014**, *24*, 1156–1178.

108. Faulwasser, T.; Bonvin, D. On the Design of Economic NMPC Based on Approximate Turnpike Properties. In Proceedings of the 54th IEEE Conference on Decision and Control, Osaka, Japan, 15–18 December 2015; pp. 4964–4970.

Article

A Study of Explorative Moves during Modifier Adaptation with Quadratic Approximation

Weihua Gao *, Reinaldo Hernández and Sebastian Engell

Biochemical and Chemical Engineering Department, TU Dortmund, Emil-Figge-Str. 70,
44221 Dortmund, Germany; reinaldo.hernandez@bci.tu-dortmund.de (R.H.);
sebastian.engell@bci.tu-dortmund.de (S.E.)
* Correspondence: weihua.gao@bci.tu-dortmund.de; Tel.: +49-231-755-5131

Academic Editor: Dominique Bonvin
Received: 31 October 2016; Accepted: 22 November 2016; Published: 26 November 2016

Abstract: Modifier adaptation with quadratic approximation (in short MAWQA) can adapt the operating condition of a process to its economic optimum by combining the use of a theoretical process model and of the collected data during process operation. The efficiency of the MAWQA algorithm can be attributed to a well-designed mechanism which ensures the improvement of the economic performance by taking necessary explorative moves. This paper gives a detailed study of the mechanism of performing explorative moves during modifier adaptation with quadratic approximation. The necessity of the explorative moves is theoretically analyzed. Simulation results for the optimization of a hydroformylation process are used to illustrate the efficiency of the MAWQA algorithm over the finite difference based modifier adaptation algorithm.

Keywords: real-time optimization; modifier adaptation; quadratic approximation

1. Introduction

In the process industries, performing model-based optimization to obtain economic operations usually implies the need of handling the problem of plant-model mismatch. An optimum that is calculated using a theoretical model seldom represents the plant optimum. As a result, real-time optimization (RTO) is attracting considerable industrial interest. RTO is a model based upper-level optimization system that is operated iteratively in closed loop and provides set-points to the lower-level regulatory control system in order to maintain the process operation as close as possible to the economic optimum. RTO schemes usually estimate the process states and some model parameters or disturbances from the measured data but employ a fixed process model which leads to problems if the model does not represent the plant accurately.

Several schemes have been proposed towards how to combine the use of theoretical models and of the collected data during process operation, in particular the model adaptation or two-step scheme [1]. It handles plant-model mismatch in a sequential manner via an identification step followed by an optimization step. Measurements are used to estimate the uncertain model parameters, and the updated model is used to compute the decision variables via model-based optimization. The model adaptation approach is expected to work well when the plant-model mismatch is only of parametric nature, and the operating conditions lead to sufficient excitation for the estimation of the plant outputs. In practice, however, both parametric and structural mismatch are typically present and, furthermore, the excitation provided by the previously visited operating points is often not sufficient to accurately identify the model parameters.

For an RTO scheme to converge to the plant optimum, it is necessary that the gradients of the objective as well as the values and gradients of the constraints of the optimization problem match those of the plant. Schemes that directly adapt the model-based optimization problem by using the update terms (called modifiers) which are computed from the collected data have been proposed [2–4]. The modifier-adaptation schemes can handle considerable plant-model mismatch by applying bias- and gradient-corrections to the objective and to the constraint functions. One of the major challenges in practice, as shown in [5], is the estimation of the plant gradients with respect to the decision variables from noisy measurement data.

Gao et al. [6] combined the idea of modifier adaptation with the quadratic approximation approach that is used in derivative-free optimization and proposed the modifier adaptation with quadratic approximation (in short MAWQA) algorithm. Quadratic approximations of the objective function and of the constraint functions are constructed based on the screened data which are collected during the process operation. The plant gradients are computed from the quadratic approximations and are used to adapt the objective and the constraint functions of the model-based optimization problem. Simulation studies for the optimization of a reactor benchmark problem with noisy data showed that by performing some explorative moves the true optimum can be reliably obtained. However, neither the generation of the explorative moves nor their necessity for the convergence of set-point to the optimum was theoretically studied. Due to the fact that the estimation of the gradients using the quadratic approximation approach requires more data than those that are required by using a finite difference approach, the efficiency of the MAWQA algorithm, in terms of the number of plant evaluations to obtain the optimum, has been questioned, in particular for the case of several decision variables. In addition, in practice, it is crucial for plant operators to be confident with the necessity of taking the explorative moves which may lead to a deterioration of plant performance.

This paper reports a detailed study of the explorative moves during modifier adaptation with quadratic approximation. It starts with how the explorative moves are generated and then the factors that influence the generation of these moves are presented. The causality between the factors and the explorative moves is depicted in Figure 1, where the blocks with a yellow background represent the factors. The use of a screening algorithm to optimize the regression set for quadratic approximations is shown to ensure that an explorative move is only performed when the past collected data cannot provide accurate gradient estimates. Simulation results for the optimization of a hydroformylation process with four optimization variables are used to illustrate the efficiency of the MAWQA algorithm, which takes necessary explorative moves, over the finite difference based modifier adaptation algorithm.

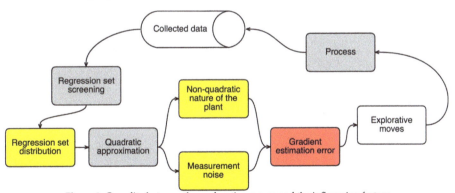

Figure 1. Causality between the explorative moves and the influencing factors.

2. Modifier Adaptation with Quadratic Approximation

Let $J_m(\mathbf{u})$ and $\mathbf{C}_m(\mathbf{u})$ represent the objective and the vector of constraint functions of a static model-based optimization problem, assumed to be twice differentiable with respect to the vector of decision variables $\mathbf{u} \in \mathbb{R}^{n_u}$

$$\min_{\mathbf{u}} \quad J_m(\mathbf{u})$$
$$\text{s.t.} \quad \mathbf{C}_m(\mathbf{u}) \leq \mathbf{0}. \tag{1}$$

At each iteration of the modifier adaptation algorithm, bias- and gradient-corrections of the optimization problem are applied as

$$\min_{\mathbf{u}} \quad J_m(\mathbf{u}) + \left(\nabla J_p^{(k)} - \nabla J_m^{(k)}\right)^T \left(\mathbf{u} - \mathbf{u}^{(k)}\right)$$

$$\text{s.t.} \quad \mathbf{C}_m(\mathbf{u}) + \mathbf{C}_p^{(k)} - \mathbf{C}_m^{(k)} + \left(\nabla \mathbf{C}_p^{(k)} - \nabla \mathbf{C}_m^{(k)}\right)^T \left(\mathbf{u} - \mathbf{u}^{(k)}\right) \leq \mathbf{0}.$$

$$(2)$$

The symbols are explained in Table 1. $\nabla J_p^{(k)}$ and $\nabla \mathbf{C}_p^{(k)}$ are usually approximated by the finite difference approach

$$\nabla J_p^{(k)} \approx \begin{bmatrix} u_1^{(k)} - u_1^{(k-1)} & \cdots & u_{n_u}^{(k)} - u_{n_u}^{(k-1)} \\ \vdots & \vdots & \vdots \\ u_1^{(k)} - u_1^{(k-n_u)} & \cdots & u_{n_u}^{(k)} - u_{n_u}^{(k-n_u)} \end{bmatrix}^{-1} \begin{bmatrix} J_p^{(k)} - J_p^{(k-1)} \\ \vdots \\ J_p^{(k)} - J_p^{(k-n_u)} \end{bmatrix}, \qquad (3)$$

where n_u is the number of dimensions of $\mathbf{u}$, $J_p^{(k-i)}$, $i = 0, \ldots, n_u$, are the plant objectives at set-points $\mathbf{u}^{(k-i)}$, $i = 0, \ldots, n_u$, and $\nabla \mathbf{C}_p^{(k)}$ is approximated similarly. The accuracy of the finite difference approximations is influenced by both the step-sizes between the set-points and the presence of measurement noise. In order to acquire accurate gradient estimations, small step-sizes are preferred. However, the use of small step-sizes leads to a high sensitivity of the gradient estimates to measurement noise.

Table 1. Symbols used in the modifier adaptation formulation.

Symbol	Description
k	Index of iteration
$\mathbf{u}^{(k)}$	Current set-point
$\nabla J_p^{(k)}$	Gradient vector of the plant objective function at $\mathbf{u}^{(k)}$
$\nabla J_m^{(k)}$	Gradient vector of the model-predicted objective function at $\mathbf{u}^{(k)}$
$\mathbf{C}_p^{(k)}$	Vector of the plant constraint values at $\mathbf{u}^{(k)}$
$\mathbf{C}_m^{(k)}$	Vector of the model-predicted constraint values at $\mathbf{u}^{(k)}$
$\nabla \mathbf{C}_p^{(k)}$	Gradient matrix of the plant constraint functions at $\mathbf{u}^{(k)}$
$\nabla \mathbf{C}_m^{(k)}$	Gradient matrix of the model-predicted constraint functions at $\mathbf{u}^{(k)}$

In the MAWQA algorithm, the gradients are computed analytically from quadratic approximations of the objective function and of the constraint functions that are regressed based on a screened set (represented by $\mathcal{U}^{(k)}$ at the kth iteration) of all the collected data (represented by $\mathbb{U}$). The screened set consists of near and distant points: $\mathcal{U}^{(k)} = \mathcal{U}_n \cup \mathcal{U}_d$, where $\mathcal{U}_n = \{\mathbf{u} : \|\mathbf{u} - \mathbf{u}^{(k)}\| < \Delta\mathbf{u}; \text{ and } \mathbf{u} \in \mathbb{U}\}$, and $\mathcal{U}_d$ is determined by

$$\min_{\mathcal{U}_d} \quad \frac{\sum_{\mathbf{u} \in \mathcal{U}_d} \|\mathbf{u} - \mathbf{u}^{(k)}\|}{\theta(\mathcal{U}_d)}$$

$$\text{s.t.} \quad \text{size}(\mathcal{U}_d) \geq C_2^{n_u+2} - 1$$

$$\mathcal{U}_d \subset \mathbb{U} \setminus \mathcal{U}_n,$$

$$(4)$$

where $\Delta\mathbf{u}$ is sufficiently large so that $\mathcal{U}_d$ guarantees robust quadratic approximations with noisy data, $\theta(\mathcal{U}_d)$ is the minimal angle between all possible vectors that are defined by $\mathbf{u} - \mathbf{u}^{(k)}$, and $C_2^{n_u+2} = (n_u + 2)(n_u + 1)/2$ is the number of data required to uniquely determine the quadratic approximations.

In the MAWQA algorithm, the regression set $\mathcal{U}^{(k)}$ is also used to define a constrained search space $\mathcal{B}^{(k)}$ for the next set-point move

$$\mathcal{B}^{(k)} : (\mathbf{u} - \mathbf{u}^{(k)})^T M^{-1} (\mathbf{u} - \mathbf{u}^{(k)}) \leq \gamma^2, \tag{5}$$

where $M = cov(\mathcal{U}^{(k)})$ is the covariance matrix of the selected points (inputs) and γ is a scaling parameter. $\mathcal{B}^{(k)}$ is a n_u-axial ellipsoid centered at $\mathbf{u}^{(k)}$. The axes of the ellipsoid are thus aligned with the eigenvectors of the covariance matrix. The semi-axis lengths of the ellipsoid are related to the eigenvalues of the covariance matrix by the scaling parameter γ. The adapted optimization (2) is augmented by the search space constraint as

$$\min_{\mathbf{u}} \quad J_{ad}^{(k)}(\mathbf{u})$$
$$\text{s.t.} \quad \mathbf{C}_{ad}^{(k)}(\mathbf{u}) \leq \mathbf{0} \tag{6}$$
$$\mathbf{u} \in \mathcal{B}^{(k)},$$

where $J_{ad}^{(k)}(\mathbf{u})$ and $\mathbf{C}_{ad}^{(k)}(\mathbf{u})$ represent the adapted objective and constraint functions in (2).

In the application of the modifier adaptation with quadratic approximation, it can happen that the nominal model is inadequate for the modifier-adaptation approach and that it is better to only use the quadratic approximations to compute the next plant move. In order to ensure the convergence, it is necessary to monitor the performance of the adapted optimization and possibly to switch between model-based and data-based optimizations. In each iteration of the MAWQA algorithm, a quality index of the adapted optimization $\rho_m^{(k)}$ is calculated and compared with the quality index of the quadratic approximation $\rho_\phi^{(k)}$, where

$$\rho_m^{(k)} = \max\left\{ \left| 1 - \frac{J_{ad}^{(k)} - J_{ad}^{(k-1)}}{J_p^{(k)} - J_p^{(k-1)}} \right|, \left| 1 - \frac{C_{ad,1}^{(k)} - C_{ad,1}^{(k-1)}}{C_{p,1}^{(k)} - C_{p,1}^{(k-1)}} \right|, \ldots, \left| 1 - \frac{C_{ad,n_c}^{(k)} - C_{ad,n_c}^{(k-1)}}{C_{p,n_c}^{(k)} - C_{p,n_c}^{(k-1)}} \right| \right\} \tag{7}$$

and

$$\rho_\phi^{(k)} = \max\left\{ \left| 1 - \frac{J_\phi^{(k)} - J_\phi^{(k-1)}}{J_p^{(k)} - J_p^{(k-1)}} \right|, \left| 1 - \frac{C_{\phi,1}^{(k)} - C_{\phi,1}^{(k-1)}}{C_{p,1}^{(k)} - C_{p,1}^{(k-1)}} \right|, \ldots, \left| 1 - \frac{C_{\phi,n_c}^{(k)} - C_{\phi,n_c}^{(k-1)}}{C_{p,n_c}^{(k)} - C_{p,n_c}^{(k-1)}} \right| \right\} \tag{8}$$

with $J_\phi^{(k)}$ and $\mathbf{C}_\phi^{(k)}$ are the quadratic approximations of the objective and the constraint functions. If $\rho_m^{(k)} \leq \rho_\phi^{(k)}$, the predictions of the adapted model-based optimization are more accurate than that of the quadratic approximations and (6) is performed to determine the next set-point. Otherwise, an optimization based on the quadratic approximations is done

$$\min_{\mathbf{u}} \quad J_\phi^{(k)}(\mathbf{u})$$
$$\text{s.t.} \quad \mathbf{C}_\phi^{(k)}(\mathbf{u}) \leq \mathbf{0} \tag{9}$$
$$\mathbf{u} \in \mathcal{B}^{(k)}.$$

The MAWQA algorithm is given as follows:

Step 1. Choose an initial set-point $\mathbf{u}^{(0)}$ and probe the plant at $\mathbf{u}^{(0)}$ and $\mathbf{u}^{(0)} + h\mathbf{e}_i$, where h is a suitable step size and $\mathbf{e}_i \in \mathbb{R}^{n_u} (i = 1, \ldots, n_u)$ are mutually orthogonal unit vectors. Use the finite difference approach to calculate the gradients at $\mathbf{u}^{(0)}$ and run the IGMO approach [3] until $k \geq C_2^{n_u+2}$ set-points have been generated. Run the screening algorithm to define the regression set $\mathcal{U}^{(k)}$. Initialize $\rho_m^{(k)} = 0$ and $\rho_\phi^{(k)} = 0$.

Step 2. Calculate the quadratic functions $J_\phi^{(k)}$ and $\mathbf{C}_\phi^{(k)}$ based on $\mathcal{U}^{(k)}$. Determine the search space $\mathcal{B}^{(k)}$ by (5).

Step 3. Compute the gradients from the quadratic functions. Adapt the model-based optimization problem and determine the optimal set-point $\hat{\mathbf{u}}^{(k)}$ as follows:

    (a) If $\rho_m^{(k)} \leq \rho_\phi^{(k)}$, run the adapted model-based optimization (6).

    (b) Else perform the data-based optimization (9).

Step 4. If $\|\hat{\mathbf{u}}^{(k)} - \mathbf{u}^{(k)}\| < \Delta\mathbf{u}$ and there exists one point $\mathbf{u}^{(j)} \in \mathcal{U}^{(k)}$ such that $\|\mathbf{u}^{(j)} - \mathbf{u}^{(k)}\| > 2\Delta\mathbf{u}$, set $\hat{\mathbf{u}}^{(k)} = \left(\mathbf{u}^{(j)} + \mathbf{u}^{(k)}\right)/2$.

Step 5. Evaluate the plant at $\hat{\mathbf{u}}^{(k)}$ to acquire $J_p(\hat{\mathbf{u}}^{(k)})$ and $\mathbf{C}_p(\hat{\mathbf{u}}^{(k)})$. Prepare the next step as follows

    (a) If $\hat{J}_p^{(k)} < J_p^{(k)}$, where $\hat{J}_p^{(k)} = J_p(\hat{\mathbf{u}}^{(k)})$, this is a performance-improvement move. Define $\mathbf{u}^{(k+1)} = \hat{\mathbf{u}}^{(k)}$ and run the screening algorithm to define the next regression set $\mathcal{U}^{(k+1)}$. Update the quality indices $\rho_m^{(k+1)}$ and $\rho_\phi^{(k+1)}$. Increase k by one and go to Step 2.

    (b) If $\hat{J}_p^{(k)} \geq J_p^{(k)}$, this is an explorative move. Run the screening algorithm to update the regression set for $\mathbf{u}^{(k)}$. Go to Step 2.

Note that the index of iteration of the MAWQA algorithm is increased by one only when a performance-improvement move is performed. Several explorative moves may be required at each iteration. The number of plant evaluations is the sum of the numbers of both kinds of moves. The next section studies why the explorative moves are required and how they contribute to the improvement of the performance on a longer horizon.

3. Analysis of the Explorative Moves

In the MAWQA algorithm, the quadratic approximations of the objective and the constraint functions are started once $C_2^{n_u+2}$ data have been collected. It can happen that the distribution of the set-points is not "well-poised" [7] to ensure that the gradients are accurately estimated via the quadratic approximations, especially when the initial set-point is far away from the optimum and the following set-point moves are all along some search direction. Interpolation-based derivative-free optimization algorithms rely on a model-improvement step that generates additional set-point moves to ensure the well-poisedness of the interpolation set. Although the MAWQA algorithm was designed without an explicit model-improvement step, the generation of explorative moves can be considered as an implicit step to improve the poisedness of the regression set for the quadratic approximations. This section gives a theoretical analysis of the explorative moves. We start with some observations from the simulation results in [6] and relate the explorative moves to the estimation error of the gradients. The factors that influence the accuracy of the estimated gradients are analyzed. It is shown that the screening of the regression set leads to very pertinent explorative moves which, on the one hand, are sufficient to improve the accuracy of the gradient estimations, and, on the other hand, are less expensive than the model-improvement step in the derivative-free optimization algorithms.

The generation of the explorative moves is presented in Figure 2 where one MAWQA iteration for the optimization of the steady-state profit of the Williams-Otto reactor with respect to the flow rate and the reaction temperature [6] is illustrated. Here the blue surface represents the real profit mapping, and the mesh represents the quadratic approximation which was computed based on the regression set (⦿: set-point moves, ●: measured profit values). The bottom part shows the contours of the profit as predicted by the uncorrected model (blue lines) , the constrained search space (dash-dot line), and the contours of the modifier-adapted profit (inside, magenta lines). Comparing the surface plot and the mesh plot, we can see that the gradient along the direction of the last set-point move is estimated well. However, a large error can be observed in the perpendicular direction. The gradient error propagates to the modifier-adapted contours and therefore, the next set-point move (⦿) points to the direction where the gradient is badly estimated. Despite the fact that the move may not improve the objective function, the data collection in that direction can later help to improve the gradient estimation.

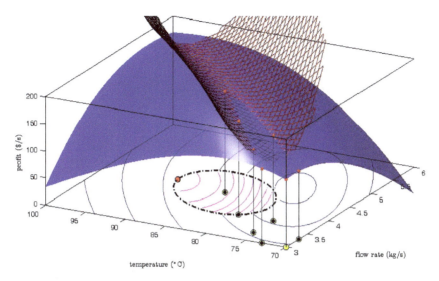

Figure 2. Illustration of one MAWQA iteration with noisy data. Surface plot: real profit mapping, mesh plot: quadratic approximation, ◉: regression set-point, ○: not chosen set-point, ●: measured profit, ⬤: next set-point move, blue contours: model-predicted profit, magenta contours: modifier-adapted profit, dash-dot line: constrained search space.

The example illustrates how the gradient error in a specific direction may lead to an explorative move along the same direction. In the MAWQA algorithm, the gradients are determined by evaluating ∇J_ϕ and $\nabla \mathbf{C}_\phi$ at $\mathbf{u}^{(k)}$. In order to be able to quantify the gradient error, we assume that the screened set $\mathcal{U}^{(k)}$ is of size $C_2^{n_u+2}$ and the quadratic approximations are interpolated based on $\mathcal{U}^{(k)}$. In the application of the MAWQA algorithm, this assumption is valid when the current set-point is far away from the plant optimum. Recall the screening algorithm, $\mathcal{U}^{(k)}$ consists of the near set $\mathcal{U}_n$ and the distant set $\mathcal{U}_d$. From (4), we can conclude that the distant set $\mathcal{U}_d$ is always of size $C_2^{n_u+2} - 1$. Step 4 of the MAWQA algorithm ensures that the near set $\mathcal{U}_n$ only consists of $\mathbf{u}^{(k)}$ until the optimized next move is such that $\|\hat{\mathbf{u}}^{(k)} - \mathbf{u}^{(k)}\| < \Delta \mathbf{u}$ and there are no points $\mathbf{u}^{(j)} \in \mathcal{U}^{(k)}$ such that $\|\mathbf{u}^{(j)} - \mathbf{u}^{(k)}\| > 2\Delta \mathbf{u}$, that is, all the points in $\mathcal{U}_d$ keep suitable distances away from $\mathbf{u}^{(k)}$ for good local approximations. The above two conditions imply that $\|\mathbf{u}^{(k)} - \mathbf{u}^*\| \leq \Delta \mathbf{u}$, where $\mathbf{u}^*$ represents the plant optimum. As a result of Step 4, when $\|\mathbf{u}^{(k)} - \mathbf{u}^*\| > \Delta \mathbf{u}$, $\mathcal{U}_n$ is always of size 1. For simplicity, a shift of coordinates to move $\mathbf{u}^{(k)}$ to the origin is performed and the points in $\mathcal{U}^{(k)}$ are reordered as $\{\mathbf{0}, \mathbf{u}^{d_1}, \ldots, \mathbf{u}^{d_n}\}$, where $n = C_2^{n_u+2} - 1$.

Let $\phi = \{1, u_1, \ldots, u_{n_u}, u_1^2, \ldots, u_{n_u}^2, \sqrt{2} u_1 u_2, \sqrt{2} u_1 u_3, \ldots, \sqrt{2} u_{n_u-1} u_{n_u}\}$ represent a natural basis of the quadratic approximation. Let $\underline{\alpha}$ represent a column vector of the coefficients of the quadratic approximation. The quadratic approximation of the objective function is formulated as

$$J_\phi(\mathbf{u}) = \alpha_0 + \sum_{i=1}^{n_u} \alpha_i u_i + \sum_{i=1}^{n_u} \alpha_{n_u+i} u_i^2 + \sqrt{2} \sum_{i=1}^{n_u-1} \sum_{j=i+1}^{n_u} \alpha_{2n_u+I(n_u,i,j)} u_i u_j, \tag{10}$$

where $I(n_u, i, j) = n_u(i-1) - (i+1)i/2 + j$. The coefficients α_i, $i = 0, \ldots, n$ are calculated via the interpolation of the $n + 1$ data sets $\{\mathbf{u}, J_p(\mathbf{u})\}$

$$
\begin{bmatrix}
1 & 0 & \cdots & 0 \\
1 & \varphi_1(\mathbf{u}^{(d_1)}) & \cdots & \varphi_n(\mathbf{u}^{(d_1)}) \\
\vdots & \vdots & \vdots & \vdots \\
1 & \varphi_1(\mathbf{u}^{(d_n)}) & \cdots & \varphi_n(\mathbf{u}^{(d_n)})
\end{bmatrix}
\begin{bmatrix}
\alpha_0 \\
\alpha_1 \\
\vdots \\
\alpha_n
\end{bmatrix}
=
\begin{bmatrix}
J_p(0) \\
J_p(\mathbf{u}^{(d_1)}) \\
\vdots \\
J_p(\mathbf{u}^{(d_n)})
\end{bmatrix}
+
\begin{bmatrix}
v_0 \\
v_1 \\
\vdots \\
v_n
\end{bmatrix},
\tag{11}
$$

$$
\underbrace{\qquad\qquad\qquad\qquad}_{\underline{M}(\phi,\mathcal{U}^{(k)})} \qquad \underbrace{\quad}_{\underline{\alpha}} \qquad \underbrace{\qquad}_{\underline{J}_p(\mathcal{U}^{(k)})} \qquad \underbrace{\quad}_{\underline{v}}
$$

where $\varphi_i(\mathbf{u})$, $i = 1,\dots,n$, represent the polynomial bases in ϕ, J_p and v represent the noise-free objective and the measurement noise. Assume $\underline{M}(\phi,\mathcal{U}^{(k)})$ is nonsingular,

$$
\underline{\alpha} = \left(\underline{M}(\phi,\mathcal{U}^{(k)})\right)^{-1} \underline{J}_p(\mathcal{U}^{(k)}) + \left(\underline{M}(\phi,\mathcal{U}^{(k)})\right)^{-1} \underline{v}.
\tag{12}
$$

The computed gradient vector at the origin via the quadratic approximation is

$$
\nabla J_\phi(0) = (\alpha_1,\dots,\alpha_{n_u})^T = \underline{\alpha}^{J_p} + \underline{\alpha}^v,
\tag{13}
$$

where $\underline{\alpha}^{J_p}$ represents the noise-free estimation and $\underline{\alpha}^v$ represents the influence of the measurement noise. From [8], a bound on the error between the noise-free estimation $\underline{\alpha}^{J_p}$ and $\nabla J_p(0)$ can be obtained and simplified to

$$
\|\underline{\alpha}^{J_p} - \nabla J_p(0)\| \leq \frac{1}{6} G \Lambda \sum_{i=1}^{n} \|\mathbf{u}^{(d_i)}\|^3,
\tag{14}
$$

where G is an upper bound on the third derivative of $J_p(\mathbf{u})$, and Λ is a constant that depends on the distribution of the regression set $\mathcal{U}^{(k)}$. Note that the bound in (14) is defined for the error between the plant gradients and the estimated gradients. It is different from the lower and upper bounds on the gradient estimates which were studied by Bunin et al. [5]. To simplify the study of Λ, assume $\|\mathbf{u}^{(d_i)} - \mathbf{u}^{(k)}\| = \Delta\mathbf{u}$. Λ is defined as

$$
\Lambda \geq \max_{0 \leq i \leq n} \max_{\|\mathbf{u}\| \leq \Delta\mathbf{u}} |\ell_i(\mathbf{u})|,
\tag{15}
$$

where $\ell_i(\mathbf{u})$, $i = 0,\dots,n$, are the Lagrange polynomial functions that are defined by the matrix determinants

$$
\ell_i(\mathbf{u}) = \frac{\det\left(\underline{M}(\phi,\mathcal{U}_i(\mathbf{u}))\right)}{\det\left(\underline{M}(\phi,\mathcal{U}^{(k)})\right)}
\tag{16}
$$

with the set $\mathcal{U}_i(\mathbf{u}) = \mathcal{U}^{(k)} \setminus \{\mathbf{u}^{(d_i)}\} \cup \{\mathbf{u}\}$. The determinant of $\underline{M}(\phi,\mathcal{U}^{(k)})$ is computed as

$$
\det\left(\underline{M}(\phi,\mathcal{U}^{(k)})\right) =
\begin{vmatrix}
\varphi_1(\mathbf{u}^{(d_1)}) & \cdots & \varphi_n(\mathbf{u}^{(d_1)}) \\
\vdots & \vdots & \vdots \\
\varphi_1(\mathbf{u}^{(d_n)}) & \cdots & \varphi_n(\mathbf{u}^{(d_n)})
\end{vmatrix}.
\tag{17}
$$

Let $vol(\phi(\mathcal{U}^{(k)}))$ represent the volume of the n-dimensional convex hull spanned by the row vectors of the matrix in (17), we have

$$
\left|\det\left(\underline{M}(\phi,\mathcal{U}^{(k)})\right)\right| = vol(\phi(\mathcal{U}^{(k)}))\, n!.
\tag{18}
$$

Except the vertex at the origin, all the other vertices of the convex hull distribute on a n-dimensional sphere with radius $\Delta\mathbf{u} + \Delta\mathbf{u}^2$. $vol(\phi(\mathcal{U}^{(k)}))$ reaches its maximal value when the vectors are orthogonal to each other. Let $\underline{v}_i$ and $\underline{v}_j$ represent any two row vectors of the matrix in (17). The angle between them

$$\cos(\theta_{i,j}^v) = \frac{\underline{v}_i \cdot \underline{v}_j}{\|\underline{v}_i\| \|\underline{v}_j\|} = \frac{u_1^{(d_i)} u_1^{(d_j)} + \ldots + u_{n_u}^{(d_i)} u_{n_u}^{(d_j)} + \left(u_1^{(d_i)} u_1^{(d_j)} + \ldots + u_{n_u}^{(d_i)} u_{n_u}^{(d_j)}\right)^2}{\Delta u + \Delta u^2}. \tag{19}$$

Note that the angle $\theta_{i,j}^v$ is different from the angle $\theta_{i,j}$ between vectors $\mathbf{u}^{d_i}$ and $\mathbf{u}^{d_j}$

$$\cos(\theta_{i,j}) = \frac{u_1^{(d_i)} u_1^{(d_j)} + \ldots + u_{n_u}^{(d_i)} u_{n_u}^{(d_j)}}{\Delta u}. \tag{20}$$

The relationship between $\theta_{i,j}^v$ and $\theta_{i,j}$ is illustrated in Figure 3, where the angle between two 3-dimensional unit vectors is changed from 0 to 180 degree and the angle between the corresponding quadratic interpolation vectors increases proportionally when $\theta \leq 90$ degree and stays in an interval of [90 98] degree from 90 to 180 degree. Recall the screening for the distant set $\mathcal{U}_d$ via (4), the consideration of the minimal angle at the denominator of the objective function ensures the choosing of the best set in terms of the orthogonality of the matrix in (17) from all the collected data. As a result of (14)–(16) and (18), the lowest bound of the error between $\underline{\alpha}^{J_p}$ and $\nabla J_p(\mathbf{0})$ based on the collected data is achieved.

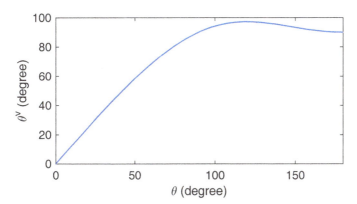

Figure 3. Illustration of the relationship between θ and θ^v.

The error due to the measurement noise $\underline{\alpha}^v$ can be calculated by Cramer's rule

$$\alpha_i^v = \frac{det\left(\underline{M}_i(\phi, \mathcal{U}^{(k)}, \underline{v})\right)}{det\left(\underline{M}(\phi, \mathcal{U}^{(k)})\right)} = \frac{\delta_{noise}}{\Delta u} \frac{det\left(\underline{M}_i(\phi, \mathcal{U}^{(k)}, \underline{\tilde{v}})\right)}{det\left(\underline{M}(\phi, \mathcal{U}^{(k)})\right)}, \tag{21}$$

where $\underline{M}_i(\phi, \mathcal{U}^{(k)}, \underline{v})$ is the matrix formed by replacing the $(i + 1)$th column of $\underline{M}(\phi, \mathcal{U}^{(k)})$ by the column vector $\underline{v}$, δ_{noise} is the level of the measurement noise, $v_i \in (-\delta_{noise}, +\delta_{noise})$, and $\underline{\tilde{v}} = \Delta u \underline{v} / \delta_{noise}$ represents the scaled vector of noises. In order to reduce $\underline{\alpha}^v$, the value of Δu should be large enough. However, from (14) the error bound will increase accordingly. The optimal tuning of Δu according to δ_{noise} and G can be a future research direction. For a given distribution of $\mathcal{U}_d$, the relative upper bound of α_i^v is related to the variance of the elements at the $(i + 1)$th column. To show that, we start from the angle between the $(i + 1)$th column vector and the first column vector

$$\cos(\beta_{i+1,1}) = \frac{\sum_{j=1}^{n} u_i^{(d_j)}}{\sqrt{n+1}\sqrt{\sum_{j=1}^{n} \left(u_i^{(d_j)}\right)^2}}, \tag{22}$$

where we use β to differentiate the angle from that formed by the row vectors. The variance of the elements at the $(i + 1)$th column is

$$Var(\{0, u_i^{(d_1)}, \ldots, u_i^{(d_n)}\}) = \frac{\sum_{j=1}^{n} \left(u_i^{(d_j)}\right)^2}{n+1} - \left(\frac{\sum_{j=1}^{n} u_i^{(d_j)}}{n+1}\right)^2. \tag{23}$$

From (22) and (23), we obtain that

$$\cos(\beta_{i+1,1}) = \frac{\sum_{j=1}^{n} u_i^{(d_j)}}{(n+1)\sqrt{Var + \left(\frac{\sum_{j=1}^{n} u_i^{(d_j)}}{n+1}\right)^2}}. \tag{24}$$

For the same mean value, the orthogonality of the $(i + 1)$th column vector to the first column vector can be quantified by the variance of the elements at the $(i + 1)$th column. As discussed before, the absolute value of the determinant of $\underline{M}(\phi, \mathcal{U}^{(k)})$ is influenced by the orthogonality. As a result, to replace a column of elements with small variance leads to a higher upper bound of the error than to replace a column of elements with large variance. Note that this is consistent with the constrained search space which is defined by the covariance matrix of the regression set.

From (14) and (21), three factors determine the gradient estimation errors

- Distribution of the regression set (quantified by Λ and the distance to the current point)
- Non-quadratic nature of the plant (quantified by G, the upper bound on the third derivative)
- Measurement noise (quantified by δ_{noise}).

Figure 4 depicts how the three factors influence the generation of the explorative moves. Assume the plant functions are approximately quadratic in the region $\|\mathbf{u} - \mathbf{u}^{(k)}\| \leq \Delta\mathbf{u}$ around the current set-point and the value of $\Delta\mathbf{u}$ is large enough, a well-distributed regression set normally leads to a performance-improvement move. If the regression set is not well-distributed but the plant functions are approximately quadratic, a performance-improvement move is still possible if the level of the measurement noise δ_{noise} is low. This is illustrated in Figure 5, where noise-free data was considered and the MAWQA algorithm did not perform any explorative moves. The explorative moves are only generated when either the plant functions deviate significantly from quadratic functions or the level of the measurement noise δ_{noise} is large. In the case shown in Figure 2, the mapping of the plant profit is approximately quadratic but considerable measurement noise was presented. As a result, the unfavourable distribution of the regression set leads to an explorative move.

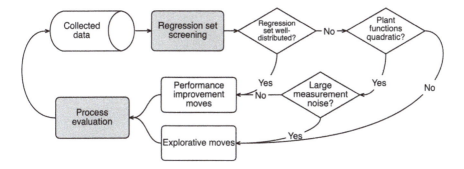

Figure 4. Illustration of the generation of explorative moves.

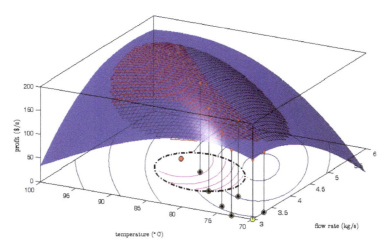

Figure 5. Illustration of one MAWQA iteration with noise-free measurements. Surface plot: real profit mapping, mesh plot: quadratic approximation, ◉: regression set-point, ○: not chosen set-point, ●: measured profit, ●: next set-point move, blue contours: model-predicted profit, magenta contours: modifier-adapted profit, dash-dot line: constrained search space.

Gao et al. [6] proved that the explorative moves can ensure an improvement of the accuracy of the gradient estimation in the following iterations. As an example, Figure 6 shows the MAWQA iteration after two explorative moves for the optimization of the Williams-Otto reactor with noisy data [6]. The mesh of the quadratic approximation well represents the real mapping (the blue surface) around the current point which locates at the center of the constrained search space (defined by the dash-dot line). The computed gradients based on the quadratic approximation are more accurate than those based on the quadratic approximation in Figure 2. As a result, a performance-improvement move (represented by ●) was obtained .

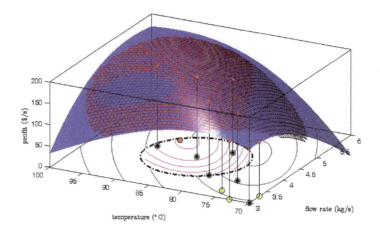

Figure 6. Illustration of the MAWQA iteration after two explorative moves. Surface plot: real profit mapping, mesh plot: quadratic approximation, ◉: regression set-point, ○: not chosen set-point, ●: measured profit, ◑: next set-point move, blue contours: model-predicted profit, magenta contours: modifier-adapted profit, dash-dot line: constrained search space.

4. Simulation Studies

The optimization of a hydroformylation process with four optimization variables is used to illustrate the efficiency of the MAWQA algorithm over the finite difference based modifier adaptation algorithm. The continuous hydroformylation of 1-dodecene in a thermomorphic multicomponent solvent (in short TMS) system is considered. This process was developed in the context of the collaborative research centre InPROMPT at the universities of Berlin, Dortmund and Magdeburg and was demonstrated on miniplant scale at TU Dortmund [9]. Figure 7 illustrates the simplified flow diagram of the TMS system together with the reaction network. The TMS system consists of two main sections: the reaction part and the separation part (here a decanter). The feed consists of the substrate 1-dodecene, the apolar solvent n-decane, the polar solvent dimethylformamide (in short DMF), and synthesis gas (CO/H$_2$). The catalyst system consists of Rh(acac)(CO)$_2$ and the bidentate phosphite biphephos as ligand. During the reaction step, the system is single phase, thus homogeneous, so that no mass transport limitation occurs. During the separation step a lower temperature than that of the reactor is used and the system exhibits a miscibility gap and separates into two liquid phases, a polar and an apolar phase. The apolar phase contains the organic product which is purified in a down-stream process, while the catalyst mostly remains in the polar phase which is recycled. The main reaction is the catalyzed hydroformylation of the long-chain 1-dodecene to linear n-tridecanal. Besides the main reaction, isomerization to iso-dodecene, hydrogenation to n-dodecane and formation of the branched iso-aldehyde take place. Hernández and Engell [10] adapted the model developed by Hentschel et al. [11] to the TMS miniplant by considering the material balances of the above components as follows:

$$V_R \frac{dC_i}{dt} = \dot{V}_{in} C_{i,in} - \dot{V}_{out} C_{i,out} + V_R C_{cat} M_{cat} \sum_{l=1}^{n_{react}} v_{i,l} r_l \tag{25}$$

$$V_R \frac{dC_j}{dt} = -k_{eff}(C_j - C_j^{eq}) + \dot{V}_{in} C_{j,in} - \dot{V}_{out} C_{j,out} + V_R C_{cat} M_{cat} \sum_{l=1}^{n_{react}} v_{j,l} r_l, \tag{26}$$

where (25) is applied to the liquid components 1-dodecene, *n*-tridecanal, iso-dodecene, *n*-dodecane, iso-aldehyde, decane, and DMF. (26) is applied to the gas components CO and H_2. The algebraic equations involved in the model are as follows:

$$C_j^{eq} = \frac{P_j}{H_{j,0}\exp\left(-E_j/RT\right)} \tag{27}$$

$$C_{cat} = \frac{C_{Rh,precursor}}{1 + K_{cat,1}C_{CO} + K_{cat,2}C_{CO}/C_{H_2}} \tag{28}$$

$$K_i = \exp\left(A_{i,0} + \frac{A_{i,1}}{T_{decanter}} + A_{i,2}T_{decanter}\right) \tag{29}$$

$$n_{i,product} = \frac{K_i}{1 + K_i}n_{i,decanter} \tag{30}$$

$$n_{i,catalyst} = \frac{1}{1 + K_i}n_{i,decanter}. \tag{31}$$

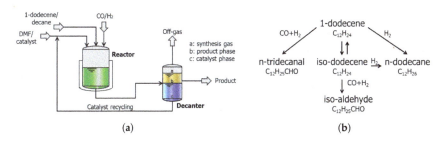

(a) (b)

Figure 7. (a) Thermomorphic multicomponent solvent (TMS) system; (b) Reaction network of the hydroformylation of 1-dodecene. Adapted from Hernández and Engell [10].

Table 2 lists all the symbols used in the model together with their explanations. The optimization problem is formulated as the minimization of the raw material and operating cost per unit of n-tridecanal produced

$$\min_{\mathbf{u}} \frac{Pr_{1-dodecene} \cdot F_{1-dodecene} + Pr_{Rh} \cdot F_{Rh} + C_{Cooling} + C_{Heating}}{F_{tridecanal}}, \tag{32}$$

where $Pr_{1-dodecene}$ and Pr_{Rh} represent the prices of 1-dodecene and of the catalyst, $F_{1-dodecene}$ and F_{Rh} are the molar flow rates, $C_{cooling}$ and $C_{heating}$ are the operating costs of cooling and heating, and $F_{tridecanal}$ is the molar flow rate of n-tridecanal, the vector of the optimization variables **u** consists of the reactor temperature, the catalyst dosage, the pressure and the composition of the synthesis gas. A sensitivity analysis was performed on the different model parameters and it was found that the gas solubility and the equilibrium constants for the catalyst species have the largest influence on the cost function. In our study of the MAWQA approach, the plant-model mismatch is created by decreasing the Henry coefficients $H_{j,0}$ by 50% and ignoring the influence of CO on the active catalyst ($K_{cat,2} = 0$) in the model that is used by the optimization. Table 3 lists the operating intervals of the optimization variables and compares the real optimum with the model optimum. In order to test the robustness of the approach to noisy data, the real cost data is assumed to be subject to a random error which is normally distributed with standard deviation σ.

Table 2. Model parameters and variables.

Symbol	Description
C_i	Concentration of 1-dodecene, n-tridecanal, iso-dodecene, n-dodecane, iso-aldehyde, decane, and DMF
C_j	Concentration of CO and H_2
C_j^{eq}	Equilibrium concentration of CO and H_2 at the G/L interface
V_R	Reactor volume
$\dot{V}_{in}$	Inflow rate
$\dot{V}_{out}$	Outflow rate
C_{cat}	Concentration of the active catalyst
M_{cat}	Molar mass of the catalyst
$v_{i,l}$	Coefficients of the stoichiometric matrix [11]
r_l	Reaction rate of the lth reaction
k_{eff}	Mass transfer coefficient
P_j	Partial pressure
T	Reaction temperature
$H_{j,0}$	Henry coefficient
$C_{Rh,precursor}$	Concentration of the catalyst precursor
$K_{cat,1\backslash 2}$	Equilibrium constants
$T_{decanter}$	Decanter temperature
$A_{i,0\backslash 1\backslash 2}$	Coefficients regressed from experimental data [12]
$n_{i,product}$	Molar flows of the components in the product stream
$n_{i,catalyst}$	Molar flow of the components in the recycled catalyst stream
$n_{i,decanter}$	Molar flow of the components in the decanter inlet stream

Table 3. Operating variables and optimum.

Operating variable	Operating Interval	Initial Set-Point	Real Optimum	Model Optimum
Reactor temperature (°C)	85~105	95.0	88.64	85.10
Catalyst dosage (ppm)	0.25~2.0	1.1	0.51	0.49
Gas pressure (bar)	1.0~3.0	2.0	3.0	3.0
CO fraction	0.0~0.99	0.5	0.55	0.61
Cost (Euro/kmol)		899.04	761.33	818.88

Simulation results of the modifier-adaptation approach using finite-difference approximation of gradient are illustrated in Figure 8. The figures on the left show the evolutions of the normalized optimization variables with respect to the index of RTO iterations. The small pulses, which are superimposed on the evolutions, represent the additional perturbations required for the finite-difference approximations of the gradients. The star symbols at the right end mark the real optima. The figures on the right show the evolutions of the cost and the number of plant evaluations with respect to the index of the RTO iteration. The inset figure zooms in on the cost evolution, and the dashed line marks the real optimum of the cost. Three cases with different combinations of the step size of the perturbation and the noise in the data are considered. In the first case a large step-size, $\Delta h = 0.1$, is used and the data is free of noise ($\sigma = 0.0$). From Figure 8a we can see that three of the four optimization variables are still away from their real optimal values after 16 iterations. The cost evolution in Figure 8b shows an oscillating behavior above the cost optimum. This indicates that the step-size is too large to enable an accurate estimation of the gradients.

In the second case a reduced step-size ($\Delta h = 0.05$) is tried. From Figure 8c we can see that the optimization variables attain their real optimal values at the 14th iteration. However, numerical errors of the simulation of the plant cause deviations during the following iterations. On the one hand, the use of a small step-size reduces the error of the finite-difference approximation of the gradients. On the other hand, the small step-size leads to a high sensitivity of the gradient approximation to errors. This is illustrated by the third case, in which the data contains a normally distributed error ($\sigma = 0.3$). The optimization variables do not reach the real optima (see Figure 8e,f).

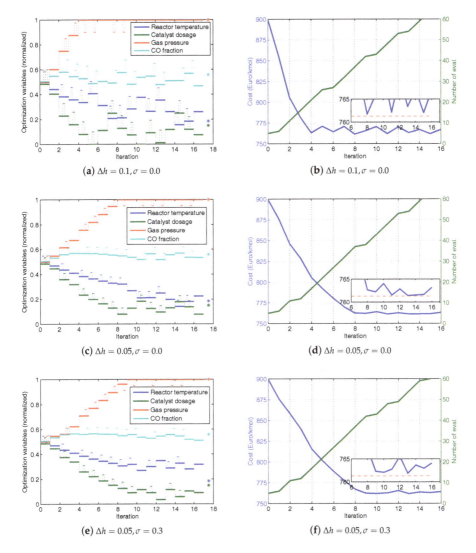

(**a**) $\Delta h = 0.1, \sigma = 0.0$

(**b**) $\Delta h = 0.1, \sigma = 0.0$

(**c**) $\Delta h = 0.05, \sigma = 0.0$

(**d**) $\Delta h = 0.05, \sigma = 0.0$

(**e**) $\Delta h = 0.05, \sigma = 0.3$

(**f**) $\Delta h = 0.05, \sigma = 0.3$

Figure 8. Modifier-adaptation optimization of the thermomorphic solvent system using finite-difference approximation of the gradients, the left figures show the evolutions of the normalized optimization variables **u** (the additional set-point perturbations are represented by the small pulses which are superimposed on the set-point evolutions; the star symbols at the end mark the real optima), the right figures show the evolutions of the cost and the number of plant evaluations (the inset figure zooms in on the cost evolution, and the dashed line marks the real optimum).

Simulation results of the MAWQA algorithm are illustrated in Figure 9. The parameters of the MAWQA algorithm are listed in Table 4. The figures on the left show the evolutions of the normalized optimization variables with respect to iteration. The small pulses, which are superimposed on the evolutions, represent the additional plant evaluations, i.e., initial probes and explorative moves. The real optima are marked by the star symbols. The figures on the right show the evolutions of the cost and the number of plant evaluations with respect to the iterations. The inset figure zooms in on the cost evolution, and the dashed line marks the real optimum of the cost. In the first 4 iterations, the modifier-adaptation approach using finite-difference approximation of gradient is run. Afterwards, enough sampled points (here $(n_u + 1)(n_u + 2)/2 = 15$) are available for the quadratic approximation and the MAWQA approach is run. In the case of noise-free data, the MAWQA approach takes 8 iterations to reach the real optima approximately (see Figure 9a). The total number of plant evaluations is 30, much less than that used in the second case of the finite-difference approximations of gradients which requires 55 plant evaluations to reach a similar accuracy. Note that the additional plant evaluations at the 10th iteration are attributed to the shrinking of the regression region by Step 4 of the MAWQA algorithm. Figure 9c,d show the optimization results in the presence of noise. The MAWQA algorithm takes 10 iterations to reach the real optima.

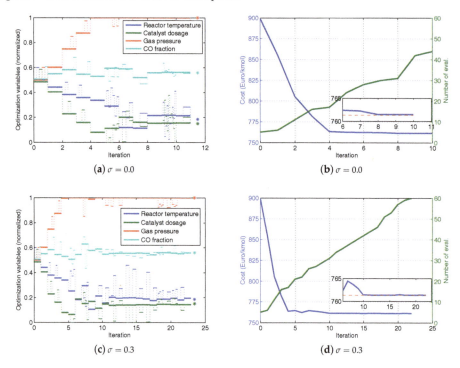

Figure 9. MAWQA optimization of the thermomorphic solvent system, the left figures show the evolutions of the normalized optimization variables (the additional plant evaluations, i.e., initial probes and unsuccessful moves, are represented by the small pulses which are superimposed on the set-point evolutions; the star symbols at the end mark the real optima), the right figures show the evolutions of the cost and the number of plant evaluations (the inset figure zooms in on the cost evolution, and the dashed line marks the real optimum).

Table 4. Parameters of MAWQA.

Description	Symbol	Value
Screening parameter	Δu	0.1
Search space parameter	γ	3
Perturbation step size	Δh	0.1

Finally, the MAWQA algorithm was tested with different values of the parameters. For each parameter, three values are considered and the costs after 30 plant evaluations are compared with the real optimum. The results are summarized in Table 5. The increase of Δu leads to a decrease of the accuracy of the computed optima. This is due to the fact that the true mapping is only locally quadratic and therefore the use of too distant points can cause large approximation errors. The value of γ influences the rate of convergence since it is directly related to the size of the search space in each iteration. The value of Δh determines the accuracy of the finite-difference approximation of the gradients at the starting stage of the MAWQA approach. In the absence of noise, a small Δh is preferred. However, the search space is also determined by the distribution of the sampled points. A small Δh leads to a more constrained search space and therefore decreases the rate of convergence. The overall influence of Δh on the rate of convergence is a combination of both effects. Note that Δh does not influence the accuracy of the optima if enough plant evaluations are performed.

Table 5. Influence of MAWQA parameters.

	Δu	Δh	γ	Cost after 30 Eval.	Deviation from the True Optimum (%)
Initial	0.1	0.1	3	761.5	0.02%
↑ Δu	0.15	0.1	3	762.5	0.15%
↑↑ Δu	0.2	0.1	3	762.9	0.21%
↑ Δh	0.1	0.15	3	761.4	0.01%
↑↑ Δh	0.1	0.2	3	763.3	0.26%
↓ γ	0.1	0.1	2	763.2	0.24%
↓↓ γ	0.1	0.1	1	772.1	1.14%

5. Conclusions

This paper focuses on the explorative moves when using the MAWQA algorithm to optimize a plant. The explorative moves are generated as a result of the estimation errors of the plant gradients. Three factors that influence the estimation errors are analyzed: the non-quadratic nature of the plant mappings, the measurement noise, and the distribution of the regression set. The screening algorithm is shown to take the accuracy of the gradient estimation into consideration and to choose the best set from the collected data. This ensures that the MAWQA algorithm takes only necessary explorative moves to improve the gradient estimations, instead of an expensive model-improvement step as in the derivative-free optimization algorithms. The simulation results for the optimization of the hydroformylation process with four decision variables demonstrate the promising performance of the MAWQA algorithm over the finite difference based modifier adaptation algorithm. Further studies will be focused on how to implement a dual control between the performance improvement and the explorative moves.

Acknowledgments: The research leading to these results has received funding from the European Commission under grant agreement number 291458 (ERC Advanced Investigator Grant MOBOCON) and by the Deutsche Forschungsgemeinschaft (DFG) via the funding of the Collaborative Research Center "Integrated Chemical processes in Liquid Multiphase Systems-InPROMPT" (TR63). The financial support by the ERC and by DFG is most gratefully acknowledged.

Author Contributions: W.G. conceived the theoretical analysis, performed the simulation studies and wrote the paper; R.H. provided the TMS model; R.H. and S.E. corrected the paper.

Conflicts of Interest: The authors declare no conflict of interest.

Abbreviations

The following abbreviations are used in this manuscript:

RTO	Real-time optimization
MAWQA	Modifier adaptation with quadratic approximation
TMS	Thermomorphic multicomponent solvent system
DMF	Dimethylformamide

References

1. Chen, C.Y.; Joseph, B. On-line optimization using a two-phase approach: An application study. *Ind. Eng. Chem. Res.* **1987**, *26*, 1924–1930.
2. Roberts, P.D. An algorithm for steady-state system optimization and parameter estimation. *Int. J. Syst. Sci.* **1979**, *10*, 719–734.
3. Gao, W.; Engell, S. Iterative set-point optimization of batch chromatography. *Comput. Chem. Eng.* **2005**, *29*, 1401–1409.
4. Marchetti, A.; Chachuat, B.; Bonvin, D. Modifier-adaptation methodology for real-time optimization. *Ind. Eng. Chem. Res.* **2009**, *48*, 6022–6033.
5. Bunin, G.A.; François, G.; Bonvin, D. From discrete measurements to bounded gradient estimates: A look at some regularising structures. *Ind. Eng. Chem. Res.* **2013**, *52*, 12500–12513.
6. Gao, W.; Wenzel, S.; Engell, S. A reliable modifier-adaptation strategy for real-time optimization. *Comput. Chem. Eng.* **2016**, *91*, 318–328.
7. Conn, A.R.; Scheinberg, K.; Vicente, L.N. *Introduction to Derivative-Free Optimization*; SIAM: Philadelphia, PA, USA, 2009.
8. Ciarlet, P.G.; Raviart, P.A. General lagrange and hermite interpolation in R^n with applications to finite element methods. *Arch. Ration. Mech. Anal.* **1972**, *46*, 177–199.
9. Zagajewski, M.; Behr, A.; Sasse, P.; Wittman, J. Continuously operated miniplant for the rhodium catalyzed hydroformylation of 1-dodecene in a thermomorphic multicomponent solvent system (TMS). *Chem. Eng. Sci.* **2014**, *115*, 88–94.
10. Hernández, R.; Engell, S. Modelling and iterative real-time optimization of a homogeneously catalyzed hydroformylation process. In Proceedings of the 26th European Symposium on Computer Aided Process Engineering; Portorož, Slovenia, 12–15 June 2016.
11. Hentschel, B.; Kiedorf, G.; Gerlach, M.; Hamel, C.; Seidel-Morgenstern, A.; Freund, H.; Sundmacher, K. Model-based identification and experimental validation of the optimal reaction route for the hydroformylation of 1-Dodecene. *Ind. Eng. Chem. Res.* **2015**, *54*, 1755–1765.
12. Schäfer, E.; Brunsch, Y.; Sadowski, G.; Behr, A. Hydroformylation of 1-dodecene in the thermomorphic solvent system dimethylformamide/decane. Phase behavior-reaction performance-catalyst recycling. *Ind. Eng. Chem. Res.* **2012**, *51*, 10296–10306.

Article

An Analysis of the Directional-Modifier Adaptation Algorithm Based on Optimal Experimental Design

Sébastien Gros

Department of Signals and Systems, Chalmers University of Technology, SE-412 96 Göteborg, Sweden;
grosse@chalmers.se; Tel.: +46-31-772-1555

Academic Editor: Dominique Bonvin
Received: 1 November 2016; Accepted: 15 December 2016; Published: 22 December 2016

Abstract: The modifier approach has been extensively explored and offers a theoretically-sound and practically-useful method to deploy real-time optimization. The recent directional-modifier adaptation algorithm offers a heuristic to tackle the modifier approach. The directional-modifier adaptation algorithm, supported by strong theoretical properties and the ease of deployment in practice, proposes a meaningful compromise between process optimality and quickly improving the quality of the estimation of the gradient of the process cost function. This paper proposes a novel view of the directional-modifier adaptation algorithm, as an approximation of the optimal trade-off between the underlying experimental design problem and the process optimization problem. It moreover suggests a minor modification in the tuning of the algorithm, so as to make it a more genuine approximation.

Keywords: modifier approach; directional-modifier adaptation; experimental design; optimality loss function

1. Introduction

Real-Time Optimization (RTO) aims at improving the performance and safety of industrial processes by means of continually-adjusting their inputs, i.e., the degrees of freedom defining their operating conditions, in response to disturbances and process variations. RTO makes use of both model-based and model-free approaches. The model-free approaches have the clear advantage of being less labor intensive, as a model of the process is not needed, but the increasing number of inputs that can be adjusted when running the process has made them decreasingly attractive.

Model-based techniques have received an increasing interest as the capability of running a large amount of computations online has become standard. Arguably, the most natural approach to model-based RTO is the two-step approach, where model parameter estimation and model-based optimization are alternated so as to refine the process model and adapt the operational parameters accordingly [1,2]. Unfortunately, the two-step approach requires the process model to satisfy very strict criteria in order for the scheme to reach optimality [3,4]. This issue is especially striking in the case of structural mismatch between the model and the process and can make the two-step scheme ineffective or even counterproductive [5–7].

The idea of not only adapting the model parameters, but also the gradient of the cost function can be traced back to [8] and allows for guaranteeing that the resulting scheme reaches optimality upon convergence [7,9,10]. Unlike the two-step approach, adapting the gradient of the cost function allows one to tackle structural model-plant mismatches efficiently, which cannot be efficiently addressed via the adaptation of the model parameters alone. The original idea has been further improved; see, e.g., [7,9–13]. These contributions have converged to the modern Modifier Adaptation (MA) approach, which has been successfully deployed on several industrial processes; see [14–17].

The MA approach has been recently further developed along a number of interesting directions; see [16,18–21].

In a run-to-run scenario where estimations of the uncertain parameters are carried out after every run, the input for any run does not only maximize the process performance for the coming run, but also influences the performance of the subsequent runs through the estimation of the process parameters. This observation is generally valid when parameter estimation is performed between runs and pertains to the MA approach. Taking this influence into account leads one to possibly depart from applying to the process an input that is optimal according to the best available estimation of the parameters at the time and adopt an input that strikes a compromise between process optimality and gathering relevant information for the next parameter estimation. In that sense, the MA approach can be construed as a mix of an optimization problem and an experimental design problem. The problem of tailoring experimental design specifically for optimization in a computationally-tractable way has been recently studied in [22], where the problem of designing inputs for a process so as to gather relevant information for achieving process optimality is tackled via an approximate optimality loss function.

The recently-proposed Directional-Modifier Adaptation (DMA) algorithm [23,24] and its earlier variant the dual-modifier adaptation approach [25] offer a practical way for the MA approach to deal with the compromise between process optimality and gaining information. Indeed, at each process run, the DMA algorithm delivers an input that seeks a compromise between maximizing the process performance and promoting the quality of the estimation of the process gradients. The DMA approach handles this compromise by adopting inputs that depart from the nominal ones in directions corresponding to the largest covariance in the estimated gradients of the process Lagrange function. The DMA algorithm is easy to deploy and has strong theoretical properties, e.g., it converges rapidly and with guarantees to the true process optimum. The directional-modifier adaptation algorithm additionally makes use of iterative schemes to update the modifiers used in the cost model, so as to reduce the computational burden of performing classical gradient estimations.

In this paper, we propose to construct the DMA algorithm from a different angle, based on a modification of the optimality loss function [22]. This construction delivers new theoretical insights into the DMA algorithm and suggests minor modifications that make the DMA algorithm a more genuine approximation of the optimal trade-off between process optimality and excitation. For the sake of simplicity, we focus on the unconstrained case, though the developments can arguably be naturally extended to constrained problems.

The paper is structured as follows. Section 2 proposes some preliminaries on the selection of an optimality loss function for the considered experimental design problem and proposes a computationally-tractable approximation, following similar lines as [22]. Section 3 investigates the MA approach as a special case of the previous developments, proposes to tackle it within the proposed theoretical framework and shows that the resulting algorithm has the same structure as the DMA algorithm, but with some notable differences. Simple examples are presented throughout the text to illustrate and support the concepts presented.

2. Optimal Experimental Design

In this paper, we consider the problem of optimizing a process in a run-to-run fashion. The process is described via the cost function $\phi(u, p)$, where u gathers the set of inputs, or degrees of freedom, available to steer the process, and p gathers the parameters available to adjust the cost function using the measurements gathered on the plant. Function ϕ is assumed to be everywhere defined and smooth. This assumption is arguably not required, but will make the subsequent analysis less involved. The N-run optimization problem can then be formulated as:

$$\min_{u_{0,\dots,N-1}} \frac{1}{N} \sum_{k=0}^{N-1} \phi(u_k, p), \tag{1}$$

where u_k is the vector of decision variables applied at run k. Here, we seek the minimization of the average process performance over the N runs. The cost function $\phi(u, p)$ associated with the process is not available in practice, such that at any run k, the input u_k is typically chosen according to the best parameter estimation $\hat{p}_k$ available at that time. It is important to observe here that the parametric cost function (1) encompasses parametric mismatch between the plant and the model, but also any structure adjusting the cost function according to the data, such as the MA approach; see Section 3.1. Ideally, one ought to seek solving the optimization model:

$$\min_{u_{0,\dots,N-1}} \frac{1}{N} \sum_{k=0}^{N-1} \mathbb{E}_{\hat{p}_k} \left[\phi\left(u_k, \hat{p}_k\right) \right], \tag{2}$$

where $\mathbb{E}_{\hat{p}_k}$ stands for the expected value over $\hat{p}_k$. For the sake of simplicity, we will focus in this paper on the two-run problem, i.e., using $N = 2$ in Problem (2). In the following, we will assume that there exists a vector of parameter p_{real} for which $\phi(u_k, p_{\text{real}})$ captures effectively the cost function of the real process. This assumption is locally fulfilled, up to a constant term, by the MA approach.

When estimations of the parameters $\hat{p}_k$ are conducted between the runs using the latest measurements gathered on the process, a difficulty in using (2) stems from the fact that it can yield an inadequate sequence of decisions $u_{0,\dots,N-1}$. We motivate this statement next, via a simple example.

2.1. Failure of Problem (2): An Example

Consider the optimization model $\phi(u) = u^2 + p^2$ yielding the the two-run problem:

$$\min_{u_{0,1}} \frac{1}{2} \sum_{k=0}^{1} \mathbb{E}_{\hat{p}_k} \left\{ u_k^2 + \hat{p}_k^2 \right\} = \min_{u_{0,1}} \frac{1}{2} \sum_{k=0}^{1} u_k^2 + \Sigma_k + \mu_k^2, \tag{3}$$

where Σ_k is the covariance of the estimation of parameter $\hat{p}_k$ and μ_k its expected value. If the distribution of the estimated parameter $\hat{p}_1$ is independent of the input u_0, then Problem (3) takes the trivial solution $u_{0,1} = 0$, which yields the best performance on the real cost function $\phi(u, p_{\text{real}})$, regardless of the actual parameter value p_{real} or its estimated value $\hat{p}_0$ available for deciding the input u_0. However, since the estimated parameter $\hat{p}_1$ is obtained from the run based on u_0, it is in fact not independent of the decision variables. Indeed, let us assume that the estimation of $\hat{p}_1$ is provided between the two runs via the least-square fitting problems:

$$\hat{p}_1 = \arg\min_{p} \frac{1}{2} \|p - \hat{p}_0\|_{\Sigma_0^{-1}}^2 + \frac{1}{2} \|y(u_0, p) - y_0^{\text{meas}}\|_{\Sigma_{\text{meas}}^{-1}}^2, \tag{4}$$

where $y_0^{\text{meas}} \in \mathbb{R}^m$ is the measurements taken on the process during or after the run based on u_0, $y(u, p)$ is the corresponding measurement model, Σ_{meas} is the covariance of the measurement noise and Σ_0 the covariance associated with the parameter estimation $\hat{p}_0$. Consider then the measurement model:

$$y(u, p) = pu. \tag{5}$$

The solution to (4) is then explicitly given by:

$$\hat{p}_1 = \left(\Sigma_0^{-1} + \Sigma_{\text{meas}}^{-1} u_0^2 \right)^{-1} \left(\Sigma_0^{-1} \hat{p}_0 + \Sigma_{\text{meas}}^{-1} u_0 y_0^{\text{meas}} \right). \tag{6}$$

Assuming that $\mu_{\hat{p}_0} = p_{\text{real}} = 0$ and $\mathbb{E}\left\{ y_0^{\text{meas}} \right\} = 0$, we then observe that if the measurement noise is independent between the various runs, we have:

$$\Sigma_1 = \left(\Sigma_0^{-1} + \Sigma_{\text{meas}}^{-1} u_0^2 \right)^{-1}. \tag{7}$$

After removing the constant terms, Problem (3) becomes:

$$\min_{u_0, u_1} \frac{1}{2}\left(u_0^2 + u_1^2\right) + \frac{1}{2}\left(\Sigma_0^{-1} + \Sigma_{\text{meas}}^{-1} u_0^2\right)^{-1}. \tag{8}$$

An interesting situation occurs for $\Sigma_{\text{meas}} \leq \Sigma_0^2$, i.e., when the covariance of the measurements is sufficiently low; see Figure 1. The solution to (8) then reads as:

$$u_0 = \pm \left(\Sigma_{\text{meas}}^{\frac{1}{2}} - \frac{\Sigma_{\text{meas}}}{\Sigma_0}\right)^{\frac{1}{2}}, \qquad u_1 = 0, \tag{9}$$

while the sequence $u_0 = u_1 = 0$ should clearly be used in order to minimize the cost of the real two-run process, even in the sense of the expected value. This trivial example illustrates a fundamental limitation of Problem (2) in successfully achieving the goal of minimizing the cost over a two- or N-run process.

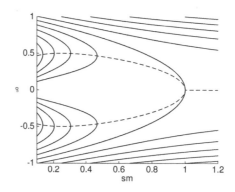

Figure 1. Illustration for Problem (8). The level curves report the cost of (8) as a function of u_0 and Σ_{meas}, with $\Sigma_0 = 1$. The dashed lines report the optimal input u_0 for various values of Σ_{meas}. For Σ_{meas} low enough, the problem has two non-zero solutions.

2.2. Modified Optimality Loss Function

A sensible approach inspired from the work presented in [22] consists of selecting the input u_0 according to:

$$u_0 = \arg\min_u \ \mathbb{E}_e\left[\phi\left(u, p_{\text{real}}\right) + \phi\left(u^*\left(\hat{p}_1\right), p_{\text{real}}\right)\right] =$$
$$\arg\min_u \ \mathbb{E}_e\left[\ \phi\left(u, p_{\text{real}}\right) + \underbrace{\phi\left(u^*\left(\hat{p}_1\right), p_{\text{real}}\right) - \phi\left(u^*\left(p_{\text{real}}\right), p_{\text{real}}\right)}_{\Delta_0}\ \right], \tag{10}$$

where Δ_0 is labeled the optimality loss function and e gathers the noise on the estimation of the process parameters and the measurement noise, i.e.:

$$\hat{p}_0 = p_{\text{real}} + e_0, \quad y_{\text{meas}} = y\left(u_0, p_{\text{real}}\right) + e_1. \tag{11}$$

Problem (10) seeks a compromise between the expected process performance at the coming run via the first term in (10) and the expected process performance at the subsequent run via the second term. The performance of the second term depends on the input selected in the first run via the parameter estimation performed between the two runs. We assume hereafter that e follows a normal, centered distribution, and we use for the estimated parameter $\hat{p}_1$ the least-square fitting problem:

$$\hat{p}_1 = \arg\min_p \; \frac{1}{2} \|p - (p_{\text{real}} + e_0)\|^2_{\Sigma_0^{-1}} + \frac{1}{2} \|y(u_0, p_{\text{real}}) + e_1 - y(u_0, p)\|^2_{\Sigma_1^{-1}}, \tag{12}$$

where $\hat{p}_1$ is the parameter estimation following the first run. The optimality loss function Δ_0 proposed in [22] was designed for the specific purpose of performing experimental design dedicated to capturing the process parameters most relevant for process optimization. However, it was not designed to be used within the two-run problem considered here. In this paper, we propose to use a slightly modified version of (10), so as to avoid a potential difficulty it poses. For the sake of brevity and in order to skip elaborate technical details, let us illustrate this difficulty via the following simple example. Consider the cost function and measurement model:

$$\phi(u, p) = \frac{1}{2}(u - p)^2, \qquad y(u, p) = up. \tag{13}$$

The least-square problem (12) reads as:

$$\hat{p}_1 = \arg\min_p \; \frac{1}{2} \|p - (p_{\text{real}} + e_0)\|^2_{\Sigma_0^{-1}} + \frac{1}{2} \|u_0 p_{\text{real}} + e_1 - u_0 p\|^2_{\Sigma_1^{-1}}, \tag{14}$$

which takes the explicit form:

$$\hat{p}_1 = p_{\text{real}} + \frac{e_0 \Sigma_1 + e_1 \Sigma_0 u_0}{\Sigma_0 u_0^2 + \Sigma_1}. \tag{15}$$

The optimality loss function Δ_0 then reads as:

$$\Delta_0(u_0) = \phi(u^*(\hat{p}_1), p_{\text{real}}) - \phi(u^*(p_{\text{real}}), p_{\text{real}}) = \frac{1}{2}\left(\frac{e_0 \Sigma_1 + e_1 \Sigma_0 u_0}{\Sigma_0 u_0^2 + \Sigma_1}\right)^2, \tag{16}$$

and has the expected value:

$$\mathbb{E}_e[\Delta_0] = \frac{1}{2}\frac{\Sigma_0 \Sigma_1}{\Sigma_0 u_0^2 + \Sigma_1}. \tag{17}$$

It is worth observing that a similar optimality loss function has also been used in [25] in order to quantify the loss of optimality resulting from uncertain parameters. Problem (10) can then be equivalently written as:

$$u_0 = \arg\min_u \; \phi(u, p_{\text{real}}) + \mathbb{E}_e[\Delta_0]. \tag{18}$$

However, since in practice, p_{real} is not available to solve Problem (18), a surrogate problem must be solved, using $p_{\text{real}} \approx \hat{p}_0$. It reads as:

$$u_0 = \arg\min_u \; \phi(u, \hat{p}_0) + \mathbb{E}_e[\Delta_0] = \arg\min_u \; \phi(u, p_{\text{real}} + e_0) + \mathbb{E}_e[\Delta_0]. \tag{19}$$

An issue occurs here, which is illustrated in Figure 2. Because the expected value of the optimality loss function computed in a stand-alone fashion in (17) misses the correlation between the control input u_0 and the initial estimation error e_0 that arises via the optimization problem (19), using (19) as a surrogate for (18) can be counterproductive in the sense that the performance of Problem (18) is worse than the one of the nominal problem.

In this paper, we address this issue by taking an approach to the optimality loss function that departs slightly from (16).

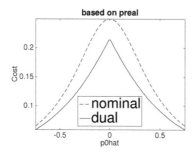 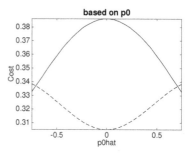

Figure 2. Comparison of the performance resulting from using the nominal input $u_0 = u^*(\hat{p}_0)$ and the one resulting from (18) or (19) on the proposed example. The displayed cost is calculated according to (10) and reads as $\mathbb{E}_e \left[\frac{1}{2} u_0^2 + \frac{1}{2} u_1^* (\hat{p}_1)^2 \right]$. The left graph displays the cost resulting from using (18), which delivers a better expected performance than using the nominal input. The right graph displays the cost resulting from using (19), where $p_{\text{real}} \approx \hat{p}_0$ is used. In this example, this approximation is detrimental to the performance of Problem (10), resulting in a worse performance than the nominal one.

2.3. Problem Formulation

For a given initial estimation $\hat{p}_0$, initial estimation error e_0 and measurement error e_1 and using $p_{\text{real}} = \hat{p}_0 - e_0$, the estimation problem solved after the first run can be formulated as:

$$\hat{p}_1(u_0, \Sigma, \hat{p}_0, e) = \arg\min_p \frac{1}{2} \|p - \hat{p}_0\|^2_{\Sigma_0^{-1}} + \frac{1}{2} \|y(u_0, p) - (y(u_0, \hat{p}_0 - e_0) + e_1)\|^2_{\Sigma_1^{-1}}, \quad (20)$$

where we use the notation:

$$e = \begin{bmatrix} e_0 \\ e_1 \end{bmatrix}, \qquad \Sigma = \begin{bmatrix} \Sigma_0 & 0 \\ 0 & \Sigma_1 \end{bmatrix}, \quad (21)$$

and consider e_0, e_1 to be uncorrelated. Defining:

$$\hat{u}_1^*(u_0, \Sigma, \hat{p}_0, e) = u^*(\hat{p}_1(u_0, \Sigma, \hat{p}_0, e)), \quad (22)$$

the modified optimality loss function can be formulated as:

$$\Delta(u_0, \Sigma, \hat{p}_0, e) = \phi(\hat{u}_1^*(u_0, \Sigma, \hat{p}_0, e), \hat{p}_0 - e_0) - \phi(u^*(\hat{p}_0 - e_0), \hat{p}_0 - e_0). \quad (23)$$

This reformulation allows for construing the optimality loss function from the point of view of the experimenter, by considering $\hat{p}_0$ as a fixed variable arising as a realization of the estimation of the unknown parameter p_{real} rather than a stochastic one. In (20) and (23), the actual parameter p_{real} is then, from the experimenter point of view, a stochastic variable, reflecting the uncertainty of the experimenter concerning the real parameter. The resulting two-run problem reads as:

$$u_0 = \arg\min_u \quad \mathbb{E}_e \left[\phi(u, \hat{p}_0 - e_0) + \Delta(u, \Sigma, \hat{p}_0, e) \right]. \quad (24)$$

We observe here that the cost function proposed in (24) is different from the original one in (19). From the optimality principle, Problem (24) delivers an expected performance that is better or no worse than the expected performance yielded by applying the nominal input $u_0 = u^*(\hat{p}_0)$. A simple example of the proposed optimality-loss approach is provided in Section 2.5. Unfortunately, solving Problem (24) is in general difficult. In the next section, we consider a second-order approximation instead, following a line also adopted in [22].

2.4. Second-Order Approximation of the Modified Optimality Loss Function

The optimality loss function (23) is difficult to use in practice. A second-order approximation of (23) can be deployed as a tractable surrogate problem in (24). We develop this second-order approximation next. We observe that the following equality trivially holds:

$$\hat{p}_1\left(u_0, \Sigma, \hat{p}_0, 0\right) = \hat{p}_0. \tag{25}$$

The sensitivity of the parameter estimations $\hat{p}_1$ to the errors e can be obtained via the implicit function theorem applied to the fitting problem (20); it reads as:

$$\left.\frac{\partial \hat{p}_1\left(u_0, \Sigma, \hat{p}_0, e\right)}{\partial e}\right|_{e=0} = F\left(u_0, \Sigma, \hat{p}_0\right)^{-1} M\left(u_0, \hat{p}_0\right), \tag{26}$$

where:

$$F\left(u_0, \Sigma, \hat{p}_0\right) = \Sigma_0^{-1} + y_p\left(u_0, \hat{p}_0\right)^\top \Sigma_1^{-1} y_p\left(u_0, \hat{p}_0\right) \tag{27}$$

is the Fisher information matrix of (20), and:

$$\begin{aligned} M\left(u_0, \hat{p}_0\right) &= \left[\begin{array}{cc} -y_p\left(u_0, \hat{p}_0\right)\Sigma_1^{-1} y_p\left(u_0, \hat{p}_0\right)^\top & y_p\left(u_0, \hat{p}_0\right)^\top \Sigma_1^{-1} \end{array} \right] \\ &= \left[\begin{array}{cc} \Sigma_0^{-1} - F\left(u_0, \Sigma, \hat{p}_0\right) & y_p\left(u_0, \hat{p}_0\right)^\top \Sigma_1^{-1} \end{array} \right]. \end{aligned} \tag{28}$$

We note that from optimality that $\Delta \geq 0$ always holds and:

$$\Delta\left(u_0, \Sigma, \hat{p}_0, 0\right) = 0, \qquad \left.\frac{\partial \Delta\left(u_0, \Sigma, \hat{p}_0, e\right)}{\partial e}\right|_{e=0} = 0, \tag{29}$$

which motivates a second-order approximation of Δ at $e = 0$. The Taylor expansion of Δ in e reads as:

$$\Delta\left(u_0, \Sigma, \hat{p}_0, e\right) = \frac{1}{2}e^\top \frac{\partial^2 \Delta\left(u_0, \Sigma, \hat{p}_0, 0\right)}{\partial e^2} e + r_3(u_0, \Sigma, \hat{p}_0, e). \tag{30}$$

We can then form the second-order approximation of the modified optimality loss function Δ.

Lemma 1. *The following equality holds:*

$$\frac{\partial^2 \Delta\left(u_0, \Sigma, \hat{p}_0, 0\right)}{\partial e^2} = \left(\frac{\partial \hat{p}_1}{\partial e} + \frac{\partial e_0}{\partial e}\right)^\top \phi_{pu}^* \left(\phi_{uu}^*\right)^{-1} \phi_{up}^* \left(\frac{\partial \hat{p}_1}{\partial e} + \frac{\partial e_0}{\partial e}\right), \tag{31}$$

where we note $\phi_{xx}^* = \phi_{xx}\left(u^*\left(\hat{p}_0\right), \hat{p}_0\right)$, and all partial derivatives are evaluated at $e = 0$.

Proof. We observe that:

$$\frac{\partial^2 \Delta\left(u_0, \Sigma, \hat{p}_0, e\right)}{\partial e^2} = \frac{\partial}{\partial e}\left(\phi_u\left(\hat{u}_1^*, \hat{p}_0 - e_0\right) u_p^*\left(\hat{p}_1\right)\frac{\partial \hat{p}_1}{\partial e} - \phi_p\left(\hat{u}_1^*, \hat{p}_0 - e_0\right)\frac{\partial e_0}{\partial e}\right. \tag{32}$$

$$\left. + \phi_u\left(u^*\left(\hat{p}_0 - e_0\right), \hat{p}_0 - e_0\right) u_p^*\left(\hat{p}_0 - e_0\right)\frac{\partial e_0}{\partial e} + \phi_p\left(u^*\left(\hat{p}_0 - e_0\right), \hat{p}_0 - e_0\right)\frac{\partial e_0}{\partial e}\right),$$

where for the sake of clarity, the arguments are omitted when unambiguous. Using the fact that $\phi_u\left(u^*\left(\hat{p}_0\right), \hat{p}_0\right) = 0$, it follows that:

$$\frac{\partial^2 \Delta\left(u_0, \Sigma, \hat{p}_0, 0\right)}{\partial e^2} = \frac{\partial \hat{p}_1}{\partial e}^\top \left(u_p^*\right)^\top \phi_{uu}^* u_p^* \frac{\partial \hat{p}_1}{\partial e} - \frac{\partial e_0}{\partial e}^\top \phi_{pu}^* u_p^* \frac{\partial \hat{p}_1}{\partial e} - \frac{\partial \hat{p}_1}{\partial e}^\top \left(u_p^*\right)^\top \phi_{up}^* \frac{\partial e_0}{\partial e} + \frac{\partial e_0}{\partial e}^\top \phi_{pp}^* \frac{\partial e_0}{\partial e} \quad (33)$$

$$- \frac{\partial e_0}{\partial e}^\top \left(u_p^*\right)^\top \phi_{uu}^* u_p^* \frac{\partial e_0}{\partial e} - \frac{\partial e_0}{\partial e}^\top \phi_{pu}^* u_p^* \frac{\partial e_0}{\partial e} - \frac{\partial e_0}{\partial e}^\top \left(u_p^*\right)^\top \phi_{up}^* \frac{\partial e_0}{\partial e} - \frac{\partial e_0}{\partial e}^\top \phi_{pp}^* \frac{\partial e_0}{\partial e},$$

where all functions are evaluated at $e = 0$. We use then the equality $u_p^* = -\left(\phi_{uu}^*\right)^{-1}\phi_{up}^*$ to get (31). $\square$

In the following, it will be useful to write $\Delta\left(u_0, \Sigma, \hat{p}_0, e\right)$ as:

$$\Delta\left(u_0, \Sigma, \hat{p}_0, e\right) = \frac{1}{2}\mathrm{Tr}\left(\phi_{pu}^*\left(\phi_{uu}^*\right)^{-1}\phi_{up}^* V\right) + r_3\left(u_0, \Sigma, \hat{p}_0, e\right), \quad (34)$$

where we note:

$$V\left(u_0, \Sigma, \hat{p}_0, e\right) = \left(\left.\frac{\partial \hat{p}_1\left(u_0, \Sigma, \hat{p}_0, e\right)}{\partial e}\right|_{e=0} + \frac{\partial e_0}{\partial e}\right) ee^\top \left(\left.\frac{\partial \hat{p}_1\left(u_0, \Sigma, \hat{p}_0, e\right)}{\partial e}\right|_{e=0} + \frac{\partial e_0}{\partial e}\right)^\top.$$

Using (28), we observe that:

$$\left.\frac{\partial \hat{p}_1\left(u, \Sigma, \hat{p}_0, e\right)}{\partial e}\right|_{e=0} + \frac{\partial e_0}{\partial e} = F\left(u_0, \Sigma, \hat{p}_0\right)^{-1}\left[\begin{array}{cc} \Sigma_0^{-1} & y_p\left(u_0, \hat{p}_0\right)^\top \Sigma_1^{-1} \end{array}\right], \quad (35)$$

such that:

$$\mathbb{E}_e\left[V\left(u_0, \Sigma, \hat{p}_0, e\right)\right] = F\left(u_0, \Sigma, \hat{p}_0\right)^{-1}\left[\begin{array}{cc} \Sigma_0^{-1} & y_p\left(u_0, \hat{p}_0\right)^\top \Sigma_1^{-1} \end{array}\right]\Sigma_1\left(\star\right) = F\left(u_0, \Sigma, \hat{p}_0\right)^{-1}. \quad (36)$$

It follows that the expected value of the optimality loss function reads as:

$$\mathbb{E}_e\left[\Delta\left(u, \Sigma, \hat{p}_0, e\right)\right] = \frac{1}{2}\mathrm{Tr}\left(\phi_{pu}^*\left(\phi_{uu}^*\right)^{-1}\phi_{up}^* F\left(u_0, \Sigma, \hat{p}_0\right)^{-1}\right) + \mathbb{E}_e\left[r_3\left(u_0, \Sigma, \hat{p}_0, e\right)\right]. \quad (37)$$

It is useful to observe that even though a modified optimality loss function has been selected here, its approximation (37) is nonetheless very similar to the one proposed in [22]. Hence, the real difference lies in its interpretation as an approximation of the modified function (23) rather than (16). Here, it is useful to introduce the following lemma:

Lemma 2. *If the following conditions hold:*

1. *the noise e has a multivariate normal and centered distribution*
2. *for all $p \in \mathbb{P}$, $u^*\left(p\right)$ exists, is smooth, unique and satisfies the Second-Order Sufficient Condition (SOSC) condition of optimality.*
3. *the parameter estimation problem (20) has a unique solution $\hat{p}_1\left(u_0, \Sigma, \hat{p}_0, e\right)$ satisfying SOSC for any e and is smooth and polynomially bounded in e*
4. *functions $u^*\left(p\right)$, $\hat{p}_1\left(u_0, \Sigma, \hat{p}_0, e\right)$ and ϕ_{up}, ϕ_{uu} are all bounded by polynomials on their respective domains.*

Then, the inequality:

$$\left|\mathbb{E}_e\left[r_3\left(u_0, \Sigma, \hat{p}_0, e\right)\right]\right| \le c\|\Sigma\|^2 \quad (38)$$

holds locally for some constant $c > 0$, where $\|.\|$ is the matrix two-norm.

Proof. Because all functions are smooth and bounded by polynomials, the function Δ is also smooth and bounded by polynomials. It follows that:

$$r_3\left(u_0, \Sigma, \hat{p}_0, e\right) = \Delta\left(u_0, \Sigma, \hat{p}_0, e\right) - \frac{1}{2}\text{Tr}\left(\phi_{pu}^* \left(\phi_{uu}^*\right)^{-1} \phi_{up}^* V\right) \tag{39}$$

is also smooth and polynomially bounded. Additionally, the bound:

$$\left|r_3\left(u_0, \Sigma, \hat{p}_0, e\right)\right| \leq c\left\|e\right\|^3 \tag{40}$$

holds locally for some $c > 0$ as a result of Taylor's theorem. Then, Inequality (38) follows directly from Lemma A1. □

Lemma 2 appears to be a special case of the delta method [26]. We can now approximate (24) as:

$$\min_{u_0}\quad \mathbb{E}_e\left[\phi\left(u_0, \hat{p}_0 - e_0\right)\right] + \frac{1}{2}\text{Tr}\left(\phi_{pu}^* \left(\phi_{uu}^*\right)^{-1}\phi_{up}^* F\left(u_0, \Sigma, \hat{p}_0\right)^{-1}\right), \tag{41}$$

using $\phi_{uu}^* = \phi_{uu}\left(u^*\left(\hat{p}_0\right), \hat{p}_0\right)$ and $\phi_{up}^* = \phi_{up}\left(u^*\left(\hat{p}_0\right), \hat{p}_0\right)$.

Algorithm 1: 2-run nominal optimal experimental design.

Input : Current parameter estimation $\hat{p}_0$, covariance Σ.

1 Compute $u^*\left(\hat{p}_0\right)$

2 Evaluate $\phi_{pu}^*\left(\phi_{uu}^*\right)^{-1}\phi_{up}^*$ and F at $u^*\left(\hat{p}_0\right), \hat{p}_0$

3 Solve:

$$\min_{u_0}\quad \mathbb{E}_e\left[\phi\left(u_0, \hat{p}_0 - e_0\right)\right] + \frac{1}{2}\text{Tr}\left(\phi_{pu}^* \left(\phi_{uu}^*\right)^{-1}\phi_{up}^* F\left(u_0, \Sigma, \hat{p}_0\right)^{-1}\right)$$

4 Apply u_0 to the process, gather measurements, perform parameter estimation update

return updated $\hat{p}_0$ and Σ, repeat

For the sake of clarity, the deployment of Problem (41) in a run-to-run algorithm is detailed in Algorithm 1.

2.5. Illustrative Example: Observability Problem

We consider again the example (13), i.e.:

$$\phi\left(u, p\right) = \frac{1}{2}\left(u - p\right)^2, \qquad y\left(u, p\right) = up. \tag{42}$$

where we consider $\hat{p}_0 = p_{\text{real}} + e_0$ as known a priori with $\mathbb{E}[e_0] = 0$, and $\hat{p}_1$ is provided by the estimation problem:

$$\hat{p}_1 = \arg\min_p\ \frac{1}{2}\left\|p - \hat{p}_0\right\|^2_{\Sigma_0^{-1}} + \frac{1}{2}\|\underbrace{u_0\left(\hat{p}_0 - e_0\right) + e_1}_{y^{\text{meas}}} - u_0 p\|^2_{\Sigma_1^{-1}}, \tag{43}$$

and takes the explicit solution:

$$\hat{p}_1 = \hat{p}_0 + \frac{e_1\Sigma_0 u_0 - e_0\Sigma_0 u_0^2}{\Sigma_0 u_0^2 + \Sigma_1}. \tag{44}$$

The optimality loss for the second run then reads as:

$$\Delta = \frac{1}{2}\left(u_1^*\left(\hat{p}_1\right) - \left(\hat{p}_0 - e_0\right)\right)^2 - \underbrace{\phi^*}_{=0} = \frac{1}{2}\frac{\left(e_0\Sigma_1 + e_1\Sigma_0 u_0\right)^2}{\left(\Sigma_0 u_0^2 + \Sigma_1\right)^2}, \tag{45}$$

and its expected value takes the form:

$$\mathbb{E}_e\left[\Delta\right] = \frac{1}{2}\frac{\Sigma_0\Sigma_1}{\Sigma_0 u_0^2 + \Sigma_1} = \frac{1}{2}F\left(u_0, \Sigma\right)^{-1}. \tag{46}$$

Ignoring the constant terms and since $\mathbb{E}[e_0] = 0$, the two-stage optimal experimental design then picks the input u_0 according to:

$$u_0 = \arg\min_u \; \frac{1}{2}\left(u - \hat{p}_0\right)^2 + \frac{1}{2}F\left(u, \Sigma\right)^{-1}. \tag{47}$$

We observe that in this simple case, the proposed approximation (41) is identical to the original problem (24) and to Problem (19). This equivalence does not hold in general. The behavior of Problem (41) in this simple case is reported in Figures 3 and 4. In particular, we observe that the expected performance of Problem (41) on this example is consistently better than the one of the nominal approach. It is important to understand here that in this specific example, the difference between Figures 2 and 4 lies in the cost function that evaluates the performance of the nominal and proposed approach. Indeed, because of the approximation $p_{\text{real}} = \hat{p}_0$, the original approach (19) appears potentially counterproductive under its targeted performance metric (10). Instead, the proposed performance metric (24) is the one that can be minimized via exploiting measurements for subsequent optimizations. In general, however, the inputs selected by (10) and (24) are different.

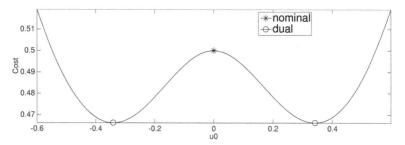

Figure 3. Comparison of the nominal and optimal experimental design on the proposed example for $\hat{p}_0 = 0$. The displayed cost is calculated according to the cost proposed in (24), which reads as $\mathbb{E}_e\left[\frac{1}{2}(u_0 - (\hat{p}_0 - e_0))^2 + \frac{1}{2}(u_1^*(\hat{p}_1) - (\hat{p}_0 - e_0))^2\right]$ in this example. It can be observed that the optimal experimental design approach has two solutions, due to the non-convexity of the problem.

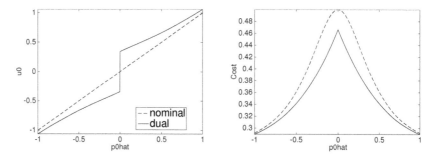

Figure 4. The left graph illustrates the nominal and optimal experimental design performance on the proposed example. The displayed cost is calculated according to the cost proposed in (24), which reads as $\mathbb{E}_e\left[\frac{1}{2}(u_0 - (\hat{p}_0 - e_0))^2 + \frac{1}{2}(u_1^*(\hat{p}_1) - (\hat{p}_0 - e_0))^2\right]$ in this example. The right graph displays the corresponding inputs. Observe that the right-hand graph ought to be compared to the right-hand graph of Figure 2.

3. Link to the Modifier Approach and the DMA Approximation

In this section, we draw a connection between the proposed developments and the well-proven modifier approach tackled via the recent Directional-Modifier Adaptation (DMA) algorithm [23,24]. In particular, we show that the DMA approach can be construed as an approximation of Problem (41).

3.1. The Modifier Approach

In the context of RTO, instead of considering uncertain model parameters, the Modifier Approach (MA) tackles the difficulty of working with uncertain process models by introducing a modification of the gradient of the cost function in the optimization problem. The MA then considers a model of the cost function in the form:

$$\phi(u, p) = \phi_0(u) + p^T u, \tag{48}$$

where p is a set of parameters that modifies the gradient of the process model. Hence, instead of refining the process model, the MA focuses on adjusting the cost gradient at the solution in order to reach optimality for the real process. At each run, measurements of the cost function can be used to improve the estimation of the process gradients via numerical differences. The measurements obtained at each run can be written as:

$$y^{\text{real}} = \frac{\phi(u_0, p_{\text{real}}) - \phi(u_{-1}, p_{\text{real}})}{\|u_0 - u_-\|}, \tag{49}$$

while the measurement model reads as:

$$y(u_0, p) = \frac{\phi(u_0, p) - \phi(u_{-1}, p)}{\|u_0 - u_-\|} = p^\top \frac{u_0 - u_{-1}}{\|u_0 - u_-\|} + \frac{\phi_0(u_0) - \phi_0(u_{-1})}{\|u_0 - u_-\|}. \tag{50}$$

Here, we consider the inputs prior to u_0 as fixed, since they are already realized, and we consider that a parameter estimation $\hat{p}_0$ is available from these previous measurements, with associated covariance Σ_0. It can be verified that:

$$\phi_{pu}^* \left(\phi_{uu}^*\right)^{-1} \phi_{up}^* = \nabla^2 \phi_0^{-1}, \qquad F(u_0, \Sigma, \hat{p}_0) = \Sigma_{\hat{p}_0}^{-1} + \Sigma_{\text{meas}}^{-1} S(u_0), \tag{51}$$

where $\Sigma_{\text{meas}} \in \mathbb{R}$ is the covariance of the measurements of the numerical gradients of the process cost function and where we have defined:

$$S(u_0) = \frac{(u_0 - u_{-1})(u_0 - u_{-1})^\top}{\|u_0 - u_-\|^2}. \tag{52}$$

Hence, Problem (41) deployed on the MA approach solves the problem:

$$\min_{u_0} \quad \phi(u_0, \hat{p}_0) + \frac{1}{2} \text{Tr} \left[\Sigma_{\hat{p}_0} \nabla^2 \phi_0^{-1} \left(I + \Sigma_{\text{meas}}^{-1} \Sigma_{\hat{p}_0} S(u_0) \right)^{-1} \right]. \tag{53}$$

3.2. DMA as an Approximation of (41)

We will consider next a 1st-order Neumann expansion to approximate Problem (53) for $u_0 \approx u_{-1}$. We observe that:

$$\left(I + \Sigma_{\text{meas}}^{-1} \Sigma_{\hat{p}_0} S(u_0) \right)^{-1} = I - \Sigma_{\text{meas}}^{-1} \Sigma_{\hat{p}_0} S(u_0) + R, \tag{54}$$

where:

$$R = \left(I + \Sigma_{\text{meas}}^{-1} \Sigma_{\hat{p}_0} S(u_0) \right)^{-1} \left(\Sigma_{\text{meas}}^{-1} \Sigma_{\hat{p}_0} S(u_0) \right)^2. \tag{55}$$

If the covariance Σ_ϕ associated with the measurements of the cost function is fixed, then $\Sigma_{\text{meas}}^{-1} = \frac{1}{2}\Sigma_\phi^{-1} \|u_0 - u_{-1}\|^2$. It follows that for $\|u_0 - u_{-1}\|$ small, the following approximation is asymptotically exact:

$$\text{Tr}\left[\Sigma_{\hat{p}_0} \nabla^2 \phi_0^{-1} \left(I + \Sigma_{\text{meas}}^{-1} \Sigma_{\hat{p}_0} S\left(u_0\right)\right)^{-1}\right] \approx \text{Tr}\left[\Sigma_{\hat{p}_0} \nabla^2 \phi_0^{-1} - \Sigma_{\text{meas}}^{-1} \Sigma_{\hat{p}_0} \nabla^2 \phi_0^{-1} \Sigma_{\hat{p}_0} S\left(u_0\right)\right] \tag{56}$$

$$= \text{Tr}\left[\nabla^2 \phi_0^{-1} \Sigma_{\hat{p}_0}\right] - \Sigma_{\text{meas}}^{-1} \left(u_0 - u_{-1}\right)^\top \Sigma_{\hat{p}_0} \nabla^2 \phi_0^{-1} \Sigma_{\hat{p}_0} \left(u_0 - u_{-1}\right). \tag{57}$$

One can then consider the following approximation of Problem (53):

$$u_0 = \arg\min_{u_0} \quad \phi_0\left(u_0\right) + \hat{p}_0^\top u_0 - \frac{1}{2}\Sigma_{\text{meas}}^{-1} \left(u_0 - u_{-1}\right)^\top \Sigma_{\hat{p}_0} \nabla^2 \phi_0^{-1} \Sigma_{\hat{p}_0} \left(u_0 - u_{-1}\right), \tag{58}$$

which is valid for $\|u_0 - u_{-1}\|$ small. The DMA approach computes a direction δu in the input space according to:

$$\max_{\delta u} \quad \delta u^T \Sigma_{\nabla \phi} \delta u \tag{59a}$$

$$\text{s.t.} \quad \|\delta u\| = 1, \quad \delta u \in C\left(U_r\right), \tag{59b}$$

where $U_r = I$ trivially holds in the unconstrained case and then solves the problem:

$$u_0 = \arg\min_{u_0} \quad \phi_0\left(u\right) + \hat{p}_0^T \left(u_0 - u_{-1}\right) - \frac{c}{2}\left(\delta u^T \left(u_0 - u_{-1}\right)\right)^2, \tag{60}$$

which is equivalent to:

$$u_0 = \arg\min_{u_0} \quad \phi_0\left(u_0\right) + \hat{p}_0^T u_0 - \frac{c}{2}\left(u_0 - u_{-1}\right)^T Q\left(u_0 - u_{-1}\right) \tag{61}$$

for the semi-positive, rank-one weighting matrix $Q = c\delta u \delta u^T$. The close resemblance of the DMA problem (61) to Problem (58) offers a deeper understanding of the procedure at play in the DMA algorithm. More specifically, Problem (58) is identical to the DMA problem (61) if:

$$\Sigma_{\text{meas}}^{-1} \Sigma_{\hat{p}_0} \nabla^2 \phi_0^{-1} \Sigma_{\hat{p}_0} = cQ. \tag{62}$$

We observe here that $\nabla \phi = \nabla \phi_0 + \hat{p}_0$, such that $\Sigma_{\nabla \phi} \equiv \Sigma_{\hat{p}_0}$ mathematically holds. Since δu is the dominant unitary eigenvector of $\Sigma_{\nabla \phi}$ and is therefore also the dominant unitary eigenvector of $\Sigma_{\nabla \phi}^2$, it follows that matrix Q is given by:

$$\max \quad \left\langle \Sigma_{\hat{p}_0}^2, Q \right\rangle \tag{63a}$$

$$\text{s.t.} \quad \|Q\| = 1, \quad \text{rank}\left(Q\right) = 1. \tag{63b}$$

Observing (62) and (63), it follows that the classical DMA method picks an input using:

- the approximation $\nabla^2 \phi_0 \approx \gamma I$ for some $\gamma > 0$
- a rank-one approximation of $\Sigma_{\hat{p}_0}^2$

According to these observations, a reasonable choice for the scaling constant c can be:

$$c = \Sigma_{\nabla \phi}^{-1} \left\| \Sigma_{\hat{p}_0} \nabla^2 \phi_0^{-1} \Sigma_{\hat{p}_0} \right\|. \tag{64}$$

It is useful to remark here that dismissing the information provided by $\nabla^2 \phi_0$ may be advantageous when ϕ_0 does not reflect adequately the curvature of the cost function of the real process. In such a case, the weighting provided by $\nabla^2\phi_0$ in (58) can arguably be misleading. Including estimations of the 2nd-order sensitivities in the MA approach has been investigated in [19].

3.3. Illustrative Example

We illustrate here the developments proposed above via a simple quadratic example, which nonetheless captures a number of observations that ought to be made. Consider the cost model:

$$\phi_0 = \frac{1}{2}u_0^\top R u_0 + f^\top u_0, \tag{65}$$

such that the nominal optimal input is trivially given by:

$$u_0 = -R^{-1}f. \tag{66}$$

Problem (53) then reads as:

$$\min_{u_0} \quad \frac{1}{2}u_0^\top R u_0 + f^\top u_0 + \frac{1}{2}\mathrm{Tr}\left[\Sigma_{\hat{p}_0}R^{-1}\left(I + \Sigma_{\nabla\phi}^{-1}\Sigma_{\hat{p}_0}S\left(u_0\right)\right)^{-1}\right], \tag{67}$$

while the approximate problem (58) reads as:

$$u_0 = \arg\min_{u_0} \quad \frac{1}{2}u_0^\top \left(R - \Sigma_{\nabla\phi}^{-1}\Sigma_{\hat{p}_0}R^{-1}\Sigma_{\hat{p}_0}\right)u_0 + \left(\hat{p}_0 + f - u_{-1}^\top\Sigma_{\nabla\phi}^{-1}\Sigma_{\hat{p}_0}R^{-1}\Sigma_{\hat{p}_0}\right)^\top u_0. \tag{68}$$

Note that Problem (68) is unbounded for $\Sigma_{\nabla\phi}I < \left(R^{-1}\Sigma_{\hat{p}_0}\right)^2$, while (67) can have a well-defined solution; see Figures 5 and 6 for an illustration. This situation occurs here when the measurement noise is small while the current parameter estimation is highly uncertain and is discontinued when the parameter estimation becomes reliable, such that $\Sigma_{\hat{p}_0}$ becomes small. Note that this can be addressed in practice via an ad hoc regularization or by, e.g., bounding the input correction $\|u_0 - u^*\left(\hat{p}_0\right)\|$ in Problem (58).

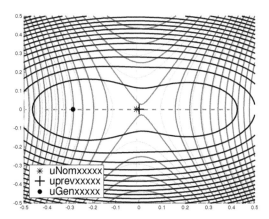

Figure 5. Example of the problem where the quadratic approximation (58) is unbounded, while (53) has a solution. The black lines report the level curves of the cost of Problem (67); the grey lines report the level curves of the cost of Problem (68); and the light grey lines report the level curves of the cost of Problem (69) with Q given by (63). In this example, ignoring the contribution of $\nabla^2\phi_0$ in the Directional-Modifier Adaptation (DMA) algorithm leads it to privilege directions (light grey dashed line) that are significantly different from the ones privileged by (67) (grey dashed line). The latter point to the solution of the original Problem (53).

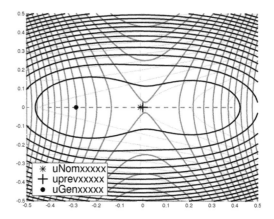

Figure 6. Example of problem where the quadratic approximation (58) is unbounded, while (53) has a solution. The black lines report the level curves of the cost of Problem (67); the grey lines report the level curves of the cost of Problem (68); and the light grey lines report the level curves of the cost of Problem (69) where $Q = \left\| \Sigma_{\hat{p}_0} \right\|^{-2} \Sigma_{\hat{p}_0}^2$ and $c = \Sigma_{\nabla\phi}^{-1} \left\| \Sigma_{\hat{p}_0} \nabla^2 \phi_0^{-1} \Sigma_{\hat{p}_0} \right\|$. Adopting a matrix Q delivering a full-rank approximation of $\Sigma_{\hat{p}_0}^2$ does not help the DMA algorithm adopting directions (see the light-grey dashed line) that point to the direction of the solution to (67); hence, ignoring $\nabla^2 \phi_0$ is problematic here.

The DMA-based problem (60) reads as:

$$u_0 = \arg\min_{u_0} \ \frac{1}{2} u_0^\top (R - cQ)\, u_0 + \left(\hat{p}_0 + f - \frac{c}{2} u_{-1}^\top Q \right)^\top u_0. \tag{69}$$

The behaviors of the DMA problem (69) and its proposed counterpart (68) are reported in Figures 5–8. In Figures 5 and 6, the two problems are compared for the setup:

$$Q = \begin{bmatrix} 0.5060 & 0 \\ 0 & 1.2358 \end{bmatrix}, \quad f = 0, \quad u_- = 0,$$

$$\hat{p}_0 = \begin{bmatrix} 5 \cdot 10^{-3} \\ 0 \end{bmatrix}, \quad \Sigma_{\hat{p}_0} = \begin{bmatrix} 0.0990 & 0 \\ 0 & 0.1638 \end{bmatrix}, \quad \Sigma_{\nabla\phi} = 0.0202, \tag{70}$$

resulting in an unbounded problem for both problems. In this case, the DMA approach (69) with a reduced choice of c would ensure a bounded problem, while a regularization or trust-region technique for Problem (68) would deliver a solution. We observe in Figures 5 and 6 that ignoring the term $\nabla^2 \phi_0$ in the DMA problem can lead the algorithm to favor a solution that departs significantly from the ones proposed by (53).

In Figure 7, the two problems are compared for the setup:

$$Q = I, \quad f = 0, \quad u_- = \begin{bmatrix} 0 \\ -0.0444 \end{bmatrix}, \quad \hat{p}_0 = \begin{bmatrix} 0.04 \\ 0 \end{bmatrix}, \quad \Sigma_{\hat{p}_0} = \begin{bmatrix} 1 & 0 \\ 0 & 0.95 \end{bmatrix}, \quad \Sigma_{\nabla\phi} = 1.5. \tag{71}$$

In this case, ignoring the term $\nabla^2 \phi_0 = Q = I$ does not yield any difficulty. However, because all parameters $\hat{p}_0$ have a very similar covariance, the rank-one approximation of $\Sigma_{\hat{p}_0}$ misleads the DMA algorithm into selecting a solution that departs significantly from the one of (53). Finally, in Figure 8, the two problems are compared for the setup:

$$Q = \begin{bmatrix} 1 & 0 \\ 0 & 0.8 \end{bmatrix}, \quad f = 0, \quad u_- = \begin{bmatrix} 0 \\ -0.05 \end{bmatrix},$$

$$\hat{p}_0 = \begin{bmatrix} 0.04 \\ 0 \end{bmatrix}, \quad \Sigma_{p_0} = \begin{bmatrix} 1 & 0 \\ 0 & 0.2 \end{bmatrix}, \quad \Sigma_{\nabla\phi} = 1.5. \tag{72}$$

In this last case, both the DMA problem (69) and (68) deliver solutions that are very close to the one of Problem (53), i.e., in this scenario, ignoring the term $\nabla^2\phi_0$ and forming a rank-one approximation do not affect the solution significantly.

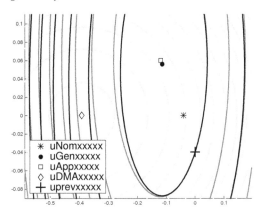

Figure 7. Illustration for Section 3.3, setup (71). The black lines report the level curves of the cost of Problem (67); the grey lines report the level curves of the cost of Problem (68); and the light grey lines report the level curves of the cost of Problem (69) with Q given by (63). In this example, the rank-one approximation for Q leads the DMA algorithm to propose a solution that is far from the one of (67).

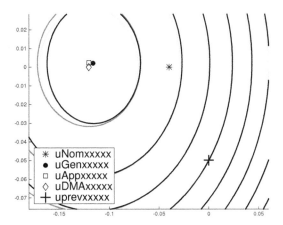

Figure 8. Illustration for Section 3.3, setup (72). The black lines report the level curves of the cost of Problem (67); the grey lines report the level curves of the cost of Problem (68); and the light grey lines report the level curves of the cost of Problem (69) with Q given by (63). In this example, all problems deliver very similar solutions.

4. Conclusions

In this paper, we have proposed a novel view of real-time optimization and of the modifier approach from an experimental design perspective. While some methods are available to handle the trade-off between process optimality and the gathering of information for the performance of future runs, this paper proposes a formal framework to construe this trade-off as an optimization problem and develops a tractable approximation of this problem. The paper then shows that the recent directional-modifier adaptation algorithm is a special formulation of this approximation. This observation allows one to further justify the directional-modifier adaptation algorithm from a theoretical standpoint and to consider a refined tuning of the algorithm. The theory presented in the paper is illustrated via simple examples.

Acknowledgments: This research was partially supported by Freiburg Institute for Advanced Studies (FRIAS), University of Freiburg, Germany. Helpful remarks have been provided by B. Houska.

Conflicts of Interest: The authors declare no conflict of interest.

Appendix A

We provide here the lemma used in Proposition 2.

Lemma A1. *If $x \in \mathbb{R}^m$ is a normally distributed, centered variable of covariance $\Sigma \in \mathbb{R}^{m \times m}$ and $f(x) : \mathbb{R}^m \to \mathbb{R}$ a smooth function polynomially bounded as:*

$$|f(x)| \leq P_{m,n}(x) \tag{A1}$$

for some n-th-order polynomial of the form $P_{m,n}(x) = \sum_{k=m}^{n} \alpha_k \|x\|^k$, then the following inequality holds locally:

$$|\mathbb{E}_x[f(x)]| \leq c \|\Sigma\|^{\mathrm{ceil}\left(\frac{m}{2}\right)}. \tag{A2}$$

Proof. We first observe that:

$$\mathbb{E}_x[P_{m,n}(x)] \leq \sum_{k=m}^{n} \beta_k \|\Sigma\|_\infty^{\frac{k}{2}} \tag{A3}$$

holds for some suite $\beta_k \geq 0$, with $\beta_k = 0$ for k odd. This is a direct consequence of the generalized Isserlis theorem [27,28], which states that the expected value of any even-order moment of a multivariate normal centered distribution is a sum of products between $k/2$ entries of the covariance matrix Σ, while odd-order moments are null. It then also holds that:

$$|\mathbb{E}_x[f(x)]| \leq \sum_{k=m}^{n} \beta_k \|\Sigma\|_\infty^{\frac{k}{2}}, \tag{A4}$$

and the inequality:

$$|\mathbb{E}_x[f(x)]| \leq c \|\Sigma\|^{\mathrm{ceil}\left(\frac{m}{2}\right)} \tag{A5}$$

holds locally. □

We observe that this Lemma appears to be a simple special case of the Theorem proposed by [26] on the delta method, restricted to the normal distribution.

References

1. Chen, C.; Joseph, B. On-line optimization using a two-phase approach: An application study. *Ind. Eng. Chem. Res.* **1987**, *26*, 1924–1930.
2. Jang, S.; Joseph, B. On-line optimization of constrained multivariable chemical processes. *Ind. Eng. Chem. Res.* **1987**, *33*, 26–35.
3. Forbes, J.; Marlin, T.; MacGgregor, J. Model adequacy requirements for optimizing plant operations. *Comput. Chem. Eng.* **1994**, *18*, 497–510.
4. Forbes, J.; Marlin, T. Design cost: A systematic approach to technology selection for model-based real-time optimization systems. *Comput. Chem. Eng.* **1996**, *20*, 717–734.
5. Agarwal, M. Feasibility of on-line reoptimization in batch processes. *Chem. Eng. Commun.* **1997**, *158*, 19–29.
6. Agarwal, M. Iterative set-point optimization of batch chromatography. *Comput. Chem. Eng.* **2005**, *29*, 1401–1409.
7. Marchetti, A. Modifier-Adaptation Methodology for Real-Time Optimization. Ph.D. Thesis, EPFL, Lausanne, Switzerland, 2009.
8. Roberts, P. An algorithm for steady-state system optimization and parameter estimation. *Int. J. Syst. Sci.* **1979**, *10*, 719–734.
9. Gao, W.; Engell, S. Comparison of iterative set-point optimization strategies under structural plant-model mismatch. *IFAC Proc. Vol.* **2005**, *16*, 401.
10. Marchetti, A.; Chachuat, B.; Bonvin, D. Modifier-adaptation methodology for real-time optimization. *Ind. Eng. Chem. Res.* **2009**, *48*, 6022–6033.
11. Roberts, P. Coping with model-reality differences in industrial process optimisation—A review of integrated system optimization and parameter estimation (ISOPE). *Comput. Ind.* **1995**, *26*, 281–290.
12. Tatjewski, P. Iterative optimizing set-point control-the basic principle redesigned. *IFAC Proc. Vol.* **2002**, *35*, 49–54.
13. François, G.; Bonvin, D. Use of convex model approximations for real-time optimization via modifier adaptation. *Ind. Eng. Chem. Res.* **2014**, *52*, 11614–11625.
14. Bunin, G.; Wuillemin, Z.; François, G.; Nakajo, A.; Tsikonis, L.; Bonvin, D. Experimental real-time optimization of a solid oxide fuel cell stack via constraint adaptation. *Energy* **2012**, *39*, 54–62.
15. Serralunga, F.; Mussati, M.; Aguirre, P. Model adaptation for real-time optimization in energy systems. *Ind. Eng. Chem. Res.* **2013**, *52*, 16795–16810.
16. Navia, D.; Marti, R.; Sarabia, R.; Gutirrez, G.; Prada, C. Handling infeasibilities in dual modifier-adaptation methodology for real-time optimization. *IFAC Proc. Vol.* **2012**, *45*, 537–542.
17. Darby, M.; Nikolaou, M.; Jones, J.; Nicholson, D. RTO: An overview and assessment of current practice. *J. Process Control* **2011**, *21*, 874–884.
18. Costello, S.; François, G.; Bonvin, D.; Marchetti, A. Modifier adaptation for constrained closed-loop systems. *IFAC Proc. Vol.* **2014**, *47*, 11080–11086.
19. Faulwasser, T.; Bonvin, D. On the Use of Second-Order Modifiers for Real-Time Optimization. In Proceedings of the 19th IFAC World Congress, Cape Town, South Africa, 24–29 August 2014.
20. Bunin, G.; François, G.; Bonvin, D. From discrete measurements to bounded gradient estimates: A look at some regularizing structures. *Ind. Eng. Chem. Res.* **2013**, *52*, 12500–12513.
21. Serralunga, F.; Aguirre, P.; Mussati, M. Including disjunctions in real-time optimization. *Ind. Eng. Chem. Res.* **2014**, *53*, 17200–17213.
22. Houska, B.; Telenb, D.; Logist, F.; Diehl, M.; Van Impe, J.F.M. An economic objective for the optimal experiment design of nonlinear dynamic processes. *Automatica* **2015**, *51*, 98–103.
23. Costello, S.; François, G.; Bonvin, D. Directional Real-Time Optimization Applied to a Kite-Control Simulation Benchmark. In Proceedings of the European Control Conference 2015, Linz, Austria, 15–17 July 2015.
24. Costello, S.; François, G.; Bonvin, D. A directional modifier-adaptation algorithm for real-time optimization. *J. Process Control* **2016**, *39*, 64–76.
25. Marchetti, A.; Chachuat, B.; Bonvin, D. A dual modifier-adaptation approach for real-time optimization. *J. Process Control* **2010**, *20*, 1027–1037.
26. Oehlert, G. A note on the delta method. *Am. Stat.* **1992**, *46*, 27–29.

27.   Withers, C. The moments of the multivariate normal. *Bull. Aust. Math. Soc.* **1985**, *32*, doi:10.1017/S000497270000976X.

28.   Vignat, C. A generalized Isserlis theorem for location mixtures of Gaussian random vectors. *Stat. Probab. Lett.* **2012**, *82*, 67–71.

Article

A Modifier-Adaptation Strategy towards Offset-Free Economic MPC

Marco Vaccari [†] and Gabriele Pannocchia [*,†]

Department of Civil and Industrial Engineering, University of Pisa, Largo Lazzarino 2, 56126 Pisa, Italy;
marco.vaccari@ing.unipi.it
* Correspondence: gabriele.pannocchia@unipi.it; Tel.: +39-050-2217838
† These authors contributed equally to this work.

Academic Editor: Dominique Bonvin
Received: 16 November 2016; Accepted: 20 December 2016; Published: 29 December 2016

Abstract: We address in the paper the problem of designing an economic model predictive control (EMPC) algorithm that asymptotically achieves the optimal performance despite the presence of plant-model mismatch. To motivate the problem, we present an example of a continuous stirred tank reactor in which available EMPC and tracking model predictive control (MPC) algorithms do not reach the optimal steady state operation. We propose to use an offset-free disturbance model and to modify the target optimization problem with a correction term that is iteratively computed to enforce the necessary conditions of optimality in the presence of plant-model mismatch. Then, we show how the proposed formulation behaves on the motivating example, highlighting the role of the stage cost function used in the finite horizon MPC problem.

Keywords: model predictive control (MPC); real-time optimization (RTO); economic model predictive control (EMPC); modifier-adaptation

1. Introduction

Optimization-based controllers, in general, and model predictive control (MPC) systems, in particular, represent an extraordinary success case in the history of automation in the process industries [1]. MPC algorithms exploit a (linear or nonlinear) dynamic model of the process and numerical optimization algorithms to guide a process to a setpoint reliably, while fulfilling constraints on outputs and inputs. The optimal steady-state setpoint is usually provided by an upper layer, named real-time optimization (RTO), that is dedicated to economic steady-state optimization. The typical hierarchical architecture for economic optimization and control in the process industries is depicted in Figure 1. For an increasing number of applications, however, this separation of information and purpose is no longer optimal nor desirable [2]. An alternative to this decomposition is to take the economic objective directly as the objective function of the control system. In this approach, known as economic model predictive control (EMPC), the controller optimizes directly, in real time, the economic performance of the process, rather than tracking a setpoint.

MPC being a model-based optimization algorithm, in the presence of plant-model mismatch or unmeasured disturbances, it can come across offset problems. Non-economically optimum stationary points can also be the result of a plant-model mismatch in model-based RTO. However, as explained later, some RTO algorithms do not use a model, i.e., extremum-seeking control [3,4], so in this case, the mismatch issue can be associated with unmeasured disturbances. The offset correction in tracking MPC algorithms has been deeply exploited and analyzed. Muske and Badgwell [5] and Pannocchia and Rawlings [6] first introduced the concept of general conditions that allow zero steady-state offset with respect to external setpoints. The general approach is to augment the nominal system with disturbances, i.e., to build a disturbance model and to estimate the state and disturbance from output measurements. A recent review about disturbance models and offset-free MPC design can also be found in [7]. Furthermore, in the RTO literature, many works are focused on plant-model mismatch issues. RTO typically proceeds using an iterative two-step approach [8,9], namely an identification step followed by an optimization step. The idea is to repeatedly estimate selected uncertain model parameters and to use the updated model to generate new inputs via optimization. Other alternative options do not use a process model online to implement the optimization [10–12]. Others utilize a nominal fixed process model and appropriate measurements to guide the iterative scheme towards the optimum. In this last field, the term "modifier-adaptation" indicates those fixed-model methods that adapt correction terms (i.e., the modifiers) based on the observed difference between actual and predicted functions or gradients [13–15]. Marchetti et al. [16] formalize the concept of using plant measurements to adapt the optimization problem in response to plant-model mismatch, through modifier-adaptation.

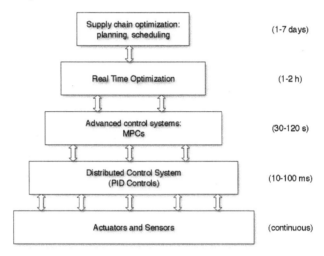

Figure 1. Typical hierarchical optimization and control structure in process systems.

As underlined above, the RTO and MPC hierarchical division issue has led to the increased interest in merging the two layers. Many works in the literature consider a combination between RTO and MPC through a target calculation level in the middle that coordinates the communication and guarantees stability to the whole structure calculating the feasible target for the optimal control problem [17,18]. There are also examples of integration between the modifier-adaptation technique and MPC [19]: in this way, the input targets calculated by the MPC are included as equality constraints into the modified RTO problem. In other cases, the target module of the MPC has been modified in various ways, including a new quadratic programming problem that is an approximation of the RTO problem [20].

Another area of the literature aimed at merging the two layers is the so-called dynamic real-time optimization (D-RTO). The objective function of the D-RTO includes an economic objective, subject to a dynamic model of the plant. The optimal control profiles are then determined from the solution of the above dynamic optimization problem and then passed to the underlined MPC layer as trajectory setpoints to follow. The advantages of this formulation in the presence of disturbances have been deeply emphasized in the literature [21,22], also in the case of model-free alternatives [23]. The D-RTO is also seen as a solution for merging economic and control layer, while advances in nonlinear model predictive control and its generalization to deal with economic objective functions taking place [24]. In this sense, a receding horizon closed-loop implementation of D-RTO can be also referred to as economic model predictive control [25].

In the presence of plant-model mismatch, also EMPC can suffer from converging to a non-economically steady-state point and also reaching a steady state different from the one indicated by the target at the same time. The main goal of this work is to build an economic MPC algorithm that, combining the previous ideas of offset-free MPC and modifier-adaptation, achieves the ultimate optimal economic performance despite modeling errors and/or disturbances. In the proposed method, there is no RTO layer because the economic cost function is used directly in the MPC formulation, which however includes a modifier-adaptation scheme.

The rest of this paper is organized as follows. A review of the related technique used in this work is presented in Section 2 along with a motivating example. The proposed method, with a detailed mathematical analysis and description, is presented in Section 3. The algorithm and several variants are then tested over the illustrative example, and the numerical results and associated discussions are reported in Section 4. Finally, Section 5 concludes the paper and presents possible future directions of this methodology.

2. Related Techniques and a Motivating Example

In order to propose an offset-free EMPC algorithm, a review of related concepts and techniques is given. Then, we present a motivating example that shows how neither the standard EMPC formulation nor an offset-free tracking MPC formulation are able to achieve the ultimate optimal economic performance.

2.1. Plant, Model and Constraints

In this paper, we are concerned with the control of time-invariant dynamical systems in the form:

$$x_p^+ = F_p(x_p, u)$$
$$y = H_p(x_p) \tag{1}$$

in which $x_p \in \mathbb{R}^n$, $u \in \mathbb{R}^m$, $y \in \mathbb{R}^p$ are the plant state, control input and output at a given time, respectively, and x_p^+ is the successor state. The plant output is measured at each time $k \in \mathbb{I}$. Functions $F_p: \mathbb{R}^n \times \mathbb{R}^m \to \mathbb{R}^n$ and $H_p: \mathbb{R}^n \to \mathbb{R}^p$ are not known precisely, but are assumed to be differentiable. In order to design an MPC algorithm, a process model is known:

$$x^+ = f(x, u)$$
$$y = h(x) \tag{2}$$

in which $x, x^+ \in \mathbb{R}^n$ denote the current and successor model states. The functions $f: \mathbb{R}^n \times \mathbb{R}^m \to \mathbb{R}^n$ and $h: \mathbb{R}^n \to \mathbb{R}^p$ are assumed to be differentiable. Input and output are required to satisfy the following input and output constraints at all times:

$$u_{\min} \leq u \leq u_{\max}, \quad y_{\min} \leq y \leq y_{\max} \tag{3}$$

in which $u_{\min}, u_{\max} \in \mathbb{R}^m$ and $y_{\min}, y_{\max} \in \mathbb{R}^p$ are the bound vectors.

2.2. Offset-Free Tracking MPC

Offset-free MPC algorithms are generally based on an augmented model [5,6,26,27]. The general form of this augmented model can be written as:

$$x^+ = F(x, u, d)$$
$$d^+ = d$$
$$y = H(x, d) \tag{4}$$

in which $d \in \mathbb{R}^{n_d}$ is the so-called disturbance. The functions $F: \mathbb{R}^n \times \mathbb{R}^m \times \mathbb{R}^{n_d} \to \mathbb{R}^n$ and H: $\mathbb{R}^n \times \mathbb{R}^{n_d} \to \mathbb{R}^p$ are assumed to be continuous and consistent with (2), i.e., $F(x, u, 0) = f(x, u)$ and $H(x, 0) = h(x)$.

Assumption 1. *The augmented system (4) is observable.*

At each time $k \in \mathbb{I}$, given the output measurement $y(k)$, an observer for (4) is defined to estimate the augmented state $(x(k), d(k))$. For simplicity of exposition, only the current measurement of $y(k)$ is used to update the prediction of $(x(k), d(k))$ made at the previous decision time, i.e., a "Kalman filter"-like estimator is used. We define symbols $\hat{x}_{k|k-1}$, $\hat{d}_{k|k-1}$ and $\hat{y}_{k|k-1}$ as the predicted estimate of $x(k)$, $d(k)$ and $y(k)$, respectively, obtained at the previous time $k-1$ using the augmented model (4), i.e.,

$$\hat{x}_{k|k-1} = F(\hat{x}_{k-1|k-1}, u_{k-1}, \hat{d}_{k-1|k-1})$$
$$\hat{d}_{k|k-1} = \hat{d}_{k-1|k-1}$$
$$\hat{y}_{k|k-1} = H(\hat{x}_{k|k-1}, \hat{d}_{k|k-1}) \tag{5}$$

Defining the output prediction error as:

$$e_k = y(k) - \hat{y}_{k|k-1} \tag{6}$$

the filtering relations can be written as follows:

$$\hat{x}_{k|k} = \hat{x}_{k|k-1} + \kappa_x(e_k)$$
$$\hat{d}_{k|k} = \hat{d}_{k|k-1} + \kappa_d(e_k) \tag{7}$$

where $\hat{x}_{k|k}$ and $\hat{d}_{k|k}$ are the filtered estimate of $x(k)$ and $d(k)$ in (4) obtained using measurement $y(k)$. We assume that Relations (5)–(7) form an asymptotically-stable observer for the augmented system (4).

Given the current estimate of the augmented state $(\hat{x}_{k|k}, \hat{d}_{k|k})$, an offset-free tracking MPC algorithm computes the steady-state target that ensures exact setpoint tracking in the controlled variable. Hence, in general, the following target problem is solved:

$$\min_{x,u,y} \ell_s(y - y_{sp}, u - u_{sp}) \tag{8a}$$

subject to

$$x = F(x, \hat{d}_{k|k}, u) \tag{8b}$$
$$y = H(x, \hat{d}_{k|k}) \tag{8c}$$
$$u_{min} \le u \le u_{max} \tag{8d}$$
$$y_{min} \le y \le y_{max} \tag{8e}$$

in which $\ell_s: \mathbb{R}^p \times \mathbb{R}^m \to \mathbb{R}$ is the steady-state cost function and $y_{sp} \in \mathbb{R}^p$, $u_{sp} \in \mathbb{R}^m$ are the output and input setpoints, respectively. We assume (8) is feasible, and we denote its (unique) solution as $(x_{s,k}, u_{s,k}, y_{s,k})$. Typically, $\ell_s(\cdot)$ is positive definite in the first argument (output steady-state error) and semidefinite in the second argument (input steady-state error), and relative input and output weights are chosen to ensure that $y_{s,k} \to y_{sp}$ whenever constraints allow it.

Let $x = \{x_0, x_1, \ldots, x_N\}$ and $u = \{u_0, u_1, \ldots, u_{N-1}\}$ be, respectively, a state sequence and an input sequence. The finite horizon optimal control problem (FHOCP) solved at each time is the following:

$$\min_{x,u} \sum_{i=0}^{N-1} \ell_{QP}(x_i - x_{s,k}, u_i - u_{s,k}) + V_f(x_N - x_{s,k}) \tag{9a}$$

subject to

$$x_0 = \hat{x}_{k|k}, \tag{9b}$$

$$x_{i+1} = F(x_i, \hat{d}_{k|k}, u_i), \qquad i = 0, \ldots, N-1 \tag{9c}$$

$$u_{min} \leq u_i \leq u_{max}, \qquad i = 0, \ldots, N-1 \tag{9d}$$

$$y_{min} \leq H(x_i, \hat{d}_{k|k}) \leq y_{max} \qquad i = 0, \ldots, N-1 \tag{9e}$$

$$x_N = x_{s,k} \tag{9f}$$

in which $\ell_{QP}: \mathbb{R}^n \times \mathbb{R}^m \rightarrow \mathbb{R}_{\geq 0}$ is a strictly positive definite convex function. $V_f: \mathbb{R}^n \rightarrow \mathbb{R}_{\geq 0}$ is a terminal cost function, which may vary depending on the specific MPC formulation, according to the usual stabilizing conditions [28]. Assuming Problem (9) to be feasible, its solution is denoted by (x_k^0, u_k^0), and the associated receding horizon implementation is given by:

$$u_k = u_{0,k}^0 \tag{10}$$

As the conclusion of this discussion, the following result holds true [5,6,29].

Proposition 1. *Consider a system controlled by the MPC algorithm as described above. If the closed-loop system is stable, then the output prediction error goes to zero, i.e.,*

$$\lim_{k \rightarrow \infty} y(k) - \hat{y}_{k|k-1} = 0 \tag{11}$$

Furthermore, if input constraints are not active at steady state, there is zero offset in the controlled variables, that is:

$$\lim_{k \rightarrow \infty} y(k) - y_{sp} = 0 \tag{12}$$

2.3. Economic MPC

As can be seen from Figure 1, setpoints (y_{sp}, u_{sp}) that enter in (8) come from the upper economic layer referred to as the RTO. This hierarchical division may limit the achievable flexibility and economic performance that many processes nowadays request. There are several proposals to improve the effective use of dynamic and economic information throughout the hierarchy. As explained in Section 1, the first approach to this merging is the D-RTO. While many D-RTO structures have been proposed throughout the literature [23,30,31], many of the two-layered D-RTO and MPC systems proposed are characterized by a lack of rigorous theoretical treatment, including the constraints. However, as can be seen in the above cited literature, the D-RTO formulations still consider the presence of both RTO and MPC in separated layers. Instead of moving the dynamic characteristic to the RTO level, the interest here is to move economic information into the control layer. This approach involves modifying the traditional tracking objective function in (9) and the target cost function in (8) directly with the economic stage cost function used in the RTO layer. In this latter case, the formulation takes the name of economic MPC (EMPC) [32]. It has to be underlined that, in this case, the economic optimization is provided only by the EMPC layer, while the RTO one is completely eliminated.

In standard MPC, the objective is designed to ensure asymptotic stability of the desired steady state. This is accomplished by choosing the stage cost to be zero at the steady-state target pair, denoted (x_s, u_s), and positive elsewhere, i.e.,

$$0 = \ell_{QP}(x_s, u_s) \le \ell_{QP}(x, u) \quad \text{for all admissible } (x, u) \tag{13}$$

In EMPC, instead, the operating cost of the plant is used directly as the stage cost in the FHOCP objective function. As a consequence, it may happen that $\ell_e(x_s, u_s) > \ell_e(x, u)$ for some feasible pair (x, u) that is not a steady state. This possibility has significant impact on stability and convergence properties. In fact, while a common approach in the tracking MPC is to use the optimal cost as a Lyapunov function for the closed-loop system to prove its stability, in the EMPC formulation, due to the fact that (13) does not hold, these stability arguments fail. Hence, for certain systems and cost functions, oscillating solutions may be economically more profitable than steady-state ones, giving rise to the concept of average asymptotic performance of economic MPC, which is deeply developed in [32,33]. Despite that, in the literature, there are also formulations of the Lyapunov-based EMPC by taking advantage of an auxiliary MPC problem solution [34,35].

In this work, we assume that operating at steady-state is more profitable than an oscillating behavior. Hence, in order to delineate the concept of convergence in EMPC, two other properties may be useful: dissipativity [32,36] and turnpike [37,38]. These properties play a key role in the analysis and design of schemes for D-RTO and EMPC. It is shown also that in a continuous-time form, the dissipativity of a system with respect to a steady state implies the existence of a turnpike at this steady state and optimal stationary operation at this steady state [39,40]. An extensive review about EMPC control methods can be found in [41,42].

The starting EMPC algorithm considered in this work is taken from [29] and includes an offset-free disturbance model as described in Section 2.2. Given the current state and disturbance estimate $(\hat{x}_{k|k}, \hat{d}_{k|k})$, the economic steady-state target is given by:

$$\min_{x,u,y} \ell_e(y, u) \tag{14a}$$

subject to

$$x = F(x, \hat{d}_{k|k}, u) \tag{14b}$$

$$y = H(x, \hat{d}_{k|k}) \tag{14c}$$

$$u_{\min} \le u \le u_{\max} \tag{14d}$$

$$y_{\min} \le y \le y_{\max} \tag{14e}$$

in which $\ell_e \colon \mathbb{R}^p \times \mathbb{R}^m \to \mathbb{R}$ is the economic cost function defined in terms of output and input. Notice that the arguments of the economic cost function are measurable quantities. Let $(x_{s,k}, u_{s,k}, y_{s,k})$ be the steady-state target triple solution to (14). Then, the FHOCP solved at each time is given by:

$$\min_{x,u} \sum_{i=0}^{N-1} \ell_e(H(x_i, \hat{d}_{k|k}), u_i) \tag{15a}$$

subject to

$$x_0 = \hat{x}_{k|k}, \tag{15b}$$

$$x_{i+1} = F(x_i, \hat{d}_{k|k}, u_i), \quad i = 0, \dots, N-1 \tag{15c}$$

$$u_{\min} \le u_i \le u_{\max}, \quad i = 0, \dots, N-1 \tag{15d}$$

$$y_{\min} \le H(x_i, \hat{d}_{k|k}) \le y_{\max}, \quad i = 0, \dots, N-1 \tag{15e}$$

$$x_N = x_{s,k} \tag{15f}$$

While several formulations of economic MPC are possible, in this work, we use a terminal equality constraint to achieve asymptotic stability [36]. We remark that the target equilibrium $x_{s,k}$ is recomputed at each decision time by the target calculation problem (14).

2.4. A Motivating Example

2.4.1. Process and Optimal Economic Performance

In order to motivate this work, we show the application of EMPC formulations to a chemical reactor to highlight how available methods are not able to achieve the optimal economic performance in the presence of modeling errors. The chemical reactor under consideration is a continuous stirred tank reactor (CSTR), in which two consecutive reactions take place:

$$A \xrightarrow{k_1} B \xrightarrow{k_2} C \tag{16}$$

The reactor is described by the following system of ordinary differential equations (ODE):

$$\dot{c}_A = \frac{Q}{V}(c_{A0} - c_A) - k_1 c_A \tag{17}$$

$$\dot{c}_B = \frac{Q}{V}(c_{B0} - c_B) + k_1 c_A - k_2 c_B$$

in which c_A and c_B are the molar concentrations of A and B in the reactor, c_{A0} and c_{B0} are the corresponding concentrations in the feed, Q is the feed flow rate, V is the constant reactor volume and k_1 and k_2 are the kinetic constants. The feed flow rate entering the reactor is regulated through a valve, i.e., Q is the manipulated variable. For the sake of simplicity, the reactor is assumed to be isothermal, so the fixed parameters of the actual system are shown in Table 1.

Table 1. Actual reactor parameters.

Description	Symbol	Value	Unit
Kinetic Constant 1	k_1	1.0	min^{-1}
Kinetic Constant 2	k_2	0.05	min^{-1}
Reactor volume	V	1.0	m^3
A feed concentration	c_{A0}	1.0	$\frac{\text{kmol}}{\text{m}^3}$
B feed concentration	c_{B0}	0.0	$\frac{\text{kmol}}{\text{m}^3}$
A price	β_A	1.0	$\frac{\text{\euro}}{\text{kmol}}$
B price	β_B	4.0	$\frac{\text{\euro}}{\text{kmol}}$

The process economics can be expressed by the running cost:

$$\ell(Q, c_B) = \beta_A Q c_{A0} - \beta_B Q c_B \tag{18}$$

where β_A, β_B are the prices for the reactants A and B, respectively, also reported in Table 1.

Using the actual process parameters reported in Table 1, we can compute the process optimal steady-state, by solving the following optimization problem:

$$\min_Q \beta_A Q c_{A0} - \beta_B Q c_B \tag{19a}$$

subject to

$$\frac{Q}{V}(c_{A0} - c_A) - k_1 c_A = 0 \tag{19b}$$

$$\frac{Q}{V}(c_{B0} - c_B) + k_1 c_A - k_2 c_B = 0 \tag{19c}$$

$$0 \leq c_A \leq c_{A0} \tag{19d}$$

$$0 \leq c_B \leq c_{A0} \tag{19e}$$

The result of this optimization is $Q_{opt} = 1.043 \text{ m}^3/\text{min}$, $c_{A,opt} = 0.511 \text{ kmol/m}^3$ and $c_{B,opt} = 0.467 \text{ kmol/m}^3$, which represents the most economic steady state that the actual process can achieve.

2.4.2. Model and Controllers

The definition of the states, input and outputs is the following:

$$x = \begin{bmatrix} c_A \\ c_B \end{bmatrix}, \quad u = \begin{bmatrix} Q \end{bmatrix}, \quad y = \begin{bmatrix} c_A \\ c_B \end{bmatrix}. \tag{20}$$

For controller design, the second kinetic constant is supposed to be uncertain, i.e., the value known by the controller is $\bar{k}_2$, instead of k_2. With these definitions, the model equations become:

$$\begin{bmatrix} \dot{x}_1 \\ \dot{x}_2 \end{bmatrix} = \begin{bmatrix} \frac{u}{V}(c_{A0} - x_1) - k_1 x_1 \\ \frac{u}{V}(c_{B0} - x_2) + k_1 x_1 - \bar{k}_2 x_2 \end{bmatrix} \tag{21}$$

We compare the closed-loop behavior of three EMPC algorithms, all designed according to Section 2.3 using the same nominal model (21), cost function and a sampling time of $\tau = 2.0 \text{ min}$. Specifically, the target optimization problem is given in (14), and the FHOCP is given in (15), where the economic cost function is:

$$\ell_e(y(t_i), u(t_i)) = \int_{t_i}^{t_i+\tau} \ell(u(t), y_2(t)) dt = \int_{t_i}^{t_i+\tau} [\beta_A u(t) c_{A0} - \beta_B u(t) y_2(t)] dt \tag{22}$$

We note that the use of the cost function integrated over the sampling time is necessary to achieve an asymptotically stable closed-loop equilibrium. As a matter of fact, if the point-wise evaluation of $\ell(\cdot)$ were used as stage cost $\ell_e(\cdot)$, the system would not be dissipative [36], i.e., the closed-loop system would not be stable. The three controllers differ in the augmented model:

- EMPC0 is the standard economic MPC and uses no disturbance model, i.e., $F(x, u, d) = f(x, u)$ and $H(x, d) = h(x) = x$.
- EMPC1 uses a state disturbance model, i.e., $F(x, u, d) = f(x, u) + d$ and $H(x, d) = h(x) = x$.
- EMPC2 uses a nonlinear disturbance model [29], in which the disturbances act as a correction to the kinetic constants, i.e., $F(x, u, d)$ is obtained by integration of the following ODE system:

$$\dot{c}_A = \frac{q}{V}(c_{A0} - c_A) - (k_1 + d_1) c_A \tag{23}$$

$$\dot{c}_B = \frac{q}{V}(c_{B0} - c_B) + (k_1 + d_1) c_A - (\bar{k}_2 + d_2) c_B$$

and $H(x, d) = h(x) = x$.

Since the state is measured, for EMPC0, we use $\hat{x}_{k|k} = x(k)$. For EMPC1 and EMPC2, we use an extended Kalman filter (EKF) to estimate the current state $\hat{x}_{k|k}$ and disturbance $\hat{d}_{k|k}$, given the current measurement of $x(k)$, with the following output noise and state noise covariance matrices:

$$R_{kf} = 10^{-8}I \quad \text{and} \quad Q_{kf} = \begin{bmatrix} 10^{-8}I & 0 \\ 0 & I \end{bmatrix} \tag{24}$$

We note that R_{kf} is chosen small because for simplicity of exposition, we are not including output noise. Furthermore, the ratio between the state covariance (upper diagonal block of Q_{kf}) and the disturbance covariance (lower diagonal block of Q_{kf}) is chosen small to ensure fast offset-free performance [6].

2.4.3. Implementation Details

In order to proceed for further calculations, a few comments on the implementation details are needed. The model in (21) has been discretized through an explicit fourth-order Runge–Kutta method with $M = 10$ equal intervals for each time step. The FHOCP in (15) is solved with a multiple shooting approach because it is very advantageous for long prediction horizons and enforces numerical stability. Simulations are performed using a code developed in Python, and the resulting nonlinear programming problems are solved with IPOPT (https://projects.coin-or.org/Ipopt) .

2.4.4. Results

Figure 2 shows the closed-loop flow rate obtained with standard EMPC0 in two cases of uncertainty on k_2. In the first case (left), $\bar{k}_2 = 0.025$, i.e., the controller model uses a value of k_2, which is half of the true value. In the second case (right), $\bar{k}_2 = 0$, i.e., the controller model ignores the second reaction. As can be seen from these plots, in both cases, the controller is unable to drive the flow rate to the most economic target.

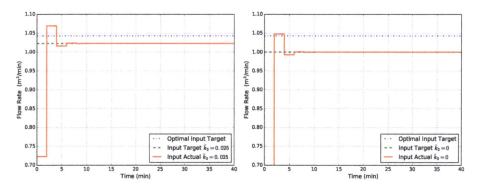

Figure 2. Closed-loop flow rate Q obtained with standard EMPC0 for two cases of uncertainty in k_2: $\bar{k}_2 = 0.025$ (**left**) and $\bar{k}_2 = 0$ (**right**).

Figure 3 shows the corresponding results obtained with EMPC1. Despite the fact that EMPC1 uses a disturbance model, which guarantees offset-free tracking, the controller is still unable to drive the flow rate to the optimal target.

Finally, Figure 4 shows the corresponding results obtained with EMPC2. In this case, the controller is able to drive the closed-loop system to the optimal steady state. The reason is that the augmented model (23) asymptotically converges to the true process because the estimated disturbance d_2 ensures that $\bar{k}_2 + d_2 \rightarrow k_2$. However, this approach requires to know exactly where the uncertainties are, in order to build an ad hoc disturbance model to correct them. Hence, it cannot be used as a general rule. With this evidence, it is clear that, at the moment, there is no general formulation for an offset-free economic MPC, and this is what motivates the present work. In the end, it has to be noted that the case $\bar{k}_2 = 0$ falls into an unmodeled dynamics problem, i.e., the second reaction is completely ignored by the model.

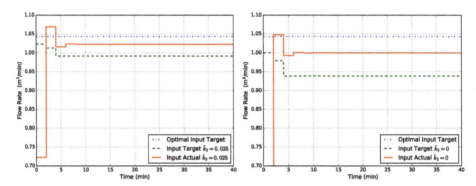

Figure 3. Closed-loop flow rate Q obtained with EMPC1 (state disturbance model) for two cases of uncertainty in k_2: $\bar{k}_2 = 0.025$ (**left**) and $\bar{k}_2 = 0$ (**right**).

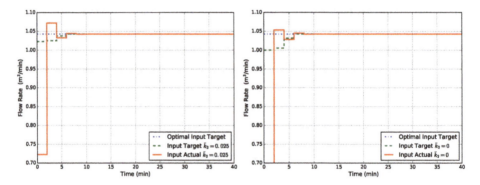

Figure 4. Closed-loop flow rate Q obtained with EMPC2 (non-linear state disturbance model) for two cases of uncertainty in k_2: $\bar{k}_2 = 0.025$ (**left**) and $\bar{k}_2 = 0$ (**right**).

3. Proposed Method

As introduced in the previous section, we now illustrate the method developed using the modifier-adaptation technique borrowed from the RTO literature. Before coming to the proposed method, we give a brief introduction to this technique, referring the interested reader to [14,16] for more details.

3.1. RTO with Modifier-Adaptation

The objective of RTO is the minimization of some steady-state operating cost function, while satisfying a number of constraints. Finding the optimal steady-state operation point for the actual process can be stated as the solution of the following problem:

$$\min_{u} \Phi_p(u) \tag{25a}$$

subject to

$$C_p(u) \leq 0 \tag{25b}$$

In the above, $\Phi_p\colon \mathbb{R}^m \to \mathbb{R}$ is the economic performance cost function of the process and $C_p\colon \mathbb{R}^m \to \mathbb{R}^{n_c}$ is the process constraint function. As explained before for the MPC case, the exact process description is unknown, and only a model can be used in the process optimization. Hence, the model-based economic optimization is represented by the problem:

$$\min_u \Phi(u, \theta) \tag{26a}$$

subject to

$$C(u, \theta) \leq 0 \tag{26b}$$

where $\Phi\colon \mathbb{R}^m \to \mathbb{R}$ and $C\colon \mathbb{R}^m \to \mathbb{R}^{n_c}$ represent the model economic cost function and the model constraint function, which may depend on uncertain parameters $\theta \in \mathbb{R}^{n_\theta}$. Due to plant-model mismatch, open-loop implementation of the solution to (26) may lead to suboptimal and even infeasible operation.

The modifier-adaptation methodology changes Problem (26) so that in a closed-loop execution, the necessary conditions of optimality (NCO) of the modified problem correspond to the necessary conditions of Process (25), upon convergence of the algorithm. The following problem shows the model-based optimization with additional modifiers [16,43]:

$$\bar{u}_h = \arg\min_u \Phi_M = \Phi(u, \theta) + (\lambda_{h-1}^\Phi)^T u \tag{27a}$$

subject to:

$$C_M = C(u, \theta) + (\lambda_{h-1}^C)^T (u - \bar{u}_{h-1}) + \epsilon_{h-1}^C \leq 0 \tag{27b}$$

in which:

$$\lambda_{h-1}^\Phi = \nabla_u \Phi_p(\bar{u}_{h-1}) - \nabla_u \Phi(\bar{u}_{h-1}, \theta) \tag{28a}$$

$$\lambda_{h-1}^C = \nabla_u C_p(\bar{u}_{h-1}) - \nabla_u C(\bar{u}_{h-1}, \theta) \tag{28b}$$

$$\epsilon_{h-1}^C = C_p(\bar{u}_{h-1}) - C(\bar{u}_{h-1}, \theta) \tag{28c}$$

In (27) and (28), $\bar{u}_{h-1} \in \mathbb{R}^m$ represents the operation point, calculated at the previous RTO iteration $h - 1$, and the modifiers $\lambda_{h-1}^\Phi \in \mathbb{R}^m$, $\lambda_{h-1}^C \in \mathbb{R}^{m \times n_c}$, and $\epsilon_{h-1}^C \in \mathbb{R}^{n_c}$ are evaluated using the information available at that point. Notice that the model parameters θ are not updated.

Marchetti et al. [16,43] demonstrated that, upon convergence, the Karush–Kuhn–Tucker (KKT) conditions of the modified problem (27) match the ones of the true process optimization problem (25). Hence, if second-order conditions hold at this point, a local optimum of the real plant can be found by the problem modified as in (27). Furthermore, a filtering procedure of the modifiers is also recommended in order to improve stability and convergence and to reduce sensitivity to measurement noise. The filtering step is given by the following equations:

$$\lambda_h^\Phi = (I - K_{\lambda^\Phi})\lambda_{h-1}^\Phi + K_{\lambda^\Phi}(\nabla_u \Phi_p(\bar{u}_h) - \nabla_u \Phi(\bar{u}_h, \theta)) \tag{29a}$$

$$\lambda_h^C = (I - K_{\lambda^C})\lambda_{h-1}^C + K_{\lambda^C}(\nabla_u C_p(\bar{u}_h) - \nabla_u C(\bar{u}_h, \theta)) \tag{29b}$$

$$\epsilon_h^C = (I - K_{\epsilon^C})\epsilon_{h-1}^C + K_{\epsilon^C}(C_p(\bar{u}_h) - C(\bar{u}_h, \theta)) \tag{29c}$$

where $K_{\lambda\Phi}$, $K_{\lambda C}$ and $K_{\epsilon C}$ (usually diagonal matrices) represent the respective first-order filter constants for each modifier. An alternative approach to the modifier filtering step (29) is to directly define the modifiers as the gradient or function differences and then filter the computed inputs to be applied to the process [44,45]. From (28) and (29), it is clear how the process gradient estimation stage is the major requirement of this method: actually, the process gradient estimation, is hidden into both $\nabla_u \Phi_p$ and $\nabla_u C_p$ for calculating λ_h^Φ and λ_h^C. This is also the major and tightest constraint for this method [46].

Before presenting the proposed technique, the example in Section 2.4 is tested on the standard hierarchical architecture RTO plus MPC. The RTO problem is modified as in Marchetti et al. [16] as follows:

$$\bar{u}_h = \arg\min_u \bar{\Phi}_M = \Phi(u, y(u, \theta) + \epsilon_{h-1}^y + (\lambda_{h-1}^y)^T (u - u_{h-1})) \tag{30a}$$

subject to

$$\tilde{C}_M = C(u, y(u, \theta) + \epsilon_{h-1}^y + (\lambda_{h-1}^y)^T (u - u_{h-1})) \leq 0 \tag{30b}$$

where ϵ_h^y and λ_h^y are updated by the following law:

$$\lambda_h^y = (I - K_{\lambda y})\lambda_{h-1}^y + K_{\lambda y}(\nabla_u y_p(\bar{u}_h) - \nabla_u y(\bar{u}_h, \theta)) \tag{31a}$$

$$\epsilon_h^y = (I - K_{\epsilon y})\epsilon_{h-1}^y + K_{\epsilon y}(y_p(\bar{u}_h) - y(\bar{u}_h, \theta)) \tag{31b}$$

Figure 5 shows the closed-loop flow rate obtained with modified RTO problem followed by tracking MPC with output disturbance model in two cases of uncertainty on k_2. The weight values used are $K_{\lambda y} = 0.2$ and $K_{\epsilon y} = 0.7$, and the RTO problem is run every 20 min. As can be seen from Figure 5, in both cases, the system achieves the optimal input value as expected by the modifier-adaptation methodology. However, the hierarchical and multi-rate nature of the standard architecture results in slow convergence towards the economically-optimal target.

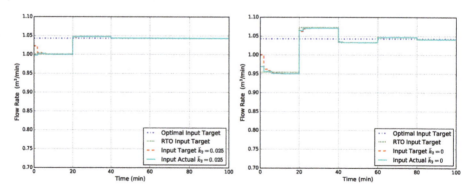

Figure 5. Closed-loop flow rate Q obtained with modified RTO followed by tracking MPC with the output disturbance model for two cases of uncertainty in k_2: $\bar{k}_2 = 0.025$ (**left**) and $\bar{k}_2 = 0$ (**right**).

3.2. Proposed Technique

Having shown that, in order to apply this technique to the EMPC, some work is needed. First of all, in order to be consistent with the offset-free augmented model and to exploit its properties, an alternative form of the modifier-adaptation technique is adopted. In this way, as illustrated in the work of Marchetti et al. [16], a linear modification of the model output steady-state function, rather than of the cost and constraint functions, independently, in the optimization problem has been preferred. To this aim, we rewrite the model constraints of the target problem (14) in a more compact form:

$$\begin{cases} x_s = F(x_s, \hat{d}_{k|k}, u_s) \\ y_s = H(x_s, \hat{d}_{k|k}) \end{cases} \Rightarrow y_s = G(u_s, \hat{d}_{k|k}) \tag{32}$$

in which $G: \mathbb{R}^{m+n_d} \to \mathbb{R}^p$. Then, the model output steady-state function is "artificially" modified as follows:

$$G_\lambda(u_s, \hat{d}_{k|k}) = G(u_s, \hat{d}_{k|k}) + (\lambda_{k-1}^G)^T(u_s - u_{s,k-1}) \tag{33}$$

where $\lambda_{k-1}^G \in \mathbb{R}^{m \times p}$ is a matrix to be defined later on and $u_{s,k-1}$ is the steady-state input target found at the previous sampling time, $k - 1$. We observe that in [16], the modified output function also includes a zero order term, which ensures that $G_\lambda(\cdot) \to G_p(\cdot)$. However, such a term is unnecessary in the present framework because the model output convergence is already achieved by the offset-free augmented model formulation. Hence, only a gradient correction of G is necessary. In order to drive the target point towards the plant optimal value, we need to calculate λ_{k-1}^G as a result of a KKT matching of the target optimization problem. In this way, similarly to what has been demonstrated in the RTO literature, the necessary condition of optimality can be satisfied.

The KKT matching is developed imposing the correspondence of the Lagrangian function gradient between the plant and model target optimization problems. The procedure is as follows.

Plant: Similarly to Model (32), a steady-state input-output map $y_{p,s} = G_p(u_s)$ can be defined also for the actual plant (1). In this way, the plant optimization steady-state problem reads:

$$\min_u \ell_e(G_p(u), u) \tag{34a}$$

subject to:

$$u_{\min} \le u \le u_{\max} \tag{34b}$$
$$y_{\min} \le G_p(u) \le y_{\max} \tag{34c}$$

The Lagrangian function associated with Problem (34) is given by:

$$\mathcal{L}_p(u, \pi_1, \pi_2, \pi_3, \pi_4) = \ell_e(G_p(u), u) + \pi_1^T(u - u_{\max}) + \pi_2^T(u_{\min} - u) + \tag{35}$$
$$\pi_3^T(G_p(u) - y_{\max}) + \pi_4^T(y_{\min} - G_p(u)), \tag{36}$$

then, the first-order necessary optimality KKT conditions for this problem are as follows. If u^* is a (local) solution to (34), there exist vectors $\pi_1^*, \pi_2^*, \pi_3^*, \pi_4^*$ satisfying the following conditions:

$$\nabla_u \ell_e(u^*, G_p(u^*)) + \pi_1^* - \pi_2^* + \nabla_u G_p(u^*)\pi_3^* - \nabla_u G_p(u^*)\pi_4^* = 0 \tag{37a}$$
$$u^* - u_{\max} \le 0 \tag{37b}$$
$$u_{\min} - u^* \le 0 \tag{37c}$$
$$G_p(u^*) - y_{\max} \le 0 \tag{37d}$$
$$y_{\min} - G_p(u^*) \le 0 \tag{37e}$$
$$\pi_1^*, \pi_2^*, \pi_3^*, \pi_4^* \ge 0 \tag{37f}$$
$$(u^* - u_{\max})_j \pi_{1,j}^* = 0 \qquad j = 1, \ldots, m \tag{37g}$$
$$(u_{\min} - u^*)_j \pi_{2,j}^* = 0 \qquad j = 1, \ldots, m \tag{37h}$$
$$(G_p(u^*) - y_{\max})_j \pi_{3,j}^* = 0 \qquad j = 1, \ldots, p \tag{37i}$$
$$(y_{\min} - G_p(u^*))_j \pi_{4,j}^* = 0 \qquad j = 1, \ldots, p. \tag{37j}$$

in which $\pi_1, \pi_2 \in \mathbb{R}^m$ are the multiplier vectors of the input bound constraints (34b), and $\pi_3, \pi_4 \in \mathbb{R}^p$ are the multiplier vectors for output bound constraints (34c).

Model: With the modification introduced in (33), the model optimization steady-state problem can be rewritten as:

$$\min_u \ell_e(G_\lambda(u, \hat{d}_{k|k}), u) \tag{38a}$$

subject to:

$$u_{\min} \leq u \leq u_{\max} \tag{38b}$$

$$y_{\min} \leq G_\lambda(u, \hat{d}_{k|k}) \leq y_{\max} \tag{38c}$$

The Lagrangian function associated with (38) is given by:

$$\mathcal{L}_m(u, \pi_1, \pi_2, \pi_3, \pi_4) = \ell_e(G_\lambda(u, \hat{d}_{k|k}), u) + \pi_1^T(u - u_{\max}) + \pi_2^T(u_{\min} - u) + \tag{39}$$

$$\pi_3^T(G_\lambda(u, \hat{d}_{k|k}) - y_{\max}) + \pi_4^T(y_{\min} - G_\lambda(u, \hat{d}_{k|k})), \tag{40}$$

then, the first-order necessary optimality KKT conditions for this problem are as follows. If u^* is a (local) solution to (38), there exist vectors $\pi_1^*, \pi_2^*, \pi_3^*, \pi_4^*$ satisfying the following:

$$\nabla_u \ell_e(G_\lambda(u^*, \hat{d}_{k|k}), u^*) + \pi_1^* - \pi_2^* + \nabla_u G_\lambda(u^*, \hat{d}_{k|k})\pi_3^* - \nabla_u G_\lambda(u^*, \hat{d}_{k|k})\pi_4^* = 0 \tag{41a}$$

$$u^* - u_{\max} \leq 0 \tag{41b}$$

$$u_{\min} - u^* \leq 0 \tag{41c}$$

$$G_\lambda(u^*, \hat{d}_{k|k}) - y_{\max} \leq 0 \tag{41d}$$

$$y_{\min} - G_\lambda(u^*, \hat{d}_{k|k}) \leq 0 \tag{41e}$$

$$\pi_1^*, \pi_2^*, \pi_3^*, \pi_4^* \geq 0 \tag{41f}$$

$$(u^* - u_{\max})_j \pi_{1,j}^* = 0 \quad j = 1, \ldots, m \tag{41g}$$

$$(u_{\min} - u^*)_j \pi_{2,j}^* = 0 \quad j = 1, \ldots, m \tag{41h}$$

$$(G_\lambda(u^*, \hat{d}_{k|k}) - y_{\max})_j \pi_{3,j}^* = 0 \quad j = 1, \ldots, p \tag{41i}$$

$$(y_{\min} - G_\lambda(u^*, \hat{d}_{k|k}))_j \pi_{4,j}^* = 0 \quad j = 1, \ldots, p. \tag{41j}$$

KKT matching: To reach the KKT matching, conditions in (41) must converge to those in (37). We recall that, due to the offset-free augmented model, upon convergence, we have: $G(u^*, \hat{d}_{k|k}) \to G_p(u^*)$. Furthermore, upon convergence from (33), we also have: $G_\lambda(u^*, \hat{d}_{k|k}) \to G(u^*, \hat{d}_{k|k})$ and therefore $G_\lambda(u^*, \hat{d}_k) \to G_p(u^*)$. Therefore, in order for (41) to match (37), Conditions (37a) and (41a) have to be the same:

$$\nabla_u \mathcal{L}_p(u^*, \pi^*) = \nabla_u \mathcal{L}_m(u^*, \pi^*) \tag{42}$$

where

$$\pi^* = [\pi_1^*, \pi_2^*, \pi_3^*, \pi_4^*].$$

We expand the LHS and RHS in (42) to obtain:

$$\nabla_u \ell_e(G_p(u^*), u^*) = \left[\frac{\partial \ell_e(\cdot, u^*)}{\partial u} + \frac{\partial \ell_e(G_p(\cdot), \cdot)}{\partial G_p} \frac{\partial G_p(u^*)}{\partial u} \right]^T \qquad \text{plant} \tag{43}$$

$$\nabla_u \ell_e(G_\lambda(u^*, \hat{d}_{k|k}), u^*) = \left[\frac{\partial \ell_e(\cdot, u^*)}{\partial u} + \frac{\partial \ell_e(G_\lambda(\cdot), \cdot)}{\partial G_\lambda} \left[\frac{\partial G(u^*, \hat{d}_{k|k})}{\partial u} + (\lambda_{k-1}^G)^T \right] \right]^T \qquad \text{model} \tag{44}$$

Then, the KKT matching condition is:

$$\frac{\partial G_p(u^*)}{\partial u} = \frac{\partial G(u^*, \hat{d}_{k|k})}{\partial u} + (\lambda_{k-1}^G)^T \Rightarrow (\lambda_{k-1}^G)^T = \frac{\partial G_p(u^*)}{\partial u} - \frac{\partial G(u^*, \hat{d}_{k|k})}{\partial u} \tag{45}$$

From (45), we also consider a filtering step and define the following update law for λ_k^G:

$$\lambda_k^G = (1 - \alpha_s)\lambda_{k-1}^G + \alpha_s \left(\nabla_u G_p(u_{s,k}) - \nabla_u G(u_{s,k}, \hat{d}_{k|k}) \right) \tag{46}$$

where α_s is a scalar first-order filter constant, chosen in the range $(0, 1]$. In order for the update law (46) to be applicable, we make the following assumption.

Assumption 2. *The gradient of the process steady-state input-output map $G_p(\cdot)$ is known at steady-state points.*

In general, the gradient of the process steady-state input-output map $G_p(\cdot)$ can be (approximately) calculated through measurements of u and y [43,47–49]. We remark that the gradient of the model steady-state input-output map $G(\cdot)$ instead can be computed from its definition (32) using the implicit function theorem. As a matter of fact, the gradient of $G(\cdot)$ can be calculated as follows:

$$\nabla_u G(\cdot) = \nabla_x H(x, d) \left[(I - \nabla_x F(x, u, d))^{-1} \nabla_u F(x, u, d) \right] \tag{47}$$

Finally, from the above discussion, the following result is established.

Theorem 1. *KKT matching of the target optimization problem: Let the MPC target optimization problem be defined in (38), with λ_k^G updated according to (46), and let $u_{s,k}$ be its solution at time k. Let the closed-loop system converge to an equilibrium, with $u_s^0 : \lim_{k\to\infty} u_{s,k}$ being the limit KKT point of the steady-state problem (38). Then, u_s^0 is also a KKT point for the plant optimization problem (34).*

3.3. Summary

Summarizing, the offset-free economic MPC algorithm proposed in this work is the following. The estimation stage is taken from the offset-free tracking MPC as described in Section 2.2. Given the current state and disturbance estimate $(\hat{x}_{k|k}, \hat{d}_{k|k})$, the economic steady-state target problem is modified in this way:

$$\min_{x,u,y} \ell_e(y, u) \tag{48a}$$

subject to

$$x = F(x, \hat{d}_{k|k}, u) \tag{48b}$$

$$y = H(x, \hat{d}_{k|k}) + (\lambda_{k-1}^G)^T(u - u_{s,k-1}) \tag{48c}$$

$$u_{\min} \leq u \leq u_{\max} \tag{48d}$$

$$y_{\min} \leq y \leq y_{\max} \tag{48e}$$

in which $u_{s,k-1}$ is the steady-state input target found at the previous sampling time $k - 1$, and λ_{k-1}^G is defined above in (46). Finally, the FHOCP solved at each time is the one defined in (15), unless differently specified in the next section.

4. Results and Discussion

Simulation results of the proposed method applied to the reactor example illustrated in Section 2.4 are here reported. We use all simulation parameters defined in Section 2.4, and in addition, we set

$\alpha_s = 0.2$ for the modifiers update law (46). The first controller that is evaluated, named EMPC1-MT, uses the same augmented system with state disturbance model as EMPC1 and the same FHOCP formulation (15). The target problem instead is the modified one reported in (48). The obtained results are shown in Figure 6. As can be seen from Figure 6, the input target has asymptotically reached the optimal value (or it is very close to it in the case $\bar{k}_2 = 0$). The actual input value, instead, reaches an asymptotic value different from the optimal target. As a matter of fact, when the economic stage cost is used in the FHOCP (15), the offset still remains, and the EMPC formulation does not seem to have gained particular advantage from the target modification. This is also why for $\bar{k}_2 = 0$, the target does not reach perfectly the optimal value: as a recursive algorithm, it is obvious how the dynamic behavior also influences the steady-state target.

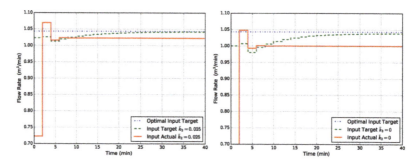

Figure 6. Closed-loop flow rate Q obtained with EMPC1-MT (state disturbance model, modified target problem) for two cases of uncertainty in k_2: $\bar{k}_2 = 0.025$ (**left**) and $\bar{k}_2 = 0$ (**right**).

We now consider another controller, named MPC1-MT, which is identical to EMPC1-MT, but uses a tracking stage cost in the FHOCP, i.e.,

$$\ell_{QP}(\hat{x}_i, u_i) = (\hat{x}_i - x_{s,k})^T Q (\hat{x}_i - x_{s,k}) + (u_i - u_{s,k})^T R (u_i - u_{s,k}) \tag{49}$$

where $Q \in \mathbb{R}^{n \times n}$ and $R \in \mathbb{R}^{m \times m}$ are positive definite weight matrices. Results are shown in Figure 7, from which we observe that the offset is completely eliminated since both the input target and the actual input value go to the optimal one. The success of the tracking function can be explained by its design: the goal is to follow the steady-state target, and with the target suitably corrected, the actual value cannot go elsewhere in an offset-free formulation since the FHOCP cost function is positive definite around $(x_{s,k}, u_{s,k})$.

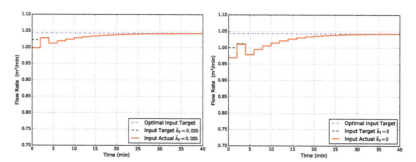

Figure 7. Closed-loop flow rate Q obtained with MPC1-MT (state disturbance model, modified target problem, tracking cost in the finite horizon optimal control problem (FHOCP)) for two cases of uncertainty in k_2: $\bar{k}_2 = 0.025$ (**left**) and $\bar{k}_2 = 0$ (**right**).

Despite the fact the MPC1-MT asymptotically reaches the optimal steady state, our primary goal is to build an offset-free economic MPC. Since now, the target problem has been adjusted by the modifier, results seem to suggest that a similar correction should be done for the FHOCP. Specifically, we consider the following modified FHOCP:

$$\min_{x,u} \sum_{i=0}^{N-1} \ell_e(H(x_i, \hat{d}_{k|k}), u_i) \tag{50a}$$

subject to:

$$x_0 = \hat{x}_{k|k}, \tag{50b}$$

$$x_{i+1} = F(x_i, u_i, \hat{d}_{k|k}) + \Theta_{x,i}(x_i, u_i), \qquad i = 0, \dots, N-1 \tag{50c}$$

$$u_{min} \leq u_i \leq u_{max}, \qquad i = 0, \dots, N-1 \tag{50d}$$

$$y_{min} \leq H(x_i, \hat{d}_{k|k}) \leq y_{max}, \qquad i = 0, \dots, N-1 \tag{50e}$$

$$x_N = x_{s,k} \tag{50f}$$

where $\Theta_{x,i}(x_i, u_i) \in \mathbb{R}^n$ is the correction term similar to λ_{k-1}^G for the target module. A KKT matching performed on the FHOCP reveals that the required modification $\Theta_{x,i}$ can be approximated as:

$$\Theta_{x,i} = (\lambda_{k-1}^x)^T(x_i - x_{s,k}) + (\lambda_{k-1}^u)^T(u_i - u_{s,k}) \tag{51}$$

where:

$$\lambda_k^x = (1 - \alpha_x)\lambda_{k-1}^x + \alpha_x\left(\nabla_x F_p(x_{p,s,k}, u_{s,k}) - \nabla_x F(x_{s,k}, u_{s,k}, \hat{d}_{k|k})\right) \tag{52a}$$

$$\lambda_k^u = (1 - \alpha_u)\lambda_{k-1}^u + \alpha_u\left(\nabla_u F_p(x_{p,s,k}, u_{s,k}) - \nabla_u F(x_{s,k}, u_{s,k}, \hat{d}_{k|k})\right) \tag{52b}$$

and $x_{p,s,k}$ is the process state in equilibrium with $u_{s,k}$ according to (1). Having chosen constant values for $\alpha_x = \alpha_u = 0.1$, simulation results obtained with this controller, named EMPC1-MT-MD, are shown in Figure 8. From Figure 8, it can be seen that the offset has disappeared for both cases of uncertainty on the kinetic constant k_2.

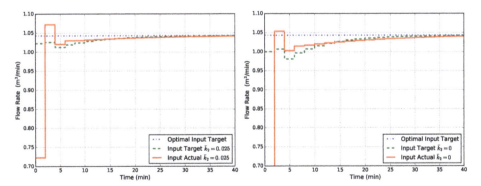

Figure 8. Closed-loop flow rate Q obtained with EMPC1-MT-MD (state disturbance model, modified target problem, modified FHOCP) for two cases of uncertainty in k_2: $\bar{k}_2 = 0.025$ (**left**) and $\bar{k}_2 = 0$ (**right**).

Furthermore, a time-varying simulation case is addressed, in which the true kinetic constant k_2 of the process is supposed to be varying during time following this step law:

$$k_2 = \begin{cases} 0.05 & \text{if } 0 \le t < 40 \\ 0.03 & \text{if } 40 \le t < 100 \\ 0.05 & \text{if } 100 \le t < 160 \\ 0.07 & \text{if } 160 \le t < 200 \end{cases} \tag{53}$$

The controller used for this example is the one named EMPC1-MT-MD, and the reaction scheme it knows is still the one defined in (21) with the $\bar{k}_2$ value fixed. Simulation results obtained with this step time-varying disturbance in (53) are shown in Figure 9 where it can be seen that the offset has disappeared for both cases of uncertainty on the kinetic constant k_2.

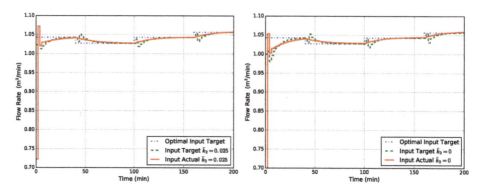

Figure 9. Closed-loop flow rate Q obtained with EMPC1-MT-MD (state disturbance model, modified target problem, modified FHOCP) for cases of unknown time-varying k_2: the MPC model uses a fixed value of $\bar{k}_2 = 0.025$ (**left**) and $\bar{k}_2 = 0.025$ (**right**).

In the end, it has to be noted that the majority of methods used for gradient estimation approximate the process gradient using a collection of previous output data to do a sort of identification [43,47–49]. Similarly, under the assumption that states are measured, i.e., $H_p(x) = x$, gradients $\nabla_x F_p(\cdot)$ and $\nabla_u F_p(\cdot)$ can be calculated if Assumption 2 holds true.

Further Comments

Currently, configurations that achieve optimal asymptotic operations are:

- EMPC2 (non-linear disturbance model). However, this is sort of an unfair choice. The disturbance has been positioned exactly where the uncertainties are, and this is cannot be considered as a general technique.
- MPC1-MT (economic modified target with tracking stage cost). This is the best general achievement at the moment and allows one to obtain offset-free economic performance for arbitrary plant-model mismatch.

As a matter of fact, it has to be underlined that, at the moment, the approximated modification term proposed in (51) works well in this example when there is no uncertainty on the first kinetic constant k_1. In other cases of uncertainty, the offset remains. Hence, further work has to be done to build a general correction strategy for the FHOCP with economic cost. Furthermore, assumptions made in this work deserve some comments. The strongest one is Assumption 2, which requires the availability of process steady-state gradients. For this purpose, we remark that gradient estimation is an active research area in the RTO literature (see, e.g., [19,43,50,51] and the references therein). Further work will investigate these approaches. In the end, it has to be noted that the proposed methodology does not add any computational burden compared to a conventional economic MPC algorithm. The modifiers can be updated after each optimization is concluded and inputs are sent to the plant, and the number of optimization variables is not augmented. Therefore, computation times are not affected.

5. Conclusions

In this paper, we addressed the problem of achieving the optimal asymptotic economic performance using the economic model predictive control (EMPC) algorithms despite the presence of plant-model mismatch.

After reviewing the standard techniques in offset-free tracking MPC and economic MPC, we presented an example where available MPC formulations fail in achieving the optimal asymptotic closed-loop performance. In order to eliminate this offset, the modifier-adaptation strategy developed in the real-time optimization (RTO) field has been taken into consideration and reviewed. Following this idea, a suitable correction to the target problem of the economic MPC algorithm has been formulated in order to achieve the necessary conditions of optimality despite the presence of plant/model mismatch. The proposed modification requires the availability of process gradients evaluated at the steady state. We then showed that the proposed modification is able to correct the steady-state target, but the actual closed-loop input may or may not converge to the optimal target depending on the finite horizon optimal control problem (FHOCP) stage cost. If such a cost is chosen to be positive definite around the target, as in tracking MPC, the optimal asymptotic behavior is achieved, although the dynamic performance may be suboptimal. For some cases of uncertainty, we showed that an economic stage cost can still be used by introducing a modification to the FHOCP.

Finally, we should remark about the main limitations of the current method and suggest future developments. First of all, the availability of process gradients should be reconsidered and relaxed as much as possible. Then, a general correction strategy for using an economic stage cost in the FHOCP, while enforcing convergence to the targets, has to be obtained.

Acknowledgments: The authors would like to thank Doug Allan and James Rawlings from the University of Wisconsin (Madison) for suggesting the illustrative example.

Conflicts of Interest: The authors declare no conflict of interest.

References

1. Qin, S.J.; Badgwell, T.A. A survey of industrial model predictive control technology. *Control Eng. Pract.* **2003**, *11*, 733–764.
2. Engell, S. Feedback control for optimal process operation. *J. Process Control* **2007**, *17*, 203–219.
3. Guay, M.; Zhang, T. Adaptive extremum seeking control of nonlinear dynamic systems with parametric uncertainties. *Automatica* **2003**, *39*, 1283–1293.
4. Guay, M.; Peters, N. Real-time dynamic optimization of nonlinear systems: A flatness-based approach. *Comput. Chem. Eng.* **2006**, *30*, 709–721.
5. Muske, K.R.; Badgwell, T.A. Disturbance modeling for offset-free linear model predictive control. *J. Process Control* **2002**, *12*, 617–632.
6. Pannocchia, G.; Rawlings, J.B. Disturbance models for offset-free model-predictive control. *AIChE J.* **2003**, *49*, 426–437.
7. Pannocchia, G. Offset-free tracking MPC: A tutorial review and comparison of different formulations. In Proceedings of the 2015 European Control Conference (ECC), Linz, Austria, 15–17 July 2015; pp. 527–532.
8. Marlin, T.E.; Hrymak, A.N. Real-time operations optimization of continuous processes. *AIChE Sympos. Ser.* **1997**, *93*, 156–164.
9. Chen, C.Y.; Joseph, B. On-line optimization using a two-phase approach: An application study. *Ind. Eng. Chem. Res.* **1987**, *26*, 1924–1930.
10. Garcia, C.E.; Morari, M. Optimal operation of integrated processing systems: Part II: Closed-loop on-line optimizing control. *AIChE J.* **1984**, *30*, 226–234.

11. Skogestad, S. Self-optimizing control: The missing link between steady-state optimization and control. *Comput. Chem. Eng.* **2000**, *24*, 569–575.

12. François, G.; Srinivasan, B.; Bonvin, D. Use of measurements for enforcing the necessary conditions of optimality in the presence of constraints and uncertainty. *J. Process Control* **2005**, *15*, 701–712.

13. Forbes, J.F.; Marlin, T.E. Model accuracy for economic optimizing controllers: The bias update case. *Ind. Eng. Chem. Res.* **1994**, *33*, 1919–1929.

14. Chachuat, B.; Marchetti, A.G.; Bonvin, D. Process optimization via constraints adaptation. *J. Process Control* **2008**, *18*, 244–257.

15. Chachuat, B.; Srinivasan, B.; Bonvin, D. Adaptation strategies for real-time optimization. *Comput. Chem. Eng.* **2009**, *33*, 1557–1567.

16. Marchetti, A.G.; Chachuat, B.; Bonvin, D. Modifier-adaptation methodology for real-time optimization. *Ind. Eng. Chem. Res.* **2009**, *48*, 6022–6033.

17. Alvarez, L.A.; Odloak, D. Robust integration of real time optimization with linear model predictive control. *Comput. Chem. Eng.* **2010**, *34*, 1937–1944.

18. Alvarez, L.A.; Odloak, D. Optimization and control of a continuous polymerization reactor. *Braz. J. Chem. Eng.* **2012**, *29*, 807–820.

19. Marchetti, A.G.; Luppi, P.; Basualdo, M. Real-time optimization via modifier adaptation integrated with model predictive control. *IFAC Proc. Vol.* **2011**, *44*, 9856–9861.

20. Marchetti, A.G.; Ferramosca, A.; González, A.H. Steady-state target optimization designs for integrating real-time optimization and model predictive control. *J. Process Control* **2014**, *24*, 129–145.

21. Kadam, J.V.; Schlegel, M.; Marquardt, W.; Tousain, R.L.; van Hessem, D.H.; van Den Berg, J.H.; Bosgra, O.H. A two-level strategy of integrated dynamic optimization and control of industrial processes—A case study. *Comput. Aided Chem. Eng.* **2002**, *10*, 511–516.

22. Kadam, J.; Marquardt, W.; Schlegel, M.; Backx, T.; Bosgra, O.; Brouwer, P.; Dünnebier, G.; Van Hessem, D.; Tiagounov, A.; De Wolf, S. Towards integrated dynamic real-time optimization and control of industrial processes. In Proceedings of the Foundations of Computer-Aided Process Operations (FOCAPO2003), Coral Springs, FL, USA, 12–15 January 2003; pp. 593–596.

23. Kadam, J.V.; Marquardt, W. Integration of economical optimization and control for intentionally transient process operation. In *Assessment and Future Directions of Nonlinear Model Predictive Control*; Springer: Berlin/Heidelberg, Germany, 2007; pp. 419–434.

24. Biegler, L.T. Technology advances for dynamic real-time optimization. *Comput. Aided Chem. Eng.* **2009**, *27*, 1–6.

25. Gopalakrishnan, A.; Biegler, L.T. Economic nonlinear model predictive control for periodic optimal operation of gas pipeline networks. *Comput. Chem. Eng.* **2013**, *52*, 90–99.

26. Maeder, U.; Borrelli, F.; Morari, M. Linear offset-free model predictive control. *Automatica* **2009**, *45*, 2214–2222.

27. Morari, M.; Maeder, U. Nonlinear offset-free model predictive control. *Automatica* **2012**, *48*, 2059–2067.

28. Rawlings, J.B.; Mayne, D.Q. *Model Predictive Control: Theory and Design*; Nob Hill Pub.: San Francisco, CA, USA, 2009.

29. Pannocchia, G.; Gabiccini, M.; Artoni, A. Offset-free MPC explained: Novelties, subtleties, and applications. *IFAC-PapersOnLine* **2015**, *48*, 342–351.

30. Würth, L.; Hannemann, R.; Marquardt, W. A two-layer architecture for economically optimal process control and operation. *J. Process Control* **2011**, *21*, 311–321.

31. Zhu, X.; Hong, W.; Wang, S. Implementation of advanced control for a heat-integrated distillation column system. In Proceedings of the 30th Annual Conference of IEEE Industrial Electronics Society (IECON), Busan, Korea, 2–6 November 2004; Volume 3, pp. 2006–2011.

32. Rawlings, J.B.; Angeli, D.; Bates, C.N. Fundamentals of economic model predictive control. In Proceedings of the 51st IEEE Conference on Decision and Control (CDC), Maui, HI, USA, 10–13 December 2012; pp. 3851–3861.

33. Angeli, D.; Amrit, R.; Rawlings, J.B. Receding horizon cost optimization for overly constrained nonlinear plants. In Proceedings of the 48th IEEE Conference on Decision and Control (CDC), Shanghai, China, 15–18 December 2009; pp. 7972–7977.

34. Heidarinejad, M.; Liu, J.; Christofides, P.D. Economic model predictive control of nonlinear process systems using Lyapunov techniques. *AIChE J.* **2012**, *58*, 855–870.

35. Ellis, M.; Christofides, P.D. On finite-time and infinite-time cost improvement of economic model predictive control for nonlinear systems. *Automatica* **2014**, *50*, 2561–2569.

36. Angeli, D.; Amrit, R.; Rawlings, J.B. On average performance and stability of economic model predictive control. *IEEE Trans. Autom. Control* **2012**, *57*, 1615–1626.

37. Faulwasser, T.; Bonvin, D. On the design of economic NMPC based on an exact turnpike property. *IFAC-PapersOnLine* **2015**, *48*, 525–530.

38. Faulwasser, T.; Bonvin, D. On the design of economic NMPC based on approximate turnpike properties. In Proceedings of the 54th IEEE Conference on Decision and Control (CDC), Osaka, Japan, 15–18 December 2015; pp. 4964–4970.

39. Faulwasser, T.; Korda, M.; Jones, C.N.; Bonvin, D. Turnpike and dissipativity properties in dynamic real-time optimization and economic MPC. In Proceedings of the 53rd IEEE Conference on Decision and Control, Los Angeles, CA, USA, 15–17 December 2014; pp. 2734–2739.

40. Faulwasser, T.; Korda, M.; Jones, C.N.; Bonvin, D. On Turnpike and Dissipativity Properties of Continuous-Time Optimal Control Problems. *arXiv* **2015**, arXiv:1509.07315.

41. Ellis, M.; Durand, H.; Christofides, P.D. A tutorial review of economic model predictive control methods. *J. Process Control* **2014**, *24*, 1156–1178.

42. Ellis, M.; Liu, J.; Christofides, P.D. *Economic Model Predictive Control: Theory, Formulations and Chemical Process Applications*; Springer: Berlin/Heidelberg, Germany, 2016.

43. Marchetti, A.G.; Chachuat, B.; Bonvin, D. A dual modifier-adaptation approach for real-time optimization. *J. Process Control* **2010**, *20*, 1027–1037.

44. Brdys, M.A.; Tatjewski, P. *Iterative Algorithms for Multilayer Optimizing Control*; World Scientific: London, UK, 2005.

45. Bunin, G.A.; François, G.; Srinivasan, B.; Bonvin, D. Input filter design for feasibility in constraint-adaptation schemes. *IFAC Proc. Vol.* **2011**, *44*, 5585–5590.

46. Navia, D.; Briceño, L.; Gutiérrez, G.; De Prada, C. Modifier-adaptation methodology for real-time optimization reformulated as a nested optimization problem. *Ind. Eng. Chem. Res.* **2015**, *54*, 12054–12071.

47. Bunin, G.A.; François, G.; Bonvin, D. Exploiting local quasiconvexity for gradient estimation in modifier-adaptation schemes. In Proceedings of the 2012 American Control Conference (ACC), Montreal, QC, Canada, 27–29 June 2012; pp. 2806–2811.

48. Serralunga, F.J.; Mussati, M.C.; Aguirre, P.A. Model adaptation for real-time optimization in energy systems. *Ind. Eng. Chem. Res.* **2013**, *52*, 16795–16810.

49. Gao, W.; Wenzel, S.; Engell, S. Modifier adaptation with quadratic approximation in iterative optimizing control. In Proceedings of the IEEE 2015 European Control Conference (ECC), Linz, Austria, 15–17 July 2015; pp. 2527–2532.

50. Brdys, M.A.; Tatjewski, P. An algorithm for steady-state optimising dual control of uncertain plants. In Proceedings of the IFAC Workshop on New Trends in Design of Control Systems, Smolenice, Slovak, 7–10 September 1994; pp. 249–254.

51. Costello, S.; François, G.; Bonvin, D. A directional modifier-adaptation algorithm for real-time optimization. *J. Process Control* **2016**, *39*, 64–76.

 *processes*

Article

On the Use of Nonlinear Model Predictive Control without Parameter Adaptation for Batch Processes

Jean-Christophe Binette * and Bala Srinivasan

Département de Génie Chimique, École Polytechnique Montréal, C.P.6079 Succ., Centre-Ville Montréal, Montréal, QC H3C 3A7, Canada; bala.srinivasan@polymtl.ca
* Correspondence: jean-christophe.binette@polymtl.ca; Tel.: +1-514-340-4711

Academic Editor: Dominique Bonvin
Received: 12 May 2016; Accepted: 22 August 2016; Published: 29 August 2016

Abstract: Optimization techniques are typically used to improve economic performance of batch processes, while meeting product and environmental specifications and safety constraints. Offline methods suffer from the parameters of the model being inaccurate, while re-identification of the parameters may not be possible due to the absence of persistency of excitation. Thus, a practical solution is the Nonlinear Model Predictive Control (NMPC) without parameter adaptation, where the measured states serve as new initial conditions for the re-optimization problem with a diminishing horizon. In such schemes, it is clear that the optimum cannot be reached due to plant-model mismatch. However, this paper goes one step further in showing that such re-optimization could in certain cases, especially with an economic cost, lead to results worse than the offline optimal input. On the other hand, in absence of process noise, for small parametric variations, if the cost function corresponds to tracking a feasible trajectory, re-optimization always improves performance. This shows inherent robustness associated with the tracking cost. A batch reactor example presents and analyzes the different cases. Re-optimizing led to worse results in some cases with an economical cost function, while no such problem occurred while working with a tracking cost.

Keywords: process optimization; batch processes; process control; constrained optimization; sensitivity; real-time optimization

---

1. Introduction

Batch processes are widely used in specialty industries, such as pharmaceuticals, due to their flexibility in operation. As opposed to continuous processes, their operating conditions vary with time, in order to meet the specifications and respect safety and environmental constraints. Additionally, in order to improve process operation efficiency, reduce cost, numerical optimization based on phenomenological models is used to obtain the time-varying schedule [1].

However, using an optimum, computed off-line, suffers from the problem of the model not exactly representing the reality. Very often, it is hard to get a precise model due to the lack of quality or quantity in the experimental data. In addition, in many cases, parameters are estimated from lab experiments, and thus are not very accurate when scaled-up to industrial processes.

To address this problem, use of measurements in the framework of optimization is recommended [2,3]. The idea is to repeatedly re-optimize, changing the optimization problem appropriately using the information obtained from measurements. The initial conditions of the optimization problem are adapted based on the current measurements. In addition, it is also possible to identify the parameters of the system from the measurements and update them. Thus, two main categories need to be distinguished, though there is a bit of inconsistency in the nomenclature reported in the literature. If only the initial conditions are updated, the schemes are referred to as Model Predictive Control (MPC) [4–11], while

Dynamic Real Time Optimization (D-RTO) schemes incorporate adaptation of both initial conditions and parameters [12].

MPC schemes incorporate feedback by re-optimization, when computation is not prohibitive [4–7]. In this case, the model is not adapted, while a new optimum is computed from the initial conditions obtained from current measurements. Most real systems are better represented by a nonlinear model [8,9] and using Nonlinear Model Predictive Control (NMPC) is more appropriate [10,11].

In D-RTO, the parameters of the model are also adapted. The major problem with the adaptation of model parameters is the persistency of excitation. The optimal input is typically not persistently exciting, and adding an excitation for the purpose of identification would cause sub-optimality [13]. Thus, in short, D-RTO is very difficult to implement except in special cases [14,15].

NMPC schemes do not get to the optimum due to plant-model mismatch, while D-RTO is not practical to implement. An intermediary solution is the robust NMPC reported in the literature [16,17]. The most known is the min-max method, that considers the worst-case scenario for optimization [18]. This method, however, is very conservative and clearly not optimal. Other methods such as the multi-stage NMPC [18] seek a compromise between conservatism and optimality. Stochastic NMPC [19] considers a probabilistic setting for the parameter uncertainties, and seeks an optimum in a stochastic sense.

The current study takes a different approach and explores the pertinence of re-optimizing with adapted initial conditions without adapting the model (NMPC) in the case of batch processes optimization with parametric errors. The main question asked is: "Given that the true optimum will not be reached due to plant-model parameter mismatch, is re-optimizing worthwhile? Will there be an improvement compared to simple implementation of the off-line optimal solution?" It is shown that NMPC re-optimization may deteriorate the performance, especially with an economic cost function. On the other hand, no such effect is present when the cost function is a squared error of the deviation from a desired trajectory feasible for the plant and the active constraints are invariant. In the absence of process noise, the tracking objective shows robustness and repeated optimization can be used even when the model is subject to small parametric errors. This paper, thus, highlights the difference in robustness between the economic and tracking objectives.

This paper first presents the basics of NMPC. Then, an analysis points out why re-optimizing without parameter adaption can give worse results. A demonstration showing that such situation does not arise for a quadratic tracking cost follows. Finally, an example is used to illustrate the different possible situations.

2. Problem Formulation—Model Predictive Control without Parameter Adaptation

Model Predictive control consists of repeatedly optimizing a given cost function based on a model of the system, using the state information obtained from the measurements. Two types of formulations are found in the literature—the receding horizon [20], typically used for continuous processes, and the diminishing horizon [21], used for batch processes. In this paper, the diminishing horizon for a batch process with fixed final time t_f will be studied. Thus, at a given time t_k, the state obtained from the measurements is x_k, and the optimization problem is given as follows:

$$
\begin{aligned}
\min_{u[t_k, t_f]} J_k &= \phi\left(x\left(t_f\right)\right) + \int_{t_k}^{t_f} L\left(x\left(t\right), u\left(t\right)\right) dt \\
s.t.\ \dot{x} &= F\left(x\left(t\right), u\left(t\right), \theta\right) + \dot{v},\ x\left(t_k\right) = x_k \\
&\quad S\left(x, u\right) \leq 0 \\
&\quad T\left(x\left(t_f\right)\right) \leq 0,
\end{aligned}
\tag{1}
$$

where J is the function to minimize, u the input variable, x the states, F the equations describing the system dynamics, v the process noise, ϕ a function representing the terminal cost evaluated, L the integral cost function, θ the parameters and S and T respectively the path and terminal constraints.

The initial conditions are obtained from the measured values, x_k. $\dot{x}$ and $\dot{v}$ represent, respectively, the differentiated states and noise.

The above formulation gets to the optimum, to the extent allowed by the sampling, when there is process noise but no parametric errors. The process noise would move the states away from the predicted value, but the repetition of the optimization assures that an optimum is found even from the deviated value.

Contrarily, this paper would consider the case where the functional form is assumed to be correct, but the parameters θ are unknown, so the error in the parameters $\theta = \theta - \theta_{real}$ is non-zero. This would also cause a variation in the states, but it might not be sufficient to simply optimize from the new states and the wrong parameters. Additionally, the excitation present in the system might not be sufficient to identify them online. In this work, the influence of such a parametric error on the operation of the NMPC would be studied.

3. Variational Analysis of Model Predictive Control without Parameter Adaptation

Let us consider an appropriate input and state parameterization (e.g., piecewise constant), where the parameterized input vector U and the parameterized states X will be used. Additionally, assume that the active constraints are invariant with respect to parametric variations and so become additional algebraic equations. These algebraic equations reduce the dimension of the search space. Let U_k represent the reduced vector of inputs from time t_k until t_f, and the states during this time interval is represented by X_k. The dynamic relationships can be written in a nonlinear static form and the dynamic optimization problem becomes the following static nonlinear programming problem:

$$
\begin{aligned}
\min_{U_k} J_k &= J\left(X_k, U_k, \theta\right) \\
X_k &= \Psi_k\left(U_k, \theta\right) + d_k ,
\end{aligned}
\tag{2}
$$

where d_k is the difference between the predicted and observed measurements, caused by process noise and parametric variations.

In what follows, variational analysis will be carried out assuming that the parametric variations are "small". Thus, higher order terms will be neglected. Thus, the results obtained are valid for "small" parametric variations. In presence of parametric uncertainties and disturbances to the system, the variation equation ΔJ can then be written as a second order development:

$$
\begin{aligned}
\Delta J = &\frac{\partial J}{\partial U}\Delta U + \frac{\partial J}{\partial d}\Delta d + \frac{\partial J}{\partial \theta}\Delta\theta + \Delta U^T\frac{\partial^2 J}{\partial\theta\partial U}\Delta\theta + \Delta d^T\frac{\partial^2 J}{\partial\theta\partial d}\Delta\theta + \Delta U^T\frac{\partial^2 J}{\partial d\partial U}\Delta d \\
&+ \frac{1}{2}\Delta U^T\frac{\partial^2 J}{\partial U^2}\Delta U + \frac{1}{2}\Delta d^T\frac{\partial^2 J}{\partial d^2}\Delta d + \frac{1}{2}\Delta\theta^T\frac{\partial^2 J}{\partial\theta^2}\Delta\theta .
\end{aligned}
\tag{3}
$$

In this equation, certain terms are constant since Δd and $\Delta\theta$ cannot be affected by manipulation on the process. Furthermore, the first term is zero by definition. Removing these terms and renaming the modifiable terms as $\widetilde{\Delta J}$, the equation becomes the following:

$$
\min_{\Delta U}\widetilde{\Delta J} = \Delta U^T\frac{\partial^2 J}{\partial\theta\partial U}\Delta\theta + \Delta U^T\frac{\partial^2 J}{\partial d\partial U}\Delta d + \frac{1}{2}\Delta U^T\frac{\partial^2 J}{\partial U^2}\Delta U.
\tag{4}
$$

The necessary condition for the variational optimization can be obtained by differentiating it with respect to the input and equating to zero. The following equation is obtained:

$$
\frac{\partial\widetilde{\Delta J}}{\partial U} = \frac{\partial^2 J}{\partial\theta\partial U}\Delta\theta + \frac{\partial^2 J}{\partial d\partial U}\Delta d + \frac{\partial^2 J}{\partial U^2}\Delta U = 0.
\tag{5}
$$

The optimal input can be calculated as:

$$\Delta U_{opt} = -\left(\frac{\partial^2 J}{\partial U^2}\right)^{-1}\left(\frac{\partial^2 J}{\partial\theta\partial U}\Delta\theta + \frac{\partial^2 J}{\partial d\partial U}\Delta d\right). \tag{6}$$

Define:

$$t_d = \left(\frac{\partial^2 J}{\partial U^2}\right)^{-\frac{1}{2}}\left(\frac{\partial^2 J}{\partial d\partial U}\right)\Delta d, \tag{7}$$

$$t_\theta = \left(\frac{\partial^2 J}{\partial U^2}\right)^{-\frac{1}{2}}\left(\frac{\partial^2 J}{\partial\theta\partial U}\right)\Delta\theta, \tag{8}$$

which are mathematical constructs that represent the parts of (6) that correspond to Δd and $\Delta\theta$ respectively. Under the standard assumption that the Hessian is positive definite, the square root exists. The units of t_θ and t_d are the same as $J^{-0.5}$ and so it is difficult to find a physical interpretation.

This paper considers the case where the parameters are not adapted principally due the absence of persistency of excitation. It is well known that the optimum cannot be reached in such a case. The following proposition goes one step further to show that it might even be harmful to re-optimize under certain circumstances.

Proposition 1. *Consider the repeated dynamic optimization problem (1) solved using the corresponding static nonlinear programming problem (2). Let the variations in the measured states be caused by both parametric variations and process noise. Furthermore, assume that the active constraints are invariant with respect to parametric variations. If the correction is only based on state measurements and the parameters are not adapted, then re-optimization will be worse than the offline solution when the terms t_θ and t_d point in opposing directions, satisfying $t_d^T t_\theta \leq -\frac{1}{2}t_d^T t_d$.*

Proof. If only Δd is measured and corrected, then:

$$\Delta U_{opt} = -\left(\frac{\partial^2 J}{\partial U^2}\right)^{-\frac{1}{2}} t_d \tag{9}$$

and:

$$\widetilde{\Delta J}_{opt} = -\frac{1}{2}t_d^T t_d - t_d^T t_\theta. \tag{10}$$

Obviously, $-\frac{1}{2}t_d^T t_d \leq 0$ while $-t_d^T t_\theta$ is sign indefinite. If t_d and t_θ point in the same direction, i.e., $\angle(t_d, t_\theta) \in \left[-\frac{\pi}{2}, \frac{\pi}{2}\right]$ rad, then $\widetilde{\Delta J}_{opt} \leq 0$. However, if they point on different directions, $\widetilde{\Delta J}_{opt}$ could still be negative as long as the first term $(-\frac{1}{2}t_d^T t_d)$ dominates. Yet, if $t_d^T t_\theta \leq -\frac{1}{2}t_d^T t_d$, $\widetilde{\Delta J}_{opt}$ is positive, making the offline solution better than the re-optimization.

In the absence of process noise, $\Delta d = \frac{\partial\Psi}{\partial\theta}\Delta\theta$, and, thus, the terms t_θ and t_d can be written as:

$$t_d = \left(\frac{\partial^2 J}{\partial U^2}\right)^{-\frac{1}{2}}\left(\frac{\partial^2 J}{\partial d\partial U}\right)\frac{\partial\Psi}{\partial\theta}\Delta\theta, \tag{11}$$

$$t_\theta = \left(\frac{\partial^2 J}{\partial U^2}\right)^{-\frac{1}{2}}\left(\frac{\partial^2 J}{\partial\theta\partial U}\right)\Delta\theta. \tag{12}$$

Since for a general cost function (such as an economic objective) there is no relationship between these two terms, the result from Proposition 1 holds. However, it will be shown in the following proposition that, for a tracking cost with a trajectory feasible for the plant, re-optimization is beneficial even if the parameters are not adapted. This, in other words, expresses the inherent robustness associated with a tracking cost function.

Proposition 2. *Consider the repeated dynamic optimization problem (1) solved using the corresponding static nonlinear programming problem (2) with the tracking cost $J = \frac{1}{2}\left(X_k - X_{ref}\right)^T\left(X_k - X_{ref}\right) +$*

$\frac{1}{2}w\left(U_k - U_{ref}\right)^T\left(U_k - U_{ref}\right)$, with X_{ref} being a trajectory feasible for the plant with U_{ref} being the corresponding input and w the weight for the input variations. *Let the variations in the measured states be caused by parametric variations only. Furthermore, assume that the active constraints are invariant with respect to parametric variations. If the correction is only based on state measurements and the parameters are not adapted, then, for small enough parametric variations, $t_\theta = t_d$, and the re-optimization will be better or equal to the offline solution, i.e., $\widetilde{\Delta J}_{opt} \leq 0$.*

Proof. If the variation in the state is caused only by parametric uncertainties, then $\Delta d = \frac{\partial \Psi}{\partial \theta}\Delta\theta$. The partial derivatives for this case are given by:

$$\frac{\partial J}{\partial u} = \left(X - X_{ref}\right)^T\frac{\partial\Psi}{\partial u} + w\left(U_k - U_{ref}\right)^T, \tag{13}$$

$$\frac{\partial^2 J}{\partial\theta\partial u} = \left(X - X_{ref}\right)^T\frac{\partial^2\Psi}{\partial\theta\partial u} + \left(\frac{\partial\Psi}{\partial u}\right)^T\frac{\partial\Psi}{\partial\theta}, \tag{14}$$

$$\frac{\partial J}{\partial d} = \left(X - X_{ref}\right)^T, \tag{15}$$

$$\frac{\partial^2 J}{\partial d\partial u} = \left(\frac{\partial\Psi}{\partial u}\right)^T. \tag{16}$$

With these, the two terms t_θ and t_d can be written as

$$t_d = \left(\frac{\partial^2 J}{\partial U^2}\right)^{-\frac{1}{2}}\left(\frac{\partial\Psi}{\partial u}\right)^T\frac{\partial\Psi}{\partial\theta}\Delta\theta, \tag{17}$$

$$t_\theta = \left(\frac{\partial^2 J}{\partial U^2}\right)^{-\frac{1}{2}}\left(X - X_{ref}\right)^T\frac{\partial^2\Psi}{\partial\theta\partial u}\Delta\theta + \left(\frac{\partial^2 J}{\partial U^2}\right)^{-\frac{1}{2}}\left(\frac{\partial\Psi}{\partial u}\right)^T\frac{\partial\Psi}{\partial\theta}\Delta\theta. \tag{18}$$

At the optimum, since X_{ref} is assumed to be feasible for the plant, $\left(X - X_{ref}\right) = 0$. Outside the optimum, $\left(X - X_{ref}\right)$ grows with $\Delta\theta$ and the first term in Equation (18) becomes proportional to $\Delta\theta^2$. For small enough parametric variations, this term can be neglected. Then, t_θ and t_d are the same and this gives:

$$\widetilde{\Delta J}_{opt} = -\frac{1}{2}t_d^T t_d - t_d^T t_\theta = -\frac{3}{2}t_d^T t_d \leq 0. \tag{19}$$

In this case, the re-optimization is always better than the offline solution.

Such a robustness result cannot be established when process noise is present. Inclusion of process noise would cause $\Delta d = \frac{\partial\Psi}{\partial\theta}\Delta\theta + v$, which would lead to an additional term in Equation (17). This in turn prevents t_θ from being equal to t_d, which could eventually lead to a potential degradation in performance. Thus, robustness can only be established mathematically for a trajectory cost without process noise.

4. Results and Discussion

4.1. Illustrative Example

To illustrate the importance of parametric errors on NMPC, six different cases will be treated. The first three will be with economical cost, while the last three will have a trajectory to follow. In both situations, cases with terminal constraint, path constraint and no constraints will be done. Barrier functions will be used to treat the constraints.

For each case, a batch reactor with two reactions is studied (inspired from Reference [12]): A → B and A + B → C. From a mass balance, the following model is derived for the system:

$$\dot{c}_A = -k_1 c_A - k_2 c_A c_B,$$
$$\dot{c}_B = k_1 c_A - k_2 c_A c_B,$$

(20)

where c_X is the concentration of X (mol/L) and k_1 and k_2 are the kinetic reaction coefficient (h^{-1}), which are obtained using the Arrhenius equation:

$$k_i = k_{i0}\exp\left(-\frac{E_i}{RT}\right).$$

(21)

Using the following scaled temperature as the input parameter:

$$u = k_{10}\exp\left(-\frac{E_1}{RT}\right)$$

(22)

and considering:

$$\alpha = \frac{E_2}{E_1}, \ \bar{k}_{10} = 1 \text{ and } \bar{k}_{20} = k_{20}\left(\frac{1}{k_{10}}\right)^{\alpha},$$

(23)

the kinetic coefficient are expressed as:

$$k_1 = \bar{k}_{10}u \text{ and } k_2 = \bar{k}_{20}u^{\alpha}.$$

(24)

The nominal values of all the parameters, as well as the constraint values, for these simulations are given in Table 1. For each case, the parameters with errors will be α and k_{10}.

Table 1. Models parameters, operating bounds, and initial conditions for Cases 1 to 6.

Parameter	Value	Units
c_{A0}	5	mol/L
c_{B0}	0	mol/L
k_{10}	5×10^3	h^{-1}
k_{20}	7×10^{16}	-
E_1	2×10^4	J/mol
E_2	1×10^5	J/mol
R	8.314	J/mol.K
α	5	-
$\bar{k}_{10}$	1	-
$\bar{k}_{20}$	0.0224	-
t_f	2	H
u_{min}	1.25	-
$c_{Af_{max}}$	0.1	mol/L
γ	0.001	-
β	0.999	-

Case 1: Unconstrained system with economical cost

The objective of the three first cases is to maximize the final concentration of B. In the first case, there are no constraints on the system, which gives the following optimization problem:

$$\max_{u(t)} J = c_B\left(t_f\right).$$

(25)

Case 2: System with terminal constraint and economical cost

The objective is to maximize the final concentration of B, in this case with a constraint on the final concentration of A:

$$\max_{u(t)} J = c_B\left(t_f\right)$$
$$s.t. c_A\left(t_f\right) \leq c_{Amax}. \tag{26}$$

The optimization is subject to a terminal constraint on c_A. The terminal constraint is included in the numerical optimization using the following barrier function, where $b\,(c)$ is a barrier function for the constraint $-c_{max} \leq 0$:

$$b\,(c) = \begin{cases} -\gamma \log\,(c - c_{max}), & c > \beta c_{min} \\ \frac{\gamma(c - \beta c_{max})}{(1-\beta)c_{max}}, & c \leq \beta c_{min} \end{cases}. \tag{27}$$

Case 3: System with path constraint and economical cost

The objective is to maximize the final concentration of B, in this case with a lower bound on the input parameter:

$$\max_{u(t)} J = c_B\left(t_f\right)$$
$$s.t.\, u \geq u_{min}. \tag{28}$$

The optimization is subject to a path constraint on u. The path constraint is included in the numerical optimization once again using a barrier function.

Case 4: Unconstrained system with trajectory cost

The objective of the three last cases is to minimize the difference between a trajectory and the concentration of B. In this case, there are no constraints on the system, which gives the following optimization problem:

$$\min_{u(t)} J = \int_{t_k}^{t_f} \left(c_B\,(t) - c_{B_{ref}}\,(t)\right)^T \left(c_B\,(t) - c_{B_{ref}}\,(t)\right) dt, \tag{29}$$

where $c_{B_{ref}}$ is the trajectory to follow. For the three tracking cases, $c_{B_{ref}}$ is a path following 90% of the maximal production (model optimum). Additionally, in those three cases, inputs are not penalized, mainly because no measurement noise was considered.

Case 5: System with terminal constraint and trajectory cost

The objective is to minimize the difference between a trajectory and the concentration of B, in this case with a constraint on the final concentration of A:

$$\min_{u(t)} J = \int_{t_k}^{t_f} \left(c_B\,(t) - c_{B_{ref}}\,(t)\right)^T \left(c_B\,(t) - c_{B_{ref}}\,(t)\right) dt$$
$$s.t. c_A\left(t_f\right) \leq c_{Amax}. \tag{30}$$

The optimization is subject to a terminal constraint on c_A. The terminal constraint is included in the numerical optimization using a barrier function. $c_{B_{ref}}$ is the trajectory to follow and not a function of time.

Case 6: System with path constraint and trajectory cost

The objective is to minimize the difference between a trajectory and the concentration of B, in this case with a lower bound on the input parameter:

$$\min_{u(t)} J = \int_{t_k}^{t_f} \left(c_B \left(t \right) - c_{B_{ref}} \left(t \right) \right)^{\text{T}} \left(c_B \left(t \right) - c_{B_{ref}} \left(t \right) \right) dt$$ (31)

$$s.t.\, u \geq u_{min}\,.$$

The optimization is subject to a path constraint on u. The path constraint is included in the numerical optimization once again using a barrier function. $c_{B_{set}}$ is the trajectory to follow and not a function of time.

4.2. Results

The terminal cost obtained for each simulation is shown in Table 2. The simulations in which the feedback re-optimization ended giving worse result than just using the offline optimization are indicated in bold. The parametric errors considered are all $\pm 20\%$ except for Case 3. This particular case was harder to optimize and a greater parametric error was required for the feedback's impact to surpass the optimization difficulties.

Table 2. Comparison of offline, re-optimization and plant optimum solutions for the six cases with parametric errors. Cost is maximized for Cases 1–3 and minimized for Cases 4–6.

Case	Parametric Error	Cost		
		Offline	Re-Optimization	Plant Optimum
1. Unconstrained, Economic cost	–	4.03	4.03	4.03
	$\bar{k}_{10}$: -20%; α: -20%	3.70	3.71	3.72
	$\bar{k}_{10}$: -20%; α: $+20\%$	**3.691**	**3.686**	3.697
2. Terminal constraint Economic cost	–	3.71	3.71	3.71
	$\bar{k}_{10}$: -20%; α: -20%	1.29	2.03	3.35
	$\bar{k}_{10}$: -20%; α: $+20\%$	**3.01**	**2.93**	3.06
3. Path constraints Economic cost	–	3.80	3.80	3.80
	$\bar{k}_{10}$: -50%; α: -50%	3.079	3.079	3.17
	$\bar{k}_{10}$: -50%; α: $+50\%$	**2.39**	**2.37**	2.40
4. Unconstrained Trajectory cost	–	0.00	0.00	0.00
	$\bar{k}_{10}$: -20%; α: -20%	1.16	0.303	0.03
	$\bar{k}_{10}$: -20%; α: $+20\%$	1.10	0.30	0.00
5. Terminal constraint Trajectory cost	–	0.00	0.00	0.00
	$\bar{k}_{10}$: -20%; α: -20%	2.84	1.49	0.03
	$\bar{k}_{10}$: -20%; α: $+20\%$	1.80	1.38	0.36
6. Path constraint Trajectory cost	–	0.21	0.21	0.21
	$\bar{k}_{10}$: -20%; α: -20%	0.20	0.16	0.02
	$\bar{k}_{1\,0}$: -20%; α: $+20\%$	2.060	1.48	0.47

Note that scenarios where re-optimization is worse than offline solution only occur with economical costs. Additional simulations have been made with different parametric errors, all leading to this same observation. All trajectory-tracking problems with a trajectory feasible for the plant always lead to the re-optimization being better. However, if a path more demanding than the maximal production was chosen for $c_{B_{set}}$, i.e., not a feasible trajectory, then the tracking problem suffers the same difficulties as the economical cost.

The simulation for a $+20\%$ error on α and -20% on $\bar{k}_{10}$ in Case 1 is shown on Figure 1. It shows how re-optimization is actually worse than the offline solution. The figure clearly shows that the input is being pulled away from its optimal value with each re-optimization.

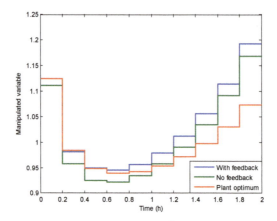

Figure 1. Input for Case 1, with perturbation in α and $\bar{k}_{1\,0}$.

5. Conclusions

Optimization is frequently used on processes, whether it is offline or online in a control method, such as NMPC. In this paper, the impact of using NMPC in presence of parametric errors is studied. An analysis of the mathematical formulation of NMPC has shown that situations can occur where online optimization could lead to results worse than the offline one. The example studied presented this case in particular. It was seen that deterioration of the performance occurred only for an economical cost, while online optimization always helped with the tracking cost. A theoretical analysis has been performed and supports this result, showing that, for a quadratic tracking cost, online re-optimization will improve performance with small parametric uncertainties.

Acknowledgments: The authors would like to thank the NSERC (Natural Sciences and Engineering Research Council of Canada) for supporting their research.

Author Contributions: J.C.B. and B.S. conceived and designed the experiments; J.C.B. performed the simulations; J.C.B. and B.S. analyzed the data; J.C.B. and B.S. wrote the paper.

Conflicts of Interest: The authors declare no conflict of interest.

Abbreviations

The following abbreviations are used in this manuscript:

MPC	Model predictive control
NMPC	Nonlinear MPC
D-RTO	Dynamic real-time optimization

References

1. Peters, N.; Guay, M.; DeHaan, D. Real-time dynamic optimization of batch systems. *J. Process Control* **2007**, *17*, 261–271. [CrossRef]
2. Srinivasan, B.; Palanki, S.; Bonvin, D. Dynamic optimization of batch processes—I. Characterization of the nominal solution. *Comput. Chem. Eng.* **2003**, *27*, 1–26. [CrossRef]
3. Bonvin, D.; Srinivasan, B.; Hunkeler, D. Control and optimization of batch processes—Improvement of process operation in the production of specialty chemicals. *IEEE Control Syst. Mag.* **2006**, *26*, 34–45. [CrossRef]
4. De Souza, G.; Odloak, D.; Zanin, A.C. Real time optimization (RTO) with model predictive control (MPC). *Comput. Chem. Eng.* **2010**, *34*, 1999–2006. [CrossRef]

5. Diehl, M.; Bock, H.G.; Schlöder, J.P.; Findeisen, R.; Nagy, Z.; Allgöwer, F. Real-time optimization and nonlinear model predictive control of processes governed by differential-algebraic equations. *J. Process Control* **2002**, *12*, 577–585. [CrossRef]

6. Lu, J. Challenging control problems and emerging technologies in enterprise optimization. *Control Eng. Pract.* **2003**, *11*, 847–858. [CrossRef]

7. Würth, L.; Hannemann, R.; Marquardt, W. Neighboring-extremal updates for nonlinear model-predictive control and dynamic real-time optimization. *J. Process Control* **2009**, *19*, 1277–1288. [CrossRef]

8. Aravind, P.; Valluvan, M.; Saranya, M. Simulation based modeling and implementation of adaptive control technique for Non Linear process tank. *Int. J. Comput. Appl.* **2013**, *68*, 16. [CrossRef]

9. Dostal, P.; Bobal, V.; Vojtesek, J.; Chramcov, B. Adaptive control of nonlinear processes using two methods of parameter estimation. *WSEAS Trans. Syst.* **2014**, *13*, 292–301.

10. Paz Suárez, L.A.; Georgieva, P.; de Feyo Azevedo, S. Nonlinear MPC for fed-batch multiple stages sugar crystallization. *Chem. Eng. Res. Des.* **2011**, *89*, 753–767. [CrossRef]

11. Revollar, S.; Vega, P.; Vilanova, R. Economic optimization of wastewater treatment plants using Non Linear model predictive control. In Proceedings of the 19th International Conference on System Theory, Control and Computing (ICSTCC), Cheile Gradistei, Romania, 14–16 October 2015.

12. Kamaraju, V.K.; Chiu, M.S.; Srinivasan, B. Reformulating real-time optimal feedback based on model uncertainty. In Proceedings of the 10th IFAC Symposium on Dynamics and Control of Process Systems, Mumbai, India, 18–20 December 2013; pp. 756–761.

13. Yuan, C.; Wang, C. Persistency of excitation and performance of deterministic learning. In Proceedings of the 30th Chinese Control Conference, Yantai, China, 22–24 July 2011.

14. Pahija, E.; Manenti, F.; Mujtaba, I.M.; Rossi, F. Assessment of control techniques for the dynamic optimization of (semi-)batch reactors. *Comput. Chem. Eng.* **2014**, *66*, 269–275. [CrossRef]

15. Jamaludin, M.Z.; Swartz, C.L.E. A bilevel programming formulation for dynamic real-time optimization. *IFAC-PapersOnLine* **2015**, *48*, 906–911. [CrossRef]

16. Nagy, Z.K.; Braatz, R.D. Open-loop and closed-loop robust optimal control of batch processes using distributional and worst-case analysis. *J. Process Control* **2004**, *14*, 411–422. [CrossRef]

17. Kadam, J.V.; Schlegel, M.; Srinivasan, B.; Bonvin, D.; Marquardt, W. Dynamic optimization in the presence of uncertainty: From off-line nominal solution to measurement-based implementation. *J. Process Control* **2007**, *17*, 389–398. [CrossRef]

18. Lucia, S.; Finkler, T.; Engell, S. Multi-stage nonlinear model predictive control applied to a semi-batch polymerization reactor under uncertainty. *J. Process Control* **2013**, *23*, 1306–1319. [CrossRef]

19. Mesbah, A.; Streif, S.; Findeisen, R.; Braatz, R.D. Stochastic nonlinear model predictive control with probabilistic constraints. In Proceedings of the 2014 American Control Conference (ACC), Portland, OR, USA, 4–6 June 2014.

20. Morari, M.; Lee, J.H. Model predictive control: Past, present and future. *Comput. Chem. Eng.* **1999**, *23*, 667–682. [CrossRef]

21. Nagy, Z.K.; Allgöwer, F. A nonlinear model predictive control approach for robust end-point property control of a thin-film deposition process. *Int. J. Robust Nonlinear Control* **2007**, *17*, 1600–1613. [CrossRef]

 *processes*

Article

Sensitivity-Based Economic NMPC with a Path-Following Approach

Eka Suwartadi [1], Vyacheslav Kungurtsev [2] and Johannes Jäschke [1,*]

[1]   Department of Chemical Engineering, Norwegian University of Science and Technology (NTNU),
      7491 Trondheim, Norway; eka.suwartadi@ntnu.no
[2]   Department of Computer Science, Czech Technical University in Prague, 12000 Praha 2, Czech Republic;
      vyacheslav.kungurtsev@fel.cvut.cz
*   Correspondence: jaschke@ntnu.no; Tel.: +47-735-93691

Academic Editor: Dominique Bonvin
Received: 26 November 2016; Accepted: 13 February 2017; Published: 27 February 2017

Abstract: We present a sensitivity-based predictor-corrector path-following algorithm for fast nonlinear model predictive control (NMPC) and demonstrate it on a large case study with an economic cost function. The path-following method is applied within the advanced-step NMPC framework to obtain fast and accurate approximate solutions of the NMPC problem. In our approach, we solve a sequence of quadratic programs to trace the optimal NMPC solution along a parameter change. A distinguishing feature of the path-following algorithm in this paper is that the strongly-active inequality constraints are included as equality constraints in the quadratic programs, while the weakly-active constraints are left as inequalities. This leads to close tracking of the optimal solution. The approach is applied to an economic NMPC case study consisting of a process with a reactor, a distillation column and a recycler. We compare the path-following NMPC solution with an ideal NMPC solution, which is obtained by solving the full nonlinear programming problem. Our simulations show that the proposed algorithm effectively traces the exact solution.

Keywords: fast economic NMPC; NLP sensitivity; path-following algorithm; nonlinear programming; dynamic optimization

---

1. Introduction

The idea of economic model predictive control (MPC) is to integrate the economic optimization layer and the control layer in the process control hierarchy into a single dynamic optimization layer. While classic model predictive control approaches typically employ a quadratic objective to minimize the error between the setpoints and selected measurements, economic MPC adjusts the inputs to minimize the economic cost of operation directly. This makes it possible to optimize the cost during transient operation of the plant. In recent years, this has become increasingly desirable, as stronger competition, volatile energy prices and rapidly changing product specifications require agile plant operations, where also transients are optimized to maximize profit.

The first industrial implementations of economic MPC were reported in [1,2] for oil refinery applications. The development of theory and stability analysis for economic MPC arose almost a decade afterwards; see, e.g., [3,4]. Recent progress on economic MPC is reviewed and surveyed in [5,6]. Most of the current research activities focus on the stability analysis of economic MPC and do not discuss its performance (an exception is [7]).

Because nonlinear process models are often used for economic optimization, a potential drawback of economic MPC is that it requires solving a large-scale nonlinear optimization problem (NLP) associated with the nonlinear model predictive control (NMPC) problem at every sample time.

The solution of this NLP may take a significant amount of time [8], and this can lead to performance degradation and even to instability of the closed-loop system [9].

To reduce the detrimental effect of computational delay in NMPC, several sensitivity-based methods were proposed [10–12]. All of these fast sensitivity approaches exploit the fact that the NMPC optimization problems are identical at each sample time, except for one varying parameter: the initial state. Instead of solving the full nonlinear optimization problem when new measurements of the state become available, these approaches use the sensitivity of the NLP solution at a previously-computed iteration to obtain fast approximate solutions to the new NMPC problem. These approximate solutions can be computed and implemented in the plant with minimal delay. A recent overview of the developments in fast sensitivity-based nonlinear MPC is given in [13], and a comparison of different approaches to obtain sensitivity updates for NMPC is compiled in the paper by Wolf and Marquardt [14].

Diehl et al. [15] proposed the concept of real-time iteration (RTI), in which the full NLP is not solved at all during the MPC iterations. Instead, at each NMPC sampling time, a single quadratic programming (QP) related to the sequential quadratic programming (SQP) iteration for solving the full NLP is solved. The real-time iteration scheme contains two phases: (1) the preparation phase and (2) the feedback phase. In the preparation phase, the model derivatives are evaluated using a predicted state measurement, and a QP is formulated based on data of this predicted state. In the feedback phase, once the new initial state is available, the QP is updated to include the new initial state and solved for the control input that is injected into the plant. The real-time iteration scheme has been applied to economic NMPC in the context of wind turbine control [16,17]. Similar to the real-time iteration scheme are the approaches by Ohtsuka [18] and the early paper by Li and Biegler [19], where one single Newton-like iteration is performed per sampling time.

A different approach, the advanced-step NMPC (asNMPC), was proposed by Zavala and Biegler [10]. The asNMPC approach involves solving the full NLP at every sample time. However, the full NLP solution is computed in advance for a predicted initial state. Once the new state measurement is available, the NLP solution is corrected using a fast sensitivity update to match the measured or estimated initial state. A simple sensitivity update scheme is implemented in the software package sIPOPT [20]. However, active set changes are handled rather heuristically; see [21] for an overview. Kadam and Marquardt [22] proposed a similar approach, where nominal NLP solutions are updated by solving QPs in a neighboring extremal scheme; see also [12,23].

The framework of asNMPC was also applied by Jäschke and Biegler [24], who use a multiple-step predictor path-following algorithm to correct the NLP predictions. Their approach included measures to handle active set changes rigorously, and their path-following advanced-step NMPC algorithm is also the first one to handle non-unique Lagrange multipliers.

The contribution of this paper is to apply an improved path-following method for correcting the NLP solution within the advanced-step NMPC framework. In particular, we replace the predictor path-following method from [24] by a predictor-corrector method and demonstrate numerically that the method works efficiently on a large-scale case study. We present how the asNMPC with the predictor-corrector path-following algorithm performs in the presence of measurement noise and compare it with a pure predictor path-following asNMPC approach and an ideal NMPC approach, where the NLP is assumed to be solved instantly. We also give a brief discussion about how our method differs from previously published approaches.

The structure of this paper is the following. We start by introducing the ideal NMPC and advanced-step NMPC frameworks in Section 2 and give a description of our path-following algorithm together with some relevant background material and a brief discussion in Section 3. The proposed algorithm is applied to a process with a reactor, distillation and recycling in Section 4, where we consider the cases with and without measurement noise and discuss the results. The paper is closed with our conclusions in Section 5.

2. NMPC Problem Formulations

2.1. The NMPC Problem

We consider a nonlinear discrete-time dynamic system:

$$\mathbf{x}_{k+1} = f(\mathbf{x}_k, \mathbf{u}_k) \tag{1}$$

where $\mathbf{x}_k \in \mathbb{R}^{n_x}$ denotes the state variable, $\mathbf{u}_k \in \mathbb{R}^{n_u}$ is the control input and $f : \mathbb{R}^{n_x} \times \mathbb{R}^{n_u} \to \mathbb{R}^{n_x}$ is a continuous model function, which calculates the next state $\mathbf{x}_{k+1}$ from the previous state $\mathbf{x}_k$ and control input $\mathbf{u}_k$, where $k \in \mathbb{N}$. This system is optimized by a nonlinear model predictive controller, which solves the problem:

$$(\mathcal{P}_{nmpc}) : \quad \min_{\mathbf{z}_l, \mathbf{v}_l} \quad \Psi(\mathbf{z}_N) + \sum_{l=0}^{N-1} \psi(\mathbf{z}_l, \mathbf{v}_l) \tag{2}$$

$$\text{s.t.} \quad \mathbf{z}_{l+1} = f(\mathbf{z}_l, \mathbf{v}_l) \quad l = 0, \dots, N-1,$$

$$\mathbf{z}_0 = \mathbf{x}_k,$$

$$(\mathbf{z}_l, \mathbf{v}_l) \in \mathcal{Z}, \quad l = 0, \dots, N-1,$$

$$\mathbf{z}_N \in \mathcal{X}_f,$$

at each sample time. Here, $\mathbf{z}_l \in \mathbb{R}^{n_x}$ is the predicted state variable; $\mathbf{v}_l \in \mathbb{R}^{n_u}$ is the predicted control input; and $\mathbf{z}_N \in \mathcal{X}_f$ is the final predicted state variable restricted to the terminal region $\mathcal{X}_f \in \mathbb{R}^{n_x}$. The stage cost is denoted by $\psi : \mathbb{R}^{n_x} \times \mathbb{R}^{n_u} \to \mathbb{R}$ and the terminal cost by $\Psi : \mathcal{X}_f \to \mathbb{R}$. Further, $\mathcal{Z}$ denotes the path constraints, i.e., $\mathcal{Z} = \{(\mathbf{z}, \mathbf{v}) \mid q(\mathbf{z}, \mathbf{v}) \leq 0\}$, where $q : \mathbb{R}^{n_x} \times \mathbb{R}^{n_u} \to \mathbb{R}^{n_q}$.

The solution of the optimization problem $\mathcal{P}_{nmpc}$ is denoted $\{\mathbf{z}_0^*, \dots, \mathbf{z}_N^*, \mathbf{v}_0^*, \dots, \mathbf{v}_{N-1}^*\}$. At sample time k, an estimate or measurement of the state $\mathbf{x}_k$ is obtained, and problem $\mathcal{P}_{nmpc}$ is solved. Then, the first part of the optimal control sequence is assigned as plant input, such that $\mathbf{u}_k = \mathbf{v}_0^*$. This first part of the solution to $\mathcal{P}_{nmpc}$ defines an implicit feedback law $\mathbf{u}_k = \kappa(\mathbf{x}_k)$, and the system will evolve according to $\mathbf{x}_{k+1} = f(\mathbf{x}_k, \kappa(\mathbf{x}_k))$. At the next sample time $k + 1$, when the measurement of the new state $\mathbf{x}_{k+1}$ is obtained, the procedure is repeated. The NMPC algorithm is summarized in Algorithm 1.

Algorithm 1: General NMPC algorithm.

---

1   set $k \leftarrow 0$
2   **while** *MPC is running* **do**
3   1. Measure or estimate x_k.
4   2. Assign the initial state: set $\mathbf{z}_0 = \mathbf{x}_k$.
5   3. Solve the optimization problem $\mathcal{P}_{nmpc}$ to find $\mathbf{v}_0^*$.
6   4. Assign the plant input $\mathbf{u}_k = \mathbf{v}_0^*$.
7   5. Inject $\mathbf{u}_k$ to the plant (1).
8   6. Set $k \leftarrow k + 1$

2.2. Ideal NMPC and Advanced-Step NMPC Framework

For achieving optimal economic performance and good stability properties, problem $\mathcal{P}_{nmpc}$ needs to be solved instantly, so that the optimal input can be injected without time delay as soon as the values of the new states are available. We refer to this hypothetical case without computational delay as ideal NMPC.

In practice, there will always be some time delay between obtaining the updated values of the states and injecting the updated inputs into the plant. The main reason for this delay is the time it requires to solve the optimization problem $\mathcal{P}_{nmpc}$. As the process models become more advanced, solving the optimization problems requires more time, and the computational delay cannot be neglected any more. This has led to the development of fast sensitivity-based NMPC approaches. One such approach that will be a adopted in this paper is the advanced-step NMPC (asNMPC) approach [10]. It is based on the following steps:

1. Solve the NMPC problem at time k with a predicted state value of time $k + 1$,
2. When the measurement x_{k+1} becomes available at time $k + 1$, compute an approximation of the NLP solution using fast sensitivity methods,
3. Update $k \leftarrow k + 1$, and repeat from Step 1.

Zavala and Biegler proposed a fast one-step sensitivity update that is based on solving a linear system of equations [10]. Under some assumptions, this corresponds to a first-order Taylor approximation of the optimal solution. In particular, this approach requires strict complementarity of the NLP solution, which ensures no changes in the active set. A more general approach involves allowing for changes in the active set and making several sensitivity updates. This was proposed in [24] and will be developed further in this paper.

3. Sensitivity-Based Path-Following NMPC

In this section, we present some fundamental sensitivity results from the literature and then use them in a path-following scheme for obtaining fast approximate solutions to the NLP.

3.1. Sensitivity Properties of NLP

The dynamic optimization Problem (2) can be cast as a general parametric NLP problem:

$$(\mathcal{P}_{NLP}) : \min_{\chi} \quad F(\chi, \mathbf{p}) \tag{3}$$
$$\text{s.t.} \quad c(\chi, \mathbf{p}) = 0$$
$$g(\chi, \mathbf{p}) \leq 0,$$

where $\chi \in \mathbb{R}^{n_\chi}$ are the decision variables (which generally include the state variables and the control input $n_\chi = n_x + n_u$) and $\mathbf{p} \in \mathbb{R}^{n_p}$ is the parameter, which is typically the initial state variable x_k. In addition, $F : \mathbb{R}^{n_\chi} \times \mathbb{R}^{n_p} \to \mathbb{R}$ is the scalar objective function; $c : \mathbb{R}^{n_\chi} \times \mathbb{R}^{n_p} \to \mathbb{R}^{n_c}$ denotes the equality constraints; and finally, $g : \mathbb{R}^{n_\chi} \times \mathbb{R}^{n_p} \to \mathbb{R}^{n_g}$ denotes the inequality constraints. The instances of Problem (3) that are solved at each sample time differ only in the parameter $\mathbf{p}$.

The Lagrangian function of this problem is defined as:

$$\mathcal{L}(\chi, \mathbf{p}, \lambda, \mu) = F(\chi, \mathbf{p}) + \lambda^T c(\chi, \mathbf{p}) + \mu^T g(\chi, \mathbf{p}), \tag{4}$$

and the KKT (Karush–Kuhn–Tucker) conditions are:

$$c(\mathbf{x}, \mathbf{p}) = 0, \quad g(\mathbf{x}, \mathbf{p}) \leq 0 \quad (primal\ feasibility) \tag{5}$$
$$\mu \geq 0, \quad (dual\ feasibility)$$
$$\nabla_x \mathcal{L}(\mathbf{x}, \mathbf{p}, \lambda, \mu) = 0, \quad (stationary\ condition)$$
$$\mu^T g(\mathbf{x}, \mathbf{p}) = 0, \quad (complementary\ slackness).$$

In order for the KKT conditions to be a necessary condition of optimality, we require a constraint qualification (CQ) to hold. In this paper, we will assume that the linear independence constraint qualification (LICQ) holds:

Definition 1 (LICQ). *Given a vector* $\mathbf{p}$ *and a point* χ*, the LICQ holds at* χ *if the set of vectors* $\left\{ \{\nabla_\chi c_i(\chi, \mathbf{p})\}_{i \in \{1, \dots, n_c\}} \cup \{\nabla_\chi g_i(\chi, \mathbf{p})\}_{i: g_i(\chi, \mathbf{p}) = 0} \right\}$ *is linearly independent.*

The LICQ implies that the multipliers (λ, μ) satisfying the KKT conditions are unique. If additionally, a suitable second-order condition holds, then the KKT conditions guarantee a unique local minimum. A suitable second-order condition states that the Hessian matrix has to be positive definite in a set of appropriate directions, defined in the following property:

Definition 2 (SSOSC). *The strong second-order sufficient condition (SSOSC) holds at χ with multipliers λ and μ if $\mathbf{d}^T \nabla_\chi^2 \mathcal{L}(\chi, \mathbf{p}, \lambda, \mu)\ \mathbf{d} > 0$ for all $\mathbf{d} \neq 0$, such that $\nabla_\chi c(\chi, \mathbf{p})^T \mathbf{d} = 0$ and $\nabla_\chi g_i(\chi, \mathbf{p})^T \mathbf{d} = 0$ for i, such that $g_i(\chi, \mathbf{p}) = 0$ and $\mu_i > 0$.*

For a given $\mathbf{p}$, denote the solution to (3) by $\chi^*(\mathbf{p}), \lambda^*(\mathbf{p}), \mu^*(\mathbf{p})$, and if no confusion is possible, we omit the argument and write simply χ^*, λ^*, μ^*. We are interested in knowing how the solution changes with a perturbation in the parameter $\mathbf{p}$. Before we state a first sensitivity result, we define another important concept:

Definition 3 (SC). *Given a vector $\mathbf{p}$ and a solution χ^* with vectors of multipliers λ^* and μ^*, strict complimentary (SC) holds if $\mu_i^* - g_i(\chi^*, \mathbf{p}) > 0$ for each $i = 1, \ldots, n_g$.*

Now, we are ready to state the result below given by Fiacco [25].

Theorem 1 (Implicit function theorem applied to optimality conditions). *Let $\chi^*(\mathbf{p})$ be a KKT point that satisfies (5), and assume that LICQ, SSOSC and SC hold at χ^*. Further, let the function F, c, g be at least $k + 1$-times differentiable in χ and k-times differentiable in $\mathbf{p}$. Then:*

- *χ^* is an isolated minimizer, and the associated multipliers λ and μ are unique.*
- *for $\mathbf{p}$ in a neighborhood of $\mathbf{p}_0$, the set of active constraints remains unchanged.*
- *for $\mathbf{p}$ in a neighborhood of $\mathbf{p}_0$, there exists a k-times differentiable function $\sigma(\mathbf{p}) = \begin{bmatrix} \chi^*(\mathbf{p})^T & \lambda^*(\mathbf{p})^T & \mu^*(\mathbf{p})^T \end{bmatrix}$, that corresponds to a locally unique minimum for (3).*

Proof. See Fiacco [25]. □

Using this result, the sensitivity of the optimal solution χ^*, λ^*, μ^* in a small neighborhood of $\mathbf{p}_0$ can be computed by solving a system of linear equations that arises from applying the implicit function theorem to the KKT conditions of (3):

$$
\begin{bmatrix} \nabla_{\chi\chi}^2 \mathcal{L}(\chi*, \mathbf{p}_0, \lambda*, \mu*) & \nabla_\chi c(\chi*, \mathbf{p}_0) & \nabla_\chi g_A(\chi*, \mathbf{p}_0) \\ \nabla_\chi c(\chi*, \mathbf{p}_0)^T & 0 & 0 \\ \nabla_\chi g_A(\chi*, \mathbf{p}_0)^T & 0 & 0 \end{bmatrix} \begin{bmatrix} \nabla_\mathbf{p}\chi \\ \nabla_\mathbf{p}\lambda \\ \nabla_\mathbf{p}\mu \end{bmatrix} = - \begin{bmatrix} \nabla_{\mathbf{p}\chi}^2 \mathcal{L}(\chi*, \mathbf{p}_0, \lambda*, \mu*) \\ \nabla_\mathbf{p} c(\chi*, \mathbf{p}_0) \\ \nabla_\mathbf{p} g_A(\chi*, \mathbf{p}_0) \end{bmatrix} . \quad (6)
$$

Here, the constraint gradients with subscript g_A indicate that we only include the vectors and components of the Jacobian corresponding to the active inequality constraints at χ, i.e., $i \in A$ if $g_i(\chi, \mathbf{p}_0) = 0$. Denoting the solution of the equation above as $\begin{bmatrix} \nabla_\mathbf{p}\chi & \nabla_\mathbf{p}\lambda & \nabla_\mathbf{p}\mu \end{bmatrix}^T$, for small $\Delta\mathbf{p}$, we obtain a good estimate:

$$
\chi(\mathbf{p}_0 + \triangle\mathbf{p}) = \chi^* + \nabla_\mathbf{p}\chi \triangle\mathbf{p}, \quad (7)
$$
$$
\lambda(\mathbf{p}_0 + \triangle\mathbf{p}) = \lambda^* + \nabla_\mathbf{p}\lambda \triangle\mathbf{p}, \quad (8)
$$
$$
\mu(\mathbf{p}_0 + \triangle\mathbf{p}) = \mu^* + \nabla_\mathbf{p}\mu \triangle\mathbf{p}, \quad (9)
$$

of the solution to the NLP Problem (3) at the parameter value $\mathbf{p}_0 + \Delta\mathbf{p}$. This approach was applied by Zavala and Biegler [10].

If $\Delta\mathbf{p}$ becomes large, the approximate solution may no longer be accurate enough, because the SC assumption implies that the active set cannot change. While that is usually true for small perturbations, large changes in $\Delta\mathbf{p}$ may very well induce active set changes.

It can be seen that the sensitivity system corresponds to the stationarity conditions for a particular QP. This is not coincidental. It can be shown that for $\triangle \mathbf{p}$ small enough, the set $\{i : \mu(\bar{\mathbf{p}})_i > 0\}$ is constant for $\bar{\mathbf{p}} = \mathbf{p}_0 + \triangle \mathbf{p}$. Thus, we can form a QP wherein we are potentially moving off of weakly-active constraints while staying on the strongly-active ones. The primal-dual solution of this QP is in fact the directional derivative of the primal-dual solution path $\chi^*(\mathbf{p}), \lambda^*(\mathbf{p}), \mu^*(\mathbf{p})$.

Theorem 2. *Let F, c, g be twice continuously differentiable in $\mathbf{p}$ and χ near $(\chi^*, \mathbf{p}_0)$, and let the LICQ and SSOSC hold at $(\chi^*, \mathbf{p}_0)$. Then, the solution $(\chi^*(\mathbf{p}), \lambda^*(\mathbf{p}), \mu^*(\mathbf{p}))$ is Lipschitz continuous in a neighborhood of $(\chi^*, \lambda^*, \mu^*, \mathbf{p}_0)$, and the solution function $(\chi^*(\mathbf{p}), \lambda^*(\mathbf{p}), \mu^*(\mathbf{p}))$ is directionally differentiable.*

Moreover, the directional derivative uniquely solves the following quadratic problem:

$$\min_{\triangle \chi} \quad \tfrac{1}{2} \triangle \chi^T \nabla_{\chi\chi}^2 \mathcal{L}(\chi^*, \mathbf{p}_0, \lambda^*, \mu^*) \triangle \chi + \triangle \chi^T \nabla_{\mathbf{p}\chi}^2 \mathcal{L}(\chi^*, \mathbf{p}_0, \lambda^*, \mu^*) \triangle \mathbf{p} \tag{10}$$

$$\text{s.t.} \qquad \nabla_\chi c_i (\chi^*, \mathbf{p}_0)^T \triangle \chi + \nabla_\mathbf{p} c_i (\chi^*, \mathbf{p}_0)^T \triangle \mathbf{p} = 0 \qquad i = 1, \ldots n_c$$

$$\nabla_\chi g_j (\chi^*, \mathbf{p}_0)^T \triangle \chi + \nabla_\mathbf{p} g_j (\chi^*, \mathbf{p}_0)^T \triangle \mathbf{p} = 0 \qquad j \in K_+$$

$$\nabla_\chi g_j (\chi^*, \mathbf{p}_0)^T \triangle \chi + \nabla_\mathbf{p} g_j (\chi^*, \mathbf{p}_0)^T \triangle \mathbf{p} \le 0 \qquad j \in K_0,$$

where $K_+ = \{j \in \mathbb{Z} : \mu_j > 0\}$ is the strongly-active set and $K_0 = \{j \in \mathbb{Z} : \mu_j = 0 \text{ and } g_j(\chi^*, \mathbf{p}_0) = 0\}$ denotes the weakly active set.

Proof. See [26] (Sections 5.1 and 5.2) and [27] (Proposition 3.4.1). □

The theorem above gives the solution of the perturbed NLP (3) by solving a QP problem. Note that regardless of the inertia of the Lagrangian Hessian, if the SSOSC holds, it is positive definite on the null-space of the equality constraints, and thus, the QP defined is convex with an easily obtainable finite global minimizer. In [28], it is noted that as the solution to this QP is the directional derivative of the primal-dual solution of the NLP, it is a predictor step, a tangential first-order estimate of the change in the solution subject to a change in the parameter. We refer to the QP (10) as a pure-predictor. Note that obtaining the sensitivity via (10) instead of (6) has the advantage that changes in the active set can be accounted for correctly, and strict complementarity (SC) is not required. On the other hand, when SC does hold, (6) and (10) are equivalent.

3.2. Path-Following Based on Sensitivity Properties

Equation (6) and the QP (10) describes the change in the optimal solutions for small perturbations. They cannot be guaranteed to reproduce the optimal solution accurately for larger perturbations, because of curvature in the solution path and active set changes that happen further away from the linearization point. One approach to handle such cases is to divide the overall perturbation into several smaller intervals and to iteratively use the sensitivity to track the path of optimal solutions.

The general idea of a path-following method is to reach the solution of the problem at a final parameter value $\mathbf{p}_f$ by tracing a sequence of solutions $(\chi_k, \lambda_k, \mu_k)$ for a series of parameter values $\mathbf{p}(t_k) = (1 - t_k) \mathbf{p}_0 + t_k \mathbf{p}_f$ with $0 = t_0 < t_1 < \ldots < t_k < \ldots < t_N = 1$. The new direction is found by evaluating the sensitivity at the current point. This is similar to a Euler integration for ordinary differential equations.

However, just as in the case of integrating differential equations with a Euler method, a path-following algorithm that is only based on the sensitivity calculated by the pure predictor QP may fail to track the solution accurately enough and may lead to poor solutions. To address this problem, a common approach is to include elements that are similar to a Newton step, which force the path-following algorithm towards the true solution. It has been found that such a corrector element can be easily included into a QP that is very similar to the predictor QP (10). Consider approximating (3) by a QP, linearizing with respect to both χ and $\mathbf{p}$, but again enforcing the equality of the strongly-active constraints, as we expect them to remain strongly active at a perturbed NLP:

$$\min_{\triangle\chi,\triangle\mathbf{p}} \tfrac{1}{2}\triangle\chi^T\nabla^2_{\chi\chi}\mathcal{L}\left(\chi^*,\mathbf{p}_0,\lambda^*,\mu^*\right)\triangle\chi + \triangle\chi^T\nabla^2_{\mathbf{p}\chi}\mathcal{L}\left(\chi^*,\mathbf{p}_0,\lambda^*,\mu^*\right)\triangle\mathbf{p} + \nabla_\chi F^T\triangle\chi + \nabla_\mathbf{p}F\triangle\mathbf{p} + \tfrac{1}{2}\triangle\mathbf{p}^T\nabla^2_{\mathbf{p}\mathbf{p}}\mathcal{L}\left(\chi^*,\mathbf{p}_0,\lambda^*,\mu^*\right)\triangle\mathbf{p} \quad (11)$$

$$\text{s.t.} \quad c_i\left(\chi^*,\mathbf{p}_0\right) + \nabla_\chi c_i\left(\chi^*,\mathbf{p}_0\right)^T\triangle\chi + \nabla_\mathbf{p}c_i\left(\chi^*,\mathbf{p}_0\right)^T\triangle\mathbf{p} = 0 \qquad i = 0,\ldots n_c$$

$$g_j\left(\chi^*,\mathbf{p}_0\right) + \nabla_\chi g_j\left(\chi^*,\mathbf{p}_0\right)^T\triangle\chi + \nabla_\mathbf{p}g_j\left(\chi^*,\mathbf{p}_0\right)^T\triangle\mathbf{p} = 0 \qquad j \in K_+$$

$$g_j\left(\chi^*,\mathbf{p}_0\right) + \nabla_\chi g_j\left(\chi^*,\mathbf{p}_0\right)^T\triangle\chi + \nabla_\mathbf{p}g_j\left(\chi^*,\mathbf{p}_0\right)^T\triangle\mathbf{p} \leq 0 \qquad j \in \{1,\ldots,n_g\}\setminus K_+.$$

In our NMPC problem $\mathcal{P}_{nmpc}$, the parameter $\mathbf{p}$ corresponds to the current "initial" state, $\mathbf{x}_k$. Moreover, the cost function is independent of $\mathbf{p}$, and we have that $\nabla_\mathbf{p}F = 0$. Since the parameter enters the constraints linearly, we have that $\nabla_\mathbf{p}c$ and $\nabla_\mathbf{p}g$ are constants. With these facts, the above QP simplifies to:

$$\min_{\triangle\chi} \quad \tfrac{1}{2}\triangle\chi^T\nabla^2_{\chi\chi}\mathcal{L}\left(\chi^*,\mathbf{p}_0+\triangle\mathbf{p},\lambda^*,\mu^*\right)\triangle\chi + \nabla_\chi F^T\triangle\chi \qquad\qquad (12)$$

$$\text{s.t.} \quad c_i\left(\chi^*,\mathbf{p}_0+\triangle\mathbf{p}\right) + \nabla_\chi c_i\left(\chi^*,\mathbf{p}_0+\triangle\mathbf{p}\right)^T\triangle\chi = 0 \quad i = 1,\ldots n_c$$

$$g_j\left(\chi^*,\mathbf{p}_0+\triangle\mathbf{p}\right) + \nabla_\chi g_j\left(\chi^*,\mathbf{p}_0+\triangle\mathbf{p}\right)^T\triangle\chi = 0 \quad j \in K_+$$

$$g_j\left(\chi^*,\mathbf{p}_0+\triangle\mathbf{p}\right) + \nabla_\chi g_j\left(\chi^*,\mathbf{p}_0+\triangle\mathbf{p}\right)^T\triangle\chi \leq 0 \quad j \in \{1,\ldots,n_g\}\setminus K_+.$$

We denote the QP formulation (12) as the predictor-corrector. We note that this QP is similar to the QP proposed in the real-time iteration scheme [15]. However, it is not quite the same, as we enforce the strongly-active constraints as equality constraints in the QP. As explained in [28], this particular QP tries to estimate how the NLP solution changes as the parameter does in the predictor component and refines the estimate, in more closely satisfying the KKT conditions at the new parameter, as a corrector.

The predictor-corrector QP (12) is well suited for use in a path-following algorithm, where the optimal solution path is tracked from $\mathbf{p}_0$ to a final value $\mathbf{p}_f$ along a sequence of parameter points $\mathbf{p}(t_k) = (1-t_k)\,\mathbf{p}_0 + t_k\,\mathbf{p}_f$ with $0 = t_0 < t_1 < \ldots < t_k < \ldots < t_N = 1$. At each point $\mathbf{p}(t_k)$, the QP is solved and the primal-dual solutions updated as:

$$\chi(t_{k+1}) = \chi(t_k) + \triangle\chi \qquad\qquad (13)$$

$$\lambda(t_{k+1}) = \triangle\lambda \qquad\qquad (14)$$

$$\mu(t_{k+1}) = \triangle\mu, \qquad\qquad (15)$$

where $\triangle\chi$ is obtained from the primal solution of QP (12) and where $\triangle\lambda$ and $\triangle\mu$ correspond to the Lagrange multipliers of QP (12).

Changes in the active set along the path are detected by the QP as follows: If a constraint becomes inactive at some point along the path, the corresponding multiplier μ_j will first become weakly active, i.e., it will be added to the set K_0. Since it is not included as an equality constraint, the next QP solution can move away from the constraint. Similarly, if a new constraint g_j becomes active along the path, it will make the corresponding linearized inequality constraint in the QP active and be tracked further along the path.

The resulting path-following algorithm is summarized with its main steps in Algorithm 2, and we are now in the position to apply it in the advanced-step NMPC setting described in Section 2.2. In particular, the path-following algorithm is used to find a fast approximation of the optimal NLP solution corresponding to the new available state measurement, which is done by following the optimal solution path from the predicted state to the measured state.

Algorithm 2: Path-following algorithm.

Input: initial variables from NLP $\chi^*(\mathbf{p}_0), \lambda^*(\mathbf{p}_0), \mu^*(\mathbf{p}_0)$
fix stepsize $\triangle t$, and set $N = \frac{1}{\triangle t}$
set initial parameter value $\mathbf{p}_0$,
set final parameter value $\mathbf{p}_f$,
set $t = 0$,
set constant $0 < \alpha_1 < 1$.
Output: primal variable χ and dual variables λ, μ along the path

```
1   for k ← 1 to N do
2       Compute step Δp = pₖ − pₖ₋₁
3       Solve QP problem ;                              /* to obtain Δχ,Δλ,Δμ  */
4       if QP is feasible then
5           /* perform update                                                  */
6           χ ← χ + Δχ;                                 /* update primal variables */
7           Update dual variables appropriately; using Equations (8) and 9 for the pure-predictor
            method or (14) and (15) for the predictor-corrector method
8           t ← t + Δt ;                               /* update stepsize */
9           k ← k + 1
10      else
11          /* QP is infeasible, reduce QP stepsize                            */
12          Δt ← α₁Δt
13          t ← t − α₁Δt
```

3.3. Discussion of the Path-Following asNMPC Approach

In this section, we discuss some characteristics of the path-following asNMPC approach presented in this paper. We also present a small example to demonstrate the effect of including the strongly-active constraints as equality constraints in the QP.

A reader who is familiar with the real-time iteration scheme [15] will have realized that the QPs (12) that are solved in our path-following algorithm are similar to the ones proposed and solved in the real-time iteration scheme. However, there are some fundamental differences between the standard real-time iteration scheme as described in [15] and the asNMPC with a path-following approach.

This work is set in the advanced-step NMPC framework, i.e., at every time step, the full NLP is solved for a predicted state. When the new measurement becomes available, the precomputed NLP solution is updated by tracking the optimal solution curve from the predicted initial state to the new measured or estimated state. Any numerical homotopy algorithm can be used to update the NLP solution, and we have presented a suitable one in this paper. Note that the solution of the last QP along the path corresponds to the updated NLP solution, and only the inputs computed in this last QP will be injected into the plant.

The situation is quite different in the real time iteration (RTI) scheme described in [15]. Here, the NLP is not solved at all during the MPC sampling times. Instead, at each sampling time, a single QP is solved, and the computed input is applied to the plant. This will require very fast sampling times, and if the QP fails to track the true solution due to very large disturbances, similar measures as in the advanced-step NMPC procedure (i.e., solving the full NLP) must be performed to get the controller "on track" again. Note that the inputs computed from every QP are applied to the plant and, not as in our path-following asNMPC, only the input computed in the last QP along the homotopy.

Finally, in the QPs of the previously published real-time iteration schemes [15], all inequality constraints are linearized and included as QP inequality constraints. Our approach in this paper, however, distinguishes between strongly- and weakly-active inequality constraints. Strongly-active inequalities are included as linearized equality constraints in the QP, while weakly-active constraints are linearized and added as inequality constraints to the QP. This ensures that the true solution path is tracked more accurately also when the full Hessian of the optimization problem becomes non-convex. We illustrate this in the small example below.

Example 1. *Consider the following parametric "NLP"*

$$\min_{x} \quad x_1^2 - x_2^2 \tag{16}$$

$$s.t. \quad -2 - x_2 + t \leq 0$$

$$-2 + x_1^2 + x_2 \leq 0,$$

for which we have plotted the constraints at $t = 0$ in Figure 1a.

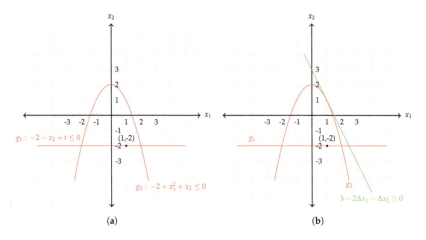

Figure 1. (a) Constraints of NLP (16) in Example 1 and (b) their linearization at $\hat{x} = (1, -2)$ and $t = 0$.

The feasible region lies in between the parabola and the horizontal line. Changing the parameter t from zero to one moves the lower constraint up from $x_2 = -2$ to $x_2 = -1$.

The objective gradient is $\nabla F(x) = (2x_1, -2x_2)$, and the Hessian of the objective is always indefinite $H = \begin{pmatrix} 2 & 0 \\ 0 & -2 \end{pmatrix}$. The constraint gradients are $\nabla g(x) = \begin{pmatrix} 0 & -1 \\ 2x_1 & 1 \end{pmatrix}$. For $t \in [0, 1]$, a (local) primal solution is given by $x^*(t) = (0, t - 2)$. The first constraint is active, the second constraint is inactive, and the dual solution is $\lambda^*(t) = (-2x_2, 0)$. At $t = 0$ we thus have the optimal primal solution $x^* = (0, -2)$ and the optimal multiplier $\lambda^* = (4, 0)$.

We consider starting from an approximate solution at the point $\hat{x}(t = 0) = (1, -2)$ with dual variables $\hat{\lambda}(t = 0) = (4, 0)$, such that the first constraint is strongly active, while the second one remains inactive. The linearized constraints for this point are shown in Figure 1b. Now, consider a change $\Delta t = 1$, going from $t = 0$ to $t = 1$.

The pure predictor QP (10) has the form, recalling that we enforce the strongly active constraint as equality:

$$\min_{\Delta x} \Delta x_1^2 - \Delta x_2^2 \tag{17}$$

$$s.t. \quad -\Delta x_2 + 1 = 0.$$

This QP is convex with a unique solution $\Delta x = (0, 1)$ resulting in the subsequent point $\hat{x}(t = 1) = (1, -1)$.

The predictor-corrector QP (12), which includes a linear term in the objective that acts as a corrector, is given for this case as

$$\min_{\Delta x} \Delta x_1^2 - \Delta x_2^2 + 2\Delta x_1 + 4\Delta x_2$$
$$s.t. - \Delta x_2 + 1 = 0 \tag{18}$$
$$-3 + 2\Delta x_1 + \Delta x_2 \leq 0.$$

Again this QP is convex with a unique primal solution $\Delta x = (-1, 1)$. The step computed by this predictor corrector QP moves the update to the true optimal solution $\hat{x}(t = 1) = (0, -1) = x^*(t = 1)$.

Now, consider a third QP, which is the predictor-corrector QP (12), but without enforcing the strongly active constraints as equalities. That is, all constraints are included in the QP as they were in the original NLP (16),

$$\min_{\Delta x} \Delta x_1^2 - \Delta x_2^2 + 2\Delta x_1 + 4\Delta x_2$$
$$s.t. \quad - \Delta x_2 + 1 \leq 0 \tag{19}$$
$$-3 + 2\Delta x_1 + \Delta x_2 \leq 0.$$

This QP is non-convex and unbounded; we can decrease the objective arbitrarily by setting $\Delta x = (1.5 - 0.5r, r)$ and letting a scalar $r \geq 1$ go to infinity. Although there is a local minimizer at $\Delta x = (-1, 1)$, a QP solver that behaves "optimally" should find the unbounded "solution".

This last approach cannot be expected to work reliably if the full Hessian of the optimization problem may become non-convex, which easily can be the case when optimizing economic objective functions. We note, however, that if the Hessian $\nabla_{xx}\mathcal{L}$ is positive definite, QP it is not necessary to enforce the strongly active constraints as equality constraints in the predictor-corrector QP (12).

4. Numerical Case Study

4.1. Process Description

We demonstrate the path-following NMPC (pf-NMPC) on an isothermal reactor and separator process depicted in Figure 2. The continuously-stirred tank reactor (CSTR) is fed with a stream F_0 containing 100% component A and a recycler R from the distillation column. A first-order reaction $A \rightarrow B$ takes place in the CSTR where B is the desired product and the product with flow rate F is fed to the column. In the distillation column, the unreacted raw material is separated from the product and recycled into the reactor. The desired product B leaves the distillation column as the bottom product, which is required to have a certain purity. Reaction kinetic parameters for the reactor are described in Table 1. The distillation column model is taken from [29]. Table 2 summarizes the parameters used in the distillation. In total, the model has 84 state variables of which 82 are from the distillation (concentration and holdup for each stage) and two from the CSTR (one concentration and one holdup).

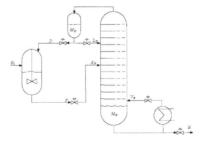

Figure 2. Diagram of continuously-stirred tank reactor (CSTR) and distillation column.

Table 1. Reaction kinetics parameters.

Reaction	Reaction Rate Constant (min^{-1})	Activation Energy (in J/mol)
$A \rightarrow B$	1×10^8	6×10^4

Table 2. Distillation Column A parameters.

Parameter	Value
α_{AB}	1.5
number of stages	41
feed stage location	21

The stage cost of the economic objective function to optimize under operation is:

$$J = p_F F_0 + p_V V_B - p_B B, \tag{20}$$

where p_F is the feed cost, p_V is the steam cost and p_B is the product price. The price setting is $p_F = 1\,\$/\text{kmol}$, $p_V = 0.02\,\$/\text{kmol}$, $p_B = 2\,\$/\text{kmol}$. The operational constraints are the concentration of the bottom product ($x_B \leq 0.1$), as well as the liquid holdup at the bottom and top of the distillation column and in the CSTR ($0.3 \leq M_{\{B,D,CSTR\}} \leq 0.7$ kmol). The control inputs are reflux flow (L_T), boil-up flow (V_B), feeding rate to the distillation (F), distillate (top) and bottom product flow rates (D and B). These control inputs have bound constraints as follows:

$$\begin{bmatrix} 0.1 \\ 0.1 \\ 0.1 \\ 0.1 \\ 0.1 \end{bmatrix} \leq \begin{bmatrix} L_T \\ V_B \\ F \\ D \\ B \end{bmatrix} \leq \begin{bmatrix} 10 \\ 4.008 \\ 10 \\ 1.0 \\ 1.0 \end{bmatrix} (\text{kmol/min}).$$

First, we run a steady-state optimization with the following feed rate $F_0 = 0.3$ (kmol/min). This gives us the optimal values for control inputs and state variables. The optimal steady state input values are $\mathbf{u}_s = \begin{bmatrix} 1.18 & 1.92 & 1.03 & 0.74 & 0.29 \end{bmatrix}^T$. The optimal state and control inputs are used to construct regularization term added to the objective function (20). Now, the regularized stage becomes:

$$J_m = p_F F_0 + p_V V_B - p_B B - p_D D + (\mathbf{z} - \mathbf{x}_s)^T \mathbf{Q}_1 (\mathbf{z} - \mathbf{x}_s) + (\mathbf{v} - \mathbf{u}_s)^T \mathbf{Q}_2 (\mathbf{v} - \mathbf{u}_s). \tag{21}$$

The weights $\mathbf{Q}_1$ and $\mathbf{Q}_2$ are selected to make the rotated stage cost of the steady state problem strongly convex; for details, see [24]. This is done to obtain an economic NMPC controller that is stable.

Secondly, we set up the NLP for calculating the predicted state variables $\mathbf{z}$ and predicted control inputs $\mathbf{v}$. We employ a direct collocation approach on finite elements using Lagrange collocation to discretize the dynamics, where we use three collocation points in each finite element. By using the direct collocation approach, the state variables and control inputs become optimization variables.

The economic NMPC case study is initialized with the steady state values for a production rate $F_0 = 0.29$ kmol/min, such that the economic NMPC controller is effectively controlling a throughput change from $F_0 = 0.29$ kmol/min to $F_0 = 0.3$ kmol/min. We simulate 150 MPC iterations, with a sample time of 1 min. The prediction horizon of the NMPC controller is set to 30 min. This setting results in an NLP with 10,314 optimization variables. We use CasADi [30] (Version 3.1.0-rc1) with IPOPT [31] as the NLP solver. For the QPs, we use MINOS QP [32] from TOMLAB.

4.2. Comparison of the Open-Loop Optimization Results

In this section, we compare the solutions obtained from the path-following algorithm with the "true" solution of the optimization problem $\mathcal{P}_{nmpc}$ obtained by solving the full NLP. To do this, we consider the second MPC iteration, where the path-following asNMPC is used for the first time to correct the one-sample ahead-prediction (in the first MPC iteration, to start up the asNMPC procedure, the full NLP is solved twice). We focus on the interesting case where the predicted state is corrupted by noise, such that the path-following algorithm is required to update the solution. In Figure 3, we have plotted the difference between a selection of predicted states, obtained by applying the path-following NMPC approaches, and the ideal NMPC approach.

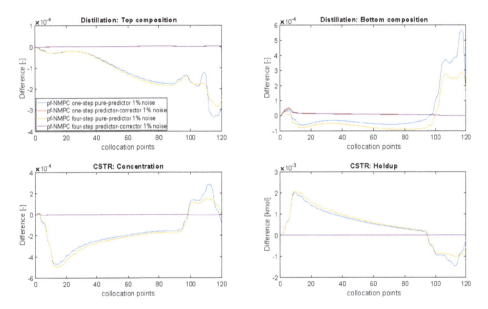

Figure 3. The difference in predicted state variables between ideal NMPC (iNMPC) and path-following NMPC (pf-NMPC) from the second iteration.

We observe that the one-step pure-predictor tracks the ideal NMPC solution worst and the four-step path-following with predictor-corrector tracks best. This happens because the predictor-corrector path-following QP has an additional linear term in the objective function and constraint for the purpose of moving closer to the solution of the NLP (the "corrector" component), as well as tracing the first-order estimate of the change in the solution (the "predictor"). The four-step path-following performs better because a smaller step size gives finer approximation of the parametric NLP solution.

This is also reflected in the average approximation errors given in Table 3. The average approximation error has been calculated by averaging the error one-norm $\left\| X_{path-following} - X_{ideal\ NMPC} \right\|_1$ over all MPC iterations.

We observe that in this case study, the accuracy of a single predictor-corrector step is almost as good as performing four predictor-corrector steps along the path. That is, a single predictor-corrector QP update may be sufficient for this application. However, in general, in the presence of larger noise magnitudes and longer sampling intervals, which cause poorer predictions, a single-step update may no longer lead to good approximations. We note the large error in the pure-predictor path-following method for the solution accuracy of several orders of magnitude.

On the other hand, given that the optimization vector χ has dimension 10,164 for our case study, the average one-norm approximation error of ca. 4.5 does result in very small errors on the individual variables.

Table 3. Approximation error using path-following algorithms. asNMPC, advanced-step NMPC (asNMPC); QP, quadratic programming.

Average Approximation Error between ideal NMPC and Path-Following (PF) asNMPC	
PF with predictor QP, 1 step	4.516
PF with predictor QP, 4 steps	4.517
PF with predictor-corrector QP, 1 step	1.333×10^{-2}
PF with predictor-corrector QP, 4 steps	1.282×10^{-2}

4.3. Closed-Loop Results: No Measurement Noise

In this section, we compare the results for closed loop process operation. We consider first the case without measurement noise, and we compare the results for ideal NMPC with the results obtained by the path-following algorithm with the pure-predictor QP (10) and the predictor-corrector QP (12). Figure 4 shows the trajectories of the top and bottom composition in the distillation column and the reactor concentration and holdup. Note that around 120 min, the bottom composition constraint in the distillation column becomes active, while the CSTR holdup is kept at its upper bound all of the time (any reduction in the holdup will result in economic and product loss).

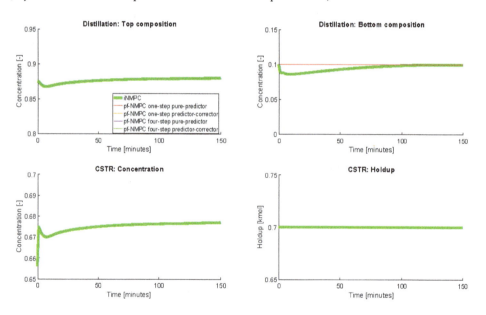

Figure 4. Recycle composition, bottom composition, reactor concentration and reactor holdup.

In this case (without noise), the prediction and the true solution only differ due to numerical noise. There is no need to update the prediction, and all approaches give exactly the same closed-loop behavior. This is also reflected in the accumulated stage cost, which is shown in Table 4.

Table 4. Comparison of economic NMPC controllers (no noise). Accumulated stage cost in $.

Economic NMPC Controller		Accumulated Stage Cost
iNMPC		−296.42
pure-predictor QP:		
	pf-NMPC one step	−296.42
	pf-NMPC four steps	−296.42
predictor-corrector QP:		
	pf-NMPC one step	−296.42
	pf-NMPC four steps	−296.42

The closed-loop control inputs are given in Figure 5. Note here that the feed rate into the distillation column is adjusted such that the reactor holdup is at its constraint all of the time.

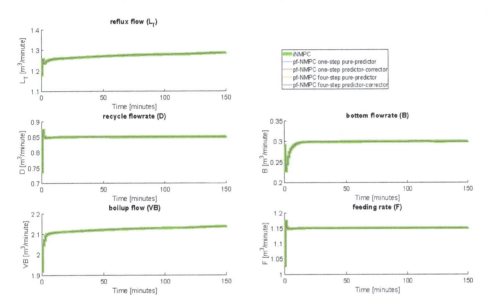

Figure 5. Optimized control inputs.

4.4. Closed-Loop Results: With Measurement Noise

Next, we run simulations with measurement noise on all of the holdups in the system. The noise is taken to have a normal distribution with zero mean and a variance of one percent of the steady state values. This will result in corrupted predictions that have to be corrected for by the path-following algorithms. Again, we perform simulations with one and four steps of pure-predictor and predictor-corrector QPs.

Figure 6 shows the top and bottom compositions of the distillation column, together with the concentration and holdup in the CSTR. The states are obtained under closed-loop operation with the ideal and path-following NMPC algorithms. Due to noise, it is not possible to avoid the violation of the active constraints in the holdup of the CSTR and the bottom composition in the distillation column. This is the case for both the ideal NMPC and the path-following approaches.

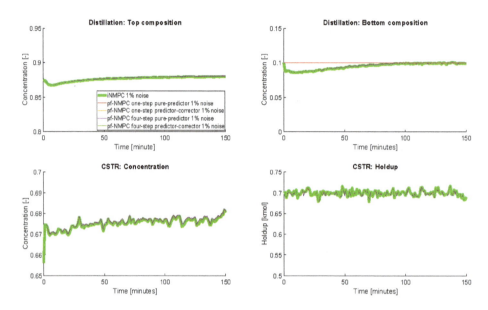

Figure 6. Recycle composition, bottom composition, reactor concentration and reactor holdup.

The input variables shown in Figure 7 are also reflecting the measurement noise, and again, we see that the fast sensitivity NMPC approaches are very close to the ideal NMPC inputs.

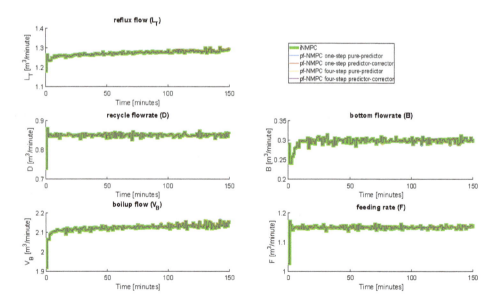

Figure 7. Optimized control inputs.

Finally, we compare the accumulated economic stage cost in Table 5.

Table 5. Comparison of economic NMPC controllers (with noise). Accumulated stage cost in $.

Economic NMPC Controller		Accumulated Stage Cost
iNMPC		−296.82
pure-predictor QP:		
	pf-NMPC one step	−297.54
	pf-NMPC four steps	−297.62
predictor-corrector QP:		
	pf-NMPC one step	−296.82
	pf-NMPC four steps	−296.82

Here, we observe that our proposed predictor-corrector path-following algorithm performs identically to the ideal NMPC. This is as expected, since the predictor-corrector path-following algorithm is trying to reproduce the true NLP solution. Interestingly, in this case, the larger error in the pure predictor path-following NMPC leads to a better economic performance of the closed loop system. This behavior is due to the fact that the random measurement noise can have a positive and a negative effect on the operation, which is not taken into account by the ideal NMPC (and also the predictor-corrector NMPC). In this case, the inaccuracy of the pure-predictor path-following NMPC led to better economic performance in the closed loop. However, it could also have been the opposite.

5. Discussion and Conclusions

We applied the path-following ideas developed in Jäschke et al. [24] and Kungurtsev and Diehl [28] to a large-scale process containing a reactor, a distillation column and a recycle stream. Compared with single-step updates based on solving a linear system of equations as proposed by [10], our path-following approach requires somewhat more computational effort. However, the advantage of the path-following approach is that active set changes are handled rigorously. Moreover, solving a sequence of a few QPs can be expected to be much faster than solving the full NLP, especially since they can be initialized very well, such that the computational delay between obtaining the new state and injecting the updated input into the plant is still sufficiently small. In our computations, we have considered a fixed step-size for the path-following, such that the number of QPs to be solved is known in advance.

The case without noise does not require the path-following algorithm to correct the solution, because the prediction and the true measurement are identical, except for numerical noise. However, when measurement noise is added to the holdups, the situation becomes different. In this case, the prediction and the measurements differ, such that an update is required. All four approaches track the ideal NMPC solution to some degree; however, in terms of accuracy, the predictor-corrector performs consistently better. Given that the pure sensitivity QP and the predictor-corrector QP are very similar in structure, it is recommended to use the latter in the path-following algorithm, especially for highly nonlinear processes and cases with significant measurement noise.

We have presented basic algorithms for path-following, and they seem to work well for the cases we have studied, such that the path-following algorithms do not diverge from the true solution. In principle, however, the path-following algorithms may get lost, and more sophisticated implementations need to include checks and safeguards. We note, however, that the application of the path-following algorithm in the advanced-step NMPC framework has the desirable property that the solution of the full NLP acts as a corrector, such that if the path-following algorithm diverges from the true solution, this will be most likely for only one sample time, until the next full NLP is solved.

The path-following algorithm in this paper (and the corresponding QPs) still relies on the assumption of linearly-independent constraint gradients. If there are path-constraints present in the discretized NLP, care must be taken to formulate them in such a way that LICQ is not violated.

In future work, we will consider extending the path-following NMPC approaches to handle more general situations with linearly-dependent inequality constraints.

Acknowledgments: Vyacheslav Kungurtsev was supported by the Czech Science Foundation Project 17-26999S. Eka Suwartadi and Johannes Jäschke are supported by the Research Council of Norway Young Research Talent Grant 239809.

Author Contributions: V.K. and J.J. contributed the algorithmic ideas for the paper; E.S. implemented the algorithm and simulated the case study; E.S. primarily wrote the paper, with periodic assistance from V.K.; J.J. supervised the work, analyzed the simulation results and contributed to writing and correcting the paper.

Conflicts of Interest: The authors declare no conflict of interest.

References

1. Zanin, A.C.; Tvrzská de Gouvêa, M.; Odloak, D. Industrial implementation of a real-time optimization strategy for maximizing production of LPG in a FCC unit. *Comput. Chem. Eng.* **2000**, *24*, 525–531.

2. Zanin, A.C.; Tvrzská de Gouvêa, M.; Odloak, D. Integrating real-time optimization into the model predictive controller of the FCC system. *Control Eng. Pract.* **2002**, *10*, 819–831,

3. Rawlings, J.B.; Amrit, R. Optimizing process economic performance using model predictive control. In *Nonlinear Model Predictive Control*; Springer: Berlin/Heidelberg, Germany, 2009; Volume 384, pp. 119–138.

4. Rawlings, J.B.; Angeli, D.; Bates, C.N. Fundamentals of economic model predictive control. In Proceeding of the 51st IEEE Conference on Conference on Decision and Control (CDC), Maui, HI, USA, 10–13 December 2012.

5. Ellis, M.; Durand, H.; Christofides, P.D. A tutorial review of economic model predictive methods. *J. Process Control* **2014**, *24*, 1156–1178.

6. Tran, T.; Ling, K.-V.; Maciejowski, J.M. Economic model predictive control—A review. In Proceeding of the 31st ISARC, Sydney, Australia, 9–11 July 2014.

7. Angeli, D.; Amrit, R.; Rawlings, J.B. On average performance and stability of economic model predictive control. *IEEE Trans. Autom. Control* **2012**, *57*, 1615–1626.

8. Idris, E.A.N.; Engell, S. Economics-based NMPC strategies for the operation and control of a continuous catalytic distillation process. *J. Process Control* **2012**, *22*, 1832–1843.

9. Findeisen, R.; Allgöwer, F. Computational delay in nonlinear model predictive control. In Proceeding of the International Symposium on Advanced Control of Chemical Proceses (ADCHEM'03), Hongkong, China, 11–14 January 2004.

10. Zavala, V.M.; Biegler, L.T. The advanced-step NMPC controller: Optimality, stability, and robustness. *Automatica* **2009**, *45*, 86–93.

11. Diehl, M.; Bock, H.G.; Schlöder, J.P. A real-time iteration scheme for nonlinear optimization in optimal feedback control. *SIAM J. Control Optim.* **2005**, *43*, 1714–1736.

12. Würth, L.; Hannemann, R.; Marquardt, W. Neighboring-extremal updates for nonlinear model-predictive control and dynamic real-time optimization. *J. Process Control* **2009**, *19*, 1277–1288.

13. Biegler, L.T.; Yang, X.; Fischer, G.A.G. Advances in sensitivity-based nonlinear model predictive control and dynamic real-time optimization. *J. Process Control* **2015**, *30*, 104–116.

14. Wolf, I.J.; Marquadt, W. Fast NMPC schemes for regulatory and economic NMPC—A review. *J. Process Control* **2016**, *44*, 162–183.

15. Diehl, M.; Bock, H.G.; Schlöder, J.P.; Findeisen, R.; Nagy, Z.; Allgöwer, F. Real-time optimization and nonlinear model predictive control of processes governed by differential-algebraic equations. *J. Process Control* **2002**, *12*, 577–585.

16. Gros, S.; Quirynen, R.; Diehl, M. An improved real-time economic NMPC scheme for Wind Turbine control using spline-interpolated aerodynamic coefficients. In Proceedings of the 53rd IEEE Conference on Decision and Control, Los Angeles, CA, USA, 15–17 December 2014; pp. 935–940.

17. Gros, S.; Vukov, M.; Diehl, M. A real-time MHE and NMPC scheme for wind turbine control. In Proceedings of the 52nd IEEE Conference on Decision and Control, Firenze, Italy, 10–13 December 2013; pp. 1007–1012.

18. Ohtsuka, T. A continuation/GMRES method for fast computation of nonlinear receding horizon control. *Automatica* **2004**, *40*, 563–574.

19. Li, W.C.; Biegler, L.T. Multistep, Newton-type control strategies for constrained nonlinear processes. *Chem. Eng. Res. Des.* **1989**, *67*, 562–577.

20. Pirnay, H.; López-Negrete, R.; Biegler, L.T. Optimal sensitivity based on IPOPT. *Math. Program. Comput.* **2002**, *4*, 307–331.

21. Yang, X.; Biegler, L.T. Advanced-multi-step nonlinear model predictive control. *J. Process Control* **2013**, *23*, 1116–1128.

22. Kadam, J.; Marquardt, W. Sensitivity-based solution updates in closed-loop dynamic optimization. In Proceedings of the DYCOPS 7 Conference, Cambridge, MA, USA, 5–7 July 2004.

23. Würth, L.; Hannemann, R.; Marquardt, W. A two-layer architecture for economically optimal process control and operation. *J. Process Control* **2011**, *21*, 311–321.

24. Jäschke, J.; Yang, X.; Biegler, L.T. Fast economic model predictive control based on NLP-sensitivities. *J. Process Control* **2014**, *24*, 1260–1272.

25. Fiacco, A.V. *Introduction to Sensitivity and Stability Analysis in Nonlinear Programming*; Academic Press: New York, NY, USA, 1983.

26. Bonnans, J.F.; Shapiro, A. Optimization problems with perturbations: A guided tour. *SIAM Rev.* **1998**, *40*, 228–264.

27. Levy, A.B. Solution sensitivity from general principles. *SIAM J. Control Optim.* **2001**, *40*, 1–38.

28. Kungurtsev, V.; Diehl, M. Sequential quadratic programming methods for parametric nonlinear optimization. *Comput. Optim. Appl.* **2014**, *59*, 475–509.

29. Skogestad, S.; Postlethwaite, I. *Multivariate Feedback Control: Analysis and Design*; Wiley-Interscience: Hoboken, NJ, USA, 2005.

30. Andersson, J. A General Purpose Software Framework for Dynamic Optimization. Ph.D. Thesis, Arenberg Doctoral School, KU Leuven, Leuven, Belgium, October 2013.

31. Wächter, A.; Biegler, L.T. On the implementation of an interior-point filter line-search algorithm for large-scale nonlinear programming. *Math. Program.* **2006**, *106*, 25–57.

32. Murtagh, B.A.; Saunders, M.A. A projected lagrangian algorithm and its implementation for sparse nonlinear constraints. *Math. Program. Study* **1982**, *16*, 84–117.

 *processes*

Article

A Feedback Optimal Control Algorithm with Optimal Measurement Time Points

Felix Jost *, Sebastian Sager and Thuy Thi-Thien Le

Institute of Mathematical Optimization, Otto-von-Guericke University Magdeburg, Universitätsplatz 2, 39106 Magdeburg, Germany; sager@ovgu.de (S.S.); thuy.lethien@ovgu.de (T.T.-T.L.)
* Correspondence: felix.jost@ovgu.de; Tel.: +49-391-67-52207

Academic Editor: Dominique Bonvin
Received: 19 November 2016; Accepted: 22 February 2017; Published: 28 February 2017

Abstract: Nonlinear model predictive control has been established as a powerful methodology to provide feedback for dynamic processes over the last decades. In practice it is usually combined with parameter and state estimation techniques, which allows to cope with uncertainty on many levels. To reduce the uncertainty it has also been suggested to include optimal experimental design into the sequential process of estimation and control calculation. Most of the focus so far was on dual control approaches, i.e., on using the controls to simultaneously excite the system dynamics (learning) as well as minimizing a given objective (performing). We propose a new algorithm, which sequentially solves robust optimal control, optimal experimental design, state and parameter estimation problems. Thus, we decouple the control and the experimental design problems. This has the advantages that we can analyze the impact of measurement timing (sampling) independently, and is practically relevant for applications with either an ethical limitation on system excitation (e.g., chemotherapy treatment) or the need for fast feedback. The algorithm shows promising results with a 36% reduction of parameter uncertainties for the Lotka-Volterra fishing benchmark example.

Keywords: feedback optimal control algorithm; optimal experimental design; sampling time points; Pontryagin's Maximum Principle

---

1. Introduction

We start by surveying recent progress of feedback via nonlinear optimal control under uncertainty, before we come to the main contribution of this paper, an investigation of the role of the measurement time grid. This can be seen as complementary and can be combined with almost all other aspects of efficient nonlinear model predictive control.

We are interested in controlling a dynamic process in an optimal way, under the assumption that model parameters are unknown. We assume that there are no systematic uncertainties, i.e., that the mathematical model represents the dynamics of the process sufficiently well and all measurement errors are normally distributed. One possible control task is controlling a dynamic system from an undesired cyclic steady state to a desired one in an optimal way. Such tasks arise in a large variety of applications in biology, chemistry, mechanics and medicine.

The dynamic system is described as a system of differential equations that involves a priori unknown model parameters. To cope with the uncertainty, optimization problems are solved on short time horizons, and new measurements are used to update the model parameters and thus the mathematical model as such. The feedback is calculated via model predictive control (MPC), an established method applicable for linear [1] as well as nonlinear models (NMPC) [2]. MPC is based on the assumption that new measurements arrive continuously, thus allowing an optimal feedback control that can be applied online. NMPC is in practice often combined with moving horizon estimation (MHE), or estimation on an expanding time horizon, which allow an update of state and parameter estimates based on new measurements [3].

NMPC and MHE are based on the calculation of optimal trajectories. As a fast feedback of the controller is important in many applications, clever approaches doing most of the necessary calculations before a new measurement arrives have been proposed in the literature. The most important numerical concepts comprise real-time iterations [4,5], multi-level iterations [6], parallel multi-level iterations [7], an exploitation of the KKT structures [8,9], adaptive control [10], automatic code export [11,12], and usage of parametric QPs [13,14]. For a benchmark problem, the continuously stirred tank reactor of [15], a speedup of approximately 150,000 has been achieved comparing the 60 seconds per iteration reported in 1997 [16] and the 400 microseconds per iteration reported in 2011 by [17]. This speedup is mainly due to the faster algorithms and only partially due to the hardware speedup. Surveys on efficient numerical approaches to NMPC and MHE can be found in, e.g., [7,18–20].

The state and parameter solutions of the maximum likelihood estimation problems are random variables, and are hence endowed with confidence regions. How the process is controlled and when and what is being measured have an important impact on the size of these confidence regions. Optimal experimental design (OED) is concerned with calculating controls and sampling decisions that minimize the size of the confidence regions of the state and parameter estimates. This special control problem is analyzed from a statistical and numerical point of view in several textbooks [21–24] and became a state of the art method in designing experiments in many fields of application. Also a lot of research has been done in sequential optimal experimental design (re-design of experiments) where iteratively optimal experimental designs are performed and parameters are estimated [25,26]. In the last decade, sequential OED has been extended by online OED in which the experiment is directly re-designed when a new measurement is taken [27–31].

Our algorithm is related in the spirit of dual control [32–34], as we want to learn model parameters at the same time as we are using them for NMPC. Note that for medical applications the situation is completely different than from industrial chemical engineering. In the latter mathematical modeling, experimental design, model calibration and analysis are typically performed beforehand with pilot plants, and the results are then transferred in a second stage such that NMPC can be applied over and over again to continuous or batch processes. For biological and medical applications a repetition is not possible, e.g., a chemotherapy treatment can only be performed once under identical conditions.

Recently, different economic objective functions have been proposed that incorporate the nested goals of excitation and exploration [35–37]. Also scenario trees [38,39] and set-based approaches [40] have been successfully applied.

In all mentioned publications the focus is on the control function, with an implicit assumption that measurements are available on a given sampling time grid. While this assumption is true for many applications in which sensors are routinely used, the situation is different in biological and medical applications, where measurements are often invasive and imply logistical, ethical, and financial overhead. In [41] we showed the large impact of optimal sampling on uncertainty reduction for patients suffering from acute myeloid leukemia. Uncertainty could be reduced by more than 50% by choosing the time points different from the standard daily routine, in an a posteriori analysis.

This motivates us to concentrate on the question of the optimal timing of measurements in a real-time algorithm. We propose a new feedback optimal control algorithm with sampling time points for the parameter and state estimation from the solution of an optimal experimental design problem. In our setting the control is assumed to be fixed for the experimental design problem, i.e., we do not excite the dynamics for the sake of information gain. Instead, we focus on determining the optimal measuring (sampling) times. The motivation considering the control $u(\cdot)$ as fixed for the experimental design problem is practically motivated by applications such as fishing or chemotherapy dosage in which there is an ethical, logistical, or financial reluctance to profit only indirectly from a system excitation. This decoupling may also be interesting for a different kind of applications for which fast feedback is necessary, as it results in a very efficient way to calculate the optimal sampling points.

Note that the question of optimal sampling of measurements is to a large extent independent from most of the aforementioned approaches to NMPC. Our approach is complementary in the sense that, e.g., the numerical structure exploitation, the treatment of systematic disturbances, the treatment of robustness, the formulation of dual control objective functions, the use of scenario trees or set-based approaches can all be combined with an adaptive measurement grid. This also applies to the nature of the underlying control task, where many extensions are possible, e.g., multi-stage processes, mixed path- and control constraints, complicated boundary conditions and so on. In the interest of a clear focus on our main results we choose a simple setting that allows to highlight the additional value of measurement grid adaptivity, and only show exemplarily the impact of one possible extension of our algorithm. We take the uncertainty with respect to model parameters into account on the level of optimal control and of the experimental design by calculating robust optimal controls and samplings, compare [42,43], and compare our new algorithm based on nominal solutions with the new algorithm with robust solutions.

Numerical results demonstrating the performance of the algorithm and underlying the theoretical finding are presented for the benchmark example called *Lotka-Volterra fishing problem*. This example is particularly suited for several reasons. First, it is prototypical for many biological, chemical, and medical processes as it captures the most basic dynamic behavior of oscillatory systems. Second, for fishing systems our basic assumption of a slow process with expensive measurements applies and processes related to sustainable fishing have been receiving increasing attention lately, e.g., [44,45]. Third, it has a prototypical objective for many medical applications, as we want to control from an undesired cyclic steady state to a desired steady state. Fourth, it is simple and small enough to visualize the impact of our approach in terms of uncertainty quantification and reduction. A transfer to larger and more complex processes is straightforward.

The paper is organized as follows: In Section 2 we give an overview over the different optimization subproblems that play a role. In Section 3 we present and discuss our novel feedback optimal control algorithm with sampling decisions from sequential optimal experimental designs, and we elaborate on the role of finite support designs. In Section 4 the theoretical findings are illustrated via numerical results for the mentioned Lotka-Volterra fishing example, followed by a discussion and conclusions.

2. On the Estimation, Control, and Design Problems

In this section, the mathematical formulation of the underlying dynamical system and of the three different types of optimization problems, i.e., parameter and state estimation, optimal control, and optimal experimental design are introduced. They are solved sequentially in our feedback optimal control algorithm with adaptive measurement grid that will be presented in Section 3. We explain the advantages of our decoupled dual control approach with respect to an efficient solution of the experimental design problem.

2.1. Nonlinear Dynamic Systems

We assume that dynamic processes can be described as an initial value problem (IVP), consisting of a system of nonlinear ordinary differential equations (ODEs) and initial values $x_0(p)$ that may also depend on the model parameters p,

$$\dot{x}(t) = f(x(t), u(t), p), \qquad x(t_0) = x_0(p), \tag{1}$$

on a time interval $t \in [t_0, t_f] = \mathcal{T}$ with $x : \mathcal{T} \mapsto \mathbb{R}^{n_x}$ the differential state vector, $u : \mathcal{T} \mapsto \mathcal{U}$ a control function with $\mathcal{U} \in \mathcal{R}^{n_u}$ a bounded set, and unknown model parameters $p \in \mathbb{R}^{n_p}$. The function f is assumed to be Lipschitz, such that (1) has a unique solution on $\mathcal{T}$ for all u and p. We calculate $x(\cdot)$ and its derivatives numerically by appropriate methods as described, e.g., in [46].

To formulate design problems and robust versions of control problems, we will need sensitivities $G = \frac{dx}{dp} : \mathcal{T} \mapsto \mathbb{R}^{n_x \times n_p}$. They can be calculated as the solution of the variational differential equations

$$\dot{G}(t) = f_x(\hat{x}(t), u(t), p)G(t) + f_p(\hat{x}(t), u(t), p), \quad G(t_0) = \frac{dx_0(p)}{dp} \tag{2}$$

with $\hat{x}(t)$ the solution of (1) and the partial derivatives $h_x(\cdot), f_x(\cdot), f_p(\cdot)$ written in short form. Note that here and in the following matrix equations are to be understood component-wise. Again, we assume unique solutions for (2).

2.2. State and Parameter Estimation Problems

The relation between the model (1) and the measured data η_i^ω for different measurement functions $\omega \in \{1, \ldots, n_\omega\}$ and time points t_i for $i \in \{1, \ldots, N\}$ can be described by the nonlinear regression

$$\eta_i^\omega = h^\omega(x^*(t_i)) + \varepsilon_i^\omega. \tag{3}$$

The state $x^*(\cdot)$ depends as the solution trajectory of (1) implicitly on the model parameters p (possibly also via the initial values $x_0(p)$). The measurements are described by the nonlinear model responses $h^\omega : \mathbb{R}^{n_x} \mapsto \mathbb{R}^{n_\eta^\omega}$ of the true, but unknown state trajectory $x^*(\cdot)$ plus some normally distributed measurement error $\varepsilon_i^\omega \sim \mathcal{N}(0, \sigma_{\omega,i}^2)$ with zero mean and variances $\sigma_{\omega,i}^2$. Note that the measurement, the model response, and the measurement error are vectors of dimension n_η^ω. Following a maximum-likelihood approach we estimate initial values and model parameters by solving the state and parameter estimation (SPE) problem in the form of a nonlinear weighted least squares problem

$$\min_{x(t),p} \frac{1}{2} \sum_{\omega=1}^{n_\omega} \sum_{i=1}^{N} w_i^\omega \frac{(\eta_i^\omega - h^\omega(x(t_i)))^2}{\sigma_{\omega,i}^2} \quad \text{s.t. (1)} \tag{4}$$

for given and fixed controls $u : \mathcal{T} \mapsto \mathcal{U}$ and weights $w_i^\omega \in \mathcal{W}$. As the measurement times t_i may be a priori unknown, we will in our analysis in Section 3.1 also look at the continuous analogue to (4). This is given by

$$\min_{x(t),p} \frac{1}{2} \sum_{\omega=1}^{n_\omega} \int_{t_0}^{t_f} w^\omega(t) \frac{(\eta^\omega(t) - h^\omega(x(t)))^2}{\sigma_\omega^2(t)} dt \quad \text{s.t. (1)}$$

By choosing the function space for $w^\omega : \mathcal{T} \mapsto \mathcal{W}$ such that we allow Borel measures $\zeta^\omega(\mathcal{T})$ on $\mathcal{T} = [t_0, t_f]$ as solutions, we can define designs ζ^ω via $d\zeta^\omega = w^\omega(t)dt$ and work with

$$\min_{x(t),p} \frac{1}{2} \sum_{\omega=1}^{n_\omega} \int_{t_0}^{t_f} \frac{(\eta^\omega(t) - h^\omega(x(t)))^2}{\sigma_\omega^2(t)} d\zeta^\omega \quad \text{s.t. (1)} \tag{5}$$

There is a large variety of algorithms to solve (4), and of alternative formulations, compare [47] for a recent survey.

2.3. Optimal Control Problems

We consider an optimal control (OC) problem of the following form

$$\min_{x(t), u: \mathcal{T} \mapsto \mathcal{U}} M(x(t_f)) \quad \text{s.t. (1)} \tag{6}$$

with a Mayer term as an objective function. Note that we omit mixed path and control constraints and other possible and practically relevant extensions in the interest of a clearer presentation. The objective function $M(\cdot)$ comprises the main goal of the control task under uncertainty, such as minimizing the deviation from a target state or minimizing the number of cancer cells, and may of course also contain a Lagrange term by adding an additional state variable. Again, there is a large variety of algorithms to solve such control problems, comprehending dynamic programming, Pontryagin's maximum principle, or direct methods, compare, e.g., [48,49].

2.4. Optimal Experimental Design Problems

We see the optimal experimental design (OED) problem as an optimal control problem with a particular structure, as suggested in [50]. The degrees of freedom in experimental design are the control functions u and the sampling decisions (or weights) w, which have been assumed to be fixed in Section 2.2. The control can be used to excite the system dynamics, and hence also the sensitivities. The sampling chooses time points or intervals with much information on the sensitivity of the model response with respect to the model parameters. We assume u to be fixed on the level of the experimental design problem for reasons to be discussed later, therefore we concentrate from now on on w as the only degree of freedom. The objective of experimental design is maximizing information gain. With the sensitivities (2), we can define the Fisher Information Matrix (FIM) as

$$F_d(t_f) = \sum_{\omega=1}^{n_\omega} \sum_{i=1}^{N} w_i^\omega \left(h_x^\omega \left(x(t_i) \right) G(t_i) \right)^T \left(h_x^\omega \left(x(t_i) \right) G(t_i) \right) \quad \in \mathbb{R}^{n_p \times n_p} \tag{7}$$

for the discrete setting of (4) and as $F(\xi)$ via the Borel measure

$$F(\xi) = \sum_{\omega=1}^{n_\omega} \int_{t_0}^{t_f} \left(h_x^\omega \left(x(t) \right) G(t) \right)^T \left(h_x^\omega \left(x(t) \right) G(t) \right) d\xi^\omega \quad \in \mathbb{R}^{n_p \times n_p} \tag{8}$$

for the continuous measurement setting of (5).

Minimizing the uncertainty of state and parameter estimates, or maximizing information gain, can now be quantified via a scalar function $\phi(\cdot)$ of the FIM or its inverse, the variance-covariance matrix. A list of different objective functions (criteria), such as trace, determinant or maximum eigenvalue can be found, e.g., in [24]. To limit the amount of measurement, either an economic penalty in the objective as suggested in [50] can be used, or a normalization via constraints, e.g.,

$$1 = \sum_{i=1}^{N} w_i^\omega \tag{9}$$

for all ω and the discrete setting of (4) and as

$$1 = \int_{t_0}^{t_f} d\xi^\omega \tag{10}$$

for all ω and the continuous measurement setting of (5). Based on our assumptions and considerations, we define the OED problem with fixed u as

$$\min_{x(t),G(t),F_d(t_f),w \in \mathcal{W}^{n_\omega N}} \phi(F_d(t_f)) \quad \text{s.t. (1,2,7,9)} \tag{11}$$

for the case of a discrete measurement grid and as

$$\min_{x(t),G(t),F(\xi),\xi} \phi(F(\xi)) \quad \text{s.t. (1,2,8,10)} \tag{12}$$

for the continuous measurement flow. Problems (11) and (12) can be solved numerically with the same methods as general optimal control problems, and with specialized ones that take the structure of the derivatives and sensitivities into account, [51]. Our assumption of a fixed u and the specific way w enters the right hand side allow an even more efficient approach, in which the expensive calculation of the states x and G is decoupled from the optimization over x and F_d, see Algorithm 1.

Algorithm 1 OED

Input: Fixed p and u, initial values $x(t_0)$, $G(t_0)$, possible measurement times $\{t_1, \dots, t_N\} \subset [t_0, t_f]$

1: Solve IVP ((1) and (2)) to obtain $x(\cdot)$ and $G(\cdot)$

2: Solve $\displaystyle\min_{F_d(t), w \in \mathcal{W}^{n_\omega N}} \phi(F_d(t_f))$ s.t. (7,9)

This decoupling is not the main motivation for our approach to optimize sequentially over u and w, but it should be exploited and might be an argument for time-critical processes.

Algorithm 1 operates with a (fine) time grid of possible time points that can be chosen to take a measurement. If one wants to leave the exact timings $t_i \in \mathbb{R}$ as degrees of freedom, one can apply a time transformation (switching time optimization), as suggested and discussed in the context of mixed-integer optimal control, e.g., in [52–54] with stage lengths $T_i := t_{i+1} - t_i$. The variables T_i become additional optimization variables, integration of x and G is performed on the interval $[0, 1]$ and the dynamics ((1) and (2)) are scaled according to

$$\dot{x}(t) = T_i \, f(x(t), u(t), p), \qquad x(t_0) = x_0(p), \tag{13}$$

$$\dot{G}(t) = T_i \, (f_x(\hat{x}(t), u(t), p) G(t) + f_p(\hat{x}(t), u(t), p)), \quad G(t_0) = \frac{dx_0(p)}{dp}. \tag{14}$$

Also continuity conditions at times t_i need to be included, and a constraint like $\sum_{i=0}^{N} T_i = t_f$ for fixed t_f. The advantage of using ((13) and (14)) is the independence of an a priori grid. However, this comes at the price of not being able to decouple the calculation of x and G from w and F any more, of higher computational costs due to the extra variables, an increased nonconvexity of the dynamics, and possibly not practically realizable (e.g., irrational) measurement times $t_i \in \mathbb{R}$. Therefore we prefer to use Algorithm 1 with a fine grid of possible measurement times.

3. A Feedback Optimal Control Algorithm With Optimal Measurement Times

We start by formulating the main algorithm, before we have a closer look at the role of optimal measurement times and one possible extension, the consideration of robustness.

As an alternative to a dual control approach which incorporates the system excitement, an optimizing control with respect to the control objective, and possibly also the choice of optimal measurement times into one single optimization problem, we propose a decoupled dual control approach. We formulate it for a shrinking horizon $[\tau, t_f]$ with respect to the control and experimental design tasks, and an expanding horizon $[t_0, \tau]$ with respect to state and parameter estimation, which can be easily adapted to a moving horizon setting if appropriate.

The algorithm iterates over time with a "current time" τ_i. It solves three subproblems that have been introduced in Section 2. The solution of the optimal control problem (6) provides a control $u^*(\cdot)$ which optimizes with respect to the main control objective. This control is applied until the next update at time τ_{i+1}. This time point τ_{i+1} is calculated by means of an optimal experimental design problem (11) as the first time point from a given fine grid of possible measurement points on which the calculated measurement weight $w^*_{k\text{new}}$ is strictly positive. At this time a new measurement is performed, with a subsequent estimation of states and parameters. Based on the modified parameters, a new optimal control is calculated, based on the modified parameters and control, new measurement weights are calculated and so forth. Naturally, previous solutions can and should be used as initialization to speed up the calculations. Depending on the time scales of the process and the calculation times, there usually is a small time gap in which the old controls need to be applied. See, e.g., [17], for details on how to deal with this situation.

Figure 1 visualizes the start of one loop to the start of the next loop of Algorithm 2 applied to the Lotka-Volterra fishing example which is described and discussed in detail in Section 4. In Figure 1a an optimal control problem is solved with the initial values $\hat{x}(15)$ and $\hat{p}$ on the interval

[15,30]. The initial values are obtained from a state and parameter estimation performed on the interval [0,15] with measurement time points derived from a optimal experimental design problem. The uncertainty tubes around the two trajectories are created by 100 simulations with parameter values randomly chosen from a normal distribution with the estimated parameters and corresponding uncertainties as mean and variance. Next, an optimal experimental design problem is solved for the optimal control strategy $u^*(t)$ and the associated solution $\hat{x}^*(t)$ obtaining optimal measurement time points on the interval [15,30] (see Figure 1b). From the optimal design w^* the time point τ_1 is chosen for which the corresponding entry $w_j^* > 0$ is the first strictly positive one. In Figure 1c the optimal control u^* is applied to the real system until time point τ_1 at which a measurement is performed and the parameters and the initial states are re-estimated with the additional measurements. With the updated values we are back at the start of the algorithm's loop and a new optimal control problem is solved with the updated values on the receding time horizon $[\tau_1, 30]$ shown in Figure 1d. For the uncertainty tubes again 100 simulations with parameter values sampled from a normal distribution with updated values for the mean and the variance were used.

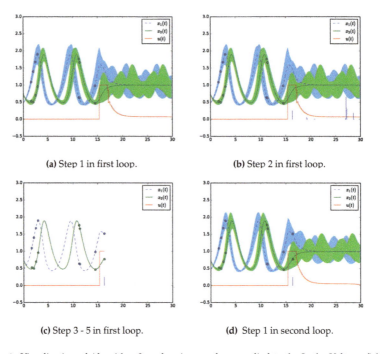

(a) Step 1 in first loop.   (b) Step 2 in first loop.

(c) Step 3 - 5 in first loop.   (d) Step 1 in second loop.

Figure 1. Visualization of Algorithm 2 performing one loop applied to the Lotka-Volterra fishing example. In Figure 1a the first step, solving an optimal control problem, of Algorithm 2 is performed on the time interval [15,30] with initial values from a parameter and state estimation on the interval [0,15] with measurements from an optimal experimental design problem. The uncertainty tubes are computed from 100 simulations with parameter samples from a normal distribution with the estimated parameters and uncertainties as mean and variance. In Figure 1b an optimal experimental design is computed on on $t \in [15,30]$ with the optimal control strategy. The strictly positive optimal sampling weights are visualized as vertical lines. Next, the optimal control strategy is performed until time point t_i at which the first sampling weight is strictly positive and a measurement is taken. Afterwards a state and parameter estimation is performed (Figure 1c). The loop starts again with solving a OCP on $[t_i,30]$ with the estimated values. The new optimal control strategy is shown in Figure 1d with uncertainty tubes computed from 100 simulations with updated mean and variance.

Algorithm 2 FOCoed

Input: Initial guess $\hat{p}$, initial values $x(t_0), G(t_0)$, possible measurement times $\{t_1, \ldots, t_N\} \subset [t_0, t_f]$

    Initialize sampling counter $i = 0$, measurement grid counter $k = 0$ and "current time" $\tau_0 = t_0$

    while stopping criterion not fulfilled **do**

1: Solve OC problem (6) on the horizon $[\tau_i, t_f]$, obtain $u^*(\cdot), \hat{x}^*(\cdot)$

2: Solve OED problem (11) on the horizon $[\tau_i, t_f]$ (hence w_j^ω fixed for $j \leq k$), obtain $w^* \in \mathcal{W}^{n_\omega N}$

3: Set $i = i + 1$, k^{new} such that $w_{k^{\text{new}}}^{\omega,*} > 0$ and $w_j^{\omega,*} = 0 \; \forall \, k < j < k^{\text{new}}$. Set $k = k^{\text{new}}$ and $\tau_i = t_k$

4: Apply u^* on $[\tau_{i-1}, \tau_i]$, measure function ω at τ_i

5: Solve SPE problem (4) on the horizon $[t_0, \tau_i]$, obtain $\hat{p}, \hat{x}(t)$

    end while

6: Solve OC problem (6) on the horizon $[\tau_i, t_f]$

The stopping criterion is formulated in a general way as it usually depends on the experimenter's choice. Possible criteria are a minimum amount of uncertainty reduction, a fixed number of measurements, or an economic penalization term as proposed in [50].

3.1. Finite Support Designs

We look at the role of finite support for optimal experimental designs in more detail, as this will allow us to choose measurement points (and hence the sampling grid) in an optimal way. It is an interesting question how optimal solutions of the discrete OED problem (11) and of the continuous analogue (12) relate to one another. The answer is given by the following theorem, which states that to every optimal design there is a discrete design with finitely many measurement points resulting in the same Fisher information matrix. This is obviously a justification for our iterative approach in Algorithm 2, using a finite number of measurements. Theorem 1 presents a property of optimal designs for the Fisher information matrix.

Theorem 1. *Let $n_\omega = 1$. For any optimal design ξ of the OED problem (12) resulting in a nonsingular Fisher information matrix of the SPE problem (5) there exist a finite number N of measurement time points $\{t_1, t_2, \ldots, t_N\} \subset \mathcal{T}$ and positive real numbers $w_1, w_2, \ldots, w_N$ with $\sum_{i=1}^{N} w_i = 1$ such that*

$$F(\xi) = F_d(t_f) = \sum_{i=1}^{N} w_i \left(h_x(x(t_i)) G(t_i) \right)^T h_x(x(t_i)) G(t_i)$$

with the bounds

$$\left\lfloor \frac{n_p}{n_\eta} \right\rfloor \leq N \leq \frac{n_p(n_p + 1)}{2}. \tag{15}$$

n_p is the number of parameters and n_η is the dimension of the model response $h(x)$.

A proof can be found in [55,56]. It is based on the set of all matrices of the form (8) being a compact, convex set. The upper bound results from the Theorem of Carathéodory [21,24] and the solution of the dual problem which is located at the boundary of the convex set [57]. The lower bound is based on the assumption of $F_d(t_f)$ having full rank n_p, and every update $w_i \left(h_x(x(t_i)) G(t_i) \right)^T h_x(x(t_i)) G(t_i)$ having rank n_η. Our setting is slightly more general, as we allow n_ω different measurement functions. However, the result carries over.

Corollary 1. *For any $n_\omega \geq 1$ Theorem 1 applies with $n_\eta = \sum_{\omega=1}^{n_\omega} n_\eta^\omega$.*

Proof. The Minkowski sum of convex, compact sets is again a convex, compact set, and hence the argument for the representability due to the Theorem of Carathéodory and the upper bound are still valid. The maximum rank of the matrix update $\sum_{\omega=1}^{n_\omega} w_i^\omega \left(h_x^\omega(x(t_i))G(t_i) \right)^T h_x^\omega(x(t_i))G(t_i)$ at time t_i is $\sum_{\omega=1}^{n_\omega} n_\eta^\omega$. The lower bound on N is the quotient of the assumed full rank n_p and this sum. □

This corollary directly implies that to every optimal solution of the continuous OED problem (12) there is an equivalent solution of the discrete OED problem (11).

We are further interested in (a posteriori) characterizing the optimal measurement times t_i with corresponding $w_i^\omega > 0$. We make the following assumptions. Let an optimal solution (x^*, G^*, w^*, μ^*) of the optimization problem (12) with $\mathcal{W} = [w^{min}, w^{max}]$ be given. Here $\mu^{\omega,*}$ is the Lagrange multiplier of the constraint (9). Let $F^{*-1}(t_f)$ exist. We call

$$\Pi^\omega(t) := F^{*-1}(t_f) \, (h_x^\omega(x(t))G(t))^T h_x^\omega(x(t))G(t) \, F^{*-1}(t_f) \in \mathbb{R}^{n_p \times n_p} \tag{16}$$

the *global information gain* matrix. Let $\phi(F(t_f)^{-1}) = \text{trace}(F^{-1}(t_f))$ be the objective function of the OED problem (12) (for other objectives similar expressions can be found in [50]).

Under the above assumptions in [50] it is shown that

$$w^{\omega,*}(t) = \begin{cases} w^{min} & \text{if} \quad \text{trace}\,(\Pi^\omega(t)) < \mu^{\omega,*}, \\ w^{max} & \text{if} \quad \text{trace}\,(\Pi^\omega(t)) > \mu^{\omega,*}. \end{cases} \tag{17}$$

The proof is based on an application of Pontryagin's maximum principle, exploiting constant adjoint variables, and matrix calculus.

We want to join Theorem 1 with this insight, and look at the special case of $w^{min} = 0, w^{max} = 1$. One particular case may arise when the lower bound on the number of support points in Theorem 1, i.e., $\left\lceil \frac{n_p}{n_\eta} \right\rceil$ is equal to one. For one single measurement it can happen that $w_i^\omega = 1$ for one index, while otherwise the normalization constraint (9) ensures that all $w_i^\omega \in [0, 1)$. For this particular case we define $\nu^{\omega,*}$ to be the maximum of $\mu^{\omega,*}$ (the Lagrange multiplier of the normalization constraint) and of the upper bound constraint $w_i^\omega \leq 1$. In most cases, however, $\nu^* = \mu^{\omega,*}$.

Lemma 1. *For any optimal design ξ of the OED problem (12) resulting in a nonsingular Fisher information matrix of the SPE problem (5) there exist a finite number N of measurement time points $\{t_1, t_2, \ldots, t_N\} \subset \mathcal{T}$ and positive real numbers $w_1^\omega, w_2^\omega, \ldots, w_N^\omega$ with $\sum_{i=1}^N w_i^\omega = 1$ for all $\omega \in 1, \ldots, n_\omega$ such that*

$$\text{trace}(\Pi^\omega(t)) \leq \nu^{\omega,*} \quad \forall \quad t \in [t_0, t_f]. \tag{18}$$

Proof. Corollary 1 states the existence and optimality of such a design. Assuming there exists $t_i \in \mathcal{T}$ with $\text{trace}(\Pi^\omega(t_i)) > \nu^{\omega,*}$, it directly follows $w_i^\omega = w^{max} = 1$ and with the normalization (9) that $w_j^\omega = 0 \, \forall j \neq i$. The local impact on the optimal objective value is given by $\text{trace}(\Pi^\omega(t_i))$, the assumption of this value being strictly larger than both multipliers is hence a contradiction to optimization theory which states that the Lagrange multiplier of the active constraints give a local estimate for the change in the optimal objective function value. □

3.2. Robustification

As mentioned in the Introduction, there are many possible extensions to Algorithm 2. Highlighting its flexibility, we exemplarily look at a possible robustification of the optimal control and of the optimal experimental design problem.

The optimization problems (6) and (12) depend on given values of the model parameters and the computed control and measurement strategies are only optimal for the specific parameter values. If the true parameter values are known or the estimated parameter values are equal to the true values the optimal strategies can be applied to the real process without loss of optimality. However, in most cases the true parameter values are not exactly known. Then, the uncertainty of parameters in the spirit of confidence regions should be included into the optimization formulations to robustify the computed optimal control and measurement strategies. We apply a robustification approach suggested in [42,43,58]. The idea is to formulate a min-max optimization problem in which the maximal value of the objective function over the parameters' confidence region is minimized. Applying Taylor expansion with respect to the parameters, a computationally feasible approximation based on first derivatives is used. It aims at preferring solutions with a "flat objective function", i.e., which is not too sensitive with respect to the parameter value p.

Again, we assume that the parameters are normally distributed random variables with mean $\hat{p}$ and variance $\Sigma_{\hat{p}}$. The confidence region of $\hat{p}$ with confidence quantile γ is defined as the set

$$\{p : \|p - \hat{p}\|_{2,\Sigma^{-1}} \leq \gamma\} \tag{19}$$

where the positive definite matrix Σ^{-1} induces the norm $\|p\|_{2,\Sigma^{-1}} := (p^T \Sigma^{-1} p)^{\frac{1}{2}}$. Now, the OED objective function in (12) is augmented to

$$\phi(F(\xi; \hat{p})) + \gamma \left\| \frac{d}{dp} \phi(F(\xi; \hat{p})) \right\|_{2,\Sigma} \tag{20}$$

and similarly the robust OC objective function is defined as

$$M(x(t_f); \hat{p}) + \gamma \left\| \frac{d}{dp} M(x(t_f); \hat{p}) \right\|_{2,\Sigma}. \tag{21}$$

No further modifications to Algorithm 2 are necessary. Note that the norms are evaluated pointwise, as Mayer term and the FIM in Problems (6) and (12) are evaluated at time t_f. However, the analysis of Section 3.1 can not be applied in a straightforward way due to the derivative term in the objective function (20), as the weights may jump as $\hat{p}$ changes locally. Intuition and numerical results hint into the direction that also for the robust case discrete designs are optimal, probably with the same bounds on the number of support points. But we only conjecture this and do not have a proof.

4. Numerical Examples

In this section we apply Algoritm 2 to the Lotka-Volterra fishing benchmark problem demonstrating the performance of the algorithm and separately analyze optimal finite support designs.

4.1. Lotka-Volterra Fishing Benchmark Problem

The Lotka-Volterra example is chosen as a well studied dynamic system representing the relation between two competing populations. The model can be modified analyzing disease spreading in an epidemiological context [59] or technological forecasting of stock markets [60] such that the model combines medical, biological and economical interests. The optimal control (OC) and optimal experimental design problem (OED) problem of the Lotka-Volterra fishing example are introduced and described in the following.

The goal of the OC problem is an optimal fishing strategy $u^*(t)$ that brings the prey $x_1(t)$ and predator $x_2(t)$ populations into a steady state (22d), by penalizing deviations from the steady state over the whole time horizon $[t_0, t_f]$. The optimal control problem of type (6) is

$$\min_{x(t),u(t)} \quad x_3(t_\mathrm{f}) \tag{22a}$$

$$\text{s.t.} \quad \dot{x}_1(t) = \ p_1\,x_1(t) - p_2\,x_1(t)\,x_2(t) - c_0\,x_1(t)\,u(t), \tag{22b}$$

$$\dot{x}_2(t) = -p_3\,x_2(t) + p_4\,x_1(t)\,x_2(t) - c_1\,x_2(t)\,u(t), \tag{22c}$$

$$\dot{x}_3(t) = (x_1(t)-1)^2 + (x_2(t)-1)^2, \tag{22d}$$

$$x(t_0) = x_0, \tag{22e}$$

$$u(t) \ \in [0,1]. \tag{22f}$$

The Lotka-Volterra OED problem is of type (11) and defined as

$$\min_{x(t),G(t),F_d(t_\mathrm{f}),w^1,w^2} \quad \operatorname{trace}(F_d^{-1}(t_\mathrm{f})) \tag{23a}$$

$$\text{s.t.} \quad \dot{x}_1(t) \ = \ p_1\,x_1(t) - p_2\,x_1(t)\,x_2(t), \tag{23b}$$

$$\dot{x}_2(t) \ = -p_3\,x_2(t) + p_4\,x_1(t)\,x_2(t), \tag{23c}$$

$$\dot{G}_{11}(t) = f_{x11}\,G_{11}(t) + f_{x12}\,G_{21}(t) + f_{p11}, \tag{23d}$$

$$\dot{G}_{12}(t) = f_{x11}\,G_{12}(t) + f_{x12}\,G_{22}(t) + f_{p12}, \tag{23e}$$

$$\dot{G}_{13}(t) = f_{x11}\,G_{13}(t) + f_{x12}\,G_{23}(t), \tag{23f}$$

$$\dot{G}_{14}(t) = f_{x11}\,G_{14}(t) + f_{x12}\,G_{24}(t), \tag{23g}$$

$$\dot{G}_{21}(t) = f_{x21}\,G_{11}(t) + f_{x22}\,G_{21}(t), \tag{23h}$$

$$\dot{G}_{22}(t) = f_{x21}\,G_{12}(t) + f_{x22}\,G_{22}(t), \tag{23i}$$

$$\dot{G}_{23}(t) = f_{x21}\,G_{13}(t) + f_{x22}\,G_{23}(t) + f_{p23}, \tag{23j}$$

$$\dot{G}_{24}(t) = f_{x21}\,G_{14}(t) + f_{x22}\,G_{24}(t) + f_{p24}, \tag{23k}$$

$$F_{11}(t_i) = F_{11}(t_{i-1}) + w_i^1\,G_{11}^2(t_i) \qquad\quad + w_i^2\,G_{21}^2(t_i), \tag{23l}$$

$$F_{12}(t_i) = F_{12}(t_{i-1}) + w_i^1\,G_{11}(t_i)\,G_{12}(t_i) + w_i^2\,G_{21}(t_i)\,G_{22}(t_i), \tag{23m}$$

$$F_{13}(t_i) = F_{13}(t_{i-1}) + w_i^1\,G_{11}(t_i)\,G_{13}(t_i) + w_i^2\,G_{21}(t_i)\,G_{23}(t_i), \tag{23n}$$

$$F_{14}(t_i) = F_{14}(t_{i-1}) + w_i^1\,G_{11}(t_i)\,G_{14}(t_i) + w_i^2\,G_{21}(t_i)\,G_{24}(t_i), \tag{23o}$$

$$F_{22}(t_i) = F_{22}(t_{i-1}) + w_i^1\,G_{12}^2(t_i) \qquad\quad + w_i^2\,G_{22}^2(t_i), \tag{23p}$$

$$F_{23}(t_i) = F_{23}(t_{i-1}) + w_i^1\,G_{12}(t_i)\,G_{13}(t_i) + w_i^2\,G_{22}(t_i)\,G_{23}(t_i), \tag{23q}$$

$$F_{24}(t_i) = F_{24}(t_{i-1}) + w_i^1\,G_{12}(t_i)\,G_{14}(t_i) + w_i^2\,G_{22}(t_i)\,G_{24}(t_i), \tag{23r}$$

$$F_{33}(t_i) = F_{33}(t_{i-1}) + w_i^1\,G_{13}^2(t_i) \qquad\quad + w_i^2\,G_{23}^2(t_i), \tag{23s}$$

$$F_{34}(t_i) = F_{34}(t_{i-1}) + w_i^1\,G_{13}(t_i)\,G_{14}(t_i) + w_i^2\,G_{23}(t_i)\,G_{24}(t_i), \tag{23t}$$

$$F_{44}(t_i) = F_{44}(t_{i-1}) + w_i^1\,G_{14}^2(t_i) \qquad\quad + w_i^2\,G_{24}^2(t_i), \tag{23u}$$

$$x(t_0) \ = x_0, \tag{23v}$$

$$F_{ij}(t_0) = 0 \quad i,j \in \{1,2,3,4\} \text{ and } i \le j, \tag{23w}$$

$$G_{ij}(t_0) = 0 \quad i \in \{1,2\},\ j \in \{1,2,3,4\}, \tag{23x}$$

$$\sum_{i=0}^{N} w_i^\omega \le 1 \quad \omega \in \{1,2\}, \tag{23y}$$

$$w_i^\omega \quad \in [0,1] \tag{23z}$$

On the time grid $t \in [t_0, t_f]$ with

$$f_{x11} = \partial f_1(t)/\partial x_1 = p_1 - p_2\, x_2, \tag{24a}$$

$$f_{x12} = -p_2\, x_1, \tag{24b}$$

$$f_{x21} = p_4\, x_2, \tag{24c}$$

$$f_{x22} = p_4\, x_1 - p_3, \tag{24d}$$

$$f_{p11} = \partial f_1(t)/\partial p_1 = x_1, \tag{24e}$$

$$f_{p12} = -x_1\, x_2, \tag{24f}$$

$$f_{p23} = -x_2, \tag{24g}$$

$$f_{p24} = x_1\, x_2. \tag{24h}$$

The solution of problem (23) provides an optimal sampling design minimizing the uncertainties of the parameters p_1, p_2, p_3 and p_4. The right upper entries of the Fisher information matrix (FIM) are considered as differential states in the optimization problem instead of all matrix entries due to symmetry properties of the FIM. Explicit values of the time horizon, the initial states, the parameters and the constants chosen for the numerical computations are given in the next subsection.

4.2. Software and Experimental Settings

Algorithm 2 is implemented as a prototype in the open-source software tool CasADi [61]. We used the version 3.1.0 together with Python 2.7.6. The finite dimensional nonlinear programs resulting from discretizing the optimal control problem (6) and optimal experimental design problem (11) are solved with IPOPT [62]. The parameter estimation problems are solved by a Gauss-Newton algorithm using IPOPT. The derivatives needed for the optimization problems and their robustifications are efficiently generated within CasADi using automatic differentiation [61]. In Subsection 4.3 the system of ODEs is solved using the in-house fixed-step explicit Runge-Kutta integrator and a single shooting method with a stepsize of 0.15. For the first state and parameter estimation problem on the time interval [0,15] the initial guess is $p = (p_1, p_2, p_3, p_4, x_1(0), x_2(0))^T = (1.5, 1.5, 1.5, 1.5, 0.0, 0.0)$. We assume that both states $h_1(t_i) = x_1(t_i)$ and $h_2(t_i) = x_2(t_i)$ can be measured and that no fishing is permitted on $t \in [0, 15]$. The pseudo-measurements are derived from a simulation with the true parameters plus a measurement error $\varepsilon_i \sim \mathcal{N}(\left(\begin{smallmatrix}0\\0\end{smallmatrix}\right), \left(\begin{smallmatrix}0.03^2 & 0\\0 & 0.03^2\end{smallmatrix}\right))$ according to Equation (3). For the OED problems only the uncertainty of the parameters is considered.

For the analysis of finite support designs in Subsection 4.4 the ODE system is solved with CVodes from the SUNDIALS suite [63] and a multiple shooting method with stepsize $h(= 12/500)$. The continuous version of the OED problem (23) is computed on the time grid [0,12] with $p = (p_1, p_2, p_3, p_4) = (1, 1, 1, 1)$. In both examples the discretization of the optimization variable $u(t)$ coincides with the time grid of the ODE problem.

4.3. Three Versions of Algorithm FOCoed applied to the Lotka-Volterra fishing problem

We apply three versions of Algorithm 2 to the control problem (22a) to stress the relevance of optimal measurement time points and the influence of parameter uncertainty during optimization.

- *with_OED*. This is Algorithm 2, i.e., using measurement time points from non-robust OED.
- *without_OED*. The OED problem in Step 2 of Algorithm 2 is omitted, and an equidistant time grid is used for measurements.
- *with_r_OED*. The OC problem in Step 1 and the OED problem in Step 2 of Algorithm 2 are replaced with their robust counterparts as described in Section 3.2.

In the following the experimental setting is described independently of the chosen version of Algorithm 2. The experiment is performed on the time interval [0,30]. From 0 to 15 a first state and parameter estimation with seven measurements, initial guesses $p_{ini} = (1.5, 1.5, 1.5, 1.5, 0.0., 0.0)^T$ is performed. From time point $t = 15$, Algorithm 2 is performed with the estimated parameter values $\hat{p}$, the state values $\hat{x}(15) = (\hat{x}_1(15), \hat{x}_2(15))^T$ and the objective function $\phi(\cdot) = \text{trace}(F^{-1}(t_f))$ of the optimization problem (11).

For a quantitative statement the three versions of Algorithm 2 are repeated 50 times with the normally distributed measurement error ε_i used for the generation of pseudo-measurements. The averaged estimated parameter values and the corresponding uncertainties after $t = 15$ and $t = 30$ are presented in Table 1 for the three different algorithm versions *with_r_OED*, *with_OED* and *without_OED*. The first column shows the objective function value of the optimal control problem (22) solved on $t \in [15, 30]$ with the true parameter values and the initial state values $x(15) = (1.25847, 0.473369, 0)^T$ as the reference solution. The last row additionally presents the averaged objective function values of the three algorithm versions and the last three columns contain the relative uncertainty and objective function value improvements between the three algorithm versions.

First of all, Table 1 indicates that the three versions of Algorithm 2 provide estimated parameters next to the true parameter values but the results qualitatively differ by means of the resulting parameter uncertainties and the optimal control objective function values. The use of measurement time points from optimal experimental designs (*with_OED*) compared to equidistant time points (*without_OED*) improves the parameter uncertainty by 15% after $t = 15$ and by 34% after $t = 30$ on average. The robustification of the OC and OED problems (*with_r_OED*) results in an improvement of the parameter uncertainties compared to version *without_OED* of 15% after $t = 15$ and of 36% after $t = 30$ on average and compared to the non-robust version *with_OED* of 0.26% after $t = 15$ and of 2.52% after $t = 30$ on average. The objective function of the optimal control problem is reduced by approximately 8%, respectively 10%, using version *with_r_OED* or version *with_OED* compared to version *without_OED*. The robustification of Algorithm 2 has a minor averaged improvement of 0.41%.

Table 1. Averaged estimated parameter values with their uncertainties and the objective function value ($M_{LV} = x_3(30)$) after 50 runs of the optimal control problem (22) solved with three versions of Algorithm 2 (*with_r_OED* (A) , *with_OED* (B) , *without_OED* (C)). $I_{ij}(\%)$ is the relative uncertainty and objective value improvement after $t = 15$ and $t = 30$ of column i compared to column j. Column *OC* contains the true parameter values with which the optimal control problem (22) is solved on $t \in [15, 30]$ and the resulting objective function value.

	At $t = 15$								
	OC	with_r_OED (A)		with_OED (B)		without_OED (C)				
	value	value	σ^2	value	σ^2	value	σ^2	I_{AC}	I_{BC}	I_{AB}
p_1	1.000	1.0074	0.0003377	0.9925	0.0003300	1.0293	0.0005090	33.65	35.17	-2.33
p_2	1.000	1.0085	0.0005540	0.9954	0.0005404	1.0267	0.0005313	-4.27	-1.71	-2.52
p_3	1.000	0.9935	0.0005861	1.0073	0.0006063	0.9758	0.0006139	4.53	1.24	3.33
p_4	1.000	0.9959	0.0006466	1.0053	0.0006635	0.9762	0.0008780	26.36	24.43	2.55
	At $t = 30$								
		with_r_OED (A)		with_OED (B)		without_OED (C)				
	value	value	σ^2	value	σ^2	value	σ^2	I_{AC}	I_{BC}	I_{AB}
p_1	1.000	1.0066	0.0002414	0.9974	0.0002418	1.0082	0.0004214	42.71	42.62	0.17
p_2	1.000	1.0065	0.0003639	1.0004	0.0003706	1.0069	0.0004624	21.30	19.85	1.81
p_3	1.000	0.9936	0.0003472	1.0029	0.0003582	0.9924	0.0005068	31.49	29.32	3.07
p_4	1.000	0.9958	0.0003575	1.0014	0.0003764	0.9937	0.0006837	47.71	44.95	5.02
M_{LV}	0.714	0.724		0.727		0.790		9.62	7.97	0.41

Figure 2 shows exemplary the solution of the Lotka-Volterra fishing problem computed with the three versions *with_r_OED*, *with_OED* and *without_OED* of Algorithm 2.

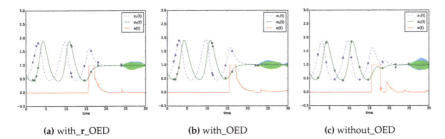

| (a) with_r_OED | (b) with_OED | (c) without_OED |

Figure 2. Visualization of three versions (*with_r_OED*, *with_OED* and *without_OED*) of the feedback optimal control Algorithm 2 applied to the Lotka-Volterra fishing example. The algorithm is performed on the time interval [15,30]. On the time interval [0,15] seven measurements are taken for a state and parameter estimation. The estimated parameters with the corresponding uncertainties and initial states serve as input for the algorithm. In Figure 2a the robust version and in Figure 2b the non-robust version of Algorithm 2 is used with measurement time points from optimal experimental designs. Figure 2c presents the solution of algorithm 2 with measurements taken on an equidistant time grid. After the last measurement time point uncertainty tubes are computed by 100 simulations with parameter values sampled from a normal distribution with the estimated parameters as mean $\hat{p} = [0.982, 0.990, 1.015, 1.023]$ and variance $\Sigma_{\hat{p}} = diag(0.000214, 0.000321, 0.000347, 0.000351)$ in Figure 2a, $\hat{p} = [1.014, 0.998, 0.981, 0.977]$ and variance $\Sigma_{\hat{p}} = diag(0.000231, 0.000325, 0.000319, 0.000334)$ in Figure 2b and $\hat{p} = [1.031, 1.047, 0.977, 0.978]$ and $\Sigma_{\hat{p}} = diag(0.000413, 0.000470, 0.000463, 0.000636)$ in Figure 2c.

4.4. Analyzing Finite Support Designs of Optimal Experimental Design Problems

In this section we demonstrate the theoretical result of Lemma 1 on the *Lotka-Volterra optimal experimental design problem.*

The optimal solution $w^{1*}(t)$ and $w^{2*}(t)$ of the OED problem are plotted in Figure 3 together with the information gain matrices

$$\Pi^1(t) = F^{-1}(t) \begin{pmatrix} G_{11}^2 & G_{11}\,G_{12} & G_{11}\,G_{13} & G_{11}\,G_{14} \\ G_{11}\,G_{12} & G_{12}^2 & G_{12}\,G_{13} & G_{12}\,G_{14} \\ G_{11}\,G_{13} & G_{12}\,G_{13} & G_{13}^2 & G_{13}\,G_{14} \\ G_{11}\,G_{14} & G_{12}\,G_{14} & G_{13}\,G_{14} & G_{14}^2 \end{pmatrix} F^{-1}(t)$$

and

$$\Pi^2(t) = F^{-1}(t) \begin{pmatrix} G_{21}^2 & G_{21}\,G_{22} & G_{21}\,G_{23} & G_{21}\,G_{24} \\ G_{21}\,G_{22} & G_{22}^2 & G_{22}\,G_{23} & G_{22}\,G_{24} \\ G_{21}\,G_{23} & G_{22}\,G_{23} & G_{23}^2 & G_{23}\,G_{24} \\ G_{21}\,G_{24} & G_{22}\,G_{24} & G_{23}\,G_{24} & G_{24}^2 \end{pmatrix} F^{-1}(t).$$

The Lagrange multipliers are also shown as horizontal lines in Figure 3a,b. Both Figures visualize the result of Lemma 1 such that the touching of the information gains' maxima is equivalent to a singular arc of the sampling decisions $w^1(t)$ and $w^2(t)$.

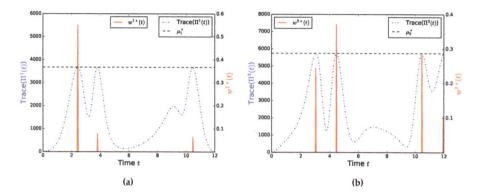

Figure 3. Visual relation between the trace of the information gain matrices $\Pi^1(t), \Pi^2(t)$, the Lagrange multipliers μ_1^*, μ_2^* and the optimized sampling decisions $w^{1*}(t), w^{1*}(t)$ of the Lotka-Volterra optimal experimental design problem. (**a**) Information gain $\Pi^1(t)$ and sampling $w^1(t)$; (**b**) Information gain $\Pi^2(t)$ and sampling $w^2(t)$.

4.5. Discussion

The measurement time points have a large impact on the uncertainty of the model parameters and consequently an impact on the optimal control solution, even if the optimizing control does not excite the system dynamics. The quantitative study of Subsection 4.3, which is summarized in Table 1, significantly shows that the optimal measurement time points taken from non-robust and robust optimal experimental designs lead to an averaged uncertainty improvement of 34%, respectively 36%, compared to equidistantly taken measurements. The qualitatively different measuring positions are visualized in Figure 2. The measurement time points of the optimal experimental designs are placed at the beginning and at the end of the time interval [0,15] in which a first state and parameter estimation is performed. During the optimal control phase starting from $t = 15$ the non-robust and robust optimal experimental designs suggest measuring once, respectively twice, at the steep descent/ascent of the populations on the interval [15,20] where a larger information content is expected compared to the equidistant time points next to the trajectories' steady state. The heterogeneity in the improvement of the parameters' uncertainties results in the used objective function $\text{trace}(F^{-1}(t_f))$ with which the averaged parameter uncertainty is minimized and not each uncertainty separately. This leads to slightly increased uncertainties of parameter p_2 after $t = 15$ by the use of optimal experimental design. A different scalar function $\phi(\cdot)$ such as the determinant or the largest eigenvalue of the information matrix might prevent this problem but this analysis is not part of the work. Besides this minor increase, the estimated parameter values are closer to the true values using optimal experimental designs in comparison to equidistant measurement time points. The uncertainty tubes in Figure 2 give an indication that the reduced uncertainty of the parameters from Algorithm 2 has an indirect positive influence on the state uncertainty leading to tighter uncertainty tubes. The visual indication is strengthened by the last row of Table 1 presenting the optimal control objective function value of the reference solution and the averaged values resulting from the three different versions (*with_r_OED*, *with_OED* and *without_OED*) of Algorithm 2. The reduced parameter uncertainties obtained from non-robust and robust optimal experimental designs lead to a 8%, respectively 10%, objective function value compared to the version *without_OED* with measurements taken on equidistant time points.

Lemma 1 is visualized for the Lotka-Volterra optimal experimental design benchmark problem in Figure 3a,b. Whenever the Lagrange multiplier μ^* is equal to the value of the information gain matrix, the sampling decision variable $w^*(t)$ is between 0 and 1.

5. Conclusions

The paper presents a novel algorithm for feedback optimal control with measurement time points for parameter estimations computed from optimal experimental design problems. It is based on a decoupled approach to dual control. The performance of the algorithm is shown by 50 runs of the Lotka-Volterra fishing benchmark example. The algorithm provides a 34% averaged reduction of parameter uncertainties while applying an optimal control strategy when measurement time points are used from optimal experimental designs compared to heuristically chosen equidistant measurement time points for parameter estimations. A robustified version of the algorithm moreover reveals a 36% averaged uncertainty reduction. Furthermore, a theoretical insight about the solution of the optimal experimental design problem is given. Therefore Pontryagin's Maximum Principle is applied to the OED problem when the sum of optimization variables is constrained by one and a connection is drawn between the trace of the information gain matrix and the Lagrange multipliers for a discrete optimal design. The algorithmic and theoretical results are demonstrated on the *Lotka-Volterra fishing* benchmark problem.

Acknowledgments: This project has received funding from the European Research Council (ERC) under the European Union's Horizon 2020 research and innovation programme (grant agreement No. 647573) and from the German BMBF under grant 05M2013 - GOSSIP, which is gratefully acknowledged.

Author Contributions: F.J. implemented the algorithm and did all numerical calculations and is the corresponding author of the article. T.T.-T.L. and S.S. contributed to the general idea, to the theoretical aspects, and to proof-reading of the manuscript.

Conflicts of Interest: The authors declare no conflict of interest. The founding sponsors had no role in the design of the study; in the collection, analyses, or interpretation of data; in the writing of the manuscript, and in the decision to publish the results.

Abbreviations

The following abbreviations are used in this manuscript:

FIM	Fisher Information Matrix
MPC	Model Predictive Control
NLP	Nonlinear Program
ODE	Ordinary Differential Equation
OC	Optimal Control
OED	Optimal Experimental Design
SPE	State and Parameter Estimation

References

1. Morari, M.; Lee, J.H. Model predictive control: Past, present and future. *Comput. Chem. Eng.* **1999**, *23*, 667–682.
2. Henson, M. Nonlinear model predictive control: Current status and future directions. *Comput. Chem. Eng.* **1998**, *23*, 187–202.
3. Rawlings, J.; Mayne, D. *Model Predictive Control: Theory and Design*; Nob Hill Publishing, LLC.: Madison, WI, USA, 2009.
4. Diehl, M.; Bock, H.; Schlöder, J. A real-time iteration scheme for nonlinear optimization in optimal feedback control. *SIAM J. Control Optim.* **2005**, *43*, 1714–1736.
5. Zavala, V.; Biegler, L. The advanced–step NMPC controller: Optimality, stability and robustness. *Automatica* **2009**, *45*, 86–93.
6. Frasch, J.; Wirsching, L.; Sager, S.; Bock, H. Mixed—Level Iteration Schemes for Nonlinear Model Predictive Control. In Proceedings of the IFAC Conference on Nonlinear Model Predictive Control, Noordwijkerhout, The Netherlands, 23–27 August 2012.
7. Frasch, J. Parallel Algorithms for Optimization of Dynamic Systems in Real-Time. Ph.D. Thesis, Otto-von-Guericke University Magdeburg, Magdeburg, Germany, 2014.

8. Steinbach, M. Fast Recursive SQP Methods for Large-Scale Optimal Control Problems. Ph.D. Thesis, Ruprecht-Karls-Universität Heidelberg, Heidelberg, Germany, 1995.
9. Frasch, J.V.; Sager, S.; Diehl, M. A parallel quadratic programming method for dynamic optimization problems. *Math. Program. Comput.* **2015**, *7*, 289–329.
10. Schlegel, M.; Marquardt, W. Detection and exploitation of the control switching structure in the solution of dynamic optimization problems. *J. Process Control* **2006**, *16*, 275–290.
11. Domahidi, A. Methods and Tools for Embedded Optimization and Control. Ph.D. Thesis, ETH Zurich, Zurich, Switzerland, 2013.
12. Houska, B.; Ferreau, H.; Diehl, M. ACADO Toolkit—An Open Source Framework for Automatic Control and Dynamic Optimization. *Optim. Control Appl. Methods* **2011**, *32*, 298–312.
13. Ferreau, H. qpOASES—An open-source implementation of the online active set strategy for fast model predictive control. In Proceedings of the Workshop on Nonlinear Model Based Control—Software and Applications, Loughborough, UK, 2007; pp. 29–30.
14. Kirches, C.; Potschka, A.; Bock, H.; Sager, S. A Parametric Active Set Method for a Subclass of Quadratic Programs with Vanishing Constraints. *Pac. J. Optim.* **2013**, *9*, 275–299.
15. Klatt, K.U.; Engell, S. Rührkesselreaktor mit Parallel- und Folgereaktion. In *Nichtlineare Regelung—Methoden, Werkzeuge, Anwendungen*; VDI-Berichte Nr. 1026; Engell, S., Ed.; VDI-Verlag: Düsseldorf, Germany, 1993; pp. 101–108.
16. Chen, H. *Stability and Robustness Considerations in Nonlinear Model Predictive Control*; Fortschr.-Ber. VDI Reihe 8 Nr. 674; VDI Verlag: Düsseldorf, Germany, 1997.
17. Houska, B.; Ferreau, H.; Diehl, M. An Auto-Generated Real-Time Iteration Algorithm for Nonlinear MPC in the Microsecond Range. *Automatica* **2011**, *47*, 2279–2285.
18. Diehl, M.; Ferreau, H.; Haverbeke, N. Efficient Numerical Methods for Nonlinear MPC and Moving Horizon Estimation. In *Nonlinear Model Predictive Control*; Magni, L.; Raimondo, D.; Allgöwer, F., Eds.; Springer Lecture Notes in Control and Information Sciences; Springer: Berlin/Heidelberg, Germany; New York, NY, USA, 2009; Volume 384, pp. 391–417.
19. Zavala, V.M.; Biegler, L.T. Nonlinear Programming Strategies for State Estimation and Model Predictive Control. In *Nonlinear Model Predictive Control*; Springer: London, UK, 2009; pp. 419–432.
20. Kirches, C.; Wirsching, L.; Sager, S.; Bock, H. Efficient numerics for nonlinear model predictive control. In *Recent Advances in Optimization and its Applications in Engineering*; Diehl, M., Glineur, F., Jarlebring, E., Michiels, W., Eds.; Springer: Berlin/Heidelberg, Germany, 2010; pp. 339–359.
21. Fedorov, V. *Theory of Optimal Experiments*; Academic Press: New York, NY, USA; London, UK, 1972.
22. Atkinson, A.; Donev, A. *Optimum Experimental Designs*; Number 8 in Oxford Statistical Sciences Series; Oxford University Press: Oxford, UK, 1992.
23. Kitsos, C. *Optimal Experimental Design for Non-Linear Models*; Springer: Heidelberg, Germany, 2013.
24. Pukelsheim, F. *Optimal Design of Experiments*; Classics in Applied Mathematics 50; Society for Industrial and Applied Mathematic (SIAM): Philadelphia, PA, USA, 2006.
25. Körkel, S.; Bauer, I.; Bock, H.; Schlöder, J. A Sequential Approach for Nonlinear Optimum Experimental Design in DAE Systems. In *Scientific Computing in Chemical Engineering II*; Springer: Berlin/Heidelberg, Germany, 1999; pp. 338–345.
26. Kreutz, C.; Timmer, J. Systems biology: Experimental design. *FEBS J.* **2009**, *276*, 923–942.
27. Stigter, J.; Vries, D.; Keesman, K. On adaptive optimal input design: A bioreactor case study. *AIChE J.* **2006**, *52*, 3290–3296.
28. Galvanin, F.; Barolo, M.; Bezzo, F. Online Model-Based Redesign of Experiments for Parameter Estimation in Dynamic Systems. *Ind. Eng. Chem. Res.* **2009**, *48*, 4415–4427.
29. Barz, T.; López Cárdenas, D.C.; Arellano-Garcia, H.; Wozny, G. Experimental evaluation of an approach to online redesign of experiments for parameter determination. *AIChE J.* **2013**, *59*, 1981–1995.
30. Qian, J.; Nadri, M.; Moroşan, P.D.; Dufour, P. Closed loop optimal experiment design for on-line parameter estimation. In Proceedings of the IEEE 2014 European Control Conference (ECC), Strasbourg, France, 24–27 June 2014; pp. 1813–1818.
31. Lemoine-Nava, R.; Walter, S.F.; Körkel, S.; Engell, S. Online optimal experimental design: Reduction of the number of variables. In Proceedings of the 11th IFAC Symposium on Dynamics and Control of Process Systems, Trondheim, Norway, 6–8 June 2016.

32. Feldbaum, A. Dual Control Theory. I. *Avtom. Telemekhanika* **1960**, *21*, 1240–1249.
33. Wittenmark, B. Adaptive dual control methods: An overview. In Proceedings of the IFAC Symposium on Adaptive Systems in Control and Signal Processing, Budapest, Hungary, 14–16 June 1995; pp. 67–72.
34. Filatov, N.M.; Unbehauen, H. *Adapive Dual Control*; Lecture Notes in Control and Information Sciences; Springer: Berlin/Heidelberg, Germany, 2004.
35. Recker, S.; Kerimoglu, N.; Harwardt, A.; Marquardt, W. On the integration of model identification and process optimization. *Comput. Aided Chem. Eng.* **2013**, *32*, 1012–1026.
36. Bavdekar, V.A.; Mesbah, A. Stochastic model predictive control with integrated experiment design for nonlinear systems. In Proceedings of the 11th IFAC Symposium on Dynamics and Control of Process Systems, Including Biosystems, Trondheim, Norway, 6–8 June 2016.
37. Telen, D.; Houska, B.; Vallerio, M.; Logist, F.; van Impe, J. A study of integrated experiment design for NMPC applied to the Droop model. *Chem. Eng. Sci.* **2017**, *160*, 370–383.
38. Lucia, S.; Andersson, J.; Brandt, H.; Diehl, M.; Engell, S. Handling uncertainty in economic nonlinear model predictive control: A comparative case study. *J. Process Control* **2014**, *24*, 1247–1259.
39. Lucia, S.; Paulen, R. Robust Nonlinear Model Predictive Control with Reduction of Uncertainty Via Robust Optimal Experiment Design. *IFAC Proc. Vol.* **2014**, *47*, 1904–1909.
40. Lucia, S.; Schliemann-Bullinger, M.; Findeisen, R.; Bullinger, E. A Set-Based Optimal Control Approach for Pharmacokinetic/Pharmacodynamic Drug Dosage Design. In Proceedings of the 11th IFAC Symposium on Dynamics and Control of Process Systems, Including Biosystems, Trondheim, Norway, 6–8 June 2016.
41. Jost, F.; Rinke, K.; Fischer, T.; Schalk, E.; Sager, S. Optimum experimental design for patient specific mathematical leukopenia models. In Proceedings of the Foundations of Systems Biology in Engineering (FOSBE) Conference, Magdeburg, Germany, 9–12 October 2016.
42. Ben-Tal, A.; Nemirovski, A. Robust Convex Optimization. *Math. Oper. Res.* **1998**, *23*, 769–805.
43. Diehl, M.; Bock, H.; Kostina, E. An approximation technique for robust nonlinear optimization. *Math. Program.* **2006**, *107*, 213–230.
44. Gjøsæter, H.; Bogstad, B.; Enberg, K.; Kovalev, Y.; Shamrai, E.A. (Eds.) Long term sustainable management of living marine resources in the Northern Seas. In Proceedings of the 17th Norwegian-Russian Symposium, Bergen, Norway, 16–17 March 2016.
45. Jana, D.; Agrawal, R.; Upadhyay, R.K.; Samanta, G. Ecological dynamics of age selective harvesting of fish population: Maximum sustainable yield and its control strategy. *Chaos Solitons Fractals* **2016**, *93*, 111–122.
46. Gerdts, M. *Optimal Control of Ordinary Differential Equations and Differential-Algebraic Equations*; University of Bayreuth: Bayreuth, Germany, 2006.
47. Kircheis, R. Structure Exploiting Parameter Estimation and Optimum Experimental Design Methods and Applications in Microbial Enhanced Oil Recovery. Ph.D. Thesis, University Heidelberg, Heidelberg, Germany, 2015.
48. Biegler, L. *Nonlinear Programming: Concepts, Algorithms, and Applications to Chemical Processes*; Series on Optimization; Society for Industrial and Applied Mathematic (SIAM): Philadelphia, PA, USA, 2010.
49. Betts, J. *Practical Methods for Optimal Control Using Nonlinear Programming*; Society for Industrial and Applied Mathematic (SIAM): Philadelphia, PA, USA, 2001.
50. Sager, S. Sampling Decisions in Optimum Experimental Design in the Light of Pontryagin's Maximum Principle. *SIAM J. Control Optim.* **2013**, *51*, 3181–3207.
51. Körkel, S. Numerische Methoden für Optimale Versuchsplanungsprobleme bei nichtlinearen DAE-Modellen. Ph.D. Thesis, Universität Heidelberg, Heidelberg, Germany, 2002.
52. Gerdts, M. A variable time transformation method for mixed-integer optimal control problems. *Optim. Control Appl. Methods* **2006**, *27*, 169–182.
53. Sager, S.; Reinelt, G.; Bock, H. Direct Methods With Maximal Lower Bound for Mixed-Integer Optimal Control Problems. *Math. Program.* **2009**, *118*, 109–149.
54. Gerdts, M.; Sager, S. Mixed-Integer DAE Optimal Control Problems: Necessary conditions and bounds. In *Control and Optimization with Differential-Algebraic Constraints*; Biegler, L., Campbell, S., Mehrmann, V., Eds.; Society for Industrial and Applied Mathematic (SIAM): Philadelphia, PA, USA, 2012; pp. 189–212.
55. Fedorov, V.; Malyutov, M. Optimal designs in regression problems. *Math. Operationsforsch. Stat.* **1972**, *3*, 281–308.

56.   La, H.C.; Schlöder, J.P.; Bock, H.G. Structure of Optimal Samples in Continuous Nonlinear Experimental Design for Parameter Estimation. In Proceedings of the 6th International Conference on High Performance Scientific Computing, Hanoi, Vietnam, 16–20 March 2015.
57.   Boyd, S.; Vandenberghe, L. *Convex Optimization*; Cambridge University Press: Cambridge, UK, 2004.
58.   Körkel, S.; Kostina, E.; Bock, H.; Schlöder, J. Numerical Methods for Optimal Control Problems in Design of Robust Optimal Experiments for Nonlinear Dynamic Processes. *Optim. Methods Softw.* **2004**, *19*, 327–338.
59.   Venturino, E. The influence of diseases on Lotka-Volterra systems. *J. Math.* **1994**, *24*, 1.
60.   Lee, S.J.; Lee, D.J.; Oh, H.S. Technological forecasting at the Korean stock market: A dynamic competition analysis using Lotka-Volterra model. *Technol. Forecast. Soc. Chang.* **2005**, *72*, 1044–1057.
61.   Andersson, J. A General-Purpose Software Framework for Dynamic Optimization. Ph.D. Thesis, Arenberg Doctoral School, KU Leuven, Leuven, Belgium, 2013.
62.   Wächter, A.; Biegler, L. On the Implementation of an Interior-Point Filter Line-Search Algorithm for Large-Scale Nonlinear Programming. *Math. Program.* **2006**, *106*, 25–57.
63.   Hindmarsh, A.; Brown, P.; Grant, K.; Lee, S.; Serban, R.; Shumaker, D.; Woodward, C. SUNDIALS: Suite of Nonlinear and Differential/Algebraic Equation Solvers. *ACM Trans. Math. Softw.* **2005**, *31*, 363–396.

Article

Performance Evaluation of Real Industrial RTO Systems

Maurício M. Câmara [1], André D. Quelhas [2] and José Carlos Pinto [1,*]

[1] Chemical Engineering Program, COPPE, Federal University of Rio de Janeiro, Cidade Universitária, Rio de Janeiro, RJ 21945-970, Brazil; mauricio@peq.coppe.ufrj.br

[2] Petrobras—Petróleo Brasileiro SA, Corporate University, Rio de Janeiro, RJ 20211-230, Brazil; quelhas@petrobras.com.br

* Correspondence: pinto@peq.coppe.ufrj.br; Tel.: +55-21-2562-8337

Academic Editor: Dominique Bonvin
Received: 4 October 2016; Accepted: 14 November 2016; Published: 22 November 2016

Abstract: The proper design of RTO systems' structure and critical diagnosis tools is neglected in commercial RTO software and poorly discussed in the literature. In a previous article, Quelhas et al. (Can J Chem Eng., 2013, 91, 652–668) have reviewed the concepts behind the two-step RTO approach and discussed the vulnerabilities of intuitive, experience-based RTO design choices. This work evaluates and analyzes the performance of industrial RTO implementations in the face of real settings regarding the choice of steady-state detection methods and parameters, the choice of adjustable model parameters and selected variables in the model adaptation problem, the convergence determination of optimization techniques, among other aspects, in the presence of real noisy data. Results clearly show the importance of a robust and careful consideration of all aspects of a two-step RTO structure, as well as of the performance evaluation, in order to have a real and undoubted improvement of process operation.

Keywords: static real-time optimization (RTO); on-line optimization; optimizing control; repeated identification and optimization; numerical methods; industrial RTO systems

1. Introduction

Real-time optimization systems (RTO) are a combined set of techniques and algorithms that continuously evaluate process operating conditions and implement business-focused decisions in order to improve process performance in an autonomous way. It relies on static real-time optimization strategies [1–5], which have been designated in the literature by real-time optimization [6], on-line optimization [7,8] and optimizing control [9], for translating a product recipe from the scheduling layer into the best set of reference values to the model predictive control (MPC) layer [10]. The two-step approach, a model-based technique, is the most common (and possibly the only) static real-time optimization strategy available in commercial RTO systems [11–13]. Its name derives from the procedure employed for determining the set of decision variables, where plant information is used to update model parameters based on the best fitting of measurements in the first step, and afterwards, the updated model is used to calculate the set of decision variable values that are assumed to lead the process to its best economic performance. RTO systems are widely used in the petrochemical industry as a part of modern day control systems [14–17], but may also be found in other sectors, such as the pulp and paper industry [18].

Great advantages are attributed to the use of a priori information in the form of a process model, and model-based techniques may present superior performance among others; generally, the more accurate the model, the better will be the RTO system performance [19,20]. Thus, such RTO applications are typically based on rigorous steady-state models of processes. However, it has long been shown that manipulation of model parameters to fit available process measurements does not necessarily guarantee the construction of an adequate model for process optimization [21,22]. For this reason, known as plant-model mismatch, some alternative procedures have been proposed (e.g., [23–26]) based on stronger mathematical requirements and constraints that guarantee the optimality of process operation. Unfortunately, these procedures demand a series of time-consuming experimental measurements in order to evaluate the gradients of a large set of functions and variables. Given the considerable impact on productivity, these implementations are virtually absent in current industrial practice. Nevertheless, commercial software is usually based on a very standard two-step structure and does not even take into account collateral improvements of this approach, such as the use of multiple datasets [27], input excitation design [28,29] or automated diagnosis [30].

In fact, plant-model mismatch is not the only vulnerability of RTO systems, whose performance can also be jeopardized by incomplete and corrupted process information, absence of knowledge regarding measurement errors and performance issues related to numerical optimization techniques [31]. In addition, the use of continuous system diagnostic tools is not common, neither in the literature, nor in commercial RTO systems. In this context, there are few works in the literature dedicated to diagnosing and criticizing the obtained results and software tools of real-time optimization. Although it is possible to find some valuable criticism about RTO implementations [32,33], the discussion is normally presented in general terms, making it hard for practitioners to distinguish process-related features from methodological limitations of the RTO approach.

The present work aims at presenting the performance evaluation of real industrial RTO systems. The characteristics of operation shared by two RTO commercial packages from two different world-class providers will be presented, which are actual implementations of the two-step RTO approach, currently in use on crude oil distillation units from two commercial-scale Brazilian petroleum refineries. The aim is not at exhausting the many aspects involved, but rather presenting some features of large-scale RTO systems that are commonly blurred due to the great amount of information required by optimization systems.

This article presents the basics of a two-step-based RTO system in Section 2. Then, it briefly presents a general description of an industrial RTO system in Section 3, along with major details about the two commercial systems discussed in this paper. The results of industrial RTO implementations are discussed in Section 4. Finally, Section 5 suggests some concluding remarks.

2. Problem Statement

The idea of optimization is to find the set of values for decision variables that renders the extreme of a function, while satisfying existing constraints. In this context, the main task of an optimization system is to tune the vector of available degrees of freedom of a process in order to reach the "best" value of some performance metric.

The vector of decision variables, $\mathbf{u}$, is a subset of a larger set of input variables, $\mathbf{I}$, that is supposed to determine how the process behaves, as reflected by the set of output variables, $\mathbf{O}$, thus establishing a mapping of $\mathbf{I} \rightarrow \mathbf{O}$. If a set of indexes $\mathbf{df}$ is used to define the vector of decision variables, thus:

$$\mathbf{u} = \mathbf{I}(\mathbf{df}), \quad \mathbf{df} \subset \left\{ 1, 2, \ldots, \dim_1(\mathbf{I}) \right\}, \tag{1}$$

where $\dim_n$ refers to the length of the n-th-dimension of an array. Common criteria used to select $\mathbf{df}$ are the easiness of variable manipulation in the plant, the requirements of the industry and the effects of the decision variables on process performance [34]. Characteristics of the feed, such as flow rate and temperature, are commonly assigned as decision variables.

Besides the identification of indexes $\mathbf{df}$ for decision variables from the set of inputs, we could identify a group that represents the expectation of some elements of $\mathbf{I}$ (e.g., vessel temperature, feed composition, heat transfer coefficients, decision variables, among others) to change along an operational scenario, being defined by a set of indexes $\mathbf{var}$. In turn, those elements supposed to remain constant (e.g., tube diameters, coolant temperature, catalyst surface area, system equilibrium states, thermodynamic constants, etc.) are represented by the set of indexes **std**. Mathematically, this can be stated as:

$$I = \left\{ I(std), I(var) \right\}, \tag{2}$$

$$var \subset \left\{ 1, 2, \ldots, \dim_1(I) \right\}, \quad std = \left\{ 1, 2, \ldots, \dim_1(I) \right\} - var. \tag{3}$$

Another important subset of input variables is external disturbances. As the system evolves with time and disturbances of a stochastic nature are present, it is convenient to establish a partition dividing disturbances into stationary and nonstationary, defining a two-time scale. When doing this, we assume that nonstationary disturbance components are "quickly" varying, and there is a regulatory control in charge of suppressing their influence, in such a way that they are irrelevant for the long-term optimization of the process [35]. Thus, there remains only the persistent and/or periodic disturbances, which have to be included in the long-term optimization. Employing a pseudo-steady-state assumption, plant dynamics may be neglected, and process evolution can be represented as a sequence of successive steady-state points. Hereafter, an element in this sequence is represented either as an array or with the help of a subscript k. Accordingly, we can state the following for the elements of I supposed to remain constant:

$$I(std, k) = I(std, 0) = I_0(std) \qquad . \tag{4}$$

The process behavior, as described by I_k and O_k, will thus present a performance metric L_k. The performance metric is the result of the mapping $\phi : (I_k, O_k) \rightarrow L_k$, where ϕ vary with the underlying process and may be defined in several ways. Nevertheless, it is conveniently represented by an economic index, such as profit, in most cases. Roughly, profit is determined as the product value minus the costs of production, such as raw material and utility costs. For example, in the work of Bailey et al. [36] applied to the optimization of a hydrocracker fractionation plant, profit was adopted as the performance metric, represented by the sum of the value of feed and product streams (valued as gasoline), the value of feed and product streams (priced as fuel), the value of pure component feeds and products and the cost of utilities. As stated above, optimization is the act of selecting the set of values for vector u that conducts the process to the most favorable $L = \phi(I, O)$, i.e., selecting a proper u^*, such that $u_{k+1}^* \rightarrow L_{k+1}^*$ given I_k and O_k at steady-state point k.

Input and output variables are related through a set of equations that express conservation balances (mass, energy, momentum), equipment design constraints, etc., expressed as a set f of equations called the process model. Another set of relationships g describes safety conditions, product specifications and other important requirements, so that f and g represent the process optimization constraints. Given the performance metric and the process optimization constraints, the static process optimization is written as the following nonlinear programming problem:

$$\begin{aligned} u_{k+1}^* := \; & \underset{u}{\arg\max} \quad \phi(I_k, O_k) \\ & \text{subject to} \quad f(I_k, O_k) = 0 \\ & \qquad\qquad\quad g(I_k, O_k) \leq 0 \end{aligned} \tag{5}$$

Process information is primarily obtained through sensors and analyzers, which translate physical and chemical properties of streams and equipment into more useful process values. The information carried by the process is represented by the whole set of process variables $Z = [I^T, O^T]^T$. Unfortunately, in any real industrial case, the full vector Z is not available, and the lack of information is related mainly to the absence of measurements due to management decisions made during the process design. These decisions are based on sensor costs and known limitations of sensor technology, as well as the lack of knowledge about the variables that constitute the real vector Z. As a consequence, the real system is known only through the elements **ms** of Z, i.e.:

$$\mathbf{Z} = \left\{ \mathbf{Z(ms), Z(um)} \right\}$$

$$\mathbf{ms} \subset \left\{ 1, 2, \ldots, \dim_1(Z) \right\} \qquad (6)$$

$$\mathbf{um} = \left\{ 1, 2, \ldots, \dim_1(Z) \right\} - \mathbf{ms} \qquad .$$

If, at steady instant k, the real plant is under the influence of $\mathbf{I}_k \neq \mathbf{I}_0$, the problem posed to the RTO system may be described in the following terms: starting from the available information set $Q_a = \{\mathbf{Z(ms}, k), \mathbf{I}_{0a}\}$, the RTO has to find out $\mathbf{u}^*_{k+1} \equiv \mathbf{I}^*_{k+1}(\mathbf{df})$ that drives the process to L^*. In a scenario of limited knowledge of the system, reflected by incomplete information of the current state $\mathbf{Z(ms}, k)$, a new expanded set of information, Q_a^+, has to be produced from Q_a, so that the optimization procedure is able to identify the right set $\mathbf{u}^*$. We assume that, in the face of the structure of the process optimization constraints (f and $\mathbf{g}$), the set of fresh measurements, $\mathbf{Z(ms}, k)$, carries an excess of information that can be used to update some elements of the vector of offsets, $\mathbf{\Theta}$, which are modifiers of $\mathbf{Z}$, so that $\mathbf{Z}^+ = \mathbf{Z} + \mathbf{\Theta}$.

Due to restrictions regarding the available information, in most problems only a subset $\theta \subset \Theta$, represented by the index **upd**, can accommodate the existing excess of information present in measurements. The remaining set of offsets, represented by the index **fix**, is supposed to be kept at (assumed) base values, as shown in the following:

$$\mathbf{\Theta} = \left\{ \mathbf{\Theta(fix), \Theta(upd)} \right\}$$

$$\mathbf{upd} \subset \left\{ 1, \ldots, \dim_1(\mathbf{\Theta}) \right\}, \quad \mathbf{fix} = \left\{ 1, \ldots, \dim_1(\mathbf{\Theta}) \right\} - \mathbf{upd} \qquad (7)$$

$$\mathbf{\Theta}_k(\mathbf{fix}) = \mathbf{\Theta}_{0a}(\mathbf{fix}) \quad \forall k \qquad .$$

It must be emphasized that this formulation implicitly assumes that the only process variables actually changing during real-world operation are the sets of measured variables and updated parameters, in such a way that it is possible to accommodate all uncertainties in the updated parameters. In other words, it is assumed that there is no plant-model mismatch.

Information provided by sensors is expected to be similar, but not equal to the "true" information produced by the process. Sensors incorporate into the process signal some features that are not related to the behavior of variables, so that the observed values of measured variables $\mathbf{Z}^{meas}(\mathbf{ms})$ are different from "true" values $\mathbf{Z(ms)}$. To cope with this kind of uncertainty, the measurement error is usually modeled as the result of two components, a deterministic (the "truth") and a stochastic one (the "noise"). Defining $\mathbf{z} = \mathbf{Z(ms)}$, a convenient form of modeling measurement errors consists in the following additive relation:

$$\mathbf{z}^{meas} = \mathbf{z}^{model} + \varepsilon \qquad , \qquad (8)$$

where $\mathbf{z}^{meas}$ represents the values of $\mathbf{z}$ acquired with the help of process instrumentation, $\mathbf{z}^{model}$ are values of $\mathbf{z}$ estimated by the process model f, which is a function of θ, and ε is the measurement error vector, being a random variable.

In an ideal scenario, the RTO implementation relies on perfect knowledge of the input set $\mathbf{I}_k$, of the process optimization constraints f and $\mathbf{g}$ and of the performance metric ϕ. In the context of the two-step RTO scheme, the adaptation step performs the task of selecting the set $\theta_k = \mathbf{\Theta}_k(\mathbf{upd})$ that better explains measurements $\mathbf{z}^{meas}_k$ in light of the plant model. In order to do that, besides the model structure, it is also necessary to take into account the probability of the occurrence of noise. In other words, it is necessary to find the set θ_k that most likely gives rise to the real corrupted measurements $\mathbf{z}^{meas}_k$. This estimation problem is successfully dealt with by the statistical approach of maximum likelihood estimation [37], as described in Equation (9), which consists of maximizing the likelihood function J^{id} under constraints imposed by the process model. It should be noted that the elements of $\mathbf{z}$

included in the objective function are those related to the indexes **obj**, where dim(**obj**) ≤ dim(**ms**), according to decisions made during the design of the RTO structure.

$$\theta_k^* := \underset{\theta}{\arg\max} \quad J^{id}\left[\mathbf{z}_k^{meas}(\mathbf{obj}), \mathbf{z}_k^{model}(\mathbf{obj})\right]$$
$$\text{subject to} \quad f(\mathbf{I}_k, \mathbf{O}_k) = 0 \tag{9}$$

If ε follows a Gaussian probability density function, such that $E[\varepsilon] = 0$, $Var[\varepsilon] = \sigma_z^2$, and $Cov[\varepsilon\varepsilon^\mathsf{T}] = \mathbf{V}_z$, the problem defined in Equation (9) becomes the weighted least squares (WLS) estimation:

$$\theta_k^* := \underset{\theta}{\arg\max} \quad J^{id} = \left[\mathbf{z}_k^{meas}(\mathbf{obj}) - \mathbf{z}_k^{model}(\mathbf{obj})\right]^\mathsf{T} \mathbf{V}_z^{-1} \left[\mathbf{z}_k^{meas}(\mathbf{obj}) - \mathbf{z}_k^{model}(\mathbf{obj})\right]$$
$$\text{subject to} \quad f(\mathbf{I}_k, \mathbf{O}_k) = 0 \tag{10}$$

where $\mathbf{V}_z$ is the covariance matrix of $\mathbf{z}^{meas}$, which is normally assumed to be diagonal (i.e., measurement fluctuations are assumed to be independent).

In summary, a typical RTO system based on the two-step approach will, at any time: (i) gather information from the plant; (ii) detect stationarity in data series, defining a new steady state k; (iii) solve the model updating problem (such as Equation (10)); and (iv) determine the best set of decision variables by solving Equation (5).

3. RTO System Description

The traditional implementation of an RTO system is based on the two-step approach, which corresponds to both commercial systems considered in this work. A typical structure of a commercial RTO system is shown in Figure 1, which relates to an application in a crude oil atmospheric distillation unit. This RTO system has the following main modules:

(a) Steady-state detection (SSD), which states if the plant is at steady state based on the data gathered from the plant within a time interval;
(b) Monitoring sequence (MON), which is a switching method for executing the RTO iteration based on the information of the unit's stability, the unit's load and the RTO system's status; the switching method triggers the beginning of a new cycle of optimization and commonly depends on a minimal interval between successive RTO iterations, which typically corresponds to 30 min to 2 h for distillation units;
(c) Execution of the optimization layer based on the two-step approach, thus adapting the stationary process model and using it as a constraint for solving a nonlinear programming problem representing an economic index.

The RTO is integrated with the following layers:

- production planning and scheduling, which transfer information to it;
- storage logistics, which has information about the composition of feed tanks;
- Distributed control system (DCS) and database, which deliver measured values.

The decision variables are implemented by the advanced control system, which will compute the proper dynamic trajectory for reaching the RTO solution.

In the present work, the discussed results are associated with two RTO systems actually running in crude oil distillation units in distinct commercial-scale refineries located in Brazil. Both RTO commercial packages are from two different world-class providers. In doing this, we aim at preferably using one for analyzing the generated data (referred to as Tool A), while the other is used to compare the systems' architecture and algorithms (referred to as Tool B). The set of data from RTO system Tool A includes the results obtained from 1000 RTO iterations, which corresponds to a three-month period. In addition, Tool A has a static process model comprised by approximately 10^5 equations.

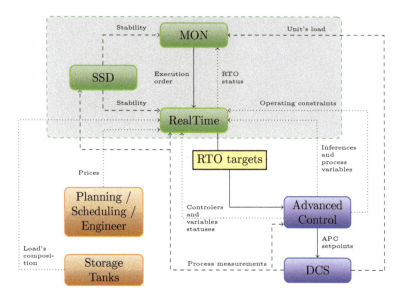

Figure 1. Topology of a real RTO system running in a crude oil distillation unit. MON, monitoring sequence; SSD, steady-state detection; APC, advanded process control; DCS, distributed control system.

4. Industrial RTO Evaluation

The evaluation of real RTO implementations is presented in this section focusing on two aspects: steady-state detection and adaptation and optimization. The former is supported by the fact that the applied process model is static, and only stationary data will render a valid process adaptation. Acting as a gatekeeper in the system, steady-state detection has a great influence on RTO performance. However, it is hardly discussed in the RTO literature. On the other hand, the latter is extensively studied in many articles. Analyses here will be mainly based on problem formulation issues and observed variability in the results.

4.1. Steady-State Detection

An important element of RTO systems refers to the mechanism that triggers the process optimization. Traditionally, it is based on the stationarity of measured process data and is accomplished by the SSD module.

4.1.1. Tool A

Tool A offers two options for detecting the steady state, shown to the user under the terms "statistical method" and "heuristic method". Formally, the former corresponds to the statistical test suggested by von Neumann [38]. This test establishes the comparison of the total variance of a signal and the variance of the difference between two successive points within this signal. The total variance of a signal x for a data window with n points is given by the sample variance (s^2), according to:

$$s^2 = \frac{1}{n-1} \sum_{i=1}^{n} \left(x_i - \overline{X} \right)^2, \tag{11}$$

where $\overline{X}$ is the sample mean, while the variance of the difference between two successive points is expressed by:

$$s_d^2 = \frac{1}{n-1} \sum_{i=2}^{n} \left(x_i - x_{i-1} \right)^2. \tag{12}$$

These two variances give rise to the statistic R [38,39], which is eventually expressed as C [40], defined as:

$$R = \frac{s_d^2}{s^2}$$
$$C = 1 - \frac{1}{2}R \quad .$$

(13)

Nevertheless, Tool A adopts this method with a slight difference. There is an extra option, where the user may define a tuning parameter, τ_{SM}, which changes the definition of R in the following way:

$$R = \frac{\max(s_d^2, \tau_{SM})}{s^2}.$$

(14)

Then, the signal is static if R is greater than a critical value R_c (or if C is lower than a critical value C_c).

The so called "heuristic method" makes use of two versions of the original signal subjected to filters with distinct cut frequencies, which are indirectly manipulated by the user when defining the parameters f_L and f_P, according to Equation (15). The filtering (or simplification) represents an exponentially-weighted moving average, or conventional first-order filter, that requires little storage and is computationally fast [41]. The signal version with a low cut frequency (X_P) is called the "heavy filter", while the other (X_L) is called the "light filter". The test is very simple and establishes that the signal is stationary if the difference between these two filtered signals is lower than a predetermined tolerance.

$$X_L(i) = f_L X(i) + (1 - f_L) X_L(i-1)$$
$$X_P(i) = f_P X(i) + (1 - f_P) X_P(i-1).$$

(15)

It is worth noting that both the "statistical method" and the "heuristic method" are somewhat combined in the method proposed by Cao and Rhinehart [41]. The method is based on the R-statistic, using a ratio of two variances measured on the same set of data by two methods and employs three first-order filter operations, providing computational efficiency and robustness to process noise and non-noise patterns. Critical values and statistical evidence of the method to reject the steady-state hypothesis, as well as to reject the transient state hypothesis have already been discussed in the literature [42,43]. This method was also modified in [44] by optimizing the filter constants so as to minimize Type I and II errors and simultaneously reduce the delay in state detection.

From a user point of view, the experience shows that the "heuristic method" is overlooked with respect to the "statistical method". This might be related to the greater dependence of this method on user inputs, where there must be a total of $3 \cdot n_{var}$ parameters, since each signal requires a value of f_L, f_P and tolerance. Besides, the tolerances are not normalized and must be provided in accordance with the unit of the original signal.

Considering the use of RTO package Tool A, each parameter in these methods is defined by the user. In the statistical method (SM), the presence of the τ_{SM} tolerance (Equation (14)) allows, in practice, the user to define what is (or will be) considered stationary. Thus, any statistical foundation claimed by the method is jeopardized by a user-defined choice based on its own definition. In the case of the heuristic method (HM), the arbitrary nature of the parameters puts the user in charge of the decision making process, directing stationarity towards its own beliefs, as it is for SM. In spite of this, given the large number of inputs, it is likely that the user will not be able to anticipate the effects of its choice on the signal shape.

4.1.2. Tool B

Tool B also presents two options for stating signals' stationarity. One of them is the R-statistic (Equation (13)), as described above for Tool A. The other option is comprised by a hypothesis test to assess whether or not the average values of two halves of a time window are identical. First, a hypothesis test is applied to the ratio between the variances. This is accomplished by means of the

F-statistic [45], where the two subsequent time intervals i and j have $n_i = n_j$ data points. If the null hypothesis of identical variances is rejected, then the mean values $\overline{X}_i$ and $\overline{X}_j$ are compared by means of the τ_{ale} variable [46,47], defined as:

$$\tau_{ale} = \frac{\overline{X}_i - \overline{X}_j}{\sqrt{\frac{s_i^2}{n_i} + \frac{s_j^2}{n_j}}}. \tag{16}$$

If the values within time intervals i and j are normal and independent, τ_{ale} will follow the Student *t*-distribution with n_{DF} degrees of freedom, determined by:

$$n_{DF} = \frac{\left(\frac{s_i^2}{n_i} + \frac{s_j^2}{n_j}\right)^2}{\frac{(s_i^2/n_i)^2}{n_i-1} + \frac{(s_j^2/n_j)^2}{n_j-1}}. \tag{17}$$

In turn, if the null hypothesis of identical variances is accepted, a second test assesses if the difference between these averages is lower than a given tolerance (ϵ). This is supported by the assumption that the *t*-statistic determined by Equations (18) and (19) follows a Student *t* with $n_i + n_j - 2$ degrees of freedom. In the particular case of Tool B, these tests always have a fixed significance level of 10%.

$$s_t = \frac{s_i^2 \left(n_i - 1\right) + s_j^2 \left(n_j - 1\right)}{n_i + n_j - 2}. \tag{18}$$

$$t = \frac{\left|\overline{X}_i - \overline{X}_j\right| - \epsilon}{\left[s_t \left(1/n_i + 1/n_j\right)\right]^{1/2}}. \tag{19}$$

The procedure applied if the null hypothesis of identical variances is accepted is similar to the method proposed by Kelly and Hedengren [48], which is also a window-based method that utilizes the Student *t*-test to determine if the difference between the process signal value minus its mean is above or below the standard deviation times its statistical critical value. In this method, non-stationary is identified with a detectable and deterministic slope, trend, bias or drift.

Besides the choice of the method and its parameters, both Tools A and B also delegate to the user the selection of which variables (or signals) will be submitted to the stationarity test. In this context, the plant is assumed at steady state if a minimum percentage of the selected variables passes the test. Again, the minimum percentage is a user-defined input.

4.1.3. Industrial Results

Let us analyze how these choices are reflected in real results. Employing Tool A, the set of signals chosen in the SSD module consists of 28 process variables, comprised by 10 flow rates and 18 temperatures. It must be stressed that the real dimension of this set of signals may vary with time as the criteria for selecting variables may also change along the operation. Such a change in criteria for selecting variables for the SSD module increases the complexity of any trial to evaluate RTO system performance enormously. Considering the test SM and the historical data of 23 days for a set of eight signals (six flow rates F and two temperatures T), Table 1 presents the percentage of time (or percentage of data points) assumed static for each variable. Percentage results are determined from two sources, computations obtained by applying test SM as it is conceived (according to Equation (13)) and data gathered from Tool A by applying test SM as it is available in the RTO package (according to Equation (14)). Analyzing Table 1, it can be seen that the frequency of points assumed static by Tool A ($r_{EE}|_{RTO}$) is much greater than that inferred by the original test SM ($r_{EE}|_{SM}$). The high percentage values of static points shown by the RTO is due to the tolerance values (τ_{SM}) that overlap the calculated values of variances by successive differences (s_d^2), as defined in Equation (14). A high value of τ_{SM} will result in a high value of the *R*-statistic, and the signal will be static for *R* values greater than the critical value R_c. Therefore, the tuning parameter τ_{SM} is defining stationarity.

Table 1. Percentage of points deemed static for the set of 8 variables. $r_{EE}|_{SM}$: percentage computed using results obtained by the *C*-statistic. $r_{EE}|_{RTO}$: percentage computed using real results obtained by the RTO system Tool A. *F*, flow rate; *T*, temperature.

Tag	$r_{EE}|_{SM}$	$r_{EE}|_{RTO}$
F1	0.0	98.3
F2	3.2	81.1
T1	0.0	97.3
T2	0.0	90.9
F3	0.0	97.1
F4	4.8	99.5
F5	0.0	90.1
F6	6.8	84.4

When analyzing Table 1, an honest question that could naturally arise is which method is right, since one method essentially never finds the variables at steady state, while the other effectively finds them at steady state continually. In fact, the observed contradiction in results just shows how the methods have different definitions for stationarity. In other words, each method and its parameterization defines stationarity differently. Furthermore, many parameters are interrelated, such as the number of window data points and critical values, and the engineer/user will be hardly aware of how its choice is affected by, e.g., control system tuning, noiseless signals and valve stiction. The right method is the one that allows the RTO to determine the true plant optimum; since this condition is unknown, the right SSD method is also unknown. In this context, a metric of assessment of RTO performance, as is discussed in Section 4.2, could be used to compare the utility of SSD methods and parameters to the improvement of process performance metric ϕ and determine the best setting for SSD.

An equivalent form to obtain the effect of τ_{SM} tolerances (as observed in Table 1 for $r_{EE}|_{RTO}$) consists of manipulating the critical values of acceptance, R_c. Figure 2 shows that, given a convenient choice of critical value R_c or its analogous C_c, levels of stationarity for $r_{EE}|_{SM}$ can be obtained similar to those observed in Table 1 for the RTO system ($r_{EE}|_{RTO}$), in an equivalent form to the use of tolerances τ_{SM}.

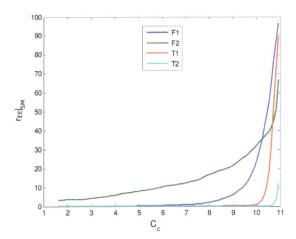

Figure 2. Percentage of values assumed static as a function of critical values C_c (the analogous of R_c as defined by Equation (13)) of the hypothesis test applied to signals of four process variables.

However, if the tolerance is used without an appropriate evaluation of the size of the data horizon, the steady-state detection might be biased towards the acceptance of stationarity. In this case, there is an increase in the inertia of transitions in detection, thus delaying changes of state. This behavior is illustrated in Figure 3, which shows successive changes in the signal of variable *F2* during a specific time interval. It can be seen that stationarity is indicated with delay, which corresponds to those moments where the signal already presents a state of reduced variability. Assuming that the visual judgment is a legitimate way of determining signal stationarity, it is clear that, in this case, dynamic data are used to update the static process model and support the determination of optimal process operating condition.

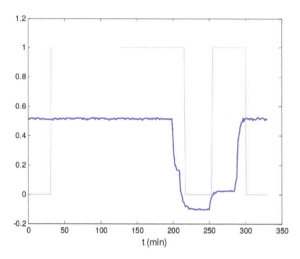

Figure 3. Normalized values of flow rate *F2* (blue line) and the corresponding indication of stationarity according to the RTO system (pink line), where one means steady and zero means unsteady.

The frequency of stationarity may seem surprisingly low as pointed out by the SM in the absence of changes in tolerances and critical values. This is due to factors uncorrelated with the process, such as the sampling interval between measurements and signal conditioning filters. When this test is applied to the values from Figure 3, results reveal no stationarity at all during the period. Even more weird is that, based on a visual inspection, the values are apparently steady within the interval comprised between the beginning and ~200 min. However, it must be noted that this method is very sensitive to short-term variability, being affected by signal preprocessing in the DCS and by the sampling interval. If one observes the signal behavior within the first 200 min with appropriate axes values, as in Figure 4, a pattern of autocorrelation can be noted, independent of the signal amplitude. The autocorrelation renders the difference between two successive points to be lower than that expected in the case of no autocorrelation, i.e., in the case that each point were due to a pure stochastic process. As a consequence, the value of s_d^2 (Equation (13)) decreases when compared to the variance in relation to the average. This is made clear from Figure 5, where the evolution of s_d^2 and $2s^2$ along the first 200 min is depicted. Thus, the values of *C* are increased beyond the critical value of acceptance.

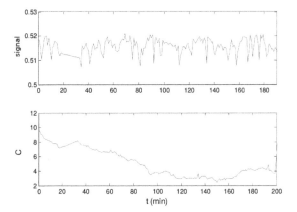

Figure 4. (**A**) Normalized values of flow rate *F2*, as shown in Figure 3, in restricted axes values; (**B**) C-statistic values for the corresponding time interval. The value of C_c according to the method is 1.64.

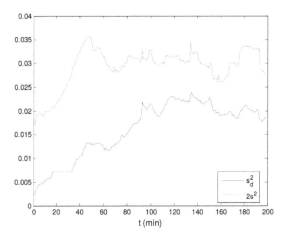

Figure 5. Evolution of s_d^2 and $2s^2$ along the first 200 min for the signal depicted in Figure 3.

4.2. Adaptation and Optimization

The decision variables for adaptation and optimization problems, $\theta = \Theta(\mathbf{upd})$ and $\mathbf{u} = \mathbf{I}(\mathbf{df})$, are selected by the user on both RTO systems. Since this choice is not based on any systematic method, it is supported by testing and experience or by the engineer/user beliefs, expectations and/or wishes. Therefore, decision variable selection is restricted to the user, and the optimizer only chooses their values.

Both commercial RTO systems discussed here make use of a recent data window in the adaptation step, which comprises a series of values along a time horizon of a certain length. The values within the moving data horizon are measurements obtained from the plant information system for each measured variable. The data window $\mathbf{Zw}$ is represented as:

$$\mathbf{Zw} = \begin{bmatrix} \mathbf{z}_{c-H}^{meas} \\ \vdots \\ \mathbf{z}_{c}^{meas} \end{bmatrix}, \tag{20}$$

where $\mathbf{z}_{c-H}^{meas}$ and $\mathbf{z}_c^{meas}$ are the set of data obtained at the first and current sampling instants of the moving window by direct observation and H is the number of successive time steps uniformly separated by a sampling time of ta, defining a data horizon from $(t_c - H\,ta)$ to t_c. Considering applications in crude oil distillation units, it is common to adopt the size of the data window as 1 h, with a sampling instant typically in the range between 0.5 and 1 min, which results in n between 120 and 60, respectively.

The model adaptation step in both RTO systems consists of a nonlinear programming model whose objective function is the weighted sum of squared errors between plant measurements and model predictions, as presented in Equation (21). The weights, w^2, are the variances of each measurement.

$$
\begin{aligned}
\theta_k^* := & \arg\min_{\theta_k} \quad J^{id} = \sum_{j=1}^{\dim(\mathbf{obj})} \frac{1}{w_i^2} \left[\overline{\mathbf{z}_k^{meas}}[\mathbf{obj}(j)] - \mathbf{z}_k^{model}[\mathbf{obj}(j)] \right]^2 \\
& \text{subject to} \quad f(\mathbf{I}_k, \mathbf{O}_k) = 0 \\
& \qquad\qquad \theta_k = \mathbf{\Theta}_k(\mathbf{upd}) \\
& \qquad\qquad \overline{\mathbf{z}_k^{meas}}[\mathbf{obj}(j)] = \frac{1}{H}\sum_{i=c-H}^{c} \mathbf{Zw}\,[i,\mathbf{obj}(j)]
\end{aligned}
\tag{21}
$$

It must be noted that there is an important difference between the objective function employed by Equation (21) and the maximum likelihood estimator shown in Equation (10) for Gaussian, zero mean and additive measurement errors. Both tools reduce the data window of each variable to only one value, which corresponds to the average of measurements within the window (most likely due to the easiness of implementation). In this case, the changes go beyond the apparent simplicity that such a modification may introduce to carry on the calculations. The resulting expression is not assured to hold the desired statistical properties that apply to a maximum likelihood estimator, i.e., unbiased and efficient estimations [37]. In addition, as shown in Equation (21), the elements w_i correspond to the standard deviation of measurements. From this, the a priori assumption of independent errors is also clear, since the expression "corresponds" to a simplification of the use of a diagonal covariance matrix.

It is noted in industrial implementations that the choice of sets **upd** and **obj** (i.e., the decision vector θ and the set of variables in the objective function) is almost always based on empirical procedures. It is interesting to note that the premises that support the choices of **obj** set are hardly observed. According to these premises, an important element is that **obj** encompasses measured variables, which are non-zero values of **Zw**, directly affected by the corruption of experimental signals. However, it may be seen in real RTO systems that there is the inclusion of updated parameters and non-measured variables (**upd** set) in the set **obj**. A typical occurrence of such a thing is the inclusion of load characterization parameters, which belong to the **upd** set and are often included in the objective function of the model adaptation problem. In this case, where there is no measured value for $\mathbf{Zw}(\mathbf{upd})$, fixed values are arbitrarily chosen for these variables. As a result, this practice limits the variation of these variables around the adopted fixed values. This approach degenerates the estimator and induces the occurrence of bias in estimated variables.

In order to take a closer look at the effects of ill-posed problems in RTO systems, we will discuss the influence of each variable in **obj** over the value of the objective function from Equation (21) with real RTO data. Assuming that Equation (10) is valid, measurement errors are independent and the knowledge of the true variance values for each measured variable is available, it is expected that the normalized effects, ct, of each variable in **obj** are similar, as defined in Equation (22). In Tool A, the number of variables in set **obj** was 49. The time interval between two successful and successive RTO iterations has a probability density with 10th, 50th and 90th percentiles of 0.80, 1.28 and 4.86, respectively. The normalized effects ct, as defined in Equation (22), are shown in Figure 6. Results show that it is common that fewer variables within **obj** have greater effects in objective function J^{id} values. For a period of three months, the RTO system from Tool A has been executed 1000 times, but achieved convergence for the reconciliation and model adaptation step in 59.7% of cases. Besides the formulation of the estimation problem, this relatively low convergence rate might be caused by the following reasons: (i) the nonlinearity of the process model that may reach hundreds of thousands of equations, since the optimization of a crude oil atmospheric distillation unit is a large-scale problem governed by complex and nonlinear physicochemical phenomena; (ii) the model is not perfect, and many parameters are assumed to remain constant during the operation, which may not be the real case; such assumptions force estimations of updated parameters to accommodate all uncertainty and may result in great variability in estimates between two consecutive RTO iterations; and (iii) the limitations of the employed optimization technique, along with its parameterization; in most commercial RTO packages, sequential quadratic programming (SQP) is the standard optimization technique, as is the case for Tool A. Regarding convergence, thresholds are empirical choices, generally represented by rules of thumb.

$$ct_j = \frac{\frac{1}{s_j^2}\left[\overline{\mathbf{Zw}}[\mathbf{obj}(j)] - \mathbf{z}[\mathbf{obj}(j)]\right]^2}{\sum_{i=1}^{\dim(\mathbf{obj})}\frac{1}{s_i^2}\left[\overline{\mathbf{Zw}}[\mathbf{obj}(i)] - \mathbf{z}[\mathbf{obj}(i)]\right]^2}. \tag{22}$$

In Table 2 are presented contribution details for variables with the 10 greatest values of the 50th percentile (median) for the considered period. The tag field indicates the nature of the variable, which may be a flow rate (F), a temperature (T) or a model parameter (θ), i.e., an unmeasured variable. Besides the comparison of the median values, the values for the 10th and 90th percentiles show greater variance in the effects of each variable. As an example, the first two variables in Table 2 vary as high as 100% among percentiles. In fact, some discrepancy among the contribution of variables in **obj** in objective function values is expected, as long as the variables are expressed with different units, and this effect is not fully compensated by the variances. Nevertheless, this fact does not explain the high variation along the operation, which can be attributed to the violation of one or more hypothesis in different operating scenarios. Even in this case, it is not possible to determine which assumptions do not hold.

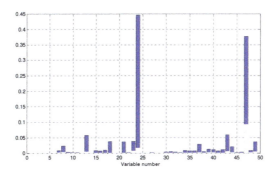

Figure 6. Interval between the first and third quartiles of the normalized effect of each variable within **obj** for the objective function from the model adaptation problem (Equation (21)). The x-axis refer to the relative position of variables in the vector **obj**.

It is not an easy task to analyze the operation of a real RTO system, since the knowledge about factors that influence and describe the plant behavior is limited. For this reason, we will put emphasis on the variability of the system's results. In doing this, we are able to compare the frequency of the most important disturbances (such as changes in the load) with the variability presented by RTO results (such as objective function values, estimated variables and the expectancy of economic performance). In this context, it is worth assessing the behavior of estimated variables that are related to the quality of the load of the unit. In refineries, the molecular characterization of the oil is not usual. In turn, physicochemical properties are used to describe both the oil and its fractions (cuts). A common analysis is the ratio between distillation fractions and their volumetric yields, which results in profiles such as ASTM-D86 (ASTM-D86 is a standard test method for the distillation of petroleum products and liquid fuels at atmospheric pressure, which evaluates fuel characteristics, in this case, distillation features).

In the conventional operation of a refinery, such profiles are not available on-line for the load, even though there are databases for oils processed by the unit. These analyses may differ from the true values due to several factors:

- the database might present lagged analyses, given the quality of oil changes with time;
- there might be changes in oil composition due to storage and distribution policies from well to final tank. Commonly, this causes the loss of volatile compounds;
- mixture rules applied to determine the properties of the load might not adequately represent its distillation profile;
- eventually, internal streams of the refinery are blended with the load for reprocessing.

Table 2. Percentile values of normalized effects (%) of the 10 most influential variables in the value of the objective function from the model adaptation problem. The rank is relative to the 50th percentile (P50).

Position in Rank	Tag	$\in$ ms	P50	P90	P10
1	T01	yes	21.53	54.83	1.15
2	T02	yes	15.99	54.33	0.19
3	F01	yes	2.37	11.39	0.10
4	T03	yes	1.95	7.49	0.48
5	T04	yes	1.68	14.21	0.35
6	T05	yes	1.41	7.01	<0.01
7	T06	yes	1.17	5.94	0.04
8	F07	yes	1.12	7.39	<0.01
9	$\theta(8)$	no	0.96	4.08	0.09
10	T07	yes	0.65	2.17	0.12

Since the characterization of the load has a huge impact in determining the quality and quantity of products, these sources of uncertainty generally motivate the use of specific parameters, called knots, that are related to the fit of the distillation profile. The distillation profile is divided into sections, and each knot represents the slope coefficient of each section of the profile. These parameters are thus included in the set of estimated parameters (**upd**). In the present case, 11 knots are the degrees of freedom of the model adaptation problem and could be used to infer the quality of the load based on available measurements and the process model for the distillation column.

The estimated knots' variability is depicted in Figure 7A by means of the distribution of estimated values for each knot, where the reference load corresponds to the knot equal to one. In addition, Figure 7B also shows the relative difference between two successive estimations of each knot. A high total variability, as well as a high amplitude for the relative difference of two successive estimations can be seen. However, considering the knowledge about the real load, such observations are incompatible with the state of the load during the operation. In the considered distillation unit, the oil load changes approximately once a week, which involves three tank transfers. Nonetheless, relative differences as high as 20% are common between two successive estimates for many knots. Considering an interval of 1.5 h between estimations, such a variability would not be expected. Besides that, as knots are independent estimates, the variation between contiguous knots might give rise to distillation profiles that do not make real physical sense.

In Table 3 are presented the lower and upper bounds applied to knots in the model adaptation problem, as well as the relative number of iterations with active constraints under convergence. From the results, one might infer that the observed variability in estimated values of knots would be higher if the bounds have allowed. These bounds deliberately force values to real physical ranges. However, this procedure alone does not guarantee real physical meaning, but only restricts the expected values to reasonable ranges. Indeed, with fewer degrees of freedom, the numerical optimization procedure would search for other "directions" to minimize the objective function, thus propagating the uncertainties to other decision variables. In summary, the approach compensates the lower flexibility to change some parameters by introducing bias in the estimates of other decision variables. Even poorer estimations, as those trapped in local minima, were further discussed in Quelhas et al. [31].

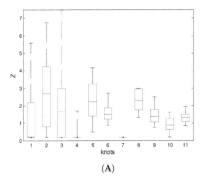

(A)

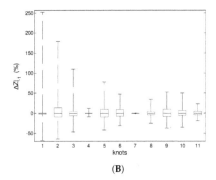

(B)

Figure 7. (**A**) Distribution of estimated values of knots; (**B**) distribution of the relative deviation between two successive estimations of a knot.

Table 3. Lower and upper bounds on the knots of the model adaptation problem and the percentage number of iterations in which the constraint is active under convergence.

Knot	Lim$_{inf}$	Lim$_{sup}$	Active Constraint (%)
1	0.2	10	42.5
2	0.2	10	13.4
3	0.2	7.5	31.5
4	0.2	7.5	81.7
5	0.2	7.5	0.7
6	0.2	7.5	0.2
7	0.2	7.5	92.1
8	0.2	3	19.4
9	0.2	3	1.2
10	0.2	3	14.6
11	0.2	3	0.3

The high variability is also reflected in the values of the objective function, as can be seen in Figure 8, where the relative difference of objective function values (J^{id}) is shown under convergence between two successive iterations, i.e.,

$$\Delta J_k^{id} = \frac{J_k^{id} - J_{k-1}^{id}}{J_{k-1}^{id}} \quad .$$

In the absence of actual short-term changes in the process (i.e., between two RTO iterations), it is not easy to explain such a high variation in terms of real changes or disturbances. Reasonable explanations could be the violation of any of the hypothesis assumed for the identification problem and/or the quality of the solution given by the employed numerical optimization technique [31].

Finally, it is worth analyzing the metric of assessment of the RTO system performance. The following two performance metrics are considered: the relative difference between the calculated profit value before, $\phi(\mathbf{u}_k)$, and after, $\phi(\mathbf{u}_{k+1}^*)$, the RTO iteration k ($\Delta\phi_k^{prev}$, Equation (23)); and the relative difference between the profit value calculated at the beginning of RTO iteration k, $\phi(\mathbf{u}_k)$, and the profit estimated by the previous iteration, $\phi(\mathbf{u}_k^*)$ ($\Delta\phi_k^{verif}$, Equation (24)). It must be emphasized that both metrics refer to profit estimates calculated by the RTO model, which will reflect real values only for a perfect model.

$$\Delta\phi_k^{prev} = \frac{\phi(\mathbf{u}_{k+1}^*) - \phi(\mathbf{u}_k)}{\phi(\mathbf{u}_k)} 100 \quad . \tag{23}$$

$$\Delta\phi_k^{verif} = \frac{\phi(\mathbf{u}_k) - \phi(\mathbf{u}_k^*)}{\phi(\mathbf{u}_k^*)} 100 \quad . \tag{24}$$

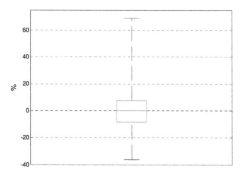

Figure 8. Distribution of the relative difference of objective function values under convergence between two successive iterations (ΔJ^{id}).

As shown in Figure 9, the most used metric of assessment of RTO performance, $\Delta\phi^{prev}$, has an optimistic bias, as it always reports positive values (as it should be for the converged RTO results). However, the results of $\Delta\phi^{verif}$, reflecting the process response over the last result, reveal that changes in decision variables are not leading to better economic performance in all RTO iterations. Even worse, they reveal the addition of useless variability to decision variables. In this context, considering the validity of the results for $\Delta\phi^{prev}$, it is worth noting its low value of only 0.01 for the 50th percentile. This reveals the clear need of analyzing RTO results to distinguish between statistically-significant results from those that are due to a common cause of variation [30,49–51]. If the dominant cause of plant variation results from the propagation of uncertainties throughout the RTO system, implementing these changes could lower profit, as is interestingly observed in the results of $\Delta\phi^{verif}$, confirmed by a negative 50th percentile.

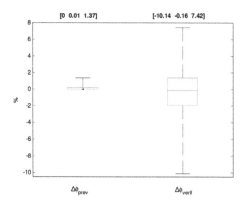

Figure 9. Distribution of the values for $\Delta\phi_{prev}$ and $\Delta\phi_{verif}$ for the RTO profit. Above the graph, the percentiles P5, P50 and P95 are indicated as [P5 P50 P95].

5. Conclusions

The implementation of optimization procedures in real time for the improvement of processes constitutes a major challenge in real-world implementations, as is the case of RTO systems. In this context, we are compelled to confirm the quotation from Bainbridge [52] that "perhaps the final irony is that it is the most successful automated systems, with rare need for manual intervention, which may need the greatest investment in human operator training".

This work has evaluated and analyzed the performance of RTO packages from two world-class providers running on crude oil distillation units from two different commercial-scale Brazilian petroleum refineries. We have briefly presented the steady-state detection methods available on these RTO packages and discussed the choice of the method and its parameters, the selection of measured signals to be submitted to the stationarity test and the tolerance criteria. It was shown that in spite of the methods available, some tuning parameters might compromise any statistical foundation eventually present, redefining stationarity in terms of the user's choice without improving the global performance of RTO. Regarding model adaptation, we have examined the problem formulation, the choice of adjustable model parameters and the selection of variables in the objective function, the convergence rate of the optimization technique and the variability of estimates. It was presented that the problem formulation lacks features to ensure unbiased and efficient estimations, which contribute to the addition of useless variability to decision variables. Finally, we have analyzed economic optimization results and showed that even though the RTO system is able to find improved values for decision variables, their implementation might not lead to better economic performance as estimated by the RTO. In practice, all choices are done on a subjective basis, supported by the operating experience of engineers, as well as empirical knowledge of software vendors. As has been shown, a possible outcome is that RTO results have an optimistic bias, in which changes in decision variables are not leading to better economic performance in all RTO iterations (Figure 9).

Given the already established conditions for model adequacy within the context of the two-step approach [22], updated parameters are just mathematical tools used by the model fitting procedure to accommodate any disagreement between model predictions and plant measurements. In other words, it is assumed that all modeling uncertainties, though unknown, might be incorporated in the vector of uncertain parameters θ. Since the plant will typically not be in the set of models obtained by spanning all of the possible values of the model parameters, the two-step approach will fail in the presence of structural plant-model mismatch. However, we should ask if the structural inability of the two-step approach is the primary source of uncertainty in RTO systems. Indeed, the disagreement in the mathematical model structure is not the only source of plant-model mismatch. The fault in steady-state detection is a source of model uncertainty and not a parametric one. This is due to the fact that derivative terms are ignored. Even for methods that theoretically are not affected by plant-model mismatch, a wrong steady-state detection will negatively impact the method's result. In addition, given the enormous amount of data and gradient estimations that would be required in a large-scale process, none of such "model-free" methods are viable for application in real industrial processes. This notwithstanding, the aforementioned disagreement may be caused by any factor that impairs information acquisition and processing in real implementations, constituting sources of uncertainty, such as: (i) measurements signals corrupted by noise with an unknown error structure; (ii) variation of the elements of input **I**, neither measured, nor estimated (**var** $\nsubseteq$ (**ms** $\cup$ **upd**)); (iii) use of the wrong default values for fixed variables; (iv) use of an inaccurate process model; (v) violation of maximum likelihood assumptions; (vi) imperfect numerical optimization method; and (vii) imperfect steady state detection or gross error filtering.

From a practical point of view, the task of diagnosing an RTO system based on the two-step approach is a challenging one. There is a very high level of uncertainty spread along all system modules. Since conclusions will likely be dependent on non-validated assumptions, the overlapping of too many possible causes of failure hampers the production of higher level diagnostics. In this context, this work illustrates some crucial features involved when evaluating RTO systems' performance, as already discussed in detail elsewhere [31]. Some results from two industrial RTO implementations are analyzed, providing some insights on common causes of performance degradation in order to have a clearer picture of the system performance and its main drawbacks. Such an analysis is a step forward towards the proper identification of existent system vulnerabilities, so that the RTO system structure and function may be improved.

Acknowledgments: The authors thank CNPq (Conselho Nacional de Desenvolvimento Científico e Tecnológico) and CAPES (Coordenação de Aperfeiçoamento de Pessoal de Nível Superior) for the financial support to this work, as well as for covering the costs to publish in open access. The authors also thank Petrobras (Petróleo Brasileiro SA) for supporting this work.

Author Contributions: A.D.Q. gathered the data and contributed analysis tools; A.D.Q., J.C.P. and M.M.C. analyzed the data; M.M.C. and A.D.Q. wrote the paper.

Conflicts of Interest: The authors declare no conflict of interest.

Abbreviations

The following abbreviations are used in this manuscript:

RTO	Real-time optimization systems
MPC	Model predictive control
MON	Monitoring sequence
SSD	Steady-state detection
APC	Advanced process control
DCS	Distributed control system
SM	Statistical method
HM	Heuristic method

References

1. Garcia, C.E.; Morari, M. Optimal operation of integrated processing systems. Part I: Open-loop on-line optimizing control. *AIChE J.* **1981**, *27*, 960–968.
2. Ellis, J.; Kambhampati, C.; Sheng, G.; Roberts, P. Approaches to the optimizing control problem. *Int. J. Syst. Sci.* **1988**, *19*, 1969–1985.
3. Engell, S. Feedback control for optimal process operation. *J. Process Control* **2007**, *17*, 203–219.
4. Chachuat, B.; Srinivasan, B.; Bonvin, D. Adaptation strategies for real-time optimization. *Comput. Chem. Eng.* **2009**, *33*, 1557–1567.
5. François, G.; Bonvin, D. Chapter One—Measurement-Based Real-Time Optimization of Chemical Processes. In *Control and Optimisation of Process Systems*; Advances in Chemical Engineering; Pushpavanam, S., Ed.; Academic Press: New York, NY, USA, 2013; Volume 43, pp. 1–50.
6. Cutler, C.; Perry, R. Real time optimization with multivariable control is required to maximize profits. *Comput. Chem. Eng.* **1983**, *7*, 663–667.
7. Bamberger, W.; Isermann, R. Adaptive on-line steady-state optimization of slow dynamic processes. *Automatica* **1978**, *14*, 223–230.
8. Jang, S.S.; Joseph, B.; Mukai, H. On-line optimization of constrained multivariable chemical processes. *AIChE J.* **1987**, *33*, 26–35.
9. Arkun, Y.; Stephanopoulos, G. Studies in the synthesis of control structures for chemical processes: Part IV. Design of steady-state optimizing control structures for chemical process units. *AIChE J.* **1980**, *26*, 975–991.
10. Darby, M.L.; Nikolaou, M.; Jones, J.; Nicholson, D. RTO: An overview and assessment of current practice. *J. Process Control* **2011**, *21*, 874–884.
11. Naysmith, M.; Douglas, P. Review of real time optimization in the chemical process industries. *Dev. Chem. Eng. Miner. Process.* **1995**, *3*, 67–87.
12. Marlin, T.E.; Hrymak, A.N. *Real-Time Operations Optimization of Continuous Processes*; AIChE Symposium Series; 1971-c2002; American Institute of Chemical Engineers: New York, NY, USA, 1997; Volume 93, pp. 156–164.

13. Trierweiler, J.O. Real-Time Optimization of Industrial Processes. In *Encyclopedia of Systems and Control*; Baillieul, J., Samad, T., Eds.; Springer: London, UK, 2014; pp. 1–11.

14. Rotava, O.; Zanin, A.C. Multivariable control and real-time optimization—An industrial practical view. *Hydrocarb. Process.* **2005**, *84*, 61–71.

15. Young, R. Petroleum refining process control and real-time optimization. *IEEE Control Syst.* **2006**, *26*, 73–83.

16. Shokri, S.; Hayati, R.; Marvast, M.A.; Ayazi, M.; Ganji, H. Real time optimization as a tool for increasing petroleum refineries profits. *Pet. Coal* **2009**, *51*, 110–114.

17. Ruiz, C.A. Real Time Industrial Process Systems: Experiences from the Field. *Comput. Aided Chem. Eng.* **2009**, *27*, 133–138.

18. Mercangöz, M.; Doyle, F.J., III. Real-time optimization of the pulp mill benchmark problem. *Comput. Chem. Eng.* **2008**, *32*, 789–804.

19. Chen, C.Y.; Joseph, B. On-line optimization using a two-phase approach: An application study. *Ind. Eng. Chem. Res.* **1987**, *26*, 1924–1930.

20. Yip, W.; Marlin, T.E. The effect of model fidelity on real-time optimization performance. *Comput. Chem. Eng.* **2004**, *28*, 267–280.

21. Roberts, P. Algorithms for integrated system optimisation and parameter estimation. *Electron. Lett.* **1978**, *14*, 196–197.

22. Forbes, J.; Marlin, T.; MacGregor, J. Model adequacy requirements for optimizing plant operations. *Comput. Chem. Eng.* **1994**, *18*, 497–510.

23. Chachuat, B.; Marchetti, A.; Bonvin, D. Process optimization via constraints adaptation. *J. Process Control* **2008**, *18*, 244–257.

24. Marchetti, A.; Chachuat, B.; Bonvin, D. A dual modifier-adaptation approach for real-time optimization. *J. Process Control* **2010**, *20*, 1027–1037.

25. Bunin, G.; François, G.; Bonvin, D. Sufficient conditions for feasibility and optimality of real-time optimization schemes—I. Theoretical foundations. *arXiv* **2013**, arXiv:1308.2620 [math.OC].

26. Gao, W.; Wenzel, S.; Engell, S. A reliable modifier-adaptation strategy for real-time optimization. *Comput. Chem. Eng.* **2016**, *91*, 318–328.

27. Yip, W.S.; Marlin, T.E. Multiple data sets for model updating in real-time operations optimization. *Comput. Chem. Eng.* **2002**, *26*, 1345–1362.

28. Yip, W.S.; Marlin, T.E. Designing plant experiments for real-time optimization systems. *Control Eng. Pract.* **2003**, *11*, 837–845.

29. Pfaff, G.; Forbes, J.F.; McLellan, P.J. Generating information for real-time optimization. *Asia-Pac. J. Chem. Eng.* **2006**, *1*, 32–43.

30. Zhang, Y.; Nadler, D.; Forbes, J.F. Results analysis for trust constrained real-time optimization. *J. Process Control* **2001**, *11*, 329–341.

31. Quelhas, A.D.; de Jesus, N.J.C.; Pinto, J.C. Common vulnerabilities of RTO implementations in real chemical processes. *Can. J. Chem. Eng.* **2013**, *91*, 652–668.

32. Friedman, Y.Z. Closed loop optimization update—We are a step closer to fulfilling the dream. *Hydrocarb. Process. J.* **2000**, *79*, 15–16.

33. Gattu, G.; Palavajjhala, S.; Robertson, D.B. Are oil refineries ready for non-linear control and optimization? In Proceedings of the International Symposium on Process Systems Engineering and Control, Mumbai, India, 3–4 January 2003.

34. Basak, K.; Abhilash, K.S.; Ganguly, S.; Saraf, D.N. On-line optimization of a crude distillation unit with constraints on product properties. *Ind. Eng. Chem. Res.* **2002**, *41*, 1557–1568.

35. Morari, M.; Arkun, Y.; Stephanopoulos, G. Studies in the synthesis of control structures for chemical processes: Part I: Formulation of the problem. Process decomposition and the classification of the control tasks. Analysis of the optimizing control structures. *AIChE J.* **1980**, *26*, 220–232.

36. Bailey, J.; Hrymak, A.; Treiber, S.; Hawkins, R. Nonlinear optimization of a hydrocracker fractionation plant. *Comput. Chem. Eng.* **1993**, *17*, 123–138.

37. Bard, Y. *Nonlinear Parameter Estimation*; Academic Press: New York, NY, USA, 1974; Volume 513.

38. Von Neumann, J.; Kent, R.; Bellinson, H.; Hart, B. The mean square successive difference. *Ann. Math. Stat.* **1941**, *12*, 153–162.

39. Von Neumann, J. Distribution of the ratio of the mean square successive difference to the variance. *Ann. Math. Stat.* **1941**, *12*, 367–395.
40. Young, L. On randomness in ordered sequences. *Ann. Math. Stat.* **1941**, *12*, 293–300.
41. Cao, S.; Rhinehart, R.R. An efficient method for on-line identification of steady state. *J. Process Control* **1995**, *5*, 363–374.
42. Cao, S.; Rhinehart, R.R. Critical values for a steady-state identifier. *J. Process Control* **1997**, *7*, 149–152.
43. Shrowti, N.A.; Vilankar, K.P.; Rhinehart, R.R. Type-II critical values for a steady-state identifier. *J. Process Control* **2010**, *20*, 885–890.
44. Bhat, S.A.; Saraf, D.N. Steady-state identification, gross error detection, and data reconciliation for industrial process units. *Ind. Eng. Chem. Res.* **2004**, *43*, 4323–4336.
45. Montgomery, D.C.; Runger, G.C. *Applied Statistics and Probability for Engineers*, 3rd ed.; John Wiley & Sons: New York, NY, USA, 2002.
46. Alekman, S.L. Significance tests can determine steady-state with confidence. *Control Process Ind.* **1994**, *7*, 62–63.
47. Schladt, M.; Hu, B. Soft sensors based on nonlinear steady-state data reconciliationin the process industry. *Chem. Eng. Process. Process Intensif.* **2007**, *46*, 1107–1115.
48. Kelly, J.D.; Hedengren, J.D. A steady-state detection (SSD) algorithm to detect non-stationary drifts in processes. *J. Process Control* **2013**, *23*, 326–331.
49. Miletic, I.; Marlin, T. Results analysis for real-time optimization (RTO): Deciding when to change the plant operation. *Comput. Chem. Eng.* **1996**, *20* (Suppl. S2), S1077–S1082.
50. Miletic, I.; Marlin, T. On-line statistical results analysis in real-time operations optimization. *Ind. Eng. Chem. Res.* **1998**, *37*, 3670–3684.
51. Zafiriou, E.; Cheng, J.H. Measurement noise tolerance and results analysis for iterative feedback steady-state optimization. *Ind. Eng. Chem. Res.* **2004**, *43*, 3577–3589.
52. Bainbridge, L. Ironies of automation. *Automatica* **1983**, *19*, 775–779.

Article

Online Optimization Applied to a Shockless Explosion Combustor

Jan-Simon Schäpel [1], Thoralf G. Reichel [2], Rupert Klein [3], Christian Oliver Paschereit [2] and Rudibert King [1,*]

[1] Department of Process Technology, Measurement and Control, Technische Universität Berlin, 10623 Berlin, Germany; jan-simon.schaepel@tu-berlin.de

[2] Department of Fluid Dynamics and Technical Acoustics, Herman Föttinger Institute, Technische Universität Berlin, 10623 Berlin, Germany; thoralf.reichel@tu-berlin.de (T.G.R.); oliver.paschereit@tu-berlin.de (C.O.P.)

[3] Department of Mathematics, Geophysical Fluid Dynamics, Freie Universität Berlin, 14195 Berlin, Germany; rupert.klein@math.fu-berlin.de

* Correspondence: rudibert.king@tu-berlin.de; Tel.: +49-30-314-24100

Academic Editor: Dominique Bonvin
Received: 27 October 2016; Accepted: 22 November 2016; Published: 30 November 2016

Abstract: Changing the combustion process of a gas turbine from a constant-pressure to a pressure-increasing approximate constant-volume combustion (aCVC) is one of the most promising ways to increase the efficiency of turbines in the future. In this paper, a newly proposed method to achieve such an aCVC is considered. The so-called shockless explosion combustion (SEC) uses auto-ignition and a fuel stratification to achieve a spatially homogeneous ignition. The homogeneity of the ignition can be adjusted by the mixing of fuel and air. A proper filling profile, however, also depends on changing parameters, such as temperature, that cannot be measured in detail due to the harsh conditions inside the combustion tube. Therefore, a closed-loop control is required to obtain an adequate injection profile and to reject such unknown disturbances. For this, an optimization problem is set up and a novel formulation of a discrete extremum seeking controller is presented. By approximating the cost function with a parabola, the first derivative and a Hessian matrix are estimated, allowing the controller to use Newton steps to converge to the optimal control trajectory. The controller is applied to an atmospheric test rig, where the auto-ignition process can be investigated for single ignitions. In the set-up, dimethyl ether is injected into a preheated air stream using a controlled proportional valve. Optical measurements are used to evaluate the auto-ignition process and to show that using the extremum seeking control approach, the homogeneity of the ignition process can be increased significantly.

Keywords: shockless explosion combustion; constant volume combustion; extremum seeking control

1. Introduction

The higher efficiency of isochoric or constant-volume combustion compared to isobaric combustion has led to many investigations about adopting this combustion type for gas turbines. Several approaches to realize such a pressure-gain combustion or approximate constant-volume combustion (aCVC) process in a gas turbine have been proposed in the last decades. Pulsed jet combustors [1], pulsed detonation engines (PDE) [2], and rotating detonation engines (RDE) [3] are the main types of these devices.

To obtain pressure-rise combustion in all these devices, the fuel is burned in a short period of time such that the gas cannot fully expand during combustion. In a pulsed jet, the chemical reaction is driven by a deflagration wave. During this deflagration process, the burned gas is given time to partially expand. Thus, no constant-volume combustion is achieved. In contrast, in a PDE, the flame speed is increased, for example, using obstacles to create a deflagration-to-detonation transition. The detonation wave propagates through the combustor at supersonic speed. As a result, the gas has almost no time to expand during the detonation phase and an aCVC is obtained. Starting the PDE with a deflagration, however, means that part of the fuel is burned in a conventional, less efficient isobaric way. To avoid the deflagration-to-detonation transition, an RDE can be used. Here, a detonation wave is created that continuously runs inside an annular combustion chamber. However, the use of a detonation wave implies a shock wave, which is associated with considerable losses.

A promising new concept to avoid these pressure peaks is the so-called shockless explosion combustion (SEC), suggested by Bobusch et al. [4,5]. This combustion concept aims for a completely simultaneous auto-ignition of the fuel and thereby further approximates the constant-volume combustion while avoiding shock waves and associated losses. To achieve such a homogeneous auto-ignition in a combustion tube, the fuel needs to be injected under ignitable conditions such that a specific ignition delay profile is produced along the tube's length (see below). When the short ignition delay after the injection is complete, the fuel ignites along the whole tube at approximately the same time, and a smooth pressure rise results without a significant expansion of the reaction mixture. If designed properly, an acoustic resonance is created inside the tube, which allows a purging and refilling with fresh gas from the compressor against an unfavorable pressure gradient and thus enables a periodic process [6].

This paper concentrates on the adjustment of the filling process as it determines whether aCVC is achieved. At the start of the filling process, a buffer of pure air is injected to separate the hot gases of the previous cycle from the fresh fuel–air mixture and to prevent premature ignition. Afterwards, the fuel is injected until 40% of the tube is filled with the reactive fuel–air mixture. In Figure 1a, a sketch of a situation is given where a constant injection profile is assumed, that is, the so-called equivalence ration ϕ is constant. In terms of constant pressure and temperature, this results in a constant ignition delay τ for every portion of the injected fuel–air mixture. Due to the substantial duration of the injection process itself, the fuel injected first will also ignite before the rest; see t_{ign}. Therefore, to achieve a homogeneous auto-ignition, the fuel that is injected over time needs to be stratified to counteract the differences in the residence time of the reactive gas. Figure 1b sketches a case where such a stratified fuel profile is used. As the ignition delay depends on the equivalence ration ϕ, one can see that this can be used to achieve a homogeneous auto-ignition with a constant ignition time t_{ign} for all fuel particles. The ignition delay on the other side is strongly influenced by the unmeasured temperature and pressure in the tube. As a result, an appropriate filling profile can only be achieved using closed-loop control to reject these disturbances.

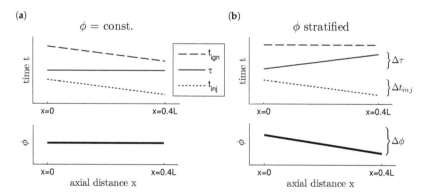

Figure 1. Sketch of the effect of equivalence ratio stratification on ignition delay time distribution (for details see text). (**a**) constant fuel profile (**b**) stratified fuel profile.

Once the fuel is injected into the tube, it is not possible to change the filling in this cycle anymore. Therefore, a controller is needed that improves the filling profile from one filling to the next, as performed in [7]. This task can be accomplished using an extremum seeking controller (ESC), which performs an online optimization. It does not require a model of the system, which is an advantage of the SEC concept because a detailed kinetic/fluid mechanic/acoustic model is far too complicated and sensitive to be used in an online optimization. Therefore, using a model-free controller, no further pressure and temperature sensors are needed to estimate the thermodynamic state in the tube that would be needed for a comprehensive model.

Many different applications of ESC, such as [8], and more theoretical works addressing stability issues [9,10] can be found in the literature. A list of possible extensions to ESC is presented in [11]. As the closed-loop bandwidth using an ESC is very low, methods to increase it are listed in [12]. In [13], we proposed using an Extended Kalman Filter to significantly speed up the single input case. An extension to the multiple input case can be found in [14]. Most of the controllers used apply a modulation of the continuous input by a dither signal and demodulation of the output to estimate the derivative of an unknown steady-state input–output map. By also estimating the Hessian matrix, it is possible to achieve higher convergence rates independent of the objective function's curvature [15]. However, it is not possible to use arbitrarily large steps due to the time separation between the dither signal and convergence speed. In this contribution, being restricted to an iterative solution from one filling to the next filling, classic ESC schemes cannot be applied. For this reason, we suggested an iterative application of an ESC in [16]. A general iterative scheme for an ESC is proposed in [17]. As the filling profile can be changed freely from one iteration to the next, Newton steps can be applied while estimating the necessary gradient and Hessian matrix using a least-squares method in a modified ESC architecture. Whereas in most applications sinusoidal dither signals are used, Tan et al. show in [18] that many other dither signals are also possible. In [19], stochastic perturbation signals are tested and considered to be a good choice to avoid sticking in local minima. These will also be used in this work. This paper focuses on the introduction and application of a variant of an ESC needed for a specific challenging process.

To experimentally investigate the concept of the SEC, an atmospheric test rig was build. This set-up allows us to investigate the auto-ignition process of dimethyl ether at atmospheric pressure and at a temperature of 920 K. An ignition delay of approximately 200 ms is observed. Such long ignition delays only allow for the investigation of single ignitions at a frequency of $\frac{4}{3}$ Hz, as the aforementioned acoustic resonance cannot be exploited for an autonomic refilling of the tube. In the future, we will move on to an SEC at a higher pressure, where this restriction should not apply. However, the control approach used here for the atmospheric test rig will work in the resonant set-up as well.

The set-up and the test procedure are described in Sections 2.1 and 2.2, respectively. The ESC formulation proposed here is given in Section 2.3 before experimental results are presented in Section 3. The paper finishes with some conclusions in Section 4.

2. Materials and Methods

2.1. The SEC Test Rig

The set-up used for the reactive ignition tests is shown as a schematic in Figure 2. The test rig allows for an investigation of a broad spectrum of possible regimes for homogeneous auto-ignition and is described in full detail in [5].

The main air flow is provided by a central air compressor with a mass flow of $m_{air} = 8.3\,g/s$. The electrical air heater heats up the air to a temperature of $T_{preheat} = 850\,K$. The inlet section of the combustion tube downstream of the fluidic switch (FDX Fluid Dynamix, Berlin, Germany) contains a fluidic diode (FDX Fluid Dynamix) and a fluidic oscillator (FDX Fluid Dynamix) (Figure 3). The diode prevents any backflow of the exhaust gas after an ignition. The fluidic oscillators are used to inject the fuel into the main stream with a high degree of turbulence to increase the homogeneity of the mixing [20]. The amount of fuel injected into the combustion tube is adjusted using a fast electric proportional valve that is able to control the fuel flow with a full-span (0%–100%) delay of less than 3 ms.

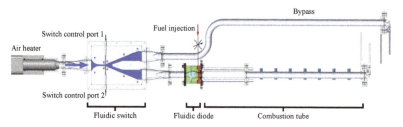

Figure 2. Schematic of the atmospheric SEC test rig.

The main air flow is provided by a central air compressor with a mass flow of $m_{air} = 8.3$ g/s. The electrical air heater heats up the air to a temperature of $T_{preheat} = 850$ K. The inlet section of the combustion tube downstream of the fluidic switch contains a fluidic diode and a fluidic oscillator (Figure 3). The diode prevents any backflow of the exhaust gas after an ignition. The fluidic oscillators are used to inject the fuel into the main stream with a high degree of turbulence to increase the homogeneity of the mixing [20]. The amount of fuel injected into the combustion tube is adjusted using a fast electric proportional valve that is able to control the fuel flow with a full-span (0%–100%) delay of less than 3 ms.

During the injection phase, the reactive gas–fuel mixture convects through the combustion tube, which has an inner diameter of 40 mm. The first section of the combustion tube, with a length of 0.5 m, is made out of quartz glass to allow for an optical measurement of the ignition times with photodiodes. For a future set-up, it is planned to detect the ignition times with ionization probes, which can be flush-mounted to the combustion tube. The second section is a stainless steel tube with multiple water-cooled, piezo-type pressure sensors connected. The ignition process takes place in the first section of the tube.

The applied flow speed of 17 m/s allows the refilling of the test section of the combustion tube within 30 ms. This time span, however, is much less than the ignition delay of dimethyl ether at atmospheric pressure of approximately 200 ms. To prevent the injected fuel from leaving the combustion tube before igniting, the air flow through the combustion tube needs to be stopped after the injection of the fuel. Regarding the air heater, an air mass flow is always required. Therefore, the air has to bypass the combustion tube after the injection process is completed. To facilitate this, a fluidic switch containing no moving parts that can redirect the main air flow into the bypass was designed. Note that the bypassing of the combustion tube is only necessary due to the high ignition delay at ambient pressure and will not be necessary at higher pressure levels, which is the focus of future work.

A real-time processor (dSpace 1202, dSpace, Paderborn, Germany) operating at 10 kHz processes all measurement data and controls the proportional valve and fluidic switch.

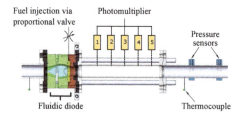

Figure 3. Section view of the injection geometry and combustion tube with sensors.

2.2. Test Procedure

The ignition tests are run at a frequency of $\frac{4}{3}$ Hz. At the beginning of each cycle, the combustion tube is purged with air; see the time span from $t = 0$ to $t = t_F$ in Figure 4. From $t = t_f$ to $t = t_A$, fuel is injected such that the optical accessible part of the tube is filled with reactive gas. The amount of fuel injected is determined by a closed-loop controller, described later. At the end of the injection, the fluidic switch redirects the main flow into the bypass. This creates a low pressure in the combustion tube such that the flap at the end of the combustion tube closes and the gas inside the combustion tube is stopped. After the ignition delay, the fuel ignites and the ignition is detected by five photodiodes. The ignition times $\tilde{t}_{ign}(x_q)$ are determined as the first time the detected signal of the q-th photodiode at position x_q exceeds a threshold. Whenever the signal of at least one photodiode does not exceed the threshold, this ignition is not evaluated but the combustion process is repeated. At $t = t_B$, the main air flow is switched back into the combustion tube, which simulates the next purging process. The system behavior is not very reproducible from one ignition cycle to the next, mainly due to the effect of the fluidic switch necessary for atmospheric operation. Therefore, the control trajectory is only recalculated every five ignition cycles. Based on the calculated ignition delays of five consecutive cycles $\tilde{t}_{ign,k,j}(x_q)$, for each position x_q the highest and lowest values are discarded to protect the controller from outliers. The remaining three ignition delays are used to calculate mean ignition delays $t_{ign,k}(x_q)$ for iteration k and for each sensor position. Only the mean ignition delays are used in the ESC.

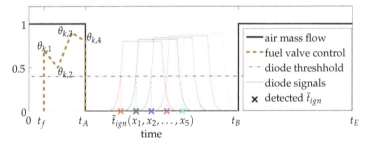

Figure 4. Example of one filling cycle showing the timings for the fuel and air injection and schematic photodiode signals.

2.3. Extremum Seeking Control

The ESC is an online optimizer that does not require a model of the system to be optimized. This means that during the optimization process, the ESC needs to estimate a local approximation of the system by evaluating the measurement information. According to this local, mostly gradient information, the optimizer then changes the input, defined by a set of parameters θ_k, such that a local optimum of an objective function dependent on the system output is found. In this paper, we will refer to a minimum without loss of generality. To guarantee that the ESC is able to converge to the optimum, it is necessary to have a system with a continuously differentiable input–output static map that is bounded. More assumptions need to be fulfilled for the most frequently used classic ESC set-up; for more details see [10,21].

While there exist many modifications to the ESC, all of them can be described with a common structure [11]. In a first step, the output of the system is evaluated to calculate the value of an objective function. This calculated value and the input of the system are used to approximate the first and possibly higher-order derivatives of the objective function with respect to the actuation. In the classic scheme, a set of high- and low-pass filters is employed to estimate the derivatives. These derivatives are then used by an optimization algorithm to modify the system input in the direction of the optimum. To estimate the derivatives, it is necessary that the input signal to the system is perturbed. In this paper, a modified ESC set-up is proposed. A schematic representation is shown in Figure 5. Details will be given below.

Applying this concept to an SEC where we need to achieve a homogeneous auto-ignition means that the fuel has to be injected into the combustion tube such that it ignites all along the tube at the same time. From the averaged ignition timings, which are detected by the five photodiodes (see Section 2.2), the variance in between the photodiodes is calculated and chosen as the objective function for the ESC that shall be minimized. A value of 0 for the variance would indicate a completely homogeneous SEC. Additionally, a fixed desired reference ignition time r is provided. As deviations from this reference ignition time are penalized, a homogeneous ignition at $t = r$ would yield the lowest objective value. The weighting parameter of the absolute ignition time was set to a small value, $W_r = 0.0125$, to keep the focus on the homogeneous ignition. In a first step, averaged ignition times $t_{ign,k}(x_q)$ are calculated for the last five ignition cycles $j = 1, \ldots, 5$ for all measurement positions x_q, discarding two outliers:

$$t_{ign,k}(x_q) = \frac{1}{3} \left(\sum_{j=1}^{5} \left(\bar{t}_{ign,k,j}(x_q) \right) - \min_{j=1\ldots5} \bar{t}_{ign,k,j}(x_q) - \max_{j=1\ldots5} \bar{t}_{ign,k,j}(x_q) \right). \tag{1}$$

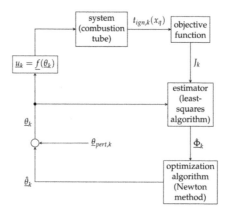

Figure 5. Schematic representation of the ESC used in this paper.

For all cycles of the k-th iteration, the same plant input $\underline{u}_k = f(\underline{\theta}_k)$ is used. With this data, the objective function J_k is determined.

$$J_k = \frac{1}{4} \sum_{q=1}^{5} \left(t_{ign,k}(x_q) - \bar{t}_{ign,k} \right)^2 + W_r (\bar{t}_{ign,k} - r)^2 \bar{t}_{ign,k} = \frac{1}{5} \sum_{q=1}^{5} t_{ign,k}(x_q). \tag{2}$$

The only input value that the ESC is allowed to adjust is the control current of the proportional valve during the injection time. To parametrize the injection profile for the k-th group of a set of five cycles, a piecewise linear function is chosen; see Figure 4. The profile of the five consecutive filling processes in the k-th iteration is defined by a set of interpolation points. To respect real-time requirements, four interpolation points are used in this study. They are concatenated in the vector $\underline{\theta}_k = (\theta_{k,1}, \cdots, \theta_{k,4})^\mathsf{T}$. Between these equidistant interpolation points, the injection profile is interpolated linearly (see Figures 4 and 5):

$$\underline{u}_k = f(\underline{\theta}_k) = \begin{pmatrix} u(t_f, \underline{\theta}_k) \\ u(t_f + \Delta t, \underline{\theta}_k) \\ \vdots \\ u(t_f + (n-1) \cdot \Delta t, \underline{\theta}_k) \end{pmatrix}, \tag{3}$$

with

$$u(t, \underline{\theta}_k) = \theta_{k,m} + (\theta_{k,m+1} - \theta_{k,m}) \left(\frac{3(t - t_f)}{t_A - t_f} + 1 - m \right),$$

$$m \in 1 \dots 3 \left| t_f + (m-1) \frac{t_A - t_f}{3} \le t < t_f + m \frac{t_A - t_f}{3} \right. \tag{4}$$

$$n = \frac{t_A - t_f}{\Delta t}, \tag{5}$$

where $\underline{u}_k$ is the discrete injection profile, $\Delta t = 0.0001$ s is the sampling interval, and t_f and t_A are the starting point and the end point of the filling process, respectively.

All combustion cycles in the present set-up are mostly independent from each other. Only the temperature in the tube will depend on previous combustions and influence the ignition delays of subsequent ignitions. This temperature distribution in the tube will change slowly from one ignition cycle to the next and is considered to be a disturbance which has to be handled by the controller.

For each set of five filling processes with the injection profile $\underline{u}_k$, the measurements are evaluated by the objective function J_k. To obtain information about the local dependency of J on $\underline{\theta}$, we propose to fit a multidimensional parabola based on all measurements up to the k-th filling process. To this end, at iteration k, every group of five cycles is approximated by

$$\hat{J}_i = \underline{\theta}_i^\mathsf{T} \mathbf{A}_k \underline{\theta}_i + \underline{b}_k^\mathsf{T} \underline{\theta}_i + c_k \ , i = 1, \dots, k, \tag{6}$$

where $\mathbf{A}_k$, $\underline{b}_k$, and c_k are the as yet unknown Hessian matrix, gradient, and constant offset, respectively. As this equation is linear regarding the unknown entries of $\mathbf{A}_k$, and $\underline{b}_k$, they can be collected in the vector $\underline{\hat{\Phi}}_k$. Equation (6) can then be formally rewritten in the form

$$\hat{J}_i = \underline{x}_i^\mathsf{T} \underline{\hat{\Phi}}_k \ , i = 1, \dots, k, \tag{7}$$

with $\underline{x}_i$ being a vector build up from $\underline{\theta}_i$. Combining Equation (7) for all iterations up to the recent cycle k of five consecutive filling processes in a matrix equation, we obtain

$$\begin{pmatrix} \hat{J}_1 \\ \vdots \\ \hat{J}_k \end{pmatrix} = \underline{\hat{J}}_k = \mathbf{X}_k \underline{\hat{\Phi}}_k = \begin{pmatrix} \underline{x}_1^\mathsf{T} \\ \vdots \\ \underline{x}_k^\mathsf{T} \end{pmatrix} \underline{\hat{\Phi}}_k. \tag{8}$$

To estimate $\underline{\hat{\Phi}}_k$, we use the least-squares algorithm, which minimizes the squared deviation between the cost function and the estimated parabola:

$$\min_{\underline{\hat{\Phi}}_k} (\underline{J}_k - \mathbf{X}_k \underline{\hat{\Phi}}_k)^\mathsf{T} \mathbf{W} (\underline{J}_k - \mathbf{X}_k \underline{\hat{\Phi}}_k), \tag{9}$$

where $\underline{J}_k$ contains the experimentally obtained objective values from k consecutive iterations. The well-known solution is given by

$$\underline{\hat{\Phi}}_k = (\mathbf{X}_k^\mathsf{T} \mathbf{W} \mathbf{X}_k)^{-1} \mathbf{X}_k^\mathsf{T} \mathbf{W} \underline{J}_k =: \mathbf{P}_k \mathbf{X}_k^\mathsf{T} \mathbf{W} \underline{J}_k, \tag{10}$$

with W being a weighting matrix. To emphasize the most recent measurements, older measurements are associated with an exponentially decreasing weight λ. By decreasing the value of λ, it is possible to further limit the influence of old values.

$$\mathbf{W} = \begin{pmatrix} \lambda^{k-1} & \cdots & & 0 \\ \vdots & \ddots & & \vdots \\ & & \lambda & \\ 0 & \cdots & & 1 \end{pmatrix} \tag{11}$$

To reduce the computational effort, the least-squares problem is solved using a recursive solution of this problem given in Equations (12)–(14). $\mathbf{P}_0$ has to be initialized with high values to account for missing system information in the beginning [22].

$$\underline{\gamma}_k = [\underline{x}_{k+1}^\mathsf{T} \mathbf{P}_k \underline{x}_{k+1} + \lambda]^{-1} \mathbf{P}_k \underline{x}_{k+1} \tag{12}$$

$$\hat{\underline{\Phi}}_{k+1} = \hat{\underline{\Phi}}_k + \underline{\gamma}_k [J_{k+1} - \underline{x}_{k+1}^\mathsf{T} \hat{\underline{\Phi}}_k] \tag{13}$$

$$\mathbf{P}_{k+1} = \lambda^{-1}[\mathbf{I} - \underline{\gamma}_k \underline{x}_{k+1}^\mathsf{T}]\mathbf{P}_k \tag{14}$$

From the fitted parameters $\hat{\underline{\Phi}}_k$ of the multidimensional parabola, the gradient and curvature at the current actuation parameter $\underline{\theta}_k$ can be recalculated according to Equation (6). Whenever the fitted parabola is positive definite, the proposed optimization algorithm calculates a Newton step. Therefore, the actuation parameters for the next injection process will be set to the minimum of the identified parabola whenever it is in range of the allowed step size; see below. If the Hessian matrix is not positive definite, the algorithm performs gradient steps with a step size σ_θ.

$$\tilde{\underline{\theta}}_{k+1} = \begin{cases} 0.5\mathbf{A}_k^{-1}\underline{b}_k, & \mathbf{A}_k > 0 \\ \hat{\underline{\theta}}_k + \sigma_\theta(2\mathbf{A}_k\hat{\underline{\theta}}_k + \underline{b}_K), & \text{otherwise} \end{cases} \tag{15}$$

Here, $\hat{\underline{\theta}}_k$ is the unperturbed control parameter of the last iteration, which differs from $\tilde{\underline{\theta}}_k$ calculated by Equation (15) in the last iteration due to its compliance to the maximum step size θ_{max}. Whenever the maximum step size is exceeded, the step size will be set to θ_{max}, while the direction of the optimization step is kept constant.

$$\hat{\underline{\theta}}_{k+1} = \begin{cases} \hat{\underline{\theta}}_k + (\tilde{\underline{\theta}}_{k+1} - \hat{\underline{\theta}}_k)\frac{\theta_{max}}{||\tilde{\underline{\theta}}_{k+1} - \hat{\underline{\theta}}_k||_2}, & ||\tilde{\underline{\theta}}_{k+1} - \hat{\underline{\theta}}_k||_2 \geq \theta_{max} \\ \tilde{\underline{\theta}}_{k+1}, & \text{otherwise} \end{cases} \tag{16}$$

This last step is necessary for stability reasons, as huge Newton steps might result for an ill-conditioned matrix $\mathbf{A}$.

As for every ESC, a perturbation needs to be applied to the actuation parameter $\hat{\underline{\theta}}_{k+1}$. Here, a vector $\underline{\theta}_{pert,k}$ with uniformly distributed random entries in a range between $[-d, d]$ is added to the calculated $\hat{\underline{\theta}}_{k+1}$; see Figure 5. Because the task of the ESC is not just to find an optimal control profile but also to keep track of it, the amplitude of the pertubation is kept constant to allow for a detection of disturbances at all times. For the application of the SEC, we chose the following values for the tuning parameters: $d = 0.5\,\text{mA}$, $\sigma_\theta = 40\,\frac{A^2}{s^2}$, $\lambda = 0.95$, and $\theta_{max} = 1\,\text{mA}$.

3. Results

For the ignition tests with the described set-up, we performed 1000 combustion cycles. However, 9% of the ignitions could not be evaluated properly because not all the photodiodes detected a signal higher than the defined threshold. With the used data acquisition system, it was not possible to store all the data at once. For this reason, the test series had to be paused after 500 cycles. During such a pause, the fuel lines close to the tube are heated up, which yields much lower ignition delays when part of this fuel is injected at the beginning of the next batch of cycles. To avoid interfering with the control algorithm after the pause, 100 filling combustion cycles were carried out with a cycle invariant injection profile. The obtained measurement data was not considered by the ESC. For every single combustion cycle, the timings for the filling and purging of the tube were set to $t_f = 0.05\,$s, $t_A = 0.08\,$s, $t_B = 0.58\,$s, and $t_E = 0.75\,$s. The desired reference ignition time r was chosen as $0.25\,$s such that the resulting range of desired ignition delays was centered inside the limits adjustable by changing the fuel concentration. The injected fuel trajectory was modified every five successful ignitions, according to the control law of the described ESC algorithm. The test series was started with a constant control value applied to the valve of 14 mA. This corresponds to a rich fuel–air mixture.

In Figure 6, the change of the input parameters $\underline{\theta}_k$, the detected ignition times, and the control error are shown as a function of the iterations. The ESC is set active after 100 iterations. It starts changing the control trajectory such that the control error decreases. The control error is calculated as the variance of the averaged ignition times of five ignitions, as explained in Section 2.2, and also takes the deviation from the desired ignition time into consideration according to Equation (2). However, for the homogeneity of an ignition, the variance of the ignition times is the best measure and is therefore also included in the diagram for every single ignition. Until the 360th iteration, the ignition always takes place at a location far downstream in the tube and is detected by the fifth photodiode first. Due to an increase in the amount of fuel injected in the beginning of the filling process and less fuel injected afterwards (see Figure 7), the ignition at the location of the fifth photodiode can be delayed. From the 360th ignition on, a quite homogeneous ignition is obtained. After achieving a homogeneous ignition, the controller is also able to adjust the ignition time towards the desired value; see Figure 6 (at around 400 iterations). From this point of time, the control trajectory is only changed slightly, which indicates that a local optimum was found by the controller. In Figure 7, the detected ignition times for a constant injection, as conducted in the beginning of the experiment, and for four consecutive injections with the converged control trajectory after 400 iterations are shown. It can be seen that the converged control trajectory found by the ESC yields significantly more homogeneous ignitions necessary for an SEC. However, among the four ignitions with the same filling profile, there is still a high deviation in the ignition times from one cycle to another. This indicates that the system behavior changes from one cycle to the next so that the ESC has no chance to further increase the quality of the SEC just using information from past combustion cycles. A high deviation between consecutive ignitions can also be observed for the pressure readings. On average, though, the pressure rise, due to the combustion, increased due to the higher homogeneity of the ignition process, as depicted in Figure 6. The highest pressure rise measured for one ignition was 0.36 bar, which was achieved for an ignition taking place within less than 2 ms.

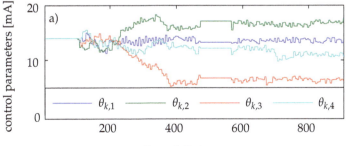

Figure 6. *Cont.*

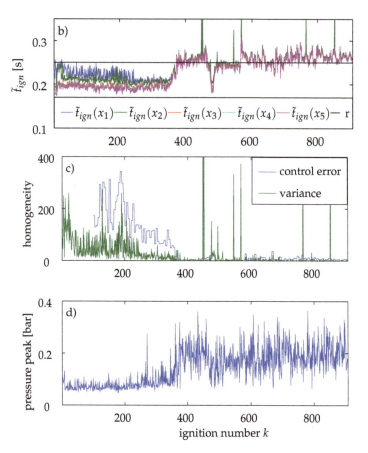

Figure 6. Experiment with 900 successful combustion cycles (9% of the ignitions are misfiring and not included in the diagram for clarity). (**a**) Control parameters defining the control profile of the fuel valve; (**b**) Ignition times detected by the photodiodes; (**c**) Homogeneity of the ignition evaluated by the variance and by the control error that is calculated for every five consecutive ignitions when the controller is active; (**d**) Maximum pressure increase due to the ignition.

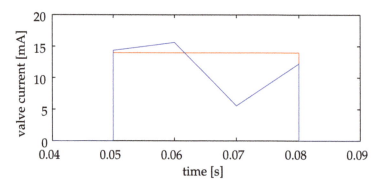

Figure 7. *Cont.*

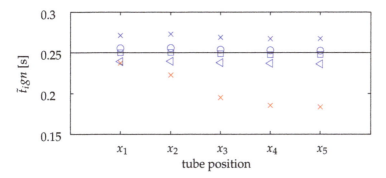

Figure 7. Example of five time-resolved combustion processes. **Red**: Injection profile and detected ignition times with initialized control trajectory; **Blue**: Injection profile and detected ignition times with converged control trajectory (ignition number 401–404). The four consecutive shots have the same injection profile. Their individual ignition timings are depicted with different markers.

4. Conclusions

In this paper, a model-free control method is presented to optimize a control input for iterative tasks where virtually no system information is available. The considered control addresses the essential challenge of SEC—the homogeneous auto-ignition of the fuel. The effectiveness of the developed ESC algorithm is demonstrated with an atmospheric test rig, which was designed to study the auto-ignition behavior at a firing frequency of $\frac{4}{3}$ Hz. A fast proportional valve was used to adjust the amount of fuel injected into the combustion tube. Using an optical measuring technique, the ignition times were detected. The variance of these ignition times, which provides a good measure for the homogeneity of the self-ignition, was used as a control target. As the chemical processes are hard to model with respect to a real-time application and are very sensitive to unmeasured quantities, such as the pressure and temperature distribution inside the combustion tube, a model-free approach was chosen. The applied ESC was able to minimize the variance using an online optimization. The first and second derivatives of the objective function were estimated by a recursive least-squares algorithm and used to perform Newton steps. However, with this method, only a local minimum can be guaranteed. Although the experiments showed that the time span of a completed ignition process could be significantly decreased below 2 ms, at the atmospheric conditions the resulting pressure rise is still not as high as would be expected for a perfect SEC. However, for combustions performed under elevated pressure, which are planned for the near future, the ignition delay will be significantly lower. For the same mixing quality, this would reduce the duration of the ignition process accordingly. As a result, the applied mixing control method presents a powerful tool to realize an SEC at relevant pressure levels.

Acknowledgments: The authors gratefully acknowledge the support of the Deutsche Forschungsgemeinschaft (DFG) as part of collaborative research center CRC 1029 "Substantial efficiency increase in gas turbines through direct use of coupled unsteady combustion and flow dynamics".

Author Contributions: Jan-Simon Schäpel built the controller, ran the experiments, and wrote the paper, supervised by Rudibert King. Thoralf Reichel was responsible for the experimental set-up. Rupert Klein and Christian Oliver Paschereit developed the concept of an SEC.

Conflicts of Interest: The authors declare no conflict of interest.

Abbreviations

The following abbreviations are used in this manuscript:

aCVC	approximate constant volume combustion
ESC	extremum seeking controller
PDE	pulsed detonation engine
RDE	rotating detonation engine
SEC	shockless explosion combustion

References

1. Putnam, A.; Belles, F.; Kentfield, J. Pulse combustion. *Prog. Energy Combust. Sci.* **1986**, *12*, 43–79.
2. Roy, G.; Frolov, S.; Borisov, A.; Netzer, D. Pulse detonation propulsion: challenges, current status, and future perspective. *Prog. Energy Combust. Sci.* **2004**, *30*, 545–672.
3. Lu, F.K.; Braun, E.M. Rotating detonation wave propulsion: experimental challenges, modeling, and engine concepts. *J. Propuls. Power* **2014**, *30*, 1125–1142.
4. Bobusch, B.C.; Berndt, P.; Paschereit, C.O.; Klein, R. Shockless Explosion Combustion: An Innovative Way of Efficient Constant Volume Combustion in Gas Turbines. *Combust. Sci. Technol.* **2014**, *186*, 1680–1689.
5. Bobusch, B.C. Fluidic Devices for Realizing the Shockless Explosion Combustion Process. Ph.D. Thesis, Technische Universität Berlin, Berlin, Germany, 2015.
6. Berndt, P.; Klein, R.; Paschereit, C.O. A Kinetics Model for the Shockless Explosion Combustion. In Proceedings of the ASME Turbo Expo 2016: Turbomachinery Technical Conference and Exposition, Seoul, Korea, 13–17 June 2016; Volume 4B.
7. Reichel, T.G.; Schäpel, J.S.; Bobusch, B.C.; Klein, R.; King, R.; Paschereit, C.O. Shockless Explosion Combustion: Experimental Investigation of a New Approximate Constant Volume Combustion Process. *J. Eng. Gas Turbines Power* **2016**, *139*, 021504–021510.
8. Tan, Y.; Moase, W.; Manzie, C.; Nesic, D.; Mareels, I. Extremum seeking from 1922 to 2010. In Proceedings of the 29th Chinese Control Conference, China, Beijing, 28–31 July 2010.
9. Krstic, M.; Wang, H.H. Design and Stability Analysis of Extremum Seeking Feedback for General Nonlinear Systems. In Proceedings of the Conference on Decision & Control, San Diego, CA, USA, 10–12 December 1997; pp. 1743–1748.
10. Tan, Y.; Nesic, D.; Mareels, I. On non-local stability properties of extremum seeking control. *Automatica* **2006**, *42*, 889–903.
11. Nesic, D.; Tan, Y.; Manzie, C.; Mohammadi, A.; Moase, W. A unifying framework for analysis and design of extremum seeking controllers. In Proceedings of the IEEE Chinese Control and Decision Conference, Taiyuan, China, 23–25 May 2012; pp. 4274–4285.
12. Krstic, M. Performance improvement and limitations in extremum seeking control. *Syst. Control Lett.* **2000**, *39*, 313–326.
13. Henning, L.; Becker, R.; Feuerbach, G.; Muminovic, R.; King, R.; Brunn, A.; Nitsche, W. Extensions of adaptive slope-seeking for active flow control. *Proc. Inst. Mech. Eng. Part I J. Syst. Control Eng.* **2008**, *222*, 309–322.
14. Gelbert, G.; Moeck, J.P.; Paschereit, C.O.; King, R. Advanced algorithms for gradient estimation in one- and two-parameter extremum seeking controllers. *J. Process Control* **2012**, *22*, 700–709.
15. Moase, W.H.; Manzie, C.; Brear, M.J. Newton-Like Extremum-Seeking for the Control of Thermoacoustic Instability. *IEEE Trans. Autom. Control* **2010**, *55*, 2094–2105.
16. Schäpel, J.S.; King, R.; Bobusch, B.; Moeck, J.; Paschereit, C.O. Adaptive Control of Mixture Profiles for a Combustion Tube. In Proceedings of the ASME Turbo Expo 2015: Turbine Technical Conference and Exposition, Montréal, QC, Canada, 15–19 June 2015; GT2015-42027.
17. Khong, S.Z.; Nesic, D.; Krstic, M. Iterative learning control based on extremum seeking. *Automatica* **2016**, *66*, 238–245.
18. Tan, Y.; Nesic, D.; Mareels, I. On the choice of dither in extremum seeking systems: A case study. *Automatica* **2008**, *44*, 1446–1450.
19. Liu, S.J.; Krstic, M. Stochastic Averaging in Continuous Time and Its Applications to Extremum Seeking. *IEEE Trans. Autom. Control* **2010**, *55*, 2235–2250.

20. Bobusch, B.C.; Berndt, P.; Paschereit, C.O.; Klein, R. Investigation of fluidic devices for mixing enhancement for the shockless explosion combustion process. In *Active Flow and Combustion Control 2014*; King, R., Ed.; Springer International Publishing: Cham, Switzerland, 2015; pp. 281–297.

21. Kristic, M.; Wang, H.H. Stability of extremum seeking feedback for general nonlinear dynamic systems. *Automatica* **2000**, *36*, 595–601.

22. Iserman, R.; Münchhof, M. *Identification of Dynamic Systems*; Springer: Berlin/Heidelberg, Germany, 2011.

Article

Integration of RTO and MPC in the Hydrogen Network of a Petrol Refinery

Cesar de Prada [1,*], Daniel Sarabia [2], Gloria Gutierrez [1], Elena Gomez [1], Sergio Marmol [3], Mikel Sola [3], Carlos Pascual [3] and Rafael Gonzalez [3]

[1]   Department of Systems Engineering and Automatic Control, University of Valladolid,
     Valladolid 47011, Spain; gloria@autom.uva.es (G.G.); elenags@cta.uva.es (E.G.)
[2]   Department of Electromechanical Engineering, University of Burgos, Burgos 09006, Spain; dsarabia@ubu.es
[3]   Petroleos del Norte, S.A, Petronor, Muskiz 48550, Spain; smarmol@repsol.com (S.M.),
     jmsola@repsol.com (M.S.); cpascual@repsol.com (C.P.); rgonzalezm@repsol.com (R.G.)
*   Correspondence: prada@autom.uva.es; Tel.: +34-983-423-164

Academic Editor: Dominique Bonvin
Received: 13 November 2016; Accepted: 29 December 2016; Published: 7 January 2017

Abstract: This paper discusses the problems associated with the implementation of Real Time Optimization/Model Predictive Control (RTO/MPC) systems, taking as reference the hydrogen distribution network of an oil refinery involving eighteen plants. This paper addresses the main problems related to the operation of the network, combining data reconciliation and a RTO system, designed for the optimal generation and redistribution of hydrogen, with a predictive controller for the on-line implementation of the optimal policies. This paper describes the architecture of the implementation, showing how RTO and MPC can be integrated, as well as the benefits obtained in terms of improved information about the process, increased hydrocarbon load to the treatment plants and reduction of the hydrogen required for performing the operations.

Keywords: real-time optimization; model predictive control; petrol refineries; hydrogen networks

---

1. Introduction

Process industries, like other industrial sectors, are compelled by the market and the regulatory norms to operate more and more efficiently. This means better product quality, higher production, fulfilment of environmental legislation, etc., with better use of resources and minimum cost. Achievement of all these aims requires, among other things, proper use of the resources and assets as well as better production management. This is why, increasingly, the topics and methods related to production optimization are gaining attention in industry. Once the basic automation layer is in operation in a factory, so that production reaches a certain degree of stability and adequate information from the process is available, the next logical step is to move up in the management of the process. This can be done, first, by enhancing the control layer to take care of interactions, constraints and future consequences of current actions in the operation of the process units, that is, incorporating Model Predictive control (MPC), and, in a second step, trying to find out the best operating conditions, considering not only technical aspects, but also the economy of the process. This requires a more global vision than considering in isolation the operation of the individual process units, because what can be good from the point of view of a specific process may not be so good for the whole factory. Real-Time Optimization (RTO) uses, such as global view, try to incorporate different aspects and interrelations among processes in a model in order to compute operational decisions that optimize process efficiency and economy.

Both layers, MPC and RTO, have different targets and normally they use different types of models, linear dynamic models in the case of MPC and non-linear first principles ones in the RTO, but they are not independent. Normally, RTO is placed on top of MPC, computing optimal values of key variables that later on are passed as set points to the MPC in a cascade structure. This architecture assumes that there exists an optimum steady state that the MPC must follow, which can be a sensible assumption in many cases. Nevertheless, it also happens quite often that, due to the plant scale or complex dynamics involved or because of the presence of significant disturbances, the plant is rarely at steady state, so some alternatives have to be used. Of course, in many cases, one can formulate a dynamic RTO, or an MPC with an economic target, merging dynamic control with economic target optimization as in [1,2], and in fact they are examples of very large dynamic optimization problems solved efficiently with state-of-the-art software and methodology [3]. However, this formulation may present stability problems and, in other cases, the computational load and the difficulties of estimating properly the process states may render the approach not very adequate for real-time operation.

In addition, other factors that contribute to the difficulties of industrial implementation of the RTO/MPC architecture are the fact that large RTO, based on rigorous models, are difficult to keep up-to-date and there is a lack of resources in industry to maintain these applications, due to limited number of qualified personnel, to the relatively frequent changes and revamping in the process and to the intrinsic difficulties of the task that is time consuming and rather specialized. The reference [4] gives a good summary of these problems. However, the benefits of RTO normally repay the efforts, not only in terms of the gains obtained through its on-line implementation, but because of other side benefits, such as improved process information, detection of groups of constraints that limit the possibility of reaching the targets, reliable feedback to upper production layers (planning), etc.

All these elements have to be taken into account when defining the approach and the implementation of the system, exploring, besides the traditional cascade RTO/MPC, other flexible alternatives in which the possibilities offered by available commercial technology have to be considered, as they provide integrated local Linear Programming (LP) based optimization with predictive multivariable controllers [5]. In the same way, one should consider the options that sometimes appear for carrying out similar solutions as the ones computed by the RTO with a specially designed control system, in line with the self-optimizing approach [6].

Besides integration of RTO with the lower layer represented by MPC, successful implementations of real-time optimization systems have to take into account that RTO normally only covers certain aspects of the operation of a large-scale process plant. In fact, there are many elements related to what should be produced or when it should be produced and at what price, that concern to the upper layer of plant planning. Then, RTO should operate in the framework and global aims defined by the planning layer of the company, receiving production aims, prices and constraints imposed by other parts of the process, that have to be considered by the RTO and MPC. This aspect concerns the information flow from top to lower layers of the control hierarchy, but additional benefits can be obtained by considering also the opposite flow by better feedback of the results of the operation to the planning layer, helping to correct gaps between what is planned and what is achieved in practice and detecting the active constraints whose removal can improve production and efficiency in a significant way.

This paper deals with these topics, presenting a large-scale optimization problem related to the management of the hydrogen distribution network of an oil refinery and discussing its real-time implementation.

Hydrogen has become an important and expensive utility required in many new processes in oil refineries for breaking long hydrocarbon chains into lighter and more valuable products and for removal of Sulphur and aromatics in order to comply with environmental legislation. Hydrogen, either imported or produced in-house, is distributed by means of a network from producer to consumer plants. In consumer plants, hydrogen is mainly used as a reactant for desulfurization, de-nitrification and de-aromatization of naphtha and diesel, in order to avoid generating acid gases when used as heating fuel or in combustion engines, thus avoiding atmosphere pollution.

In recent years, when heavier fuels are being processed and also due to more strict environmental regulations, hydrogen requirements have experienced a steady increase, gaining significant importance in the refinery global economic balance. An efficient use of H_2 in the daily operation is desired not only for its high production cost, but also because the economic penalty is even higher in scenarios where hydrogen production capacity is the bottleneck for oil processing capacity. Nevertheless, decisions related to hydrogen management are not easy as there are many interrelated plants and constraints involved in the operation of the network, not only from a modelling and optimization perspective, but also from a practical point of view because, quite often, several operators in different control rooms are in charge.

The approach to deal with the hydrogen network optimal management is driven by an operational framework where hydrogen production must always exceed consumption, with reactors operating with excess hydrogen, because hydrogen deficit is extremely damaging for catalysts which are very expensive and accumulation in a buffer vessel is not sensible. One of the main problems to perform appropriate decisions regarding the management of hydrogen networks is the lack of information on many variables and the uncertainty associated with the existing measurements. Because of this, data reconciliation has been used as a way to estimate unknown magnitudes and to correct inconsistencies in the data, before a model based optimization procedure could be applied to determine the best use of hydrogen in the network.

The optimal management of hydrogen in oil refineries has been studied mainly from a design viewpoint as in [7], as well as integrated with other utility systems in the refinery operation, as in [8], but has received less attention from the perspective of real-time operation and control.

This paper tries to contribute to the automated optimal operation of the hydrogen networks in oil refineries and is organized as follows: First, the process is described in Section 2, showing the architecture, operation and targets of the main plants and the functioning of the network as a whole. Next, Section 3 presents a Data Reconciliation and Real-Time Optimization system developed with the purpose of achieving the optimal management of the hydrogen network. Then, Section 4 is devoted to discussing the ways in which the system is implemented in the refinery, in particular through the use of a predictive Dynamic Matrix Controller (DMC) operating on several H_2 production and consumption plants. Finally, Section 5 presents and evaluates the results achieved, as well as the integration of the operation of RTO and MPC layers as a decision Support System (DSS) supervising the network performance. To conclude, the Discussion section centers on the future perspectives and challenges of process optimization.

2. Process Description

The process taken as reference is the refinery of Petronor, a company of the Repsol group located in Muskiz, in northern Spain. The refinery processes crude oil in standard distillation circuits but, as with many other modern installations, incorporates additional ones as well. Among them, conversion units transform heavy hydrocarbons into more valuable light ones, besides other units dedicated to the removal of Sulphur from the processed products in order to comply with the environmental legislation. Both conversion and desulphurization processes use hydrogen as raw material of the chemical reactions involved, so this product has become one of the most important utilities in a petrol refinery.

High purity hydrogen is produced in steam-reforming furnaces in two plants, named H3 and H4, in the refinery under consideration. Additionally, two platformer plants (P1 and P2) generate lower purity hydrogen as a byproduct of the catalytic reforming process, which increases the octane number of naphtha. From these four plants, hydrogen is distributed to the consumer ones using several interconnected networks at different purities and pressures, as can be seen in the schematic of Figure 1. The network interconnects a total of eighteen plants, four producers and fourteen consumers.

NET_PETR

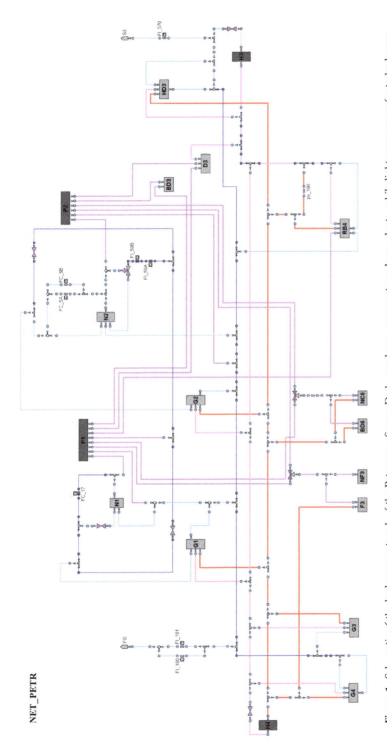

Figure 1. Schematic of the hydrogen network of the Petronor refinery. Dark grey boxes represent producer plants, while light grey ones refer to hydrogen consumer units.

A simplified schematic of a typical consumer plant can be seen in Figure 2, in this case a hydrodesulphurization one (HDS) dedicated to the removal of Sulphur from its hydrocarbon feed. Before entering the reactors, the hydrocarbon feed (HC) (black lines) is mixed with hydrogen (blue lines) coming from the distribution network: in the diagram from two producer plants (H4 and H3) and the Low Purity distribution Header (LPH), as well as with recycled hydrogen streams (R, F_{OUT_Z}). This mixture reacts endothermically under high temperature in the reactors where sulfur is converted into hydrogen sulfide H_2S, which can be removed later on by absorption on an amine solution. It is important to remark that the feed to the reactors must contain an excess of hydrogen required to prevent shortening the life of the expensive catalysts. As a consequence of this, the reactor output has still surplus hydrogen. In addition, other light end gases generated in the reactor are also present in the mixture (a mixture of CH_4, C_2H_6, C_3H_8 and other gases) which are considered as impurities.

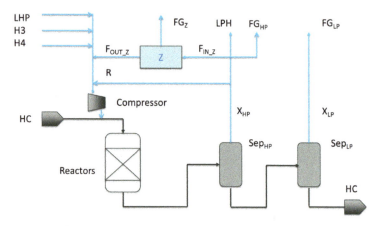

Figure 2. Simplified schematic of a typical desulphurization plant showing the hydrocarbon and hydrogen feeds, the reactor, separation units, membranes and main streams.

Hydrogen and light ends are separated from the treated hydrocarbon stream in high-pressure separation units (Sep_{HP}). Most of the hydrogen rich gas from the HP separator, with purity X_{HP}, is recycled (R) into the reactor inlet, but a certain HP purge is usually needed to avoid the accumulation of light ends in the system, either to the Fuel-gas (FG_{HP}) network of the refinery, where the gases are burnt in furnaces, or to the Low Purity distribution Header (LPH) to be reused later on. Also, some of the recycled hydrogen (F_{IN_Z}) can be fed to a set of membranes (Z) in order to increase its purity, with the low purity retentate flow (FG_Z) being sent to the fuel gas network. Referring to Figure 2, the hydrocarbon outflow of the high-pressure separators still contains hydrogen that is further removed in medium or low pressure separation units (Sep_{LP}), but this hydrogen is sent to the fuel gas network (FG_{LP}) due to its low purity (X_{LP}) that prevents it from being reused in the reactors in a profitable way.

The hydrogen purity at the reactors' input depends on the ratio of flow rates coming from the different producer plants (H3, H4, P1, P2), distribution headers (e.g., low-purity header LPH) and recycles, with the mixture having to satisfy several operational constraints, that must be achieved by proper management of the plant.

Thus, from the point of view of the hydrogen network, these plants operate with a feed of hydrogen from different sources that is partially consumed in the reactors, partially sent to the Fuel Gas (FG) network and partially reused, either internally or recycled from the low purity header LPH.

The global operation of the network outside the plants can be better explained using Figure 3, which is a simplified representation where only a small number of producer and consumer plants are represented. As mentioned above, the producer plants are of two types: the ones that generate controllable flows of fresh high purity hydrogen (H3 and H4) and the ones that generate hydrogen of lower purity as a by-product (P1 and P2) so that their flows can be considered as non-controllable disturbances to the network. The generated hydrogen is distributed to the consumer plants through the corresponding headers. The hydrogen demand of every plant depends on the amount and quality of the hydrocarbons being treated, which may experience strong changes every two or three days according to the crude that is being processed. Excess hydrogen from these plants is partially collected in the low purity header and recycled back to the consumer plants, while the rest goes to the fuel gas network, where it is mainly burnt in furnaces.

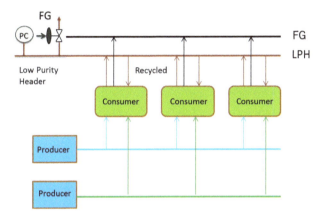

Figure 3. Schematic of producer and consumer plants with the main hydrogen distribution headers and fuel gas network.

2.1. Process Operation

Both plants and networks are operated from control rooms equipped with Distributed Control Systems (DCS) implementing basic controls (flow, pressure, ...) and several MPCs (DMC) in charge of more complex multivariable tasks, such as sulfur removal in the plants. In the past, operators decided on key variables such as hydrocarbon inflow, use of membranes and fresh hydrogen feed to the plants in a largely decentralized way with the overall operation relying on the experience of the production managers. This provides flexibility in the operation, but limits the possibilities of implementing coordinated functioning and optimization.

The main network operation aims are:

- Distribute the available fresh hydrogen and the recycled hydrogen (including internal plant recycles) so that the requirements of hydrogen at the reactors' inputs in all plants are satisfied.
- Be as close as possible to the production targets of hydrocarbon feeds to the plants established by the refinery planning system.
- Balance the hydrogen that is produced and the hydrogen that is consumed so that the hydrogen losses to fuel gas are minimized.

They are listed in order of importance: proper distribution of hydrogen fulfilling operation constraints is a must for the operation of the plants, so it goes on top. Then, production should be increased as much as possible and this target should be achieved with minimum hydrogen losses, or equivalently, with minimum fresh hydrogen production. These aims, far from being independent, are linked together: good distribution and reuse of hydrogen allows reduced losses to fuel gas, increasing the hydrogen available for a further increase in hydrocarbon production when hydrogen capacity is a limiting factor or for reducing fresh hydrogen production if the production targets were already met.

In order to achieve these targets, the main decision variables are the fresh hydrogen production of H3 and H4 plants, the hydrocarbon feed to the fourteen consumer plants and the hydrogen distribution and reuse in the network, including the use of membranes where available. Hydrogen from the platformer plants P1 and P2, being a by-product of their operation, can be considered a disturbance more than a decision variable.

The overall operation is framed by the specific production targets given by the planning system of the refinery that change according to the market conditions and crudes available, and it is constrained by the physical and operational limitations imposed by the equipment.

3. Data Reconciliation and RTO

Safe and optimal operation of this system is a difficult problem due not only to its large scale, complexity and interrelated aims, but also because of the presence of significant disturbances that affect the process and the fact that the information available about many key variables is limited and unreliable.

Uncertainty is mainly caused by:

- The changes in hydrogen consumption in the reactors of the hydrotreating plants, which depend not only on the amount of hydrocarbons being processed, but also on its sulphur content; the sulphur product specification; and the type of hydrocarbon processed, in particular its light-cyclic-oil (LCO) content.
- The use of orifice-plate differential pressure flow meters for gas streams is common in the process industry, but creates particular problems when installed in hydrogen streams. These meters provide volumetric flow measurements. In order to be converted to mass flow, they need to be compensated in temperature, pressure and molecular weight, as the operating conditions normally differ from the calibration ones of the instruments. Pressure and temperature are normally available, but molecular weight of the streams is not, which prevents proper computation of the mass flow, normally expressed as Nm^3/h. In addition, few hydrogen purity analysers are installed in the process and the molecular weight of the streams experience significant variations for small changes in purity or light ends composition (which is unknown). This is due to the low value of H_2 molecular weight, 2 g/mol, as compared to those of the main impurities, CH_4, C_2H_6, and C_3H_8, which are 16, 30 and 44 respectively. This is an important difference as opposed to other gas networks, such as the networks of natural gas, where composition can be assumed constant.

3.1. Data Reconciliation

In spite of these difficulties, decisions about the operation of the process can be improved if a model is available and better process information can be obtained from plant measurements.

A first principles model of the hydrogen behavior in the network and associated plants is available from previous work [9,10]. It was developed to provide support in process optimization and it is based on mass balances of hydrogen and light ends (considered as a single pseudo-component) in the pipes and units. In addition, it incorporates other equations for compressors, membranes, separation units (including a solubility model), etc., some of which are reduced order models fitted to experimental data or with some adjustable parameters. Taking into account the much faster dynamics of the hydrogen compared to the dynamics of the hydrogen of the reactors, the hydrogen distribution model is static and contains flows, purities, molecular weights of hydrogen and light ends of all streams and hydrogen consumption in the reactors as main variables.

When data present significant uncertainty, data reconciliation is the first step to be applied in a model based approach to process optimization. The target is to estimate consistent values of all plant variables from available on-line measurements based on a process model. Data reconciliation requires redundancy in measurements, taking advantage of the fact that the core of the model, being based on mass balances, does not present structural errors. Accurate, consistent, and robust estimations are looked for, irrespective of process disturbances, measurement noise, etc., while at the same time enabling the update of certain unknown model parameters.

The benefits of implementing data reconciliation are three-fold:

- It provides information about unknown important variables such as hydrogen consumption in reactors, molecular weights, purities, etc.
- It allows for reliable computation of Key Performance Indicators (KPIs) and Resource Efficiency Indicators (REIs) to perform process supervision.
- It provides consistent measurements and a model to be used in process optimization.

Data reconciliation is formulated as a large optimization problem searching for the values of variables and parameters that satisfy the model equations and constraints and that, simultaneously, minimize a function of the deviations (e) between model and measurements, properly normalized.

When a sum of squared errors is used as the cost function to be minimized in data reconciliation, one of the main obstacles to obtain adequate solutions is the presence of gross errors, generated usually by faulty instruments, which may distort the estimation, spreading the errors among other variables. Instruments with gross errors can be detected by a combination of data analysis and repeated execution of the data reconciliation and removed [11]. Nevertheless, this procedure is slow and implies additional difficulties for industrial implementation. An alternative is the use of robust estimators that substitute the least squares cost function with another cost function that coincides with it for small errors, but for larger ones grows at lower speeds, such as the Fair function [12] ((Equation 1a), first term of the sum), limiting the spread of errors among other variables and increasing robustness. In our case, the robust data reconciliation has been formulated as:

$$\min_{\{F_i, X_i, MW_i, \varepsilon_i, p_i\}} \sum_{j \in M} \alpha_j c^2 \left[\frac{|e_j|}{c} - \log\left(1 + \frac{|e_j|}{c}\right) \right] + \sum \alpha_i \varepsilon_i^2 + \sum \alpha_k R_k \tag{1a}$$

$$e_j = \eta_j (F_i - \beta_i F_{i,mea}) \quad \beta_i = \sqrt{\frac{T_d + 273}{(P_d + 1)MW_i}} \sqrt{\frac{(P_i + 1)MW_d}{T_i + 273}}$$
$$e_j = \eta_j (X_i - X_{i,mea})$$

s.t.

model equations

operational and range constraints $\qquad$ (1b)

$$F_{i,min} - \varepsilon_{Fi} \le F_i \le F_{i,max} + \varepsilon_{Fi} \quad \varepsilon_{Fi} \ge 0$$
$$X_{i,min} - \varepsilon_{Xi} \le X_i \le X_{i,max} + \varepsilon_{Xi} \quad \varepsilon_{Xi} \ge 0$$
$$MW_{i,min}^{imp} - \varepsilon_{Wi} \le MW_i^{imp} \le MW_{i,max}^{imp} + \varepsilon_{Wi} \quad \varepsilon_{Wi} \ge 0$$

The cost Equation 1a includes three terms: the sum of the Fair functions of the normalized errors e, the sum of penalty terms of possible range violations ε of variables to help to assure a feasible solution and the sum of regularization terms R to favor smooth changes over time of some model parameters. The coefficients α are possible weighting/removal terms and c is a tuning parameter of the Fair function. In the equations, e represents errors between the model and measurements of flows F and hydrogen purities X, with η normalization factors and β compensation factors for flows. MW refers to molecular weights, and P and T to pressures and temperatures, with the sub-index d indicating design values and imp impurities. Finally, p represents model adjustable parameters. The minimization of Equation 1a is performed under the constraint of the network model and a set of operational and range constraints Equation 1b which includes slack variables ε to help avoiding infeasibilities. Main decision variables are flows, purities and molecular weights of all streams and hydrogen consumption rates in the reactors.

The data reconciliation problem is a large Non-Linear Programming (NLP) problem that is formulated and solved with a simultaneous approach in the General Algebraic Modeling System (GAMS) environment using the Interior Point Optimizer (IPOPT) as the optimization algorithm. The implementation involves more than 4400 variables and 4700 equality and inequality constraints.

It takes less than five Central Processing Unit (CPU) minutes in a PC with i7 processor and 8 Gb RAM, giving robust results against gross errors and helping to detect faulty instruments.

3.2. Real-Time Optimization (RTO)

After the data reconciliation step, once the model incorporates the estimated parameters and reliable estimations of variables are available, it is possible to search for the best way of operating the process according to the aims specified in Section 2.1, regarding feasible hydrogen distribution, achievement of hydrocarbon production targets and minimization of fresh hydrogen generation or losses. The formulation of the optimization incorporates additional constraints oriented to keep the operation of the control rooms as undisturbed as possible. Because of that, it assumes as fixed quantities many specific values related to the current operation of the units, such as specific hydrogen consumption or specific generation of light ends and its molecular weight in reactors; specific reactor quench flows for temperature management or separation factors; and specific purge flows and its properties in separation units. In the same way, the state of functioning or stopping the plants and the current structure of the network are respected, assuming that they are mainly imposed either by maintenance or global production planning reasons.

Under these assumptions, the optimal redistribution is formulated as the RTO problem:

$$\max J = \sum_i \mathrm{p}_{HCi} HC_i - \sum_j \mathrm{p}_{Hi} F_{Hi} - \sum_k \mathrm{p}_{Rk} R_k \qquad (2a)$$

s.t.
Process model
Process constraints
Refinery planning specifications

where the three terms of the cost Equation (2a) aim to maximize the hydrocarbon load (HC_i) to consumer plants, minimize the use of fresh hydrogen generated in the steam reforming plants (F_{Hj}) and minimize the internal recycles of hydrogen (R_k) in the consumer plants, which is linked to the operation of the recycle compressors. Here, p_{HC}, p_H and p_R stand for prices associated with hydrocarbons, fresh hydrogen and compressors in order to provide an economic meaning to the cost function.

The problem has to be solved under the constraints imposed by the model and operation of the units, taking also into account the targets coming from the refinery planning. Constraints apply mainly to pipes' capacity, recycle purity in the consumer plants, ratio hydrogen/hydrocarbon at the reactors' input, operating range of membranes, producer plants' capacity, reciprocating and centrifugal compressors' capacity, etc. Main decision variables include production of fresh hydrogen, feeds to consumer plants, hydrogen flows and recirculation, purges, purities and membranes operation.

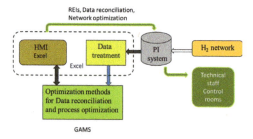

Figure 4. Block diagram of the data reconciliation and RTO showing the information flows and main components.

Again, the problem is a NLP one and has been formulated in the GAMS environment above mentioned. It involves nearly 2000 variables and more than 1800 equality and inequality constraints and is solved with a simultaneous approach and the IPOPT algorithm in less than one minute CPU time. The execution follows that of the data reconciliation according to the block diagram of Figure 4, running every two hours, and its results are available in the Excel HMI and through the Osisoft PI system.

4. System Implementation

The implementation of the hydrogen network optimal management system in the refinery followed three stages. In the first one, data reconciliation and process optimization run off-line, following the schematic of Figure 4. The system is built around an Excel application in a dedicated PC that performs different tasks: Process data are read at regular intervals from a real-time data base connected to the process (PI system) and then analyzed and treated to eliminate inconsistencies, outliers, prepare ranges of variables, etc. One important part of the analysis concerns the state of functioning of the plants and possible structural changes in the network. Rules for detecting if a plant is operating or stopped exist, as well as other ones based on valve openings that identify different ways of operating the hydrogen network using different paths, activated manually. This means that the model has to be adjusted automatically to the structural changes. For this purpose, the model includes a set of binary variables that activate or deactivate groups of equations corresponding to different operating modes. Nevertheless, these binary variables are fixed by the data analysis before the computation of the data reconciliation takes place, so that the type of optimization problem solved is NLP and not Mixed Integer Non Linear Programming (MINLP).

The application reads 171 flows and 18 purity measurements, plus other variables and configuration parameters from the PI (temperatures, pressures, valve openings, etc.) totaling around 1000 variables, averaging them in two-hour periods to smooth the effects of transients and disturbances. Once data are analyzed and filtered, they are passed to the GAMS environment, which runs the data reconciliation problem and gives back estimations of all model variables consistent with the model and constraints and as close as possible to the process measurements. These estimations can be visualized in the Excel Human Machine Interface (HMI) in different formats.

Notice that no steady state detector is normally in operation. This is due to two reasons: on one hand, pressure controllers in headers and consumer plants help to maintain mass balances fairly well, operating with time constants no greater than a few minutes, which is small compared with the two-hour average of the data. On the other hand, due to the large scale of the process, it is very unlikely that all variables are sensibly constant for reasonable time periods, so waiting for the green light of steady state detectors will lead to not running the system, except for short time intervals. A more flexible approach has been taken assuming that the fast system dynamics above mentioned and data averaging allow the obtainment of sensible results.

After the data reconciliation step, the system calls GAMS again to perform the network optimization as presented in Section 3.2. The optimal values of the process variables can be seen as well in the Excel HMI.

4.1. Validation and Implementation Problems

The data reconciliation system has been validated analyzing trends for periods of several days in different seasons with the technical staff of the refinery. Consistency in the estimated values of the variables, stability of the solutions and correspondence with the measured values, were some of the criteria used. During the validation, faulty instruments were detected and corrections and updates in the model were made. Particular attention was devoted to the rules that analyze the raw data from the PI and convert them into useful information for the model and the data reconciliation constraints.

In the same way, the results of the open loop execution of the RTO problem (2) were studied, which provide clues and directions on how to run the network optimally. The analysis of the way in which the network operates by the refinery team and the results of the RTO, lead to the identification of several action patterns and partial aims required for an optimal management of the process. The most important ones can be summarized as follows:

- Losses from the HP separators of a plant to fuel gas, required to avoid light ends accumulation, should be made at the lowest hydrogen purity compatible with the one required at the reactor input and the H_2/HC minimum ratio, see Figure 2. This implies controlling the HP separators' purity X_{HP} at these minimums, sending the gas to the FG purge from those plants that operate with the lowest purity, while, in the others, the excess hydrogen is sent to the LPH for recycle.
- As excess hydrogen is recycled to the Low Purity Header (LPH), hydrogen unbalance in the network, that is, hydrogen generated minus hydrogen consumed in the reactors, reflects in the LPH pressure (see Figure 3). This pressure is maintained with a pressure controller venting gases to the fuel gas network. Then, production of fresh hydrogen could be modified so that the adjustments of the unbalance performed by the LPH pressure controller are made with minimum average valve opening compatible with non-saturated pressure control. This is similar to the so-called valve-position control. In this way, losses to fuel gas from LPH are minimized while guaranteeing that enough hydrogen to the consumer plants is provided to cover the demand, as the pressure is maintained.
- Maximization of the hydrocarbon load to the consumer plants, which is the most important target, can be made until either maximum hydrogen capacity is reached or another technical constraint is faced.
- Sending higher purity hydrogen (H4) to lower purity header (H3) should be minimized as purity degrades.

At the same time, the automated implementation of the RTO calculations to the plant control system is not easy and presents several important problems:

- The models used in the data reconciliation and RTO are static, with results updated every two hours, but the implementation of the optimal values has to be applied to the process taking into account the time evolution of variables. In particular, HC load and hydrogen production have to be changed dynamically at a higher frequency to balance hydrogen production and consumption.
- In the same line, due to the presence of disturbances, changing aims, etc., constraints' fulfilment requires dynamic actions to be performed at a higher rate.
- Possible changes in hydrogen flows interact among them so that a proper implementation of the RTO solution would require multivariable control to take care of the interactions.

These requirements of dynamic and multivariable actions lead in a natural way to the implementation of a MPC layer between the RTO and the basic control system of the network and plants implemented in the control room DCS, as in Figure 5a. Nevertheless, this architecture does not solve the problem of a fast update of the optimization targets and requires maintaining and operating in real-time the large-scale system composed by the data reconciliation and RTO. A dynamic RTO executed with a shorter sampling time or an economic MPC merging the economic and production targets Equation 2a with dynamic MPC control could be more appropriate but it is not realistic due to the large scale of the system.

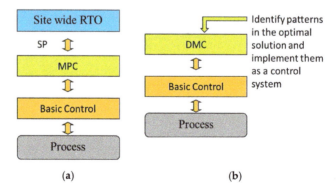

Figure 5. (**a**): traditional RTO/MPC implementation; (**b**): implementing patterns of the optimal solution by means of the DMC software.

4.2. Implementation in the DMC Environment

In view of the existence of the problems and solution patterns of the optimal network management mentioned in the previous sub-section, an alternative approach that combines these patterns, offering a simpler implementation, is presented next. It can be considered as stage two of the system implementation and it is shown schematically in Figure 5b. It takes advantage of the extended functionality of the commercial MPC used in the refinery, DMCPlus (Dynamic Matrix Control) from AspenTech [5], that mixes local LP optimizers and a predictive controller to implement the patterns that define the optimal operation and to perform multivariable control of several plants simultaneously.

In a certain way, it follows the path of the self-optimizing control [6], which substitutes the on-line optimization layer by a control system such that maintaining, in their set points, the so-called self-optimizing variables, keeps the system close to its economic optimum in spite of disturbances. Nevertheless, the formulation mentioned above is different because here there are no self-optimizing variables but the selection of targets that define the optimal operation in cascade with a standard DMC controller. Yet, the basic idea is to implement, as a control system, as much as possible of the optimal management solutions and keep its implementation as simple as possible. The commercial DMC is composed of two layers: an unconstraint DMC controller, which uses a linear step response model of the process linking controlled variables with manipulated ones and disturbances; and a LP optimizer that constitutes the second layer, as in Figure 6a. The LP uses the same model as the controller but in steady state, and includes a linear cost function of the manipulated variables that is minimized at every sampling time under a set of constraints. Both layers are executed at the same rate and the results of the LP are passed as future Set Point (SP) targets to the DMC controller, as can be seen in Figure 6b.

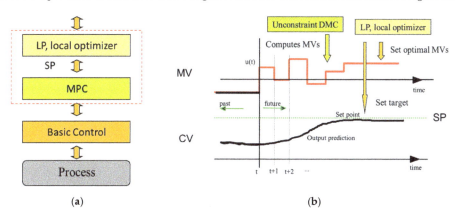

(a)   (b)

Figure 6. (**a**): Control layers showing the two components of the DMC: Local optimizer and MPC acting on the basic control system; (**b**): Predictions of controlled and manipulated variables with set points and the final targets set by the LP optimizer.

The optimal action patterns defined in Section 4.1 can be implemented in the LP layer of a DMC in terms of partial aims in the LP cost function. At the same time, as they involve the joint on-line manipulation of several process plants, and in order to keep the implementation as simple of possible, only the most important ones from the point of view of hydrogen consumption and hydrocarbon processed were included in the design of the DMC. At present, it controls the operation of six plants: two hydrogen producers H3 and H4 and four consumers G1, G3, G4 and HD3, as can be seen in Figure 7.

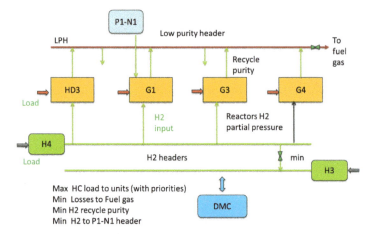

Figure 7. Diagram of the DMC controlling the operation of two hydrogen producers H3 and H4 and four consumers G1, G3, G4 and HD3, with the main controlled hydrogen flows and HC loads.

The controller was developed and implemented by the refinery team and is based on linear models obtained by identification using data from step-tests that forms a dynamic matrix such as the one in Figure 8, involving 12 manipulated variables and 29 controlled ones. The main manipulated variables refer to the set points of hydrocarbon loads to the consumer units, fresh hydrogen production, hydrogen feed to the consumers from the high purity collector and supply of hydrogen from one of the platformer plants. The main controlled variables are hydrogen partial pressure in the reactors of the consumer plants, losses to fuel gas from the Low Purity Header (valve opening), recycle purity and HP losses to FG from some plants, hydrocarbon loads and valve openings to avoid control saturation. They are organized in four sub-controllers, so that each one can be disconnected without affecting the rest of them in case it is required due to process conditions or maintenance actions.

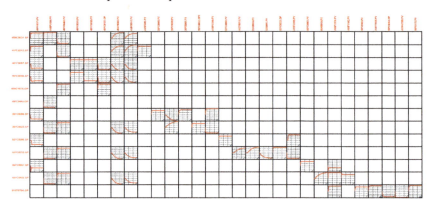

Figure 8. Dynamic matrix of the DMC controller.

The LP layer minimizes a cost function that plays with four aims:

- Maximize hydrocarbon loads to the consumer plants
- Minimize losses from the LPH to FG
- Minimize hydrogen purity in the recycles of the consumer plants
- Minimize hydrogen transfers from higher to lower purity headers

These four objectives are combined in a single linear cost function assigning different weights to the variables associated with them that reflect their relative importance and priority. This cost function is optimized under the constraints imposed by the dynamic matrix model and range constraints in the model variables. The solutions are given as targets to the predictive controller, as in Figure 6, which computes the corresponding dynamic actions and passes them to the lower basic control layer of the control room.

4.3. Planning, RTO and DMC Integration

The DMC is operating in the refinery, giving consistent improvements for several months. Its implementation represented a big step forward in the automation and optimal management of the hydrogen network of the refinery. Nevertheless, it covers only a subset of the total number of process plants and headers involved in the hydrogen network and it does not consider all possible hydrogen management strategies or non-linear effects. This is why further benefits can be obtained by additional use of the global information obtained from the data reconciliation and use of the network wide RTO solutions in a Decision Support System (DSS), which corresponds to stage three of the system implementation.

Main aims of the DSS can be summarized as:

- Provide reliable and full information about the process functioning
- Supervise the operation of the DMC and the hydrogen network
- Identify ways in which the operation of the hydrogen network can be improved
- Suggest changes that improve the DMC operation
- Report to the planning system on the achievable targets and limiting constraints

Notice that both RTO and DMC have to operate in the framework of the refinery planning system, which sets production and quality targets for the various refinery products every two or three days according to the market and crude to be processed. This information is read from the PI system by the RTO and DMC and it is used in both to fix many operation ranges, targets and priorities. One example is the allowed range for the hydrocarbon load of a certain diesel HDS plant that should be maximized within that range, and the indication that increasing it has higher priority than the hydrocarbon load of other naphtha HDS. Nevertheless, that information does not cover all parameters involved in the RTO and DMC optimization problems. In particular, hydrocarbon prices in Equation (2a) or the weights of the four aims involved in the LP cost function of the DMC are not given explicitly. The reason is that assigning proper prices to intermediate hydrocarbon streams is not an easy task, mainly when the crude and outcomes of the refinery change frequently. Because of that, the HC prices in Equation (2a) and the weights of the LP have been considered as weighting factors reflecting the relative priorities of the products and aims involved. The way in which they are tuned includes extensive off-line tests in simulation to find sets of parameters that respond to different priorities of the several aims involved, combined with the on-line use of the priorities read from the planning system, which are associated with the selection of a specific set of parameters. The control room operators can activate buttons in the consoles of the DCS that modify the priorities and the cost function accordingly. Notice that, in this way, the cost functions themselves do not have a real economic meaning, but meaningful economic interpretation can be obtained from the values of the process variables proposed by the optimization.

The proposed system therefore operates taking into account the modules and interrelations displayed in Figure 9. More than in a hierarchy, RTO and DMC operate in parallel, with the aim of using the RTO calculations to improve the operation of the DMC and to be a guide for other corrections. The PI real-time information system is at the core of the information flow, allowing the results of the Data Reconciliation/RTO to be used on-line by the different departments involved.

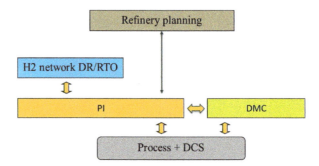

Figure 9. Block diagram of the main elements involved in the hydrogen network management.

The software has been tested off-line extensively, incorporating updates, corrections and improvements, and it is now functioning on-line in the refinery.

5. Results

The benefits obtained from the implementation of the system can be classified in four types:

- Improved network information
- Increased hydrocarbon production
- Better use of hydrogen
- Integrated network management

Improved network information is the result of data reconciliation that provides reliable values of all process variables. This is important as a help to daily operation, because many of them were not available previously, e.g., hydrogen consumption in the reactors or purity of many streams. The estimated values of the main variables are now accessible to all staff in a dedicated application in the PI system in different formats, e.g., the one in Figure 10. A significant part of the success of the data reconciliation step is due to the incorporation of robust estimators in the formulation of the problem that allow the obtainment of sensible solutions in spite of the presence of faulty instruments, as it is very difficult to not have something wrong in the plant instrumentation. Several estimators were tested, for instance, the Redescending, Fair and Welsh estimators, [12] with the Fair function selected finally for its simplicity and good behavior.

However, the data reconciliation results are also important for other purposes, such as helping in the detection and correction of faulty instruments, as they allow one to focus attention on those instruments that present consistent deviations between what is measured and what is estimated. At the same time, the data reconciliation provides coherent values for other computations, among them, the possible revamping of the network structure and the updated model for RTO calculations or the computation of efficiency indicators in the network management. This last point is particularly important.

Supervision of the network operation is made using Resource Efficiency Indicators (REIs) that were defined in the MORE project [13]. They are computed thanks to the availability of process values provided by the data reconciliation. Among them, the most useful ones are those that relate the actual value of a resource to the optimum one computed from the RTO solution, as they measure how well the process is reaching the targets computed by the optimization.

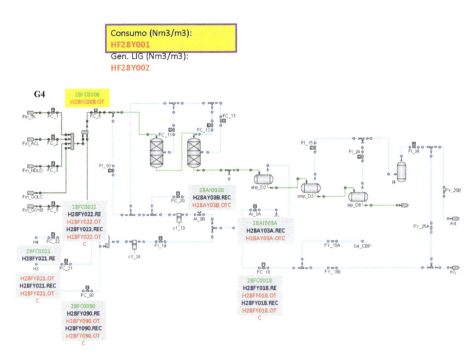

Figure 10. Schematic of a consumer plant showing the tags of measured, reconciled and optimized key variables and REIs. They can be further displayed graphically.

Two of them are displayed for one week of operation in Figure 11 and refer to the ratio between the optimal and actual fresh hydrogen production (in blue) and the ratio between the actual and optimal hydrocarbon load to the consumers (in red), as shown in Equation 3. They are defined in such a way that they indicate better operation when they are close to one.

$$REI_1 = \text{optimal } H_2 \text{ production/actual } H_2 \text{ production}$$
$$REI_2 = \text{actual HC load/optimal HC load}$$

(3)

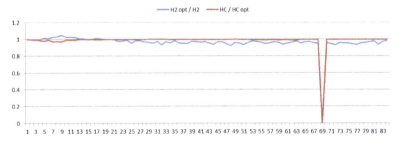

Figure 11. Two REIs showing the distance to the optimal achievable targets for one week of operation.

In the figure, we can observe that, for that week, the HC load is very close to the optimal value that can be attained according to the network conditions, while some savings of hydrogen are still possible. Notice that the hydrogen index in day one exceeds unity in day one because the hydrogen index on hydrocarbon has dropped, so both indicators have to be analyzed jointly. The graph also shows a short stop on day six.

Other REIs are also computed, but the information provided by them suffers from the fact that they depend on the type of hydrocarbons being processed or the product specifications, which make them less useful for supervising the efficiency of the operation. As an example, Figure 12 displays two of them: the specific use of makeup hydrogen (in blue) and the specific hydrogen consumption in the reactors (in red) of a certain HDS, for six days of operation. As can be seen, they experience stronger changes coinciding with the change of hydrocarbon processed around days two and five than during daily operation. However, the distance between the two curves gives useful information about the efficiency of the operation in the plant regarding the use of the hydrogen.

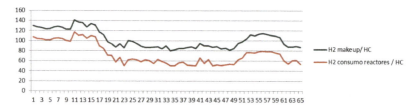

Figure 12. Two REIs showing specific use of hydrogen and specific hydrogen consumption in reactors of a HDS plant. Figures given in % of a certain scale.

Improvements in the amounts of hydrocarbon processed and the use of hydrogen are also important benefits of the implementation of the system. Nevertheless, quantifying them is not easy. A sensible evaluation implies measuring something (costs, resources, ...) before and after the implementation of a new system and comparing results in both situations to compute the gains. However, this procedure requires performing the comparison in the same conditions, i.e., setting a base line. The problem when evaluating the system described in this paper is that the raw material, targets and operating conditions change quite often, as seen in the example of Figure 12, and it is very difficult to find similar situations in the eighteen plants involved in the hydrogen network for sensible periods of time. This is due mainly to the change in the crude being processed every few days, which may imply a noticeable variation in its properties, in particular hydrogen demand.

Keeping this in mind, it is possible to perform evaluations of the results, disconnecting and connecting again the DMC for short periods of time when the operating conditions do not change significantly, and comparing the values before and after. Based on this procedure, it is possible to estimate a saving of 2.5% in the hydrogen production, while the increment of hydrocarbon loads is more difficult to estimate by this procedure, because the operators tend to be kept constant. In any case, there has been a clear improvement of the operating conditions since the online DMC started functioning, in the sense that hydrogen availability is no longer a bottleneck for production. Nevertheless, this period coincided with an average supply of lighter crudes to the refinery, so it is difficult to assign numbers to both factors. At the same time, indicators such as REI_2 in Equation (3) provide values close to one for long periods of time, as in Figure 11, indicating that hydrocarbon production, which is the most valuable target, approached the maximum feasible according to the operating conditions and the targets fixed by the refinery planning.

In addition to providing indicators to supervise the behavior of the network under the DMC, improvements to the network operation can be obtained by the analysis of the results of the RTO optimization compared to the actual operating conditions. At present, the teams involved in the analysis are the ones that have developed the system, but the trend is to move it to the personnel responsible for the network management in the control rooms. For this purpose, the main results are displayed in the PI information system for every plant as in Figure 11, where, by clicking on the different tags, one obtains displays of trends of the measured, estimated, optimized variables and REIs, facilitating the analysis to the staff involved in decision making in the refinery.

Below are two of the main points where the analysis is focused:

- One is the hydrogen distribution strategies. Notice that the RTO considers the whole network, while the DMC only considers a subset of the plants and headers and does not manipulate certain elements as e.g., the membranes. This means that sometimes there is room for further improvements, implementing a different hydrogen redistribution policy, as the feasible set of actions is larger in the RTO. For instance, in the case of the membranes, as the DMC does not manipulate them, the operators fix their behavior according to local needs, while the RTO can compute the best way of operating them according to the global aims.
- The second refers to the identification of persistent active constraints in the optimization that stop further changes in some variables that could improve the attainment of the targets. Examples include the maximum compressor capacity in a recycle or minimum hydrogen purity in a high-pressure separator. The limiting values of the constraints can be structural or operational, and should be analyzed individually to see the convenience of changing them. In order to select the important ones, the value of the associated Lagrange multipliers can be used as they provide the sensitivities of the cost function w.r.t. the constraints, indicating the benefits that could be obtained by every unit change in the value of the constraint. Referring to the above examples, the compressor capacity is a structural decision that is linked to a unit revamping, but the minimum hydrogen purity is operational and could be relaxed, for instance, at the end of life of the reactor catalyzer.

The results of the analysis can be implemented or not considering the efforts involved and expected benefits, which require familiarity with the process and global views of the problems. This is not a problem with the technical staff, but further training is required with the constraint analysis and the interpretation of the Lagrange multipliers.

The implementation of the results of the analysis follows two paths:

- The application of the hydrogen redistribution strategy, deciding, for instance, on a different use of the membranes or proportions in the hydrogen feed sources. Notice that changes in the global strategy of hydrogen distribution can help the DMC to reach its own aims. At the same time, this can help to evaluate the convenience of extending the DMC to other plants or controlled and manipulated variables not included within its scope.
- The possible changes on some DMC constraints. As an illustrative example, we will mention the ratio hydrogen/hydrocarbon in a plant. Data reconciliation estimates its current value, which is imposed as a lower bound to the RTO as a way to protect catalyst life. However, the DMC may use other limiting expressions, e.g., the linearized model of the hydrogen partial pressure obtained experimentally in a certain operating point. If the last one is consistently active and the ratio hydrogen/hydrocarbon is not, one may decide to change the DMC constraint accordingly, obtaining more space for improvements, while keeping a safe operation.

Finally, the forth benefit obtained from the system refers to the implementation of feedback to the upper planning layer. The identification of gaps between the targets given by the planning system of the refinery and what the RTO/DMC compute as feasible targets according to the current condition is valuable information for better tuning and improvements of models in the planning layer. In the same way, the detection of active constraints and sensitivity analysis complement this information that can be relevant when deciding changes in the elements of the plant, such as the compressors' capacity that was mentioned above.

6. Discussion

Development and implementation of the system described above have been the outcome of a fruitful cooperation between the industrial and academic teams over several years which is giving clear benefits in terms of better process information, increased production, and savings in the use of hydrogen and smoother operation. Overall, the system implemented in the refinery is a clear improvement in the efficiency of the use of resources and represents a significant step forward to further integration with other advanced systems in the refinery and enhancements of its functionality.

Nevertheless, the project is still under development, and several problems are open to further research. Among them, model maintenance appears as a key one to maintain the system alive for a long period of time. Revamping or major changes are not infrequent in all process plants, and this requires model (and optimization) adaptation, which should be generated automatically from some type of schematic.

The RTO system could also be improved in two directions: One is by incorporating a measure of the uncertainty present in the process, either using stochastic optimization of the modifier adaptation approaches, as we are aware that the two-step approach of data reconciliation and RTO can lead to suboptimal targets in the presence of structural errors. The other one is considering plant dynamics at this level, so that the non-linear effects could be better taken into account.

Regarding the analysis of the RTO solutions and decisions about their implementation, the development of on-line tools, such as predictive simulation, could help to better evaluate and increase the confidence in the results.

Finally, the current model could also be used as the base for studies on the convenience of larger structural changes in the hydrogen network, using superstructures and MINLP software to discover possible optimal solutions not considered at present.

Acknowledgments: The authors wish to express their gratitude to project DPI2015-70975P of Spanish MINECO/FEDER UE, as well as to the EU FP7-NMP project MORE under GA 604068, for the financial support for this study. They also wish to thank Petronor management for their involvement and help.

Author Contributions: S.M. and M.S. implemented the DMC, E.G. worked in the network modelling, G.G. performed the GAMS implementation, D.S. performed the Excel implementation, C.P. provided operation requirements, R.G. and C. de P. directed the project. All people participated in the analysis of data and results.

Conflicts of Interest: The authors declare no conflict of interest.

References

1. Engell, S. Feedback control for optimal process operation. *J. Process Control* **2007**, *17*, 203–219. [CrossRef]
2. González, A.I.; Zamarreño, J.M.; de Prada, C. Nonlinear model predictive control in a batch fermentator with state estimation. In Proceedings of the European Control Conference, Porto, Portugal, 4–7 September 2001.
3. Amrit, R.; Rawlings, J.B.; Biegler, L.T. Optimizing process economics online using model predictive control. *Comput. Chem. Eng.* **2013**, *58*, 334–343. [CrossRef]
4. Darby, M.L.; Nikolaou, M.; Jones, J.; Nicholson, D. RTO: An overview and assessment of current practice. *J. Process Control* **2011**, *21*, 874–884. [CrossRef]
5. AspenTech. Available online: http://www.aspentech.com/products/aspenONE-APC-Family/ (accessed on 4 January 2017).
6. Skogestad, S. Plantwide control: The search for the self-optimizing control structure. *J. Proc. Control* **2000**, *10*, 487–507. [CrossRef]
7. Towler, G.P.; Mann, R.; Serriere, A.J.-L.; Gabaude, C.M.D. Refinery hydrogen management: Cost analysis of chemically-integrated facilities. *Ind. Eng. Chem. Res.* **1996**, *35*, 2378–2388. [CrossRef]
8. Zhang, J.; Zhu, X.X.; Towler, G.P. A simultaneous optimization strategy for overall integration in refinery planning. *Ind. Eng. Chem. Res.* **2001**, *40*, 2640–2653. [CrossRef]
9. Sarabia, D.; de Prada, C.; Gómez, E.; Gutiérrez, G.; Cristea, S.; Mendez, C.A.; Sola, J.M.; González, R. Data reconciliation and optimal management of hydrogen networks in a petro refinery. *Control Eng. Pract.* **2012**, *20*, 343–354. [CrossRef]

10. Gomez, E. A Study on Modelling, Data Reconciliation and Optimal Operation of Hydrogen Networks in Oil Refineries. Ph.D. Thesis, University of Valladolid, Valladolid, Spain, 2016.

11. Tong, H.; Crowe, C.M. Detection of gross errors in data reconciliation by principal component analysis. *AIChE J.* **1995**, *41*, 1712–1722. [CrossRef]

12. Nicholson, B.; Lopez-Negrete, R.; Biegler, L.T. On-line state estimation of nonlinear dynamic systems with gross errors. *Comput. Chem. Eng.* **2014**, *70*, 149–159. [CrossRef]

13. Real-Time Monitoring and Optimization of Resource Efficiency in Integrated Processing Plants. EU FP7-NMP Project MORE, GA 604068. 2014. Available online: http://www.more-nmp.eu/ (accessed on 4 January 2017).

Article

Real-Time Optimization under Uncertainty Applied to a Gas Lifted Well Network

Dinesh Krishnamoorthy [1], Bjarne Foss [2] and Sigurd Skogestad [1,*]

[1] Department of Chemical Engineering, Norwegian University of Science and Technology (NTNU), 7491 Trondheim, Norway; dinesh.krishnamoorthy@ntnu.no

[2] Department of Engineering Cybernetics, Norwegian University of Science and Technology (NTNU), 7491 Trondheim, Norway; bjarne.foss@ntnu.no

* Correspondence: skoge@ntnu.no; Tel.: +47-913-716-69

Academic Editor: Dominique Bonvin
Received: 21 November 2016; Accepted: 8 December 2016; Published: 15 December 2016

Abstract: In this work, we consider the problem of daily production optimization in the upstream oil and gas domain. The objective is to find the optimal decision variables that utilize the production systems efficiently and maximize the revenue. Typically, mathematical models are used to find the optimal operation in such processes. However, such prediction models are subject to uncertainty that has been often overlooked, and the optimal solution based on nominal models can thus render the solution useless and may lead to infeasibility when implemented. To ensure robust feasibility, worst case optimization may be employed; however, the solution may be rather conservative. Alternatively, we propose the use of scenario-based optimization to reduce the conservativeness. The results of the nominal, worst case and scenario-based optimization are compared and discussed.

Keywords: real-time optimization (RTO); uncertainty; worst case optimization; scenario tree; gas lift optimization

1. Introduction

The offshore production of oil and gas is a complex process where a lot of decisions have to be taken to meet the goals in the short, medium and long run, ranging from planning and asset management to small corrective actions. Accounting for all the goals and constraints as a whole is a very challenging and unrealistic task. Thus, the operation of an oil and gas is typically decomposed into various decision making processes in a hierarchical fashion that reflects their short-, medium- and long-term impact [1], as shown in Figure 1. The long-term decisions involve selecting an investment strategy, operation model, infrastructure etc, which is typically known as asset management. Then, there are decisions taken on a horizon of one to five years such as selecting drilling schedules and production and injection strategies, known as reservoir management. This is followed by decisions that have to be taken on a decision horizon, ranging from a few hours to days known as *Daily Production Optimization*. This decision making step would typically constitute selecting the production target from each well, allocation of resources among the wells such as the available gas lift, power, etc. Thus, from a process systems perspective, this step is equivalent to real-time optimization (RTO). This is followed by a control and automation layer that accounts for fast corrective actions. This paper is concerned with the real-time optimization layer in this hierarchical framework.

Decision Horizon

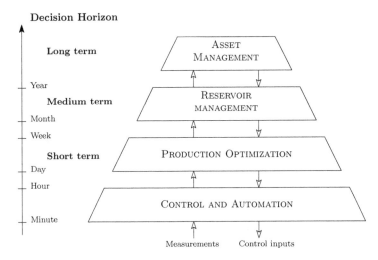

Figure 1. Typical multilevel control hierarchy in oil and gas operations as described in [1].

Daily production optimization generally seeks to maximise the oil and gas production and reduce the cost of production by choosing optimal setpoints for well production rates, gas lift rates, etc. A mathematical model is typically employed when optimizing the performance of the process. To this end, a model is used to predict the outcome of the decision variables on the production, e.g., a model may describe a production network by predicting the oil flow rate for various gas lift rates or choke openings. Due to the complexity of the system and difficulty in modelling the multiphase reservoir inflow and pressure drop in pipelines, models used in production optimization are inherently uncertain and hence the model may fail to accurately predict the outcome. However, uncertainty is simply ignored in most of the works in production optimization. The most common approach is to solve what is known as the deterministic problem with nominal models, where all the uncertain parameters are assumed to take their expected value. The quality of the optimal solution is heavily affected when data and model uncertainty are disregarded, and this approach has serious flaws for constrained optimization problems, which is the case in most real applications. Most uncertainty can be assumed to arise from the following sources [2]:

- Model uncertainty—in which the underlying structure of the model is uncertain due to lack of knowledge or model simplification.
- Parametric uncertainty—where the parameters are outdated or have insufficient excitation to be determined accurately.
- Measurement error—any model to some extent relies on measured data which have a certain degree of uncertainty.

All the above sources of uncertainty are typical to an oil and gas production network. If special precautions are not taken, the solution to the optimization problem might be meaningless and thus has to be disregarded. The uncertainty in the system threatens the relevance of the solution in two facets [3]:

1. The calculated optimal solution, which is thought to be feasible, might actually violate the problem constraints and therefore be infeasible when implemented.
2. When the optimal solution is feasible, the solution may be far from the actual optimal value, and hence is suboptimal.

In a technological survey [4], the authors state that the handling of model uncertainty is a key challenge for the success of production optimization. This challenge is twofold. The first relates the need to identify and characterize the uncertainty and the second is to handle the uncertainties in the production optimization problem. In this paper, we are concerned with the latter where we explicitly account for the uncertainty in the production optimization problem. We employ robust worst case optimization, which provides a robust, feasible, yet conservative solution. In order to reduce the conservativeness without affecting the robust feasibility, we apply scenario tree-based optimization as introduced in [5,6]. The main contribution of this paper is the control oriented modelling of a gas lifted well production network suitable for dynamic optimization and the application and comparison of worst case and scenario-based optimization methods for the production optimization problem under uncertainty.

The paper is organized as follows. A brief summary of previous work is given in Section 2. Section 3 describes the gas lifted well process considered in this paper. The optimization problem is formalized in Section 4. The results are presented and discussed in Sections 5 and 6, respectively. The methods and software used in this work are described in Section 7 before concluding the paper in Section 8.

2. Previous Work

In many offshore oil and gas production networks, the production is often constrained by processing capacity and other such processing constraints. It was pointed out in [7] that not a lot of work has been done to provide robust procedures to formulate and solve such constrained optimization problems. Interest in the field of optimization of such oil and gas production networks has been steadily increasing, and many mathematical tools that assist in decision making have been proposed. To name a few, see [8–12] and the references therein. Most of the works found in literature only consider the deterministic problem and hence disregard any uncertainty present in the system. There are only a very few published works that consider the problem of daily production optimization under uncertainty. For example, Elgsæter et al. suggested a structured approach for changing the setpoint in the presence of uncertainty [13]. Although the uncertainty was not considered directly in the optimization problem itself, but merely to assess the solution, uncertainty was explicitly handled in the optimization problem in [14] by formulating the optimization solution as a priority list between the wells. A two-stage optimization formulation for production optimization under uncertainty, which defines an operational strategy rather than a single operating point, was suggested in [15] and was demonstrated using static models. Very recently, the production optimization problem was reformulated as a robust optimization problem following the row-wise and column-wise framework with cardinality constraints in [16], where a level of protection against the uncertainty is sought at the cost of conservativeness.

However, not a lot of research has been carried out that aims to reduce the conservativeness of the solution. Most of the works above also consider a static problem, where the system dynamics are ignored and static models are used. Dynamic optimization using a multiple shooting algorithm and generalized reduced gradient method was presented in [12,17]; however, uncertainty was disregarded in both of the works. To this end, this work presents a dynamic optimization problem that explicitly handles uncertainty in the daily production optimization problem.

In terms of modelling, gas lifted well models were developed and studied in [18–20] to name a few. The dynamic models used in all these works are based on the mass balance between the different phases in the well tubing and annulus. Similar models have also been used in studies for gas lift instabilities and riser slugging [21]. However, most of these models found in literature have some minor differences in the assumptions used to fit the purpose of the respective applications. For example, the frictional pressure drop in pipes have been assumed to be negligible in [18], whereas some other works explicitly include the frictional pressure drop term. Some works consider simple linear reservoir inflow models such as in [12,20], whereas nonlinear reservoir inflow models have been used in [19]. Some works, such as [22,23], consider partial differential equations for the pressure and flow dynamics in the pipe, which are discretized and solved, whereas ordinary differential equations for mass balance have been used in many other works. Despite the minor differences, the dynamic responses of such simple models based on mass balances have been verified and have been shown to match the results from commercial high fidelity simulators such as OLGA (a dynamic multiphase simulation software from Schlumberger) with sufficient accuracy (see [12,20,24]).

3. Process Description

In many oil wells, when the reservoir pressure is not sufficient to lift the fluids economically to the surface, artificial lift methods are deployed. Gas lift is one such commonly used artificial lift method, where compressed gas is injected at the bottom of the well via the annulus to reduce the fluid mixture density. This reduces the hydrostatic pressure drop in the well and the pressure at the well bottom decreases, thereby increasing the flow from the reservoir. However, injecting too much gas increases the frictional pressure drop, which has a counter effect on the flow rate. At a certain point, the benefit of reduced hydrostatic pressure drop is overcome by the increase in the frictional pressure drop [25]. Hence, each well has a desirable gas lift injection rate. Additionally, there might be constraints on the total gas available for gas lift or total produced gas capacity constraints that must not be violated. The objective is then to find the optimal gas lift injection rates for each well such that the total oil production is maximized.

3.1. Modelling of Gas Lifted Wells

In this section, we give a brief description of the gas lifted well model that is used in the optimization problem. The model to describe production from each gas lifted well can be given in four parts: (i) mass balance of the different phases; (ii) density models; (iii) pressure models and (iv) flow models. The mass balances in each well is given by:

$$\dot{m}_{ga} = w_{gl} - w_{iv}, \tag{1a}$$

$$\dot{m}_{gt} = w_{iv} - w_{pg} + w_{rg}, \tag{1b}$$

$$\dot{m}_{ot} = w_{ro} - w_{po}, \tag{1c}$$

where m_{ga} is the mass of gas in the annulus, m_{gt} is the mass of gas in the well tubing, m_{ot} is the mass of oil in the well tubing, w_{gl} is the gas lift injection rate, w_{iv} is the gas flow from the annulus into the tubing, w_{pg} and w_{po} are the produced gas and oil flow rates, respectively, and w_{rg} and w_{ro} are the gas and oil flow rates from the reservoir.

The densities ρ_a (density of gas in the annulus) and ρ_m (fluid mixture density in the tubing) are given by:

$$\rho_a = \frac{M_w p_a}{T_a R}, \tag{2a}$$

$$\rho_w = \frac{m_{gt} + m_{ot} - \rho_o L_r A_r}{L_w A_w}, \tag{2b}$$

where M_w is the molecular weight of the gas, R is the gas constant, T_a is the temperature in the annulus, ρ_o is the density of oil in the reservoir, L_r and L_w are the length of the well above and below the injection point, respectively, and A_r and A_w are the cross-sectional area of the well above and below the injection point, respectively.

The annulus pressure p_a, wellhead pressure p_{wh}, well injection point pressure w_{iv} and the bottom hole pressure p_{bh} are given by:

$$p_a = \left(\frac{T_a R}{V_a M_w} + \frac{g L_a}{L_a A_a} \right) m_{ga}, \tag{3a}$$

$$p_{wh} = \frac{T_w R}{M_w} \left(\frac{m_{gt}}{L_w A_w + L_r A_r - \frac{m_{ot}}{\rho_o}} \right), \tag{3b}$$

$$p_{wi} = p_{wh} + \frac{g}{A_w L_w} (m_{ot} + m_{gt} - \rho_o L_r A_r) H_w, \tag{3c}$$

$$p_{bh} = p_{wi} + \rho_w g H_r, \tag{3d}$$

where L_a and A_a are the length and cross sectional area of the annulus, L_a is the length of the annulus, T_w is the temperature in the well tubing, H_r and H_w are the vertical height of the well tubing below and above the injection point, respectively, and g is the acceleration of gravity constant. The cross-sectional area of the annulus and the tubing are computed using their respective diameters, D_a and D_w.

The flow through the downhole gas lift injection valve, w_{iv}, total flow through the production choke, w_{pc}, produced gas and oil flow rate, and the reservoir oil and gas flow rates are given by:

$$w_{iv} = C_{iv} \sqrt{\rho_a max(0, p_{ai} - p_{wi})}, \tag{4a}$$

$$w_{pc} = C_{pd} \sqrt{\rho_w max(0, p_{wh} - p_m)}, \tag{4b}$$

$$w_{pg} = \frac{m_{gt}}{m_{gt} + m_{ot}} w_{pc}, \tag{4c}$$

$$w_{po} = \frac{m_{ot}}{m_{gt} + m_{ot}} w_{pc}, \tag{4d}$$

$$w_{ro} = PI(p_r - p_{bh}), \tag{4e}$$

$$w_{rg} = GOR \cdot w_{ro}, \tag{4f}$$

where C_{iv} and C_{pc} are the valve flow coefficients for the downhole injection valve and the production choke, respectively, PI is the reservoir productivity index, p_r is the reservoir pressure, p_m is the manifold pressure and GOR is the gas–oil ratio. Note that there is no pressure coupling between the wells in the present formulation.

Among the several parameters that describes the production network, some may not be accurately known. In this work, we assume that the GOR is uncertain, but their expected value $\mathbb{E}_0(GOR)$ and the range of values or variance σ are assumed to be known:

$$GOR \in \left\{ \mathbb{E}_0(GOR) \pm \sigma \right\} = \mathcal{U}. \tag{5}$$

As seen from Equations (1a)–(4f), the gas lifted well is modelled as a semi-explicit index-1 DAE (differential algebraic equation) of the form

$$\dot{x}_i = f_i(x_i, z_i, u_i, p_i), \tag{6a}$$

$$g_i(x_i, z_i, u_i, p_i) = 0 \qquad \forall i \in \mathcal{N} = \{1, \cdots, n_w\}, \tag{6b}$$

where $f_i(x_i, z_i, u_i, p_i)$ is the set of differential Equations (1a)–(1c) and $g_i(x_i, z_i, u_i, p_i)$ is the set of algebraic Equations (2a)–(4f), and the subscript i refers to any individual well from a set of $\mathcal{N} = \{1, \cdots, n_w\}$ wells. Note that, for convenience, the subscript i has been removed from the Equations (1a)–(4f), which represents the model for each gas lifted well.

The differential states x_i, algebraic states z_i, decision variables u_i, and the uncertain parameters p_i are then given by:

$$x_i = \begin{bmatrix} m_{ga_i} & m_{gt_i} & m_{ot_i} \end{bmatrix}^T, \tag{7a}$$

$$z_i = \begin{bmatrix} p_{a_i} & \rho_{m_i} & p_{a_i} & p_{wi_i} & p_{wh_i} & p_{bh_i} & w_{iv_i} & w_{pc_i} & w_{pg_i} & w_{po_i} \end{bmatrix}^T, \tag{7b}$$

$$u_i = \begin{bmatrix} w_{gl_i} \end{bmatrix}^T, \tag{7c}$$

$$p_i = \begin{bmatrix} GOR_i \end{bmatrix}^T \in \mathcal{U}_i. \tag{7d}$$

The combined system of n_w wells is then denoted by:

$$\dot{\mathbf{x}} = f(\mathbf{x}, \mathbf{z}, \mathbf{u}, \mathbf{p}), \tag{8a}$$

$$g(\mathbf{x}, \mathbf{z}, \mathbf{u}, \mathbf{p}) = 0, \qquad\qquad \forall \mathbf{p} \in \mathcal{U}, \tag{8b}$$

where the combined states $\mathbf{x}$, $\mathbf{z}$ and control input $\mathbf{u}$ are described by the vectors

$$\mathbf{x} = \begin{bmatrix} x_1^T & x_2^T & \cdots & x_{n_w}^T \end{bmatrix}^T, \tag{9a}$$

$$\mathbf{z} = \begin{bmatrix} z_1^T & z_2^T & \cdots & z_{n_w}^T \end{bmatrix}^T, \tag{9b}$$

$$\mathbf{u} = \begin{bmatrix} u_1^T & u_2^T & \cdots & u_{n_w}^T \end{bmatrix}^T. \tag{9c}$$

The combined parameters and the uncertainty set $\mathbf{p}$ and $\mathcal{U}$ are given by

$$\mathbf{p} = \begin{bmatrix} p_1^T & p_2^T & \cdots & p_{n_w}^T \end{bmatrix}^T, \tag{10a}$$

$$\mathcal{U} = \mathcal{U}_1 \times \mathcal{U}_2 \times \cdots \times \mathcal{U}_{n_w}. \tag{10b}$$

Note that the dynamic models (6) and (8) could be easily written as an explicit ODE (ordinary differential equations) by simply eliminating the algebraic variables.

4. Optimization under Uncertainty

For a production network with a set of $\mathcal{N} = \{1, \cdots, n_w\}$ wells, our objective is to find the optimal gas lift injection rate that maximizes the profit, subject to total gas capacity constraints. The profit is computed based on the earnings from the oil production and reducing the costs associated with compressing the gas for gas lift. The economic objective can then be written as:

$$J_{profit} = \alpha_o \sum_{i=1}^{n_w} w_{po_i} - \alpha_{gl} \sum_{i=1}^{n_w} w_{gl_i}, \tag{11}$$

where α_o is the price of oil, and α_{gl} is the cost of compressing the gas for gas lift injection.

Before this can be posed as a standard optimization problem, the infinite dimensional optimal control problem is first discretized into a finite dimensional nonlinear programming problem (NLP) divided into N equally spaced sampling intervals in $\mathcal{K} = \{1, \cdots, N\}$. This is done using third order direct collocation, which gives a polynomial approximation of the system (8) as shown in Figure 2. The set of three collocation points and the initial state in each interval $[k, k+1]$ is denoted by the index

$c \in \mathcal{C} = \{0, 1, 2, 3\}$, and the location of these points are computed using the Radau scheme (see [26]). The discretized states $\tilde{\mathbf{x}} = (\mathbf{x}_{k,c} | k \in \mathcal{K}, c \in \mathcal{C})$ and $\tilde{\mathbf{z}} = (\mathbf{z}_{k,c} | k \in \mathcal{K}, c \in \mathcal{C})$ are then given by:

$$\tilde{\mathbf{x}} = \begin{bmatrix} \mathbf{x}_{1,1}^T & \mathbf{x}_{1,2}^T & \mathbf{x}_{1,3}^T & \mathbf{x}_{2,1}^T & \cdots & \mathbf{x}_{N-1,3}^T & \mathbf{x}_{N,1}^T & \mathbf{x}_{N,2}^T & \mathbf{x}_{N,3}^T \end{bmatrix}^T, \tag{12a}$$

$$\tilde{\mathbf{z}} = \begin{bmatrix} \mathbf{z}_{1,1}^T & \mathbf{z}_{1,2}^T & \mathbf{z}_{1,3}^T & \mathbf{z}_{2,1}^T & \cdots & \mathbf{z}_{N-1,3}^T & \mathbf{z}_{N,1}^T & \mathbf{z}_{N,2}^T & \mathbf{z}_{N,3}^T \end{bmatrix}^T, \tag{12b}$$

where $\mathbf{x}_{k,c}$ represents the combined states for n_w wells Equation (9a) at time instant k and the collocation point c in the interval $[k, k+1]$. To ensure continuity of the states between two consecutive time intervals, the final state variables $\mathbf{x}_{k,3}$ and the initial conditions of the next time interval $\mathbf{x}^0$ must be equal, where the vector of initial states at each interval is represented by:

$$\mathbf{x}^0 = \begin{bmatrix} \mathbf{x}_{1,0}^T & \mathbf{x}_{2,0}^T & \cdots & \mathbf{x}_{N,0}^T & \mathbf{x}_{N+1,0}^T \end{bmatrix}^T. \tag{13}$$

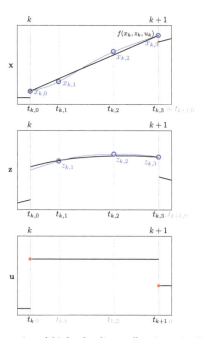

Figure 2. Schematic representation of third order direct collocation using Radau scheme showing the polynomial approximation of dynamic system (8) for a single sampling interval $[k, k+1]$. Note that the differential state has one additional collocation point at $t_{k,0}$, which is used to ensure state continuity by enforcing shooting gap constraints. The control input $\mathbf{u}$ is piecewise constant over the interval $[k, k+1]$.

The control inputs $\tilde{\mathbf{u}} = (\mathbf{u}_k | k \in \mathcal{K})$, which are discretized at each sampling interval, are assumed to be piecewise constant over each interval and hence are not discretized at the collocation points:

$$\tilde{\mathbf{u}} = \begin{bmatrix} \mathbf{u}_1^T & \mathbf{u}_2^T & \cdots & \mathbf{u}_N^T \end{bmatrix}^T. \tag{14}$$

Note that the parameters $\mathbf{p}$ are assumed to be time invariant. The discretized system dynamics at any time instant k can then be written as

$$\mathbf{F}(\tilde{\mathbf{x}}_k, \mathbf{x}^0{}_k, \tilde{\mathbf{z}}_k, \tilde{\mathbf{u}}_k, \mathbf{p}) = 0. \tag{15}$$

Once the system has been discretized, the daily production optimization problem can be posed as a standard NLP problem, divided into N equally spaced sampling intervals in $\mathcal{K} = \{1, \cdots, N\}$ on a prediction horizon from $k = 1$ to $k = N$. The vector of decision variables for the NLP problem over this prediction horizon is then given by:

$$\theta = \left[\cdots \; \underbrace{\mathbf{x}_{k,0}^T}_{\mathbf{x}^0_k} \; \underbrace{\mathbf{x}_{k,1}^T \; \cdots \; \mathbf{x}_{k,3}^T}_{\tilde{\mathbf{x}}_k} \; \underbrace{\mathbf{z}_{k,1}^T \; \cdots \; \mathbf{z}_{k,3}^T}_{\tilde{\mathbf{z}}_k} \; \underbrace{\mathbf{u}_k^T}_{\tilde{\mathbf{u}}_k} \; \cdots \right]^T \qquad \forall k \in \mathcal{K}, \qquad (16)$$

$$\min_{\theta} J = -\sum_{k=1}^{N} J_{profit} + \gamma \sum_{k=1}^{N} \|\Delta u\|_2, \qquad (17a)$$

s.t.

$$\mathbf{F}(\tilde{\mathbf{x}}_k, \mathbf{x}^0_k, \tilde{\mathbf{z}}_k, \tilde{\mathbf{u}}_k, \mathbf{p}) = 0 \qquad \forall k \in \mathcal{K}.\forall \mathbf{p} \in \mathcal{U}, \qquad (17b)$$

$$\sum_{i=1}^{n_w} w_{pg_i} \leq w_{gMax} \qquad \forall i \in \mathcal{N}, \qquad (17c)$$

$$x_l \leq \mathbf{x}_{k,c} \leq x_h \qquad \forall k \in \mathcal{K}, \forall c \in \mathcal{C}, \qquad (17d)$$

$$z_l \leq \mathbf{z}_{k,c} \leq z_h \qquad \forall k \in \mathcal{K}, \forall c \in \mathcal{C}, \qquad (17e)$$

$$u_l \leq \mathbf{u}_k \leq u_h \qquad \forall k \in \mathcal{K} \qquad (17f)$$

$$\Delta u_l \leq \Delta \mathbf{u}_k \leq \Delta u_h, \qquad \forall k \in \mathcal{K} \qquad (17g)$$

$$x_{k,3} = \mathbf{x}^0_{k+1} \qquad \forall k \in \mathcal{K}, \qquad (17h)$$

$$x_{1,0} = x_0. \qquad (17i)$$

The objective function is comprised of the economic cost function Equation (11) and in addition penalizes the control effort using the tuning parameter γ. The total gas capacity constraints are implemented in Equation (17c), where w_{gMax} is the maximum gas capacity. The discretized dynamic model is implemented as state constraints Equation (17b). Upper and lower bound constraints on the differential and algebraic states are implemented at each collocation point and the upper and lower bound constraints on decision variables are implemented at each sample as shown in Equations (17d)–(17f). Rate of change constraints on the decision variables are implemented in Equation (17g). The shooting gap constraints to ensure state continuity are implemented in Equation (17h). The initial conditions are enforced in Equation (17i). The uncertain parameter GOR can take any value from a bound uncertainty set, $\mathcal{U} = \{\mathbb{E}_0(GOR) \pm \sigma\}$.

In the nominal optimization case, the uncertainty is ignored in the optimization problem. The uncertain parameters are assumed to take their expected values. In this case, the optimization problem Equation (17) is solved with

$$GOR_i = \mathbb{E}_0(GOR_i) \qquad \forall i \in \mathcal{N}. \qquad (18)$$

In the case of constrained optimization, the optimal solution is the one where the gas capacity constraints are active. If the true realization of the uncertain parameters is higher than the expected value, then the optimal solution provided by the deterministic optimization may lead to infeasibility when implemented.

To ensure robust feasibility, the uncertain parameters may be assumed to take their worst case realization in the optimization problem. This was first introduced in 1973 by Soyster where every uncertain parameter in convex programming was taken equal to its worst case value within a set [27]. Since then, optimization for the worst case value of the parameters within a set has become effectively known as *Robust Optimization*. A static robust optimization approach for gas lift well optimization using the robust counterpart formulation, as described in [3], was recently presented in [16]. However, since the uncertainty is simple in the considered problem, the worst case can be easily determined a priori without explicitly formulating the robust counterpart. Therefore, we do not formulate the optimization problem using the robust counterpart, but simply take the a priori computed worst case values for all the uncertain parameters. For the application considered in the paper, we know that the worst case scenario occurs when the GOR of all the wells takes its maximum realization simultaneously. Therefore, we simply choose the worst case GOR as shown in Equation (19). To avoid further confusion, we call this approach "worst case optimization" instead of "robust optimization".

The worst case optimization problem (17) can then be solved with

$$GOR_i = \|\mathcal{U}_i\|_\infty = \mathbb{E}_0(GOR_i) + \sigma_i \qquad \forall i \in \mathcal{N}, \tag{19}$$

since the worst case always occurs for the maximum GOR value for each individual well. However, the robust solution will be overly conservative, since the probability that all the uncertain parameters taking its worst case realization will be low. This leads to a suboptimal solution, since the constraints may not be active, and thus there is spare capacity left.

4.1. Scenario Optimization

The robust formulation does not take into account the fact that new information will be available in the future. This makes the solution conservative as illustrated in [5]. Closed loop or feedback min–max MPC (model predictive control) scheme was proposed in [5] to overcome this problem, where the cost function is minimised over a sequence of control policies rather than control inputs. This problem may be rather difficult to solve due to its infinite dimension. A multistage NMPC (nonlinear model predictive control) framework was proposed in [6], where the uncertainty is represented by a tree of discrete scenarios as shown in Figure 3. In other words, we consider M different models, where each model has a different value for the uncertain parameters to represent how the uncertainty influences state propagation over time. At each sample, we assume that the uncertain parameters can take any discrete value from this subset of M different models. We then design different control input profiles for all the scenarios. By doing so, we explicitly take into account the fact that new information will be available in the future and the decision variables can counteract the effect of the uncertainty.

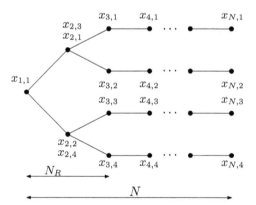

Figure 3. Scenario tree representation of the uncertainty evolution with two models ($M = 2$) and a robust horizon of two samples ($N^R = 2$). The notation $x_{k,j}$ represents the state x at sample k for j^{th} scenario.

The main drawback of this approach is that the size of the problem grows exponentially over the prediction horizon, with the number of uncertain parameters and the different values of the uncertainties that are considered in the scenario tree design. To overcome this problem, it may be sensible to stop the branching of the scenarios after a certain number of samples, $N_R \leq N$ in the prediction horizon (known as Robust Horizon). The uncertain parameters are assumed to remain constant after the robust horizon until the end of the prediction horizon, as depicted in Figure 3. This is reasonable, since the far future does not have to be represented accurately because the corresponding optimal trajectory will be refined later anyway [6].

Each path from the root node to the leaf is called a scenario and the total number of scenarios is given by $S = M^{N_R}$. Therefore, the scenario-based optimization approach optimizes over all the discrete set of scenarios $S = \{1, \cdots, S\}$. In order to model the real-time decision making accurately, the so-called *non-anticipativity constraints* have to be imposed on the decision variables. This is to reflect the fact that the decision variables cannot anticipate the future, and hence the decision variables that branch at the same node must take the same value.

Once the necessary preliminaries have been introduced, the scenario-based optimization problem can be formalized:

$$\min_{\theta_j} \sum_{j=1}^{S} \omega_j J_j, \tag{20a}$$

s.t.

$$\mathbf{F}(\tilde{\mathbf{x}}_{k,j}, \mathbf{x}^0_{k,j}, \tilde{\mathbf{z}}_{k,j}, \tilde{\mathbf{u}}_{k,j}, \mathbf{p}_j) = 0 \qquad \forall k \in \mathcal{K}, \forall \mathbf{p}_j \in \mathcal{U}, \forall j \in \mathcal{S}, \tag{20b}$$

$$\sum_{i=1}^{n_w} w_{pg_i,j} \leq w_{gMax} \qquad \forall j \in \mathcal{S}, \forall i \in \mathcal{N}, \tag{20c}$$

$$x_l \leq x_{k,c,j} \leq x_h \qquad \forall k \in \mathcal{K}, \forall c \in \mathcal{C}, \forall j \in \mathcal{S}, \tag{20d}$$

$$z_l \leq z_{k,c,j} \leq z_h \qquad \forall k \in \mathcal{K}, \forall c \in \mathcal{C}, \forall j \in \mathcal{S}, \tag{20e}$$

$$u_l \leq \mathbf{u}_{k,j} \leq u_h \qquad \forall k \in \mathcal{K}, \forall j \in \mathcal{S}, \tag{20f}$$

$$\Delta u_l \leq \Delta \mathbf{u}_{k,j} \leq \Delta u_h \qquad \forall k \in \mathcal{K}, \forall j \in \mathcal{S}, \tag{20g}$$

$$x_{k,3,j} = \mathbf{x}^0_{k+1,j} \qquad \forall k \in \mathcal{K}, \forall j \in \mathcal{S}, \tag{20h}$$

$$x_{1,0} = x_0 \tag{20i}$$

$$\sum_{j=1}^{S} \chi_j u_j = 0 \qquad \forall j \in \mathcal{S}, \tag{20j}$$

where S is the number of scenarios, and J_j is the cost of each scenario with its probability or weight ω_j. The cost of each scenario is given by Equation (17a) and GOR_j is a subset of $\mathcal{U} = \{\mathbb{E}_0(GOR) \pm \sigma\}$ with M discrete values. Note that all the variables have an extra subscript j compared to Equation (17), where j represents each scenario. In addition, nonanticipativity constraints are included in Equation (20j), where χ is the non-anticipativity constraint which enforces that all the decision variables that branch at the same parent node have to be equal. For example, the nonanticipativity constraints for the scenario tree in Figure 3 are written as

$$u_{2,1} = u_{2,2} = u_{2,3} = u_{2,4} \tag{21a}$$

$$u_{3,1} = u_{3,2} \tag{21b}$$

$$u_{3,3} = u_{3,4} \tag{21c}$$

5. Simulation Results

In this work, we consider a network of two gas lifted oil wells ($n_w = 2$) producing to a common manifold as shown in Figure 4. The process is assumed to be constrained by a maximum gas capacity of $w_{gMax} = 8kg/s$. Therefore, we have a DAE system with six differential Equations (1a)–(1c) and 24 algebraic Equations (2a)–(4f), two decision variables and two uncertain parameters. The parameter values used in the simulation are summarised in Table 1.

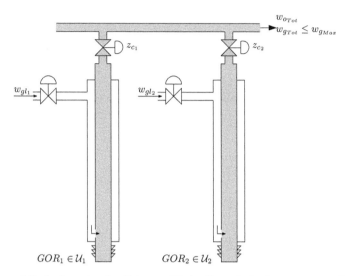

Figure 4. Production network with two gas lifted wells producing to a common manifold.

Table 1. List of parameters and their corresponding values used in the results.

Parameter	Units	Well 1	Well 2	Comment
L_w	[m]	1500	1500	Length of well
H_w	[m]	1000	1000	Height of well
D_w	[m]	0.121	0.121	Diameter of well
L_r	[m]	500	500	Length of well below injection
H_r	[m]	100	100	Height of well below injection
D_r	[m]	0.121	0.121	Diameter of well below injection
L_a	[m]	1500	1500	Length of annulus
H_a	[m]	1000	1000	Height of annulus
D_a	[m]	0.189	0.189	Diameter of annulus
ρ_o	[kg/m^3]	900	800	Density of Oil
$C_i v$	[m^2]	1×10^{-4}	1×10^{-4}	Injection valve characteristic
$C_p c$	[m^2]	1×10^{-3}	1×10^{-3}	Production valve characteristic
p_m	[bar]	20	20	Manifold pressure
p_r	[bar]	150	155	Reservoir pressure
PI	[kg·s^{-1}·bar^{-1}]	2.2	2.2	Productivity index
T_a	[°C]	28	28	Annulus temperature
T_w	[°C]	32	32	Well tubing temperature
M_w	[g]	20	20	Molecular weight of gas
GOR	[kg/kg]	0.1 ± 0.1	0.15 ± 0.01	Gas–Oil ratio

An optimizing control structure with integrated optimization and control [28] was chosen, where the control system uses an online dynamic optimization based on a nonlinear model of the plant and solves for the optimal trajectory over a prediction horizon. The dynamic optimization problem in this work was solved with a prediction horizon $N = 60$ and a sampling time of $T_s = 300$ s. The first control input is then applied to the plant.

For the deterministic optimization case, the expected value of the GOR was used in the optimization problem, and, for the worst case optimization, the maximum value of the GOR was used in the optimization problem. In the case of scenario-based optimization, four different possible values of the GOR were used in the optimization problem (see Table 2), and a robust horizon of $N_R = 1$ was chosen.

Table 2. GOR (Gas-Oil ratio) values used in the optimizer for nominal, worst case and scenario-based approach.

Well	Nominal	Worst Case	Scenario-Based			
GOR well 1	0.1	0.2	0.05	0.1	0.15	0.2
GOR well 2	0.15	0.16	0.145	0.15	0.155	0.16

The optimization problem considered here computes the optimal gas lift rate for each well. We assume that we have perfect low level controllers that adjust the gas lift choke z_{gl} to provide the desired gas lift rates. We also assume that perfect state feedback is available for the dynamic optimization. These assumptions are justified, since the main focus in this work is to compare the nominal, worst case and scenario-based optimization approaches. The control structure used in this work is shown in Figure 5.

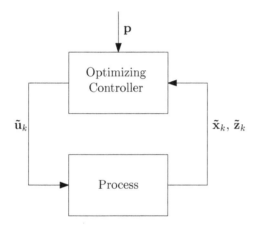

Figure 5. Schematic representation of the optimizing control structure. The Dynamic RTO (Real-time optimization) for nominal, worst case or scenario-based approach computes the optimal gas lift rates for the two wells and sets the process at each iteration.

The simulation starts with the true GOR the same as the nominal GOR. At sampling instant $N = 15$, true GOR gradually increases to 0.15 and 0.155 in well 1 and well 2, respectively, and remains constant at these values until $N = 45$. At sampling instant $N = 45$, the GOR suddenly increases to 0.2 and 0.16 (worst case realization) in wells 1 and 2, respectively. The true GOR profile is shown is Figure 6f.

The system is first simulated for the nominal optimization case, where the optimization assumes the GOR to be at its nominal value. When the true GOR is at its nominal value, there is no plant model mismatch and the total gas capacity constraints are active as expected. However, when the true GOR in the system increases, this leads to constraint violation.

Then, the system is simulated with the worst case optimization, where the optimizer assumes GOR to take its worst case value. When the true GOR is at its nominal value, we see that the optimal solution implemented is rather conservative. The gas capacity constraints are no longer active and there is spare capacity that can be utilised. When the GOR increases, we see that the constraints are not violated, even when the GOR does take its worst case value at $N = 45$. The solution is robust feasible at the cost of conservativeness.

Finally, the system is simulated with the scenario-based optimization with four different GOR values as shown in Table 2. All the scenarios are assumed equally probable and are therefore provided with equal weights for all the scenarios. When the GOR is at its nominal value, the optimizer solves for the optimal inputs that are feasible for all the possible scenarios, and we see that the gas capacity constraints are not active. However, the solution is less conservative than the worst case optimization. As the GOR increases, the implemented solution proves to be robust feasible, and the constraints are satisfied even when the GOR takes its worst case value. However, when the true GOR assumes its worst case value, the total oil produced is less than the worst case optimization. This is due to the fact that there is no plant model mismatch in the worst case optimization case, whereas in the scenario tree optimization, the optimal solution is computed that maximises the oil rate for the other scenarios in addition to the worst case scenario.

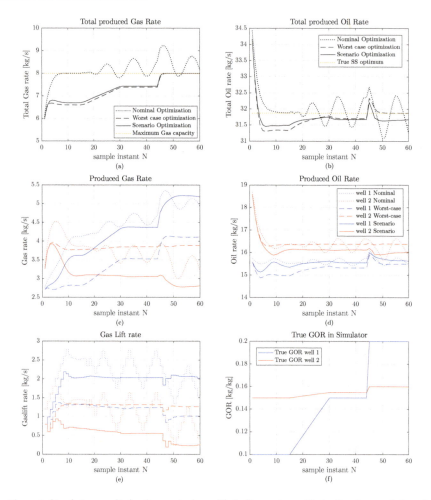

Figure 6. Simulation results for the nominal case (dotted), worst case (dashed) and scenario-based optimization (solid). (**a**) The total gas rates are shown in black and the maximum gas capacity constraint shown in yellow, (**b**) the total oil rates are shown in black and the true steady-state optimum for the oil rate is shown in yellow, (**c**) the gas rates from individual wells are shown in blue and red for well 1 and well 2, respectively, (**d**) The oil rates from individual wells are shown in blue and red for well 1 and well 2, respectively, (**e**) The gas lift rates from individual wells are shown in blue and red for well 1 and well 2, respectively. (**f**) The true GOR (gas-oil ratio) realization used in the simulator are shown in blue and red for well 1 and well 2, respectively.

6. Discussion

The case study consists of two wells with one constraint and one uncertain parameter (*GOR*) with a given nominal value and variance. In the nominal case, since well 1 has a marginally lower expected GOR, one would prioritize well 1 over well 2 to utilise the maximum gas capacity and maximise oil rate. In the worst case, however, since well 2 now has lower expected GOR, one would then prioritize well 2 over well 1. This is seen in the true optimal gas lift rates in Table 3, where well 1 is prioritized over well 2 for the nominal case and vice versa for the worst case realization. This is similar to an observation made by [15] for a static oil production optimization case.

Table 3. Results–loss evaluations for the different scenarios for nominal, worst case and scenario-based optimization.

Optimization	True GOR		True Optimum		Computed Optimum		Potential	Obtained	Loss
	Well 1	Well 2	Well 1	Well 2	Well 1	Well 2	Tot Oil	Tot Oil	
	[kg/kg]	[kg/kg]	[kg/s]	[kg/s]	[kg/s]	[kg/s]	[kg/s]	[kg/s]	[kg/s]
Nominal case	0.05	0.145	3.337	1.5117	2.663	1.518	31.879	31.7	0.179
	0.1	0.15	2.563	1.429	2.563	1.429	31.879	31.879	0
	0.15	0.155	1.788	1.348	infeasible	infeasible	31.879	infeasible	-
	0.2	0.16	1.014	1.266	infeasible	infeasible	31.879	infeasible	-
Worst case	0.05	0.145	3.337	1.5117	1.324	1.32	31.879	30.69	1.189
	0.1	0.15	2.563	1.429	1.318	1.329	31.879	31.33	0.549
	0.15	0.155	1.788	1.348	1.235	1.317	31.879	31.69	0.189
	0.2	0.16	1.014	1.266	1.014	1.266	31.879	31.879	0
Scenario tree	0.05	0.145	3.337	1.5117	2.048	0.7046	31.879	31.12	0.759
	0.1	0.15	2.563	1.429	2.036	0.6904	31.879	31.49	0.389
	0.15	0.155	1.788	1.348	2.038	0.5616	31.879	31.67	0.209
	0.2	0.16	1.014	1.266	2.007	0.2697	31.879	31.68	0.199

In the nominal optimization, when the true GOR increases, the solution imminently becomes infeasible and violates the total gas capacity constraints. The optimizer then tries to correct and reduces the gas lift rates for both of the wells. Once the total gas is below the constraint, the optimizer then increases the gas lift rates for both of the wells. This is because the optimizer "thinks" the oil rate can be maximized based on the model. The implemented solution then keeps oscillating around the constraint. Such a behaviour is clearly unacceptable.

To ensure robust feasibility, worst case optimization was then employed. The results of the worst case optimization shows that the robust solution is very conservative. Scenario-based optimization was then performed to reduce the conservativeness. When the true GOR is at its nominal value, the loss for worst case optimization is 0.549 kg/s as opposed to 0.389 kg/s for the scenario-based optimization. This shows that when the actual GOR is far away from its worst case values, the scenario optimization performs significantly better and is able to reduce the conservativeness of the robust solution since it considers different possible scenarios. However, in the unlikely event that the true GOR of all the wells approach their worst case values, the loss for the worst case optimization approaches 0 as opposed to 0.199 kg/s for the scenario-based optimization. This is due to the fact that scenario tree also considers other scenarios in its optimization problem, whereas there is no plant model mismatch in the worst case optimization. The steady state loss computed for the different realizations of the GOR using nominal, worst case and scenario-based optimization is given in Table 3.

The scenario-based optimization approach presented here assumes equal weights/ probabilities for all the different scenarios included in the optimization problem. This makes the optimal solution balance all the possible scenarios equally. This is a viable approach if no information about the uncertainty is known. However, as we get more measurements, information about the true uncertainty is revealed. Updating the weights for the different scenarios based on the measurements could perhaps significantly improve the performance of the scenario-based optimization compared to the worst case optimization even more.

7. Materials and Methods

The dynamic optimization problem considered in this work is discretized into an NLP problem using a third order direct collocation scheme in CasADi v3.0.1 (an open-source tool developed at the Optimization in Engineering Center, K.U.Leuven, Leuven, Belgium) [29] using the MATLAB R2016a (Mathworks Inc., Natick, MA, USA) programming environment. The NLP problem is then solved using IPOPT version 3.12.2 (an open-source tool developed at the Department of Chemical Engineering, Carnegie Mellon University, Pittsburgh, PA, USA) [30], running with a mumps linear solver on a 2.6 GHz workstation with 16 GB memory. The plant (simulator) was implemented in Simulink and solved with an ode45 solver. At each iteration, the first sample of the computed optimal solution is implemented in Simulink R2016a (Mathworks Inc., Natick, MA, USA). After the simulation is completed, the states from the Simulink model are fed back to the optimizer, which is used as the initial value for the next iteration. The data transfer between Simulink and the optimizer is carried out by reading and writing data to the common MATLAB workspace.

8. Conclusions

To our knowledge, this paper is the first publication considering a dynamic scenario-based optimization approach for the daily production optimization problem. A detailed modelling framework for the gas lifted well system that is suitable for dynamic optimization problems was presented. The scenario-based optimization approach was shown to reduce the conservativeness of the solution compared to the worst case optimization while being robust feasible. However, to improve the performance of the scenario-based approach, the weights for the different scenarios to reflect the uncertainty realization must be included as shown in [31]. A natural further step is also to explore systems with pressure coupling between wells and more extensive subsea completions.

Acknowledgments: This work was supported by the SUBPRO (Subsea production and processing) consortium, which is a collaboration between the Norwegian University of Science and Technology (NTNU), the Norwegian Research Council and major industry partners under the Project code 237893.

Author Contributions: D.K. developed the models and performed the simulations and wrote the paper. B.F. and S.S supervised the work and analysed the simulation results and contributed to writing and correcting the paper.

Conflicts of Interest: The authors declare no conflict of interest.

Abbreviations

The following abbreviations are used in this manuscript:

RTO	Real-Time Optimization
DAE	Differential Algebraic Equations
ODE	Ordinary Differential Equations
NLP	Nonlinear Programming Problem
NMPC	Nonlinear Model Predictive Control
GOR	Gas–Oil Ratio
PI	Productivity Index
DPO	Daily Production Optimization

References

1. Foss, B.A.; Jensen, J.P. Performance analysis for closed-loop reservoir management. *SPE J.* **2011**, *16*, 183–190.
2. Elgsæter, S.M. Modeling and Optimizing the Offshore Production of Oil and Gas under Uncertainty. Ph.D. Thesis, Norwegian University of Science and Technology (NTNU), Trondheim, Norway, 2008.

3.   Ben-Tal, A.; Nemirovski, A. Robust solutions of linear programming problems contaminated with uncertain data. *Math. Program.* **2000**, *88*, 411–424.

4.   Bieker, H.P.; Slupphaug, O.; Johansen, T.A. Real time production optimization of offshore oil and gas production systems: A technology survey. In *Intelligent Energy Conference and Exhibition*; Society of Petroleum Engineers: Amsterdam, The Netherlands, 2006.

5.   Scokaert, P.; Mayne, D. Min-max feedback model predictive control for constrained linear systems. *IEEE Trans. Autom. Control* **1998**, *43*, 1136–1142.

6.   Lucia, S.; Finkler, T.; Engell, S. Multi-stage nonlinear model predictive control applied to a semi-batch polymerization reactor under uncertainty. *J. Proc. Control* **2013**, *23*, 1306–1319.

7.   Wang, P.; Litvak, M.; Aziz, K. Optimization of production operations in petroleum fields. In *SPE Annual Technical Conference and Exhibition*; Society of Petroleum Engineers: San Antonio, TX, USA, 2002.

8.   Gunnerud, V.; Foss, B. Oil production optimization—A piecewise linear model, solved with two decomposition strategies. *Comput. Chem. Eng.* **2010**, *34*, 1803–1812.

9.   Camponogara, E.; Nakashima, P.H. Solving a gas-lift optimization problem by dynamic programming. *Eur. J. Oper. Res.* **2006**, *174*, 1220–1246.

10. Camponogara, E.; Nakashima, P. Optimizing gas-lift production of oil wells: piecewise linear formulation and computational analysis. *IIE Trans.* **2006**, *38*, 173–182.

11. Codas, A.; Camponogara, E. Mixed-integer linear optimization for optimal lift-gas allocation with well-separator routing. *Eur. J. Oper. Res.* **2012**, *217*, 222–231.

12. Codas, A.; Jahanshahi, E.; Foss, B. A two-layer structure for stabilization and optimization of an oil gathering network. *IFAC-PapersOnLine* **2016**, *49*, 931–936.

13. Elgsæter, S.M.; Slupphaug, O.; Johansen, T.A. A structured approach to optimizing offshore oil and gas production with uncertain models. *Comput. Chem. Eng.* **2010**, *34*, 163–176.

14. Bieker, H.P.; Slupphaug, O.; Johansen, T.A. Well management under uncertain gas or water oil ratios. In *Digital Energy Conference and Exhibition*; Society of Petroleum Engineers: Houston, TX, USA, 2007.

15. Hanssen, K.G.; Foss, B. Production Optimization under Uncertainty-Applied to Petroleum Production. *IFAC-PapersOnLine* **2015**, *48*, 217–222.

16. Hülse, E.O.; Camponogara, E. Robust formulations for production optimization of satellite oil wells. *Eng. Optim.* **2016**, 1–18.

17. Sharma, R.; Glemmestad, B. On generalized reduced gradient method with multi-start and self-optimizing control structure for gas lift allocation optimization. *J. Proc. Control* **2013**, *23*, 1129–1140.

18. Eikrem, G.O.; Imsland, L.; Foss, B. Stabilization of Gas-lifted Wells Based on State Estimation. 2004. Available online: http://folk.ntnu.no/bjarnean/pubs/conference/conf-75.pdf?id=ansatte/Foss_Bjarne/pubs/conference/conf-75.pdf (accessed on 14 December 2016).

19. Peixoto, A.J.; Pereira-Dias, D.; Xaud, A.F.; Secchi, A.R. Modelling and Extremum Seeking Control of Gas Lifted Oil Wells. *IFAC-PapersOnLine* **2015**, *48*, 21–26.

20. Jahanshahi, E. Control Solutions for Multiphase Flow: Linear and Nonlinear Approaches to Anti-slug Control. Ph.D. Thesis, Norwegian University of Science and Technology (NTNU), Trondheim, Norway, 2013.

21. Jahanshahi, E.; Skogestad, S. Simplified Dynamic Models for Control of Riser Slugging in Offshore Oil Production. *Oil Gas Facil.* **2014**, *3*, 80–88.

22. Alstad, V. Studies on Selection of Controlled Variables. Ph.D. Thesis, Norwegian University of Science and Technology (NTNU), Trondheim, Norway, 2005.

23. Krishnamoorthy, D.; Bergheim, E.M.; Pavlov, A.; Fredriksen, M.; Fjalestad, K. Modelling and Robustness Analysis of Model Predictive Control for Electrical Submersible Pump Lifted Heavy Oil Wells. *IFAC-PapersOnLine* **2016**, *49*, 544–549.

24. Eikrem, G.O.; Aamo, O.M.; Foss, B.A. On instability in gas lift wells and schemes for stabilization by automatic control. *SPE Prod. Oper.* **2008**, *23*, 268–279.

25. Golan, M.; Whitson, C.H. *Well Performance*, 2nd ed.; Tapir: Trondheim, Norway, 1995.

26. Biegler, L.T. *Nonlinear Programming: Concepts, Algorithms, and Applications to Chemical Processes*; SIAM: Philadelphia, PA, USA, 2010; Volume 10.

27. Soyster, A.L. Technical note—Convex programming with set-inclusive constraints and applications to inexact linear programming. *Oper. Res.* **1973**, *21*, 1154–1157.

28. Skogestad, S.; Postlethwaite, I. *Multivariable Feedback Control: Analysis and Design*, 2nd ed.; Wiley: New York, NY, USA, 2007.
29. Andersson, J. A General-Purpose Software Framework for Dynamic Optimization. Ph.D. Thesis, Arenberg Doctoral School, KU Leuven, Department of Electrical Engineering (ESAT/SCD) and Optimization in Engineering Center, Kasteelpark Arenberg, Belgium, 2013.
30. Wächter, A.; Biegler, L.T. On the implementation of an interior-point filter line-search algorithm for large-scale nonlinear programming. *Math. Program.* **2006**, *106*, 25–57.
31. Lucia, S.; Paulen, R. Robust nonlinear model predictive control with reduction of uncertainty via robust optimal experiment design. *IFAC Proc. Vol.* **2014**, *47*, 1904–1909.

Article

Combined Estimation and Optimal Control of Batch Membrane Processes

Martin Jelemenský [1,*], Daniela Pakšiová [1], Radoslav Paulen [2], Abderrazak Latifi [3] and Miroslav Fikar [1]

[1] Faculty of Chemical and Food Technology, Slovak University of Technology in Bratislava, Radlinskeho 9, 81237 Bratislava, Slovakia; daniela.paksiova@stuba.sk (D.P.); miroslav.fikar@stuba.sk (M.F.)

[2] Department of Chemical and Biochemical Engineering, Technische Universität Dortmund, Emil-Figge-Strasse 70, 44221 Dortmund, Germany; radoslav.paulen@bci.tu-dortmund.de

[3] Laboratoire Réactions et Génie des Procédés, CNRS-ENSIC, Université de Lorraine, 1 rue Grandville, 54001 Nancy, France; Abderrazak.Latifi@ensic.inpl-nancy.fr

* Correspondence: martin.jelemensky@stuba.sk; Tel.: +421-259-325-730

Academic Editor: Dominique Bonvin
Received: 13 October 2016; Accepted: 10 November 2016; Published: 18 November 2016

Abstract: In this paper, we deal with the model-based time-optimal operation of a batch diafiltration process in the presence of membrane fouling. Membrane fouling poses one of the major problems in the field of membrane processes. We model the fouling behavior and estimate its parameters using various methods. Least-squares, least-squares with a moving horizon, recursive least-squares methods and the extended Kalman filter are applied and discussed for the estimation of the fouling behavior on-line during the process run. Model-based optimal non-linear control coupled with parameter estimation is applied in a simulation case study to show the benefits of the proposed approach.

Keywords: batch diafiltration; membrane fouling; time-optimal operation; fouling estimation

1. Introduction

In the last few decades, an increased focus has been given to the membrane technology, which is used both in production and down-stream processing. Membrane technologies are exploited in a variety of processes, such as in membrane reactors, membrane distillation, diafiltration, dialysis, electrolysis, etc. All of these employ principles of membrane separation [1]. There are, however, certain limitations for the application. The major obstacle is the membrane fouling, which refers to the blockage of membrane pores during filtration, causing a decrease in the production rate. Although membrane fouling is an inevitable phenomenon occurring during the filtration process, it can be controlled and its influence alleviated [2].

There are several operational approaches to deal with membrane fouling. These mainly include scheduling of membrane cleaning cycles and on-line fouling control strategies [2]. These techniques usually require mathematical models for predicting the fouling behavior. The first attempt to describe the fouling behavior in a unified model was presented by Hermia [3] who developed four types of fouling behavior. Few works have then been devoted to model-based optimal control of membrane-assisted processes [4,5] and membrane fouling and cleaning [6,7]. However, optimal control requires knowledge of process model parameters. Thus, in the case of unknown parameters in the model, on-line parameter estimation may be performed in order to improve the process control performance. For this purpose, several methods can be applied, such as common least-squares or some more advanced methods. In Charfi et al. [8], an estimation of the fouling mechanism model proposed by Hermia was conducted for microfiltration and ultrafiltration in a membrane bioreactor using experimental data reported in the literature.

Parameter identifiability has to be addressed before the actual estimation step. If a model is non-identifiable, the estimated parameters will lead to errors in subsequent model predictions [9]. The identifiability test also provides a guideline for how to simplify the model structure or indicates when more measurements are needed to allow for unique identifiability [10].

Recently, the optimal control of a diafiltration process in the presence of fouling was proposed [11]. The obtained control law depends mainly on the parameters of membrane flux and fouling. In the subsequent work, an on-line control strategy was considered that incorporated parameter estimation using the extended Kalman filter (EKF) [12]. In this paper, we focus more broadly on the optimal operation of a diafiltration process under fouling where parameter estimation is used to determine the parameters of the fouling model. Compared to the work [12], in this paper, we provide a comparison of the estimation of the unknown parameters using several optimization-based (least-squares and moving-horizon estimation), as well as recursive (recursive least-squares estimation and extended Kalman filter) methods by considering also measurement and process noise, and we assess their performance on the highly non-linear estimation problem that arises from the nature of the employed process model. In addition, the identifiability test is also performed in order to reveal whether the model parameters can be estimated based on available measurements.

The paper is organized as follows. In the next section, the general formulation of a batch diafiltration process is introduced. In Section 3, we provide a detailed analysis of the membrane fouling phenomena, and we also discuss the modeling of the membrane fouling. Section 4 provides the definition of the problem of the optimal operation of the diafiltration process. In Section 5, a review of identifiability detection methods is given with the main focus on non-linear models described by ordinary differential equations (ODEs). The results and implications of the performed identifiability tests are presented. An introduction is then given to the considered parameter estimation problem, and four different estimation methods are briefly presented. Finally, a simulation study is provided in Section 6 with a detailed discussion and analysis of the obtained results.

2. Process Description

In this paper, we consider the batch diafiltration process shown in Figure 1. The batch process operates under constant pressure and temperature. The overall batch process consists of a feed tank and a membrane module. We consider that the process solution consist of a solvent (water), macro-solute (high molecular weight component) and micro-solute (low molecular weight component). The process solution is brought from the feed tank to the membrane by means of mechanical energy (e.g., pump). The membrane is designed to retain the macro-solute, while the micro-solute can easily pass through the membrane pores. The stream rejected by the membrane is called the retentate and is taken back into the feed tank. The stream that leaves the system is called the permeate, and its flow-rate is defined as $q = AJ$, where A is the membrane area and J is the permeate flux per unit area of the membrane. The flow rate of the permeate stream is a function of both concentrations of the individual solutes and of time, in the case of the occurrence of fouling phenomena.

The control of the batch diafiltration process can be achieved by adjusting the flow-rate of the solvent (diluent) into the feed tank. Then, the control variable α is defined as the ratio between the inflow into the feed tank and the outflow from the membrane module. Traditional approaches to the operation of the diafiltration process consider sequences of operating regimes, which differ in the rate of diluent addition:

1. Concentration mode: During this mode, no diluent is added into the feed tank, i.e., $\alpha = 0$.
2. Constant-volume diafiltration mode: Here, the rate of inflow of the diluent is kept the same as the rate of permeate outflow, i.e., $\alpha = 1$.
3. (Pure) Dilution mode: In this mode, a certain amount of diluent can be added instantaneously into the feed tank. This can be represented as $\alpha \to \infty$.

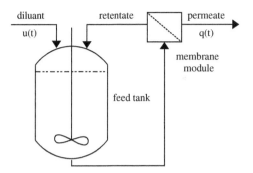

Figure 1. Schematic representation of a generalized ultrafiltration/diafiltration process.

Regarding the practical applicability of the pure dilution mode, as will be shown further, the optimal operation would involve the pure dilution mode as an initial or a final step. In both of these cases, the pure dilution step can be performed out of the batch as a pre-/post-treatment of the separated solution.

The process model [13] is constituted by the solutes mass balance equations, which have the following form:

$$\frac{dc_i}{dt} = \frac{c_i q}{V}(R_i - \alpha), \quad c_i(0) = c_{i,0}, \quad i = 1, 2, \tag{1}$$

where V is the volume in the feed tank and c_i denotes the concentration of the i-th solute; $i = 1$ for macro-solute; and $i = 2$ for micro-solute. R_i is the observed rejection coefficient of the i-th solute, which describes the ability of the membrane to retain the solute. The total mass balance is defined as follows:

$$\frac{dV}{dt} = \alpha q - q = (\alpha - 1)AJ, \quad V(0) = V_0, \tag{2}$$

where V_0 is the initial volume of the process solution.

In many cases, the rejection coefficient R_i is a function of concentrations. In this paper, we will consider that the rejections are ideal, given and constant for both solutes ($R_1 = 1$ and $R_2 = 0$). This means that the membrane is perfectly impermeable to macro-solute and that only the micro-solute can pass through the membrane. Moreover, since only the micro-solute can pass through the membrane, the mass of macro-solute in the system will not change and remains constant, such that $c_1(t)V(t) = c_{1,0}V_0$. Based on these assumptions, we can eliminate the differential equation for the volume (2), and the model has now the following form:

$$\frac{dc_1}{dt} = c_1^2 \frac{AJ}{c_{1,0}V_0}(1 - \alpha), \quad c_1(0) = c_{1,0}, \tag{3}$$

$$\frac{dc_2}{dt} = -c_1 c_2 \frac{AJ}{c_{1,0}V_0}\alpha, \quad c_2(0) = c_{2,0}. \tag{4}$$

3. Membrane Fouling

One of the major obstacles in the field of membrane-assisted processing is the membrane fouling. The membrane fouling is caused by the deposit of the solutes in/on the membrane pores. The main consequence of the membrane fouling is the decrease in the permeate outflow due to the blockage of the pores. The most important factors that cause the membrane fouling are the feed properties and membrane material. Moreover, membrane fouling can increase when the concentration polarization effect takes place. In [14], the authors have shown that during the membrane filtration, the retained macro-solute can form a gel layer over the membrane surface. The formation of such a gel layer can increase the interactions between the solutes and the membrane surface, which eventually lead to membrane fouling. Further, the process variables, such as temperature and pressure, may also contribute to membrane fouling [15].

As mentioned above, the main consequence of the membrane fouling is the decrease in the permeate flow rate, which results in the increase of the overall processing time. If the membrane becomes heavily fouled, cleaning must be performed. In some cases, even replacement of the membrane module must be carried out, which leads to the increase of the production costs.

In the past three decades, the modeling of membrane fouling became very important. In 1982, Hermia [3] derived a unified fouling model for dead-end filtration in terms of total permeate flux and time, which has the following form:

$$\frac{\mathrm{d}^2 t}{\mathrm{d}V_p^2} = K \left(\frac{\mathrm{d}t}{\mathrm{d}V_p} \right)^n, \tag{5}$$

where V_p is the permeate volume, t is time and K represents the fouling rate constant. From the above unified fouling model, four classical fouling models can be derived for different values of the fouling parameter n. The four models are cake filtration ($n = 0$), intermediate blocking ($n = 1$), internal blocking ($n = 3/2$) and the complete blocking model ($n = 2$). By integration of (5), we obtain the differential equation for the permeate flux [16,17], which is expressed as:

$$\frac{\mathrm{d}J}{\mathrm{d}t} = -KA^{2-n}J^{3-n}. \tag{6}$$

This equation can be solved to give an explicit solution $J(t, K, n, A, J_0)$ if the parameters A, K and n are constant and J_0 is the initial flux at time $t = 0$. However, this model holds only for dead-end filtration mode. In order to account for the dynamics of the cross-flow system, which is considered in this paper, we propose to substitute the initial flux $J_0(t = 0)$ with the flux of an unfouled membrane $J_0(c_1, c_2)$.

In Figure 2, we show the graphical representation of the four standard fouling models. The models differ in the way that the solutes deposit on/in the membrane surface. In the following subsections, we will briefly discuss the individual fouling models.

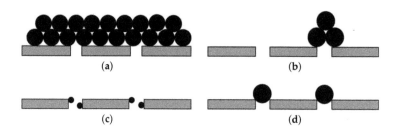

Figure 2. Graphical representation of the four classical fouling models developed by Hermia. (a) Cake filtration model ($n = 0$); (b) intermediate blocking model ($n = 1$); (c) internal blocking model ($n = 3/2$); (d) complete blocking model ($n = 2$).

3.1. Cake Filtration Model

The cake filtration model considers that the solutes brought to the membrane surface will form a multi-layered cake formation shown in Figure 2a. The multi-layered formation is caused by the repeating deposit of the solutes on the membrane surface. The parameter n is set to zero, and the permeate flux has the following form:

$$\frac{1}{J^2} = \frac{1}{J_0^2} + 2KA^2t. \tag{7}$$

where J in $\text{m}^3/\text{s}/\text{m}^2$ is the permeate flow per unit area of the membrane and J_0 is the flux of an unfouled membrane.

3.2. Intermediate Blocking Model

The intermediate fouling model also considers that the solute will block all of the pores. However, in this case, the solutes can also deposit on each other, as illustrated in Figure 2b. To derive the model, the parameter n is equal to one, and the permeate flux is of the form:

$$\frac{1}{J} = \frac{1}{J_0} + KAt. \tag{8}$$

3.3. Internal Blocking Model

The aforementioned fouling models do not consider the fouling to take place inside the membrane pores. This is not the case with an internal blocking model (Figure 2c). This type of fouling results in the decrease of the diameter of the membrane pores, which leads to the decrease of the permeate flow. For the internal blocking model, the parameter n is equal to $3/2$, and the permeate flux is derived as:

$$\frac{1}{\sqrt{J}} = \frac{1}{\sqrt{J_0}} + \frac{1}{2}KA^{1/2}t. \tag{9}$$

3.4. Complete Pore Blocking Model

The complete pore blocking model considers that all of the solutes brought to the membrane surface will block the membrane pores (Figure 2d). Therefore, the permeate flow will be reduced. Moreover, the blockage of the pores is caused only if the molecules of the solutes are larger than the membrane pores. The complete blocking model can be derived from (5) if $n = 2$ and is of the following form:

$$\ln J = \ln J_0 - Kt, \tag{10}$$

Note that unlike in the previous cases, the permeate flux does not depend on the membrane area.

4. Optimization Problem

The main operational objective of the diafiltration plant is to process as much solution as possible. This can only be achieved by pursuing the time-optimal batch recipes with tight scheduling. Consequently, as scheduling is here usually a rather trivial task, we concentrate on the time-optimal control problem of a batch membrane process in the presence of membrane fouling.

4.1. Problem Definition

The objective is to identify such a time-dependent function $\alpha(t)$ that will drive the system from the initial concentrations to the required final concentrations in the minimum time. The optimization problem reads as:

$$\mathcal{J}^* = \min_{\alpha(t)} \int_0^{t_f} 1 \, dt, \tag{11}$$

$$s.t. \, \dot{c}_1 = \frac{c_1^2 AJ}{c_{1,0} V_0}(1 - \alpha), \quad c_1(0) = c_{1,0}, \quad c_1(t_f) = c_{1,f}, \tag{12}$$

$$\dot{c}_2 = -\frac{c_1 c_2 AJ}{c_{1,0} V_0}\alpha, \quad c_2(0) = c_{2,0}, \quad c_2(t_f) = c_{2,f}, \tag{13}$$

$$J = J(t, J_0(c_1, c_2), K, n), \tag{14}$$

$$\alpha \in [0, \infty). \tag{15}$$

We assume that this optimization problem is feasible, i.e., the process design ensures that the final conditions can be met within admissible input trajectories. This optimization problem can be approximately solved using various numerical methods [18] of dynamic optimization (e.g., control vector parametrization or complete discretization). However, an analytical solution is available. This was shown in [19] and is briefly reviewed in the following.

4.2. Nominal Optimal Operation

In our recent study [19], we derived analytically the complete optimal operation for a diafiltration process in the presence of membrane fouling using Pontryagin's minimum principle [20,21]. The optimal operation is an explicit non-linear control strategy defined on three time intervals as follows:

1. In the first interval, the control is kept on the boundaries (e.g., minimum or maximum) until the singular curve is reached:

$$S(t, c_1, c_2, K, n) = J + c_1 \frac{\partial J}{\partial c_1} + c_2 \frac{\partial J}{\partial c_2} = 0. \tag{16}$$

    The minimum control action ($\alpha = 0$) is applied if the initial concentrations lie to the left side of the singular surface ($S(0, c_{1,0}, c_{2,0}, K, n) < 0$) in the state diagram. Conversely, the maximum ($\alpha \to \infty$) control action is applied when the initial concentrations are on the right of the singular curve ($S(0, c_{1,0}, c_{2,0}, K, n) > 0$).

2. Once the singular curve is reached, the singular control is applied, which forces the states to stay on the singular curve:

$$\alpha(t, c_1, c_2, K, n) = \frac{\frac{\partial S}{\partial c_1} c_1}{\frac{\partial S}{\partial c_1} c_1 + \frac{\partial S}{\partial c_2} c_2} + \frac{\frac{\partial S}{\partial t}}{\frac{c_1 A J}{c_{10} V_0} \left(\frac{\partial S}{\partial c_1} c_1 + \frac{\partial S}{\partial c_2} c_2 \right)}. \tag{17}$$

    This step is terminated once the ratio of the concentrations is equal to the ratio of the final concentrations or once the final concentration of the micro-solute is reached.

3. In the last step, the control is kept on one of the boundaries similar to the first step with the difference that the operation mode to be applied is determined by the final time constraints. The concentration mode ($\alpha = 0$) is applied if the final concentration of the micro-solute has been reached. The dilution mode with $\alpha \to \infty$ is applied once the ratio of the final concentrations is equal to the final one. Both steps are performed until the final concentrations are reached.

For a particular case of initial and final concentrations, any of the three steps can be missing. For instance, if initial (respectively final) concentrations lie on the singular case, then the first (respectively last) step will be skipped. Another case would occur if the singular case cannot be reached before the control has to switch from the first to the last step, so the optimal operation will consist entirely of saturated control arcs.

4.3. Optimal Operation with Imperfect Knowledge of Fouling Model Parameters

It can be easily shown that the optimal control structure does not depend on the unknown fouling parameters in the first and last step of the optimal operation. This comes from the fact that, on the one hand, the initial flux is not influenced by the fouling, as $J(0) = J_0$, and on the other hand, the last step is determined by the active constraints, which are independent of the fouling behavior.

These observations imply that one can distinguish two cases in the on-line optimal operation under imperfect knowledge of the fouling model:

1. If the operation starts with the concentration mode, the a priori knowledge of unknown parameters K and n should be improved during this step by parameter estimation, such that the

switching time can be determined accurately. If this estimation is successful, the optimal singular surface is followed thereafter.

2. Should the optimal operation commence with a pure dilution step, the entry point to the singular surface would be known exactly, as it only depends on J_0. In other words, the amount of the diluent that should be added at the beginning of the operation does not depend on the parameters of the fouling model. It would then be again necessary to improve the knowledge about the unknown parameters in order to maintain the singular-surface condition.

Clearly, the on-line parameter estimation will yield adequate results only if (a) a sufficient amount of data can be gathered and if (b) significant sensitivity is present between measured outputs and estimated parameters on the particular arc of the optimal solution. The first condition requires that the optimal concentration mode, respectively singular arc, lasts sufficiently long, which will likely result in the negligible suboptimality of the on-line control strategy. The latter condition suggests the provision of the persistence of excitation in the system. This might be critical should the parameter estimation be required to yield accurate parameter estimates when the system resides on the singular arc. For example, if the optimal singular flux is constant, then the set of obtained flux measurements will not bring enough new information about the fouling behavior. This case will further be addressed in Section 6 where the interesting question is to find out what the trade-off is between the insensitivity of the objective function to the control on the singular arc and the inaccuracy of parameter estimates.

5. Parameter Estimation Problem

In this section, we will discuss parameter identifiability and parameter estimation techniques. Several studies have employed standard estimation methods to obtain the fouling parameters necessary for the control of membrane processes. In [8], the authors have proposed to employ the least-squares method to identify the fouling rate constant (K) for the standard fouling models. However, this procedure was performed completely off-line with the necessity of initial probing runs to obtain the experimental measurements of flux based on which the fouling rate constant could be determined. Moreover, only the fouling rate constant was estimated with a fixed type of fouling model. Since the derived optimal control depends also on the information of the type of fouling model, the estimation of both the unknown fouling parameters (K, n) is followed in this work. Furthermore the estimation is performed on-line, which eliminates the necessity of any initial experiments.

The on-line estimation is coupled with the aforementioned optimal feedback control law, which is updated iteratively with the estimated values of the parameters of the fouling model. In our recent paper [12], we have introduced this strategy using EKF. In this paper, we provide an assessment of the performance of some other commonly-used model-based estimators.

5.1. Problem Definition

We will consider that the process dynamics is described by a set of ODEs with initial conditions and expressed in the following form:

$$\dot{c}_1 = \frac{c_1^2 A J}{c_{1,0} V_0}(1 - \alpha), \qquad\qquad c_1(0) = c_{1,0}, \qquad\qquad (18)$$

$$\dot{c}_2 = -\frac{c_1 c_2 A J}{c_{1,0} V_0}\alpha, \qquad\qquad c_2(0) = c_{2,0}, \qquad\qquad (19)$$

$$\dot{\tau} = 1, \qquad\qquad \tau(0) = 0, \qquad\qquad (20)$$

where τ replaces the explicit appearance of time with a new state, and the permeate flux J is defined as follows:

$$J(\tau, J_0(c_1, c_2), n, K, A) = J_0\left(1 + K(2 - n)(AJ_0)^{2-n}\tau\right)^{(1/(n-2))}, \qquad (21)$$

We will rewrite the above differential equations into the following compact form:

$$\dot{x} = f(x, \theta, u), \tag{22}$$

where $x = (c_1, c_2, \tau)^T$ is the vector of state variables, $\theta = (K, n)^T$ is the vector of estimated parameters and u is the control action. For the estimation of the unknown parameters, we assume that the concentrations of the individual solutes (c_1, c_2) and also the permeate flux (J) can be measured.

5.2. Identifiability Problem

The problem of the parameter identifiability of dynamic models is a special case of the observability problem. It is often the case that the parameters of a model have unknown values. These values can be estimated from observing the input-output behavior.

Before the model parameters can be estimated, the identifiability analysis must be performed. The property of identifiability is the ability to deduce the values of the model parameters uniquely in terms of known quantities based on input and output variables and their time derivatives. In order to investigate identifiability of (18) to (20), we will first introduce a definition of identifiability.

Definition 1. *A dynamic system described by (22) and (25) is identifiable if the parameter vector θ can uniquely be determined from the given system input u and the measurable system output y. If no solution can be found for the given vector of unknown parameters θ, then the model is non-identifiable.*

The identifiability analysis also distinguishes whether the parameter vector can uniquely be identified or not. In this regard, a system is said to be structurally globally identifiable if for any admissible input and any two parameter vectors θ_1 and θ_2, $y(u, \theta_1) = y(u, \theta_2)$ holds if and only if $\theta_1 = \theta_2$. A system is said to be structurally locally identifiable if for any parameter vector θ within an open neighborhood of some point, $y(u, \theta_1) = y(u, \theta_2)$ holds if and only if $\theta_1 = \theta_2$.

There are many well-established methods for determining the identifiability of linear systems. However, fewer methods are applicable for non-linear systems. The most common methods for the identifiability test include: the direct test [22], the identifiability of the corresponding linearized system [22], the similarity transformation method [23,24], power series expansion [25], the generating series approach [26] and differential algebra [27]. Two of these methods are used for the identifiability analysis in this work.

5.2.1. Identifiability of the Corresponding Linearized System

Local linearization of the non-linear models can be considered for the identifiability test. However, the identifiability of the linearized model is only a necessary condition [22].

There are several methods for the identifiability of linear systems. One method is to consider parameters as dummy state variables with time derivatives equal to zero. The observability rank test can then be applied where the observability matrix O of a linear system $\dot{x} = A(\theta)x + B(\theta)u$, $y = C(\theta)x$,

$$O = \begin{bmatrix} C & CA & \cdots & CA^{n-1} \end{bmatrix}^T, \tag{23}$$

should be of full rank n, where n is the dimension of the vector of state variables. Rigorously speaking, this approach can only serve to detect the non-identifiability of the parameters.

5.2.2. Generating Series Approach

This approach is based on the computation of Lie derivatives, which allows one to expand the output variables with respect to input variables. By computing Lie derivatives, a set of resulting coefficients is formed, which is then used to compute the parametric solution. Based on this solution, the identifiability of the model is checked. A drawback of this method is that the sufficient number of Lie derivatives to be considered is unknown. In order to easily visualize the structural identifiability problem and to assist in the solution, identifiability tableau is proposed [26]. This tableau expresses the dependency between parameters by using the Jacobian matrix of exhaustive summary, i.e., a set of relations that depends only on the parameters. The tableau is represented by a "0 – 1" matrix, which represents whether there is a dependency between Lie derivatives and the parameters "1", or not "0". The identifiability is then checked by examining whether there is a unique "1" in a row of the tableau. If so, then there exists a unique dependency between the Lie derivative and a parameter. Thus, the corresponding parameter is structurally identifiable [9,28].

5.3. Software Tools for the Identifiability Test

There are few frameworks and software tools available that assist in identifiability analysis [29,30]. To the authors knowledge, there are three common software tools that use one of the above-mentioned methods for testing global identifiability of non-linear systems. These are DAISY [31], COMBOS [30] and GenSSI. The open-source tool GenSSI implements the generating series approach and is chosen here for the identifiability analysis of the parameters. This is due to the model structure, which must be strictly polynomial in order to be implemented in DAISY and in COMBOS. In our case, the model of the diafiltration process with fouling does not satisfy this requirement.

GenSSI module is written in MATLAB and can be used for any general linear, non-linear ODE or differential algebraic system. To run the identifiability test, the user needs to specify the model equations, input and output variables, initial conditions, parameters to be identified and the number of Lie derivatives. In the case of the detection of non-identifiability, GenSSI also provides information on individual parameters and their global or local identifiability. This information can guide the proper reformulation of the model [9,28].

Results and Discussion

The identifiability problem was solved for the membrane fouling process described by (3) and (4) using both the observability matrix test and generating series approach. The results showed that the parameters K, n in the membrane fouling model are not observable with the vector of measurement $y = (c_1, c_2, J)^T$. This is due to the fact that parameters enter the process equations via J only, and therefore, there are infinitely many combinations that can lead to actual J. Therefore, a new measurement must be added, which is a different function of the estimated parameters. For this reason, the time derivative of the flux $\dot{J}$ is considered as a new measurement. Based on the results given by GenSSI, the augmented model of membrane fouling, which also considers the time-derivative of the flux as a measured variable, is globally identifiable. This means that the two parameters K, n can be identified based on the measured variables from any given initial conditions. The identifiability of the parameters was also confirmed by using the observability matrix.

It is usually not possible to measure the derivative of the flux directly. Therefore, an approximation of the third order is considered, which reads as:

$$\frac{dJ}{dt} \approx \frac{J_{k-3} - 6J_{k-2} + 3J_{k-1} + 2J_k}{6T_s}. \tag{24}$$

where T_s represents the sampling time. Different approximations were tested; the third order is a good compromise between accuracy and complexity.

Then, the considered measured outputs in discrete-time samples (k) are as follows:

$$y_k = h(x_k, \theta) = (c_1, c_2, J, \dot{J})^T. \tag{25}$$

This form of output equation is further considered for parameter estimation.

5.4. Parameter Estimation Methods

Different parameter estimation methods are discussed in the following subsections. They mainly differ in the consideration of the parameter estimation problem as non-linear (least-square method), mildly non-linear (least-squares method with moving horizon) or almost linear (recursive least-squares method and EKF). Note that this consideration implies whether the non-linear programming problem (NLP) needs to be solved with each newly-gathered measurement or whether a recursive approach is sufficient, where only a few mathematical operation (e.g., matrix-vector multiplications) are performed. Here, a critical point is presented by the tendency of the recursive methods to rapidly diverge should the process (and its model) exhibit strong non-linear behavior.

5.4.1. Weighted Least-Squares Method

One of the most used methods for parameter estimation is the weighted least-squares (WLS) method. Compared to the standard least-squares method, the WLS method considers that different measured outputs can contribute differently to the estimation of unknown parameters based on their variability and statistical significance [32]. For the on-line parameter estimation, it must be, however, considered that with each new measurement, a new NLP problem must be solved, and moreover, if a large set of experimental points is available, numerical problems can occur due to the gradually increasing complexity of the optimization problem. The optimization problem that needs to be solved in each sampling time is as follows:

$$\hat{\theta}_k = \arg\min_{\theta} \sum_{j=0}^{k} (\boldsymbol{y}_j - \hat{\boldsymbol{y}}_j)^T \boldsymbol{R}^{-1} (\boldsymbol{y}_j - \hat{\boldsymbol{y}}_j) \tag{26}$$

$$\text{s.t. (18) to (20),} \tag{27}$$

$$\hat{\boldsymbol{y}}_j = h(\boldsymbol{x}_j, \boldsymbol{\theta}), \tag{28}$$

$$\theta_{\min} \le \theta \le \theta_{\max}, \tag{29}$$

where $\boldsymbol{y}$ represents the vector of obtained measurements, $\boldsymbol{R}$ is the covariance matrix for the measurement noise and $\theta_{\min}$, $\theta_{\max}$ are the minimum and maximum values of the parameters, respectively.

5.4.2. Weighted Least-Squares Method with Moving Horizon

The weighted least-squares method with moving horizon [33] is very similar to the previously-discussed method. However, in this case, not the whole measurement set is considered, but only recent measurements on a constant moving horizon (MH) contribute actively to the estimation. The influence of the past measurements, gathered prior to the moving horizon, is not neglected, but rather considered through the parametric covariance matrix P as a priori knowledge of the parameters, similarly to Bayesian estimation. The covariance matrix then penalizes a drift of the new estimates from their a priori values in the objective function [34]. In [35], it has also been shown that the moving-horizon estimation is equivalent to the extended Kalman filter if the first-order approximation of dynamics and no constraints are considered. A distinct advantage of this method is that since a fixed-length horizon of measured outputs is considered, the NLP problem that needs to be solved, when new measurements are gathered, is of approximately fixed complexity and might be easier to solve than the optimization problem in WLS estimation. The resulting non-linear problem reads as:

$$\hat{\theta}_k = \arg\min_{\theta} \, (\theta - \hat{\theta}_{k-MH})^T P_{k-MH}^{-1}(\theta - \hat{\theta}_{k-MH}) + \sum_{j=k-MH}^{k} (y_j - \hat{y}_j)^T R^{-1}(y_j - \hat{y}_j) \qquad (30)$$

s.t. (18) to (20), $\qquad\qquad\qquad\qquad\qquad\qquad\qquad\qquad\qquad\qquad\qquad$ (31)

$$\hat{y}_j = h(x_j, \theta), \qquad\qquad\qquad\qquad\qquad\qquad\qquad\qquad\qquad (32)$$

$$\theta_{min} \leq \theta \leq \theta_{max}. \qquad\qquad\qquad\qquad\qquad\qquad\qquad\qquad\qquad (33)$$

It is worth mentioning that the matrix P can be either selected as a constant matrix or one can apply the extended Kalman filter method to update the matrix P in each sampling time to improve the convergence.

5.4.3. Recursive Least-Squares Method

The recursive least-squares method (RLS) iteratively finds parameter estimates that minimize the linearized least-squares objective function [36]. The parameter estimates are calculated at each sampling time based on the a priori knowledge of the parameters (through parametric covariance matrix) and the current measured outputs. The advantage of the method is that during the estimation, no NLP problem has to be solved. On the other hand, RLS does not explicitly consider the constraints on the estimated parameters in the updates of the covariance matrix, and thus, the a priori knowledge of parameters might be biased.

In order to apply the RLS method, we consider a Taylor expansion of the output function (25) to the first order:

$$\hat{y}_k = h(x_k, \theta) \approx h(x_k, \hat{\theta}_{k-1}) + \left(\frac{\partial h(x_k, \theta)}{\partial x_k}\bigg|_{\hat{\theta}_{k-1}} \frac{\partial x}{\partial \theta}\bigg|_{\hat{\theta}_{k-1}} + \frac{\partial h(x_k, \theta)}{\partial \theta}\bigg|_{\hat{\theta}_{k-1}} \right)^T (\hat{\theta}_k - \hat{\theta}_{k-1}), \qquad (34)$$

$$\approx h(x_k, \hat{\theta}_{k-1}) + \varphi_k^T(\hat{\theta}_k - \hat{\theta}_{k-1}), \qquad\qquad\qquad (35)$$

where $(\partial x / \partial \theta)$ is the matrix of parametric sensitivities, which can be propagated in time as follows:

$$\dot{s} = \frac{\mathrm{d}}{\mathrm{dt}} \frac{\partial x}{\partial \theta}\bigg|_{\hat{\theta}_{k-1}} = \frac{\partial f(x, \theta, u)}{\partial x}\bigg|_{\hat{\theta}_{k-1}} \frac{\partial x}{\partial \theta}\bigg|_{\hat{\theta}_{k-1}} + \frac{\partial f}{\partial \theta}\bigg|_{\hat{\theta}_{k-1}}, \qquad s(0) = \frac{\partial x_0}{\partial \theta}\bigg|_{\hat{\theta}_{k-1}}, \qquad (36)$$

for the given $u(t)$. Here, we can observe that the sensitivity of the system needs to be ideally solved at each sampling time from the initial conditions at $t = 0$. This can impose significant computational burden and certain numerical problems, since many states and parameters are present in the problem. This does not, however, present a significant issue in the present study.

The estimation error (ϵ) can be defined via the difference between the measured and calculated outputs as:

$$\epsilon = y_k - \hat{y}_k = y_k - h(x_k, \hat{\theta}_k) - \varphi_k^T \hat{\theta}_k + \varphi_k^T \hat{\theta}_{k-1}, \qquad (37)$$

The overall RLS algorithm [37] is then, using (34), defined as follows:

$$\hat{\theta}_k = \left(I + L_k \varphi_k^T \right)^{-1} \left(\hat{\theta}_{k-1} + L_k \left[y_k - h(x_k, \hat{\theta}_{k-1}) + \varphi_k^T \hat{\theta}_{k-1} \right] \right), \qquad (38)$$

$$L_k = P_{k-1} \varphi_k \left(\varphi_k^T P_{k-1} \varphi_k + R \right)^{-1}, \qquad\qquad\qquad (39)$$

$$P_k = P_{k-1} - P_{k-1} \varphi_k \left(\varphi_k^T P_{k-1} \varphi_k + R \right)^{-1} \varphi_k^T P_{k-1}, \qquad\qquad (40)$$

where I is the identity matrix and L is the so-called gain matrix.

5.4.4. Extended Kalman Filter

The Extended Kalman Filter is one of the most used methods for joint state and parameter estimation of nonlinear systems [38,39]. The main idea is the use of the prediction-correction principle where the non-linear model is used for the prediction (denoted by the superscript $^-$), and its linearized counterpart around the current estimate is exploited in the propagation of the covariance matrix P and in the subsequent correction step (denoted by the superscript $^+$) with the discrete system measurements. Compared to the recursive least-squares method, one can additionally account for the nonlinearity and the noise that affects the system dynamics using EKF. This can prove to be highly advantageous if parametric uncertainty influences the measurements strongly. Similarly to the recursive least-squares method, the absence of the treatment of the constraints and severe nonlinearities can lead to the divergence of the estimator. On the other hand, the advantage of EKF lies in its simpler implementation, where no parametric sensitivities are required, and in increased tuning capabilities, which might yield faster and more robust convergence.

To formulate the EKF algorithm, the estimated parameters are first represented by new dummy state variables with zero dynamics:

$$\frac{d\hat{\theta}}{dt} = 0, \quad \hat{\theta}(0) = \hat{\theta}_0, \tag{41}$$

and the dynamics of a new state vector is constructed using the dynamics of state and parameter estimates:

$$\dot{\tilde{x}} = \tilde{f}(\tilde{x}, u) = (f^T(\hat{x}, \hat{\theta}, u), 0^T)^T, \quad \text{with } \tilde{x} = (\hat{x}^T, \hat{\theta}^T)^T. \tag{42}$$

The observer dynamics then reads in the following form:

$$\dot{\tilde{x}}^- = \tilde{f}(\tilde{x}^-, u), \qquad\qquad\qquad \tilde{x}^-(t_{k-1}) = \tilde{x}_{k-1}^+, \tag{43}$$

$$\dot{\tilde{P}}^- = F\tilde{P}^- + \tilde{P}^- F^T + Q, \qquad\qquad \tilde{P}^-(t_{k-1}) = \tilde{P}_{k-1}^+, \tag{44}$$

with initial estimates $\tilde{x}^-(t_0) = \tilde{x}_0$ and $\tilde{P}^-(t_0) = \tilde{P}_0$ and with the update at measurement instants k defined as:

$$\tilde{x}_k^+ = \tilde{x}^-(t_k) + L_k[y_k - \tilde{h}(\tilde{x}^-(t_k))], \tag{45}$$

$$L_k = \tilde{P}^-(t_k)C_k^T \left[C_k\tilde{P}^-(t_k)C_k^T + R\right]^{-1}, \tag{46}$$

$$\tilde{P}_k^+ = (I - L_k C_k)\tilde{P}^-(t_k). \tag{47}$$

The state transition and observation matrices are defined by the following Jacobians:

$$F = \left.\frac{\partial \tilde{f}(\tilde{x}, u)}{\partial \tilde{x}}\right|_{\tilde{x}^-(t), u(t)}, \qquad C_k = \left.\frac{\partial \tilde{h}(\tilde{x})}{\partial \tilde{x}}\right|_{\tilde{x}^-(t_k)}. \tag{48}$$

Matrices Q, P denote, respectively, the covariance matrix of the noise affecting the state dynamics and the covariance of the estimated states and parameters. These matrices can also be thought of as tuning knobs of the estimation algorithm affecting its estimation performance and convergence.

5.4.5. General Assessment of the Presented Estimation Methods

The presented estimation methods differ in several aspects. One can distinguish them based on the level of accounting for the nonlinearity of the process model and the number of tuning parameters. The WLS method is the only method here that employs the fully-nonlinear model and does not approximate the estimation problem. It does not require tuning of any parameters if we assume that the information on the variance of the measurement noise is available based on the employed sensor equipment. A price to pay for this rigorousness is usually reflected in the computational time when measurements are obtained on some large time horizon. The WLSMH method uses an approximation to the full-horizon estimation problem and employs an approximation here that is parametrized by the tuning factor P. The RLS method works with the assumption that a linearized process model represents the behavior of the process within the the subsequent sampling instants. This method can be regarded as residing on the other side of the spectrum of the estimation methods compared to WLS method, as it provides a computationally-efficient estimator, which only approximates the behavior of the optimal estimator. A similar behavior can be expected from the EKF algorithm. This can additionally account for the nonlinearity of the process model (via tuning parameter Q), so even further simplifications can be made for the linearization of the estimation problem (see the previous section).

6. Case Study

Here, we present the simulation results obtained with different estimation techniques presented above. We will consider the batch diafiltration process that operates under limiting flux conditions, and the permeate flux for the unfouled membrane reads as:

$$J_0(c_1) = k \ln \left(\frac{c_{\lim}}{c_1} \right), \tag{49}$$

where k is the mass transfer coefficient and $c_{\lim}$ is the limiting concentration for the macro-solute. Note that the permeate flux depends only on the concentration of the macro-solute. The overall separation goal is to drive the system from the initial $[c_{1,0}, c_{2,0}]$ to the final point $[c_{1,f}, c_{2,f}]$ in the minimum time described by (11) to (15). The initial process volume is considered to be $V_0 = 0.1 \, \text{m}^3$. The parameters for the limiting flux model are $k = 4.79 \, \text{m/s}$, $c_{\lim} = 319 \, \text{mol/m}^3$ and the membrane area $1 \, \text{m}^2$. The a priori unknown fouling rate is $K = 2$ units. As the degree of nonlinearity of the model is strongly dependent on the nature of the fouling behavior, represented by the a priori unknown parameter n (see Section 3), we will study the cases when $n = \{0, 1, 1.5\}$.

We first study the case where $[c_{1,0}, c_{2,0}] = [10 \, \text{mol/m}^3, 100 \, \text{mol/m}^3]$ and $[c_{1,f}, c_{2,f}] = [100 \, \text{mol/m}^3, 1 \, \text{mol/m}^3]$. The time-optimal operation, as stated above, follows a three-step strategy. In the first step, the concentration mode is applied, followed with a singular arc:

$$S(\tau, J_0(c_1), K, n) = J \left(1 + k + k(n-2) J^{\frac{5-2n}{n-2}} K\tau (AJ_0)^n \right) = 0, \tag{50}$$

and in the last step, pure dilution mode is performed. The switching times between the individual control arcs are determined by the fine precision of the numerical integration around the roots of the singular surface equation. The on-line estimation of the unknown parameters is performed where the samples of the measured process outputs (25) are assumed to be available with the sampling time ($T_s = 0.01 \, \text{s}$). This means that the optimal control is updated at each sampling time based on the considered measured outputs. Based on our observations, the chosen sampling time did not pose any computational challenges in the estimation of the parameters. However, in the case of the application on a real process, this sampling time can pose computational difficulties for optimization-based estimation (WLS and WLSMH) since an optimization problem needs to be solved in each sampling time. In the case of the WLSMH method, the initial computing time for one estimation was observed to be approximately 10 s, and once the true values were reached, the computational time decreased to 2 s. For this reason, such a low sampling time is more adequate for recursive methods (RLS and EKF) where no non-linear optimization problem is needed to be solved.

For each studied estimation method (WLS, WLSMH, RLS and EKF), three simulations were performed, with $n = \{0, 1, 1.5\}$. For the WLSMH method, the moving horizon was set to $MH = 2$. The length of the horizon is traditionally defined using the sampling instants (steps) as its units. The covariance matrices were tuned for all of the considered simulations as follows

$$P_0 = \text{diag}(0.1, 0.01), \tag{51}$$

$$\tilde{P}_0 = \text{diag}[\text{diag}(0.001, 0.001, 0.001), P_0], \tag{52}$$

$$R = \text{diag}(10^{-4}, 10^{-4}, 10^{-8}, 10^{-4}), \tag{53}$$

$$Q = \text{diag}(0.001, 0.001, 0.001, 0.3, 0.1). \tag{54}$$

For the WLSMH method, the covariance matrix P was updated using the EKF run in parallel. In our simulations with the RLS method, a different matrix P_0 had to be chosen for a different value of n; otherwise, a divergent behavior was observed. We attribute this behavior to the strong non-linearities of the process model. Further, due to the non-linear behavior, the choice of P was very sensitive to the overall estimation. The noise in the measured data was simulated as a random normally-distributed Gaussian with the covariance matrix R (the noise covariance of the approximation of the flux derivative is determined empirically from the simulation data). The same evolution of the random noise is used in all presented simulations. According to our observations, the estimation performance is significantly influenced by the choice of R. A small change in the covariance matrix R can cause a big difference in the rate of estimation convergence. The chosen variances represent 1% standard deviations of the measurement noise. The actual magnitudes depend on the employed units of the process variables. Hence, the flux varies in the range $[0, 0.06]\,\text{m/h}$.

The parameter estimation methods discussed in Section 5.4 were implemented in the MATLAB R2016a environment. For the optimization-based (WLS, WLSMH) methods, the built-in NLP solver fmincon was chosen. The tolerances for the optimized variables and the objective function were both set to 1×10^{-4}. The ordinary differential equations describing the process model and sensitivity equations were solved using the MATLAB subroutine ode45. The values for the relative and absolute tolerances were set to 1×10^{-8} and 1×10^{-6}, respectively. The precision on detecting the switching times by numerical integration was determined with the same tolerances as set by the subroutine ode45. All of the reported results were obtained on the workstation Intel Xeon CPU X5660 with 2.80 GHz and 16 GB RAM.

Table 1 presents a comparison of the rate of suboptimality of the processing time (δ_{tf}^*) achieved for the on-line control strategy with different estimation methods for different fouling models. We also show the values of normalized root mean squared error (NRMSE) for the estimated parameters ($\mathcal{R}_{\hat{\theta}}$) and for the concentrations and flux ($\mathcal{R}_{\hat{x}}$) and the cumulative computational time (t_c) needed for the used estimators. We can observe that the optimality loss for the different estimation techniques is negligible, and the same loss is achieved with all employed estimators. The highest optimality loss occurs in the case of $n = 0$. The increased optimality loss could be caused here because the value $n = 0$ is used as the lower bound for the estimated parameters, and thus, at least, local convergence problems could occur due to this hard constraint. We can observe that the NRMSE for the estimated parameters for the WLS and WLSMH is higher compared to the recursive methods (RLS and EKF). This was caused due to the high oscillations in the beginning of the estimation of the parameters. The NRMSEs for the concentrations and flux ($\mathcal{R}_{\hat{x}}$) indicate that the difference in the trajectories' profile in the case of ideal and estimated concentrations and flux is small. The highest difference in all cases was observed only in the EKF method. A possible explanation is that the estimated parameters using the rest of the methods (WLS, WLSMH and RLS) converged exactly or reasonably close with negligible difference to the true values of the parameters on the second interval. If we compare the WLS and WLSMH methods, we can notice a significant decrease in the computational time. This was expected since in the case of the WLS method, every new measurement increases the complexity of the optimization problem that needs to be solved, whereas the complexity remains the same for WLSMH, since only a constant amount of measurements is considered. Simulations with a larger horizon were also performed for WLSMH ($MH = 5, 10, 20$). Although the convergence of the estimated parameters was slightly faster and smoother when compared to the case with $MH = 2$, the computational time increased significantly.

Table 1. Comparison of the rate of the suboptimality of final processing times, the normalized root mean squared error for unknown parameters and concentrations and the computational time for different estimation techniques. MH, moving horizon; RLS, recursive least-squares.

Estimation	$n = 0$				$n = 1$				$n = 1.5$			
Method	δ_{tf}^* (h)	$\mathcal{R}_{\hat{\theta}}$	$\mathcal{R}_{\hat{x}}$	t_c (h)	δ_{tf}^* (h)	$\mathcal{R}_{\hat{\theta}}$	$\mathcal{R}_{\hat{x}}$	t_c (h)	δ_{tf}^* (h)	$\mathcal{R}_{\hat{\theta}}$	$\mathcal{R}_{\hat{x}}$	t_c (h)
WLS	0.21	0.24	0.17	3.73	0.10	0.46	0.16	4.71	0.09	0.14	0.24	23.33
WLSMH	0.21	0.48	0.23	0.55	0.10	0.64	0.46	1.28	0.09	0.29	0.74	8.52
RLS	0.21	0.11	1.65	0.04	0.10	0.03	1.15	0.04	0.09	0.04	1.25	0.13
EKF	0.21	0.09	5.26	0.01	0.10	0.05	3.18	0.01	0.09	0.07	2.82	0.01

In the case of recursive methods, the computational time was low, since no NLP problem had to be solved and only the current measurements were considered. Overall, we can conclude that all of the estimation methods discussed in this paper were able to estimate the unknown fouling parameters either exactly or with only minor differences. This eventually resulted also in minor differences in the concentration and control trajectories. Further, based on the results, we can also conclude that the best method for on-line estimation is the EKF method. This is due to the fact that no NLP problem has to be solved at each sampling time, and the cumulative computational time is the lowest of all of the proposed methods. Moreover, compared to the RLS method, the EKF does not require different covariance matrices for the individual fouling models as discussed previously. Finally, the EKF method has a satisfactory convergence on the second interval, which leads to accurate information about the singular control.

The time-varying profiles of the unknown fouling parameters (K, n) are shown in Figure 3. We can observe that in the case of the WLS and WLSMH methods, the parameters converged quickly to a close neighborhood of the true values of the parameters ($K = 2$ and $n = 1.5$) prior to the switching time (vertical black dashed line) of the optimal control to the singular arc. The WLS method was able to estimate the true values of the parameters in the first few samples. However, in the case of WLSMH, the estimation needed more time, and we can observe that the parameter values were oscillating for the first two hours. This was due to the NLP solver falling into local minima. This can also be attributed to the chosen length of the moving horizon and the possibly imperfect choice of the initial covariance matrix P_0. To overcome the issue of NLP solver falling into local minima, one can employ global optimizers. However, based on our observations, the local minima were only hit in the first samples of the estimation when only a few measured outputs were considered. When the recursive methods (RLS, EKF) were used, we can observe that the parameters converged almost to the true values of the parameters. The difference in the estimated and true values of the parameters is attributed to the strong nonlinearity of the process model. Moreover, the performance of these methods also strongly depends on the choice of the covariance matrices. Overall, we can conclude that all of the estimation methods were able to estimate the unknown fouling parameters or converge almost to true values of the parameters even before switching to the singular surface where singular control is applied. As a result, the theoretical optimality of the diafiltration process was almost restored when using the proposed estimators and coupling them within the feedback control law. Similar behavior for parameter estimation was also observed for other fouling models.

Figure 4 shows the concentration, flux and control trajectories for the ideal and estimated cases together with the considered measurements of concentrations and flux. The figures show only one of the estimation method (EKF) for $n = 1.5$ as the worst case scenario since all other cases, the trajectories are closer to the ideal ones. In Figure 4a, we show the considered measured outputs (denoted by the circle and cross) and the ideal and estimated concentration trajectories. However, due to the small sampling time, we only display some of the measured points. The considered measured flux with ideal and estimated parameters is shown in Figure 4b. Moreover, in Figure 4c,d, the optimal concentration state diagram and the optimal control profile are shown. In all figures, the solid lines represent the optimal scenario with a perfect knowledge of parameters. Further, we can observe that the estimated and ideal trajectories in the first step when the control is constant ($\alpha = 0$) are identical. This behavior was expected since the control in the first step does not depend on the unknown fouling parameters. The difference in the second interval is negligible. This was due to the convergence of the parameters during the first step. For this reason, the singular control in the second step is calculated with almost the true value of the parameters. The measured concentration of the macro-solute (blue dashed line in Figure 4a) shows the increasing difference to the ideal one at the singular step. However, this has only a minor impact on the overall optimal operation. Based on the results, we can conclude that by using the estimated parameters obtained by all estimation techniques, the overall operation is very close to optimal one with only minor differences in the processing and switching times. Moreover, it should be also mentioned that even if satisfactory convergence was obtained with the EKF method, different Kalman filter methods, like the unscented Kalman filter [40], could be also employed for the parameter estimation.

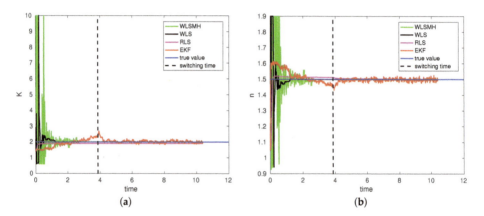

Figure 3. Estimation of the fouling parameters K, n for the three chosen cases together with the optimal switching time. (**a**) Estimation of the fouling parameter K; (**b**) estimation of the fouling parameter n.

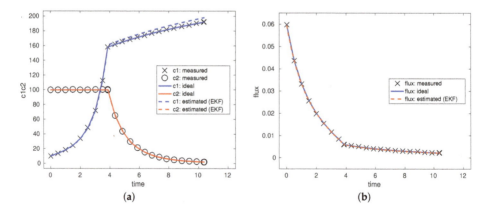

Figure 4. *Cont.*

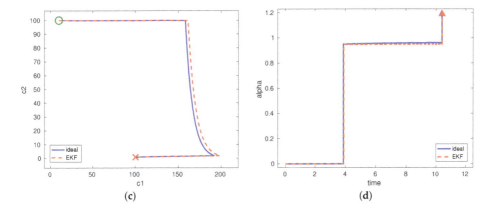

Figure 4. Concentration state diagram and optimal control profile for ideal and estimated fouling parameters ($K = 2$ and $n = 1.5$) by employing the EKF method. (**a**) Measured, ideal and estimated concentrations; (**b**) measured, ideal and estimated flux; (**c**) concentration state diagram; (**d**) optimal control profile.

Next, we study the case where the initial concentrations are $[c_{1,0}, c_{2,0}] = [130 \, \text{mol/m}^3, 100 \, \text{mol/m}^3]$, while the same final concentrations have to be met as in the previous cases. The optimal control strategy starts with pure dilution in the first step and in the last step, which follows after an operation on a singular arc. We use the same estimators as before, with the same tuning matrices.

In Figure 5, we show the results of the estimation of the unknown fouling parameters using the WLS method and the corresponding concentration state diagram and control profile of the on-line control strategy. As stated above (Section 4), the entry to the singular arc (50) can be determined without the knowledge of fouling parameters as $J = J_0$. On the singular arc, the estimation of the unknown fouling parameters commences. We can observe in Figure 5a,b that the unknown fouling parameters were estimated accurately in the first three hours of operation where the overall time-optimal operation was approximately 37 hours. The suboptimality of the on-line control strategy w.r.t. the ideal one is $\delta_{tf}^* = 0.025$. The oscillations in the first minutes of the operation were mainly caused by a small set of measured outputs. A similar behavior was observed in the previous case. Once the amount of measured outputs is increased, we can observe a quick convergence of the estimated parameters towards the true values. The comparison of ideal and estimated concentrations and control trajectories is shown in Figure 5c,d. As we can observe, the differences in the concentrations and control trajectories for ideal and estimated cases are negligible. This is due to the quick convergence of the estimated fouling parameters. We also performed simulations with the rest of the estimation methods.

In the case of the recursive methods (EKF and RLS), by using the same covariance matrices (51) to (54) as in the previous case, the estimated parameters diverged in the first hour of the batch and were not able to converge to the true values of the parameters. The same behavior was also observed in the case of the WLSMH method, since the covariance matrix P was updated based on the EKF method. The reasons for the divergence of the WLSMH, RLS and EKF methods was mainly caused due to the high sensitivity of the choice of the covariance matrices and the strong non-linearities of the process model. Other reasons for the possible divergence issues as discussed in Section 4.3 are the insufficient amount of measured outputs, since the estimation starts at the singular surface, and insignificant sensitivity between the measured outputs and the estimated parameters on the singular surface. This was caused by almost constant flux on the singular surface.

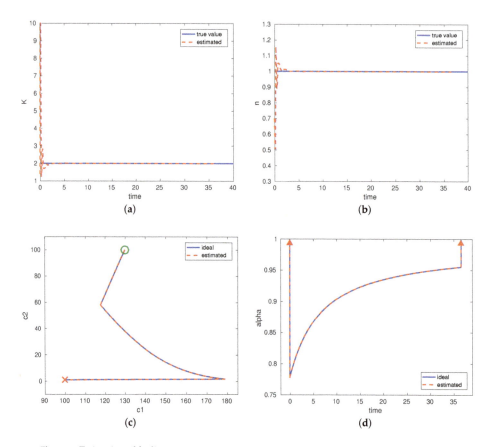

Figure 5. Estimation of fouling parameters, concentration state diagram and optimal control profile for ideal and estimated fouling parameters ($K = 2$ and $n = 1$) using the WLS estimation method. (a) Estimation of the fouling parameter K; (b) estimation of the fouling parameter n; (c) Concentration state diagram; (d) optimal control profile.

Overall, we can conclude that even if in the first step, pure dilution mode has to be applied and the estimation of unknown fouling parameters is only performed during the singular control, the differences between the ideal and estimated trajectories are negligible. The results indicate that the estimated parameters converged reasonably close to the true values of the parameters in the first hours of operation. For this reason, the overall operation is very close to the optimal one with only negligible differences in the case when the WLS method is applied. However, in the rest of the estimation methods, strong divergence of the estimated parameters was observed.

7. Conclusions

In this paper, we studied the time-optimal operation of a diafiltration process in the presence of membrane fouling. The optimal operation and control is an explicit non-linear control law defined over concentration regions. According to the theory, the optimal operation is defined as a three-step strategy with concentration or pure dilution mode in the first and the last step and with a singular arc in the middle step.

In the paper, we provided a detailed analysis on the problems related to the observation of the parameters based on the measured outputs. Based on the analysis, we conclude that by taking into account the concentrations and flux as measured outputs, both parameters could not be estimated at the same time. Therefore, the derivative of flux w.r.t. to time had to be considered as a new measured outputs. Based on the analysis, four standard parameter estimation methods were discussed for the estimation of the unknown fouling parameters on-line during the separation. The crucial reason for estimating the parameters on-line is that the singular surface and control depend on the fouling parameters. The first two methods (WLS and WLSMH) were able to estimate the parameters exactly, whereas the recursive methods (RLS and EKF) converged almost to the true values of the parameters. However, the convergence was satisfactory and resulted in minor differences in the concentration and control profiles compared to the ideal case. Based on the results, we conclude that by using the EKF estimation method, we improve the convergence with the lowest computational time compared to other discussed methods. If the optimal operation starts with a pure dilution mode, only WLS and WLSMH were able to converge to the true values of the parameters, whereas the recursive methods (RLS and EKF) diverged completely from the true values. A possible remedy for the future could be to inject some dither signal into singular dilution rate to increase the excitation of the process.

All of the results presented in this paper are based on simulation results where the process noise was also considered in the simulations. Future research directions will be focused on experimental implementation of the proposed estimation techniques on a laboratory membrane process.

Acknowledgments: The authors gratefully acknowledge the contribution of the Scientific Grant Agency of the Slovak Republic under Grant 1/0053/13, the Slovak Research and Development Agency under the project APVV-15-0007 and also the international cooperation of the Slovak Research and Development Agency under the project APVV SK-FR-2015-0001. This contribution/publication is also the partial result of the Research & Development Operational Programme for the project University Scientific Park Slovak University of Technology in Bratislava, ITMS 26240220084, supported by the Research 7 Development Operational Programme funded by the ERDF.

Author Contributions: M.J. performed simulations and wrote most of the paper. D.P. performed identifiability tests and wrote the corresponding section. R.P. provided substantial background on the parameter estimation methods. A.L. and M.F. contributed to writing and correcting the paper.

Conflicts of Interest: The authors declare no conflict of interest.

References

1. Paulen, R.; Fikar, M. *Optimal Operation of Batch Membrane Processes*; Springer: Cham, Switzerland, 2016; p. 158.
2. Nakajima, H. (Ed.) *Mass Transfer—Advances in Sustainable Energy and Environment Oriented Numerical Modeling*; InTech: Rijeka, Croatia, 2014; p. 522.
3. Hermia, J. Constant pressure blocking filtration laws-application to power-law non-Newtonian fluids. *Trans. Inst. Chem. Eng.* **1982**, *60*, 183–187.
4. Parvasi, P.; Mostafazadeh, A.K.; Rahimpour, M.R. Dynamic modeling and optimization of a novel methanol synthesis loop with hydrogen-permselective membrane reactor. *Int. J. Hydrog. Energy* **2009**, *34*, 29–37.
5. Bui, V.A.; Vu, L.T.T.; Nguyen, M.H. Simulation and optimisation of direct contact membrane distillation for energy efficiency. *Desalination* **2010**, *259*, 29–37.
6. Blankert, B.; Betlem, B.H.L.; Roffel, B. Dynamic optimization of a dead-end filtration trajectory: Blocking filtration laws. *J. Membr. Sci.* **2006**, *285*, 90–95.
7. Zondervan, E.; Roffel, B. Dynamic optimization of chemical cleaning in dead-end ultrafiltration. *J. Membr. Sci.* **2008**, *307*, 309–313.
8. Charfi, A.; Amar, N.B.; Harmand, J. Analysis of fouling mechanisms in anaerobic membrane bioreactors. *Water Res.* **2012**, *46*, 2637–2650.
9. Chis, O.; Banga, J.R.; Balsa-Canto, E. GenSSI: A software toolbox for structural identifiability analysis of biological models. *Bioinformatics* **2011**, *27*, 2610–2611.
10. Saccomani, M.P. Examples of testing global identifiability of biological and biomedical models with the DAISY software. *Comput. Methods Programs Biomed.* **2010**, *40*, 402–407.

11. Jelemenský, M.; Sharma, A.; Paulen, R.; Fikar, M. Time-optimal operation of diafiltration processes in the presence of fouling. In Proceedings of the 12th International Symposium on Process Systems Engineering and 25th European Symposium on Computer Aided Process Engineering, Copenhagen, Denmark, 31 May–4 June 2015; Gernaey, K.V., Huusom, J.K., Gani, R., Eds.; Elsevier: Copenhagen, Denmark, 2015; pp. 1577–1582.

12. Jelemenský, M.; Klaučo, M.; Paulen, R.; Lauwers, J.; Logist, F.; Van Impe, J.; Fikar, M. Time-optimal control and parameter estimation of diafiltration processes in the presence of membrane fouling. In Proceedings of the 11th IFAC Symposium on Dynamics and Control of Process Systems, Trondheim, Norway, 6–8 June 2016; Volume 11, pp. 242–247.

13. Kovács, Z.; Fikar, M.; Czermak, P. Mathematical modeling of diafiltration. In Proceedings of the International Conference of Chemical Engineering, San Francisco, CA, USA, 20–22 October 2009; Pannonia University: Veszprem, Hungary, 2009; pp. 135.

14. Baker, R.W. *Membrane Technology and Applications*, 3rd ed.; Wiley: Hoboken, NJ, USA, 2012.

15. Zhao, Y.; Wu, K.; Wang, Z.; Zhao, L.; Li, S.S. Fouling and cleaning of membrane—A literature review. *J. Environ. Sci.* **2000**, *12*, 241–251.

16. Bolton, G.; LaCasse, D.; Kuriyel, R. Combined models of membrane fouling: Development and application to microfiltration and ultrafiltration of biological fluids. *J. Membr. Sci.* **2006**, *277*, 75–84.

17. Vela, M.C.V.; Blanco, S.A.; García, J.L.; Rodríguez, E.B. Analysis of membrane pore blocking models applied to the ultrafiltration of PEG. *Sep. Purif. Technol.* **2008**, *62*, 489 – 498.

18. Goh, C.J.; Teo, K.L. Control parameterization: A unified approach to optimal control problems with general constraints. *Automatica* **1988**, *24*, 3–18.

19. Jelemenský, M.; Sharma, A.; Paulen, R.; Fikar, M. Time-optimal control of diafiltration processes in the presence of membrane fouling. *Comput. Chem. Eng.* **2016**, *91*, 343–351.

20. Pontryagin, L.S.; Boltyanskii, V.G.; Gamkrelidze, R.V.; Mishchenko, E.F. *The Mathematical Theory of Optimal Processes*; Wiley (Interscience): New York, NY, USA, 1962.

21. Bryson, A.E., Jr.; Ho, Y.C. *Applied Optimal Control*; Hemisphere Publishing Corporation: Washington, DC, USA, 1975.

22. Miao, H.; Xia, X.; Perelson, A.S.; Wu, H. On identifiability of nonlinear ODE models and applications in viral dynamics. *SIAM* **2011**, *53*, 3–39.

23. Godfrey, K.R.; Evans, N.D. Structural identifiability of nonlinear systems using linear/nonlinear splitting. *Int. J. Control* **2003**, *76*, 209–2016.

24. Godfrey, K.R.; Evans, N.D. Identifiability of some nonlinear kinetics. In Proceedings of the 3rd Workshop on Modelling of Chemical Reaction Systems, Heidelberg, Germany, 24–26 July 1996.

25. Pohjanpalo, H. System identifiability based on the power series expansion of the solution. *Math. Biosci.* **1978**, *41*, 21–33.

26. Chis, O.; Banga, J.R.; Balsa-Canto, E. Structural identifiability of systems biology models: A critical comparison of methods. *PLoS ONE* **2011**, *6*, e27755.

27. DiStefano, J., III. *Dynamic Systems Biology Modeling and Simulation*; Academic Press: Cambridge, MA, USA, 2015; p. 884.

28. Chis, O.; Banga, J.R.; Balsa-Canto, E. *GenSSI: Generating Series Approach for Testing Structural Identifiability*; CSIC: Madrid, Spain, 2011.

29. Maiwald, T.; Timmer, J. Dynamical modeling and multi-experiment fitting with PottersWheel. *Bioinformatics* **2008**, *24*, 2037–2043.

30. Meshkat, N.; Kuo, C.; DiStefano, J., III. On finding and using identifiable parameter combinations in nonlinear dynamic systems biology models and COMBOS: A novel web implementation. *PLoS ONE* **2014**, *9*, e110261.

31. Bellu, G.; Saccomani, M.P.; Audoly, S.; D'Angio, L. DAISY: A new software tool to test global identifiability of biological and physiological systems. *Comput. Methods Programs Biomed.* **2007**, *88*, 52–61.

32. Galrinho, M.; Rojas, C.; Hjalmarsson, H. A weighted least-squares method for parameter estimation in structured models. In Proceedings of the 53rd IEEE Conference on Decision and Control, Los Angeles, CA, USA, 15–17 December 2014; pp. 3322–3327.

33. Gulan, M.; Salaj, M.; Rohaľ-Ilkiv, B. Nonlinear model predictive control with moving horizon estimation of a pendubot system. In Proceedings of the 2015 International Conference on Process Control (PC), Strbske Pleso, Slovakia, 9–12 June 2015; pp. 226–231.

34. Kühl, P.; Diehl, M.; Kraus, T.; Schlöder, J.P.; Bock, H.G. A real-time algorithm for moving horizon state and parameter estimation. *Comput. Chem. Eng.* **2011**, *35*, 71–83.

35. Haverbeke, N. Efficient Numerical Methods for Moving Horizon Estimation. Ph.D. Thesis, Katholieke Universiteit Leuven, Leuven, Belgium, 2011.

36. Ding, F. Coupled-least-squares identification for multivariable systems. *IET Control Theory Appl.* **2013**, *7*, 68–79.

37. Ljung, L. *System Identification: Theory for the User*, 2nd ed.; Prentice Hall PTR: Upper Saddle River, NJ, USA, 1999.

38. Kalman, R.E. A new approach to linear filtering and prediction problems. *Trans. ASME J. Basic Eng.* **1960**, *82*, 35–45.

39. Bavdekar, V.A.; Deshpande, A.P.; Patwardhan, S.C. Identification of process and measurement noise covariance for state and parameter estimation using extended Kalman filter. *J. Process Control* **2011**, *21*, 585–601.

40. Wan, E.A.; van der Merwe, R. The unscented Kalman filter for nonlinear estimation. In Proceedings of the IEEE 2000 Adaptive Systems for Signal Processing, Communications, and Control Symposium, Lake Louise, AB, Canada, 1–4 October 2000 .

Article

Model Predictive Control of the Exit Part Temperature for an Austenitization Furnace

Hari S. Ganesh, Thomas F. Edgar * and Michael Baldea

McKetta Department of Chemical Engineering, University of Texas at Austin, Austin, TX 78712, USA;
hariganesh@utexas.edu (H.S.G.); mbaldea@che.utexas.edu (M.B.)
* Correspondence: tfedgar@austin.utexas.edu; Tel.: +1-512-471-3080

Academic Editor: Dominique Bonvin
Received: 9 August 2016; Accepted: 6 December 2016; Published: 15 December 2016

Abstract: Quench hardening is the process of strengthening and hardening ferrous metals and alloys by heating the material to a specific temperature to form austenite (austenitization), followed by rapid cooling (quenching) in water, brine or oil to introduce a hardened phase called martensite. The material is then often tempered to increase toughness, as it may decrease from the quench hardening process. The austenitization process is highly energy-intensive and many of the industrial austenitization furnaces were built and equipped prior to the advent of advanced control strategies and thus use large, sub-optimal amounts of energy. The model computes the energy usage of the furnace and the part temperature profile as a function of time and position within the furnace under temperature feedback control. In this paper, the aforementioned model is used to simulate the furnace for a batch of forty parts under heuristic temperature set points suggested by the operators of the plant. A model predictive control (MPC) system is then developed and deployed to control the the part temperature at the furnace exit thereby preventing the parts from overheating. An energy efficiency gain of 5.3% was obtained under model predictive control compared to operation under heuristic temperature set points tracked by a regulatory control layer.

Keywords: model predictive control; energy efficiency; iron and steel; austenitization

---

1. Introduction

Countries around the world are aiming for economic growth that is inclusive, smart and sustainable. Research and innovation are key drivers to realize this transition [1–6]. Studies on power technologies and technological innovation as a means to achieve a more efficient energy-intensive industry, with reduced CO_2 emissions are reported in the literature [7–12]. The iron and steel industry is not only energy-intensive but also one of the largest CO_2 emitters [4,13,14]. The United States has the third largest national iron and steel sector in the world with annual crude steel production of 80.5 million metric tonnes (Mt) in 2010 [15]. The iron and steel industry is the fourth largest industrial user of energy in the US with yearly demands of 2 quadrillion BTU (quads), which is roughly 2% of the overall domestic energy consumption [16–18]. For an individual steel processing plant, reheating and heat treating furnaces account for 65% to 80% of the overall energy use [19,20]. The energy demand is intensified due to inherent furnace inefficiencies (20%–60%) and ineffective control strategies [20]. Therefore, any improvement in energy efficiency of steel processing furnaces through optimization, restructuring of processes and applying advanced control strategies will have a direct impact on overall energy consumption and related CO_2 emissions.

Model predictive control (MPC), originally developed to meet specialized control needs of oil refineries and power plants, has now found applications in food processing, pharmaceutical, polymer, automotive, metallurgical, chemical and aerospace industries [21–23]. The success of MPC can be attributed, as summarized by Qin et al. [23], to its ability to solve complex multiple-input, multiple-output (MIMO) control problems

1. without violating input, output and process constraints,
2. accounting for disturbances,
3. by preventing excess movement of input variables, and
4. by controlling as many variables as possible in case of faulty or unavailable sensors or actuators.

In this work, we describe the development and implementation of an MPC system for controlling the temperatures of the parts exiting an industrial austenitization furnace using a model-based case study. The key to our approach is feedback control of the temperature of the metal parts (which can be measured in practice via a combination of non-contact temperature sensing and soft sensing/state observation). We show that, in this manner, the energy usage of the system is reduced considerably compared to the current regulatory control scheme (which is effectively open-loop with respect to product temperatures). To this end, we rely on the radiation-based nonlinear model of the furnace developed in Heng et al. [24] to develop a hierarchical, multi-rate control structure, whereby the setpoints of regulatory controllers are set by a multiple input, single output MPC that is computed at a much lower frequency than the regulatory control moves.

2. Process and System Description

Depending on the application, steel is forged into the desired shape and heat treated (e.g., annealed, quenched, and tempered) to improve its mechanical properties such as strength, hardness, toughness and ductility [25–28]. Among the heat treating processes, quench hardening is commonly employed to strengthen and harden the workpieces. Quench hardening consists of first heating finished or semi-finished parts made of iron or iron-based alloys to a high temperature, in an inert atmosphere, such that there is a phase transition from the magnetic, body-centered cubic (BCC) structure to a non-magnetic, face-centered cubic (FCC) structure called austenite (austenitization), followed by rapid quenching in water, brine or oil to introduce a hardened phase having a body-centered tetragonal (BCT) crystal structure called martensite [28–31]. This process is usually followed by tempering in order to decrease brittleness (increase toughness) that may have increased during quench hardening [28,32,33]. In this process of strengthening, austenitization is the energy-intensive step, where the workpieces have to be heated from typically 300 K to 1100 K in a furnace fired indirectly (to avoid oxidation) by radiant tube burners that require a large amount of fuel [27]. The part temperatures, especially the core, cannot typically be sensed and measured while the part is being processed inside the furnace. Nevertheless, the temperatures of the parts after exiting the furnace can be measured by non-contact ultrasonic measurements [34–36]. In practice, the operators tend to overheat the parts such that a minimum temperature threshold is exceeded, thereby causing excess fuel consumption. Another reason for overheating is that even if a single portion of the part does not transform to austenite completely during heat treatment, that portion will be very soft in the quenched product resulting in the entire part not meeting the quality standards. Therefore, the monetary gain in energy minimization while heating will be counter-balanced by the loss due to scrapping of defective parts. The temperature sensing limitations, combined with high energy usage, make austenitization furnaces primary targets for advanced model-based analysis and control.

The austenitization furnace considered in this work is operated in a continuous manner under temperature feedback control (see Figure 1). Metal parts are loaded on to trays placed on a conveyor belt, which transports the parts through the furnace that is heated by combustion of natural gas in radiant tube burners on the ceiling and floor. After exiting the furnace, the parts are placed into an oil quench bath to induce the crystal structure change. Nitrogen is used as the inert blanket gas to prevent surface oxidation and flows counter current to the direction of motion of the conveyor belt. The furnace operates at temperatures in excess of 1000 K and the residence time of the parts is in the order of hours. Due to sensing limitations (equipment for the aforementioned ultrasonic measurements is not available in the plant), the part temperatures are currently indirectly controlled by controlling the furnace temperature—a scheme that is effectively open-loop with respect to part temperature control. The temperature set points of the local feedback controllers are set heuristically by process operators.

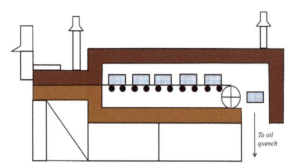

Figure 1. Prototype furnace schematic for roller hearth furnace based on a design by AFC-Holcroft [37]. The hatched rectangles are the parts that are heated in the furnace.

A two-dimensional (2D) radiation-based semi-empirical model of the furnace under consideration was developed in Heng et al. [24]. The model neglects the interactions between parts, which are cylindrical with ogive top shapes, and are loaded on a tray. The ensemble of a tray and its contents is modeled as a rectangular structure with equivalent metal mass and referred as to a "part." The mass of the conveyor belt is much smaller than that of the part. Hence, the conveyor belt is excluded from the model. Nevertheless, the movement of the parts inside the furnace is captured. There is only surface-to-surface radiation interaction and no gas-to-surface radiation interaction since nitrogen is a diatomic molecule [38]. The gas-to-surface heat transfer is assumed to occur only through convection, and surface-to-surface heat transfer is assumed to occur only though radiation. The furnace is discretized into a series of *control volumes* to calculate a discretized gas temperature profile within the furnace. For temperature control purposes, adjacent burners are grouped together and the fuel flow rates are adjusted simultaneously for each group. The furnace is divided into four such groups (four control valves) of twelve burners each referred to as *temperature control zones*. The middle insulating surface of the ceiling of each zone is assumed to host the temperature sensor used for control (see Figure 2). The inputs to the model are the dimensions of the steel parts and its physical properties, the mass flow rate of fuel to the burners, feedback control zone temperature set points, flow rate of nitrogen, and the temperature of the surrounding air. The model evaluates the energy consumption of the furnace and the temperature distribution within the parts as a function of time and part position within the furnace.

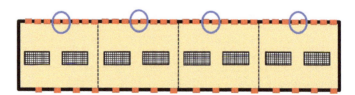

Figure 2. The schematic of the 2D model of the roller hearth heat treating furnace. On the furnace walls, the red and black lines represent burner and insulation surfaces respectively. The checkered rectangles are the parts that are heated in the furnace. Each side of a part is a design/load/part surface. Parts enter from the left hand side of the furnace schematic and exit from the right hand side. Nitrogen is injected from the right hand side and exits from the left hand side. The dotted lines indicate boundaries between temperature control zones of the furnace. The circled insulation surfaces are assumed to host the temperature sensors for control purposes.

We now follow the discussion of Heng et al. [24] to present an overview of the furnace model. In this model, the geometric elements of the furnace are discretized into a set of surfaces, namely, burner, insulation and load/part (see Figure 2). The overall energy balance of a surface i can be written as:

$$Q_{net,i} = Q_{radiation,i} + Q_{convection,i} \quad i = 1, \dots, N_s, \tag{1}$$

where N_s is the total number of surfaces (that change as the parts are loaded on to and unloaded from the furnace). $Q_{net,i}$, $Q_{radiation,i}$ and $Q_{convection,i}$ are the total heat transfer, radiative heat transfer and convective heat transfer, respectively, to surface i. The following two relationships are used for radiation heat transfer term [38]:

$$Q_{radiation,i} = \frac{\sigma T_i^4 - J_i}{\frac{1-\epsilon_i}{\epsilon_i A_i}}, \tag{2}$$

$$Q_{radiation,i} = \sum_{j=1}^{N_s} \frac{J_i - J_j}{(A_i F_{i,j})^{-1}}, \tag{3}$$

where T_i is the temperature of surface i, J_i is the radiosity of surface i, A_i is the area of surface i, $F_{i,j}$ is the view factor from surface j to surface i, σ is the Stefan–Boltzmann constant and ϵ_i is the emissivity of surface i. Radiosity J_i is defined as the net amount of heat leaving surface i via radiation and view factor $F_{i,j}$ is defined as the proportion of the heat due to radiation that leaves surface j and strikes surface i.

For burner surfaces, Equation (2) is substituted into Equation (1) to obtain:

$$Q_{net,i} - h_{furn} A_i (T_i - T_w^\infty) = \frac{\sigma T_i^4 - J_i}{\frac{1-\epsilon_i}{\epsilon_i A_i}}, \tag{4}$$

where h_{furn} is the heat transfer coefficient of the furnace and T_w^∞ is the temperature of gas in control volume w. The term, $h_{furn} A_i (T_i - T_w^\infty)$, captures the convective heat transfer between a burner surface i and the gas in control volume w. The heat transfer coefficient of furnace h_{furn} is calculated from a Nusselt number correlation for forced convection in turbulent pipe flow [38]. For a burner surface, the heat duty $Q_{net,i}$ and surface temperature T_i are input variables determined by solving a system of nonlinear differential algebraic equations (DAE) that capture the dynamics of the burner system.

For insulation surfaces, Equation (3) is substituted into Equation (1) to obtain:

$$Q_{net,i} - h_{furn} A_i (T_i - T_w^\infty) = \sum_{j=1}^{N_s} \frac{J_i - J_j}{(A_i F_{i,j})^{-1}}. \tag{5}$$

Note that, for the insulation surfaces, $Q_{net,i}$ and T_i are output variables. The insulating wall is modeled as a solid material with uniform thickness. $Q_{net,i}$ is used as a Neumann type boundary condition at the inner surface to solve the one-dimensional unsteady state heat equation (parabolic partial differential equation) by an implicit Euler finite difference scheme:

$$Q_{net,i} = -k_{ins} A_i \frac{dT_i}{d\vec{x}_i}, \tag{6}$$

where T_i is the temperature of the inner surface of insulation i, A_i is the area of insulation surface i, k_{ins} is the thermal conductivity of insulating material (brick) and $\vec{x}_i$ is the inward unit normal vector to the insulating surface i. The other boundary condition is the balance between heat conduction through the wall to the outer surface and convective heat transfer between the outer surface and the ambient air, expressed as:

$$k_{ins} A_i \frac{dT_{ins,out,i}}{d\vec{x}_i} = -h_{air} A_i (T_{ins,out,i} - T_{air}), \tag{7}$$

where $T_{ins,out,i}$ is the temperature of the outer surface of insulation i and h_{air} and T_{air} are the convective heat transfer coefficient and the temperature, respectively, of the ambient air. The view factor matrix, $F_{i,j}$, is calculated using Hottel's crossed string method [39].

Part surfaces are treated similarly to insulating surfaces, except that the furnace heat transfer coefficient h_{furn} is replaced by the part heat transfer coefficient h_{part}:

$$Q_{net,i} - h_{part} A_i (T_i - T_w^\infty) = \sum_{j=1}^{N_s} \frac{J_i - J_j}{(A_i F_{i,j})^{-1}}. \tag{8}$$

The part heat transfer coefficient h_{part} is obtained from a Nusselt number correlation for external flow over a square cylinder [38]. A part is assumed to be a uniform solid. The two-dimensional unsteady state heat equation is solved by a second-order accurate Crank–Nicolson finite difference method to obtain the spatial temperature distribution of a part. The net heat flux, $Q_{net,i}$, of the four surfaces encompassing a part are used to define the boundary conditions:

$$Q_{net,i} = -k_{part} A_i \frac{dT_i}{d\vec{n}_i}, \tag{9}$$

where k_{part} is the thermal conductivity of part, T_i and A_i are the temperature and area of part surface i and $\vec{n}_i$ is the inward unit normal vector to part surface i.

At each time step, the model evaluates the energy usage of the furnace by solving Equations (4), (5) and (8) for the heat duties and the temperatures of insulation and part surfaces using a dual iterative numerical scheme explained in Heng et al. [24]. The computed heat duties are then used to define the boundary conditions to determine the part temperature distribution for all the parts processed in the furnace. Additionally, a linear control strategy is adopted, wherein a proportional-integral (PI) controller controls the temperature of each zone to a given set point by appropriately adjusting the mass flow rate of fuel to the burners of the respective zone. The temperature set points of the PI controllers directly affect the temperature distribution of the parts in the furnace and thus the energy consumption of the system.

3. Model Predictive Control Development

In our system, model predictive control is implemented as a two-layer hierarchical structure. The inner layer is the aforementioned regulatory control that manipulates the mass flow rate of fuel to control the zone temperatures. This multiple-input, single output system is then considered in the outer layer, whereby the model predictive controller adjusts the temperature set points of the regulatory layer to control the minimum temperatures of parts at exit. Note that the time interval for control action of model predictive control is larger than that of regulatory control, as will be explained below. The block diagram of the implementation of model predictive control in the heat treating furnace is shown in Figure 3.

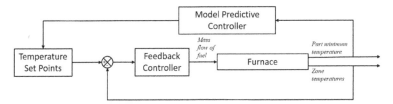

Figure 3. Block diagram for model predictive control implementation on the heat treating furnace. For the regulatory controller, zone temperatures are the controlled variables, and the fuel flow rates to the burners are the manipulated variables. In the case of the model predictive controller, the part minimum temperature at exit is the controlled variable and the zone temperature set points of the feedback controllers are the manipulated variables.

Let $T_{sp,\psi}(k)$, $\forall~\psi \in [1,4]$ be the temperature set point of zone ψ at sampling instant k, and $T_{min}(k)$ be the part minimum temperature at exit of the furnace. Let $T_{sp,ss,\psi}$, $\forall~\psi \in [1,4]$ be the steady-state temperature set point of zone ψ and $T_{min,ss}$ be the steady-state part minimum temperature. Additionally, let $y(k)$ be the deviation variable of part minimum temperature at time instant k, defined as: $y(k) \triangleq T_{min}(k) - T_{min,ss}$ and $u_{\psi}(k)$ be the deviation variable of zone ψ temperature set point at k, defined as: $u_{\psi}(k) \triangleq T_{sp,\psi}(k) - T_{sp,ss,\psi}$, $\forall~\psi \in [1,4]$.

3.1. Construction of MPC Step-Response Model

The step-response model of a stable process with four inputs and one output can be written as:

$$
\begin{aligned}
y(k+1) = y(0) &+ \sum_{i=1}^{N-1} S_{1,i}\Delta u_1(k-i+1) + S_{1,N}u_1(k-N+1) \\
&+ \sum_{i=1}^{N-1} S_{2,i}\Delta u_2(k-i+1) + S_{2,N}u_2(k-N+1) \\
&+ \sum_{i=1}^{N-1} S_{3,i}\Delta u_3(k-i+1) + S_{3,N}u_3(k-N+1) \\
&+ \sum_{i=1}^{N-1} S_{4,i}\Delta u_4(k-i+1) + S_{4,N}u_4(k-N+1),
\end{aligned}
\tag{10}
$$

where $y(k+1)$ is the output variable at the $k+1$ sampling instant, $y(0)$ is the initial value of the output variable, and $\Delta u_{\psi}(k-i+1)$ for $\psi \in [1,4]$ denotes the change in the input ψ from one sampling instant to the next: $\Delta u_{\psi}(k-i+1) = u_{\psi}(k-i+1) - u_{\psi}(k-i)$. Both u and y are deviation variables defined earlier in this paper. The model parameters are the N step-response coefficients, $S_{\psi,i}$ to $S_{\psi,N}$, for each input ψ, $\forall~\psi \in [1,4]$. Therefore, the total number of step-response coefficients are $4N$, where N is selected based on the process time constants.

The response of the output variable $y(k)$ for a step input ΔT_{step} of 20 K in each zone temperature set point is shown in Figure 4. The furnace takes about 25 h to process a batch of 40 parts with part residence time being roughly 4 h. The time difference between the exit of successive parts is the control time step Δt_{MPC}, which is around 32 min. The design variable N, which is the number of step-response coefficients for each control input was taken as 19. The step-response coefficients can be calculated from the step-response data [40]. It can be inferred from Figure 4 that the zone 3 temperature set point has the dominant effect on the part exit temperature, and zone 1 has the least.

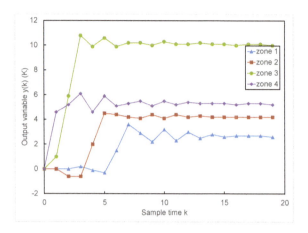

Figure 4. The response of the output variable $y(k)$ (deviation variable of part minimum temperature at exit) for a step input ΔT_{step} of 20 K for each of the zone temperature set points. k is the sampling time (around 32 min).

3.2. Optimization Formulation

Following the derivation of MPC from Seborg et al. [40], the vector of control actions $\Delta U(k)$ for next M sampling instants (the *control horizon*) is calculated at each sampling instant k by minimizing the objective function shown below, subject to the input, output and process constraints. The optimization problem formulation is:

$$
\begin{aligned}
\underset{\Delta U(k)}{\text{minimize}} \quad & J = \hat{E}(k+1)^T Q \hat{E}(k+1) + \Delta U(k)^T R \Delta U(k) \\
\text{subject to} \quad & u_\psi(k+j) \geq u_{min},\ \psi \in [1,4] \text{ and } j \in [0, k+M-1] \\
& u_\psi(k+j) \leq u_{max},\ \psi \in [1,4] \text{ and } j \in [0, k+M-1] \\
& u_\psi(k+j) - u_{\psi+1}(k+j) \leq u_{diff},\ \psi \in [1,3] \text{ and } j \in [0, k+M-1] \\
& \textit{System Model} \ (\text{Equation (10)}),
\end{aligned}
\tag{11}
$$

where Q and R are the output and input weighting matrices, respectively, that allow the output and input variables to be weighted according to their relative importance. $\hat{E}(k+1)$ is the *predicted error* vector of length P (*prediction horizon*) between the target and the model predictions (including bias correction) at $k+1$ sampling instant. u_{min} and u_{max} are the lower and upper bounds of the zone temperature set points u_ψ, $\psi \in [1,4]$ respectively, and u_{diff} is the minimum possible positive temperature difference between consecutive zones in the direction of part movement in order to prevent loss of heat from parts to the furnace while processing. Note that u_{min}, u_{max} and u_{diff} are deviation variables. Once $\Delta U(k)$ is computed, the furnace simulation proceeds for the control time interval Δt_{MPC}, during which the sample time is updated from k to $k+1$ and the entire procedure is repeated.

4. Furnace Simulation under Model Predictive Control

We simulate the furnace for a batch of forty parts using the same parameters and operating conditions as those in Heng et al. [24] under temperature feedback control. Additionally, instead of operating at a constant heuristic temperature set points suggested by the operators of the plant, the supervisory model predictive controller changes the zone temperature set points to control the part temperature at exit of the furnace (see Figure 3). The lower-layer temperature tracking controllers use the above trajectory as the control target. At the regulatory level, a linear control strategy is adopted wherein the fuel mass flow rate of a zone is manipulated to minimize the error between the measured value of the respective zone temperature and its set point determined by the MPC. All the burners in a zone are adjusted simultaneously, i.e., the furnace has only four control valves for regulatory control. In practice, a butterfly valve is used to manipulate the fuel flow rate. This valve does not close fully, i.e., the mass flow rate of fuel to the burners does not drop below a certain lower limit. In addition, when the valve is fully open, the upper bound of fuel flow rate is reached. Each control zone operates independently of other zones. However, adjustments to fuel flow rate of one zone will affect the temperatures of other zones due to long range radiation interactions. The furnace operating conditions and the parameters used in the simulation are listed in Table 1. The local control sampling time is 4 min for the 25 h furnace operation. The upper level model predictive controller functions at a much longer time interval, with a sampling time of 32.5 min, correlated with the rate of input/output of parts to the furnace. Within this time period, there are about eight control moves for the inner level temperature tracking controllers to bring the zone temperatures closer to the trajectory determined by the MPC. The setpoint for the MPC controller is the part minimum temperature at exit of the furnace. Note that non-contact ultrasonic measurements can be used to measure the value of minimum part temperature at the exit of the furnace [34–36]. However, non-contact measurements of the part temperatures, while the part is being processed inside the furnace, would be inaccurate due to the interference of the ultrasonic signal with the furnace walls. We use a constant target value of 1088 K, a temperature that ensures complete transformation from pearlite (mixture of ferrite and cementite) to austenite for a steel with 0.85% carbon content.

Table 1. List of parameters used in the heat treating furnace simulation.

Furnace Details	
Length of the furnace	16 m
Height of the furnace/length of the side walls	2 m
Length of each discretized furnace surface except the side walls	0.25 m
Total number of furnace surfaces	130
Length of a part	1.25 m
Ordinate of a part	0.75 m
Height of a part	0.5 m
Process Conditions	
Number of parts processed	40
Inlet temperature of parts	300 K
Inlet temperature of blanket gas	400 K
Number of points in the x-direction for Crank–Nicolson method	6
Number of points in the y-direction for Crank–Nicolson method	6
Total time of furnace operation	25 h
Feedback control time interval	4 min
Model Predictive Control Details	
Target minimum part temperature at exit	1088 K
Lower bound of temperature set points	900 K
Upper bound of temperature set points	1300 K
Temperature set point difference between subsequent zones	30 K
Model predictive control time interval	32.5 min

As a base case, we consider a simulation where only the regulatory control layer is employed, with the temperature set points, $T_{sp,ss,\psi} \ \forall \ \psi \in [1,4]$, taken to be same as the heuristic temperature set points of Heng et al. [24]: 1000 K, 1150 K, 1200 K, 1250 K for zones 1 to 4, respectively. Furnace operation under these set points results in an exit part minimum temperature at constant part input rate of 1126 K. This is the steady state value of the output variable $T_{min,ss}$.

Then, we consider the furnace operation under the proposed MPC scheme. Figure 5 illustrates the variation of output and input variables with respect to time of furnace operation in this case. The model predictive controller is turned on only after about 4 h of furnace operation when the first part exits the furnace, at which point the furnace begins to operate in a regime characterized by constant rates of input and output of parts. Note that the furnace is not completely full during the last 4 h of operation as well. The plots in the top row of Figure 5 show the zone temperature setpoints (as set by the MPC) and the zone temperatures maintained by the regulatory control layer at these setpoints within minimal variations (in general within 5 K). The step-response plot in Figure 4 indicates that zone 3 and zone 4 temperature set points have dominant effects on exit part temperature. This aspect is also reflected in Figure 5, where it can be seen that the set point variations are higher in zones 3 and 4 to meet the target. It is also observed that the zone temperatures exhibit periodic oscillations around their set points. This effect can be attributed to the periodic entry of cold parts into the furnace in zone 1 and periodic removal of hot parts from the furnace in zone 4. The thermal gradient is the maximum when a cold part enters the furnace. Therefore, the part acts as a heat sink resulting in a rapid decrease in the temperature of zone 1. This disturbance is propagated to other zones of the furnace due to long range zone-to-zone radiation interactions. Moreover, additional harmonics in the temperature variations are caused by parts exiting the furnace. The plots in the bottom row of Figure 5 show the corresponding changes in the manipulated variable, i.e., the mass flow rate of fuel to the burners. The dashed lines in these plots represent the lower and upper bounds of the fuel flow rate.

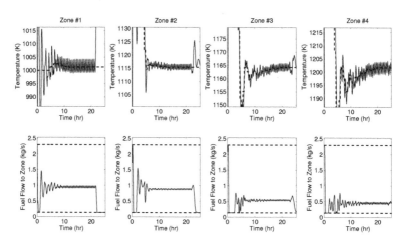

Figure 5. Zone temperatures and mass flow rate of fuel to the burners as a function of time for zones 1 to 4 (solid lines). The dashed lines in the plots of the **top** row indicate the zone temperatures setpoints and the dashed lines in the plots of **bottom** row indicate the upper and lower bounds of fuel flow rate to the burners.

Figure 6 shows the exit conditions of all the processed parts exiting the furnace sequentially. The quantities plotted are the total change in part enthalpy and its temperature distribution details. The red curve represents the average of part temperature distribution of all parts at exit, yellow curves are its standard deviation and the green curve represents the minimum of the temperature of all the parts at exit, which is the target for the model predictive controller. The temperature set point changes made by the model predictive controller drive the part minimum temperature from around 1125 K for the first part to the target value of 1088 K. The two-tiered control strategy keeps the exit conditions relatively stationary once part minimum temperature reaches its target.

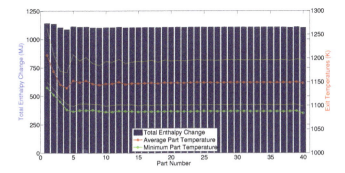

Figure 6. Part exit conditions of all 40 parts processed under model predictive control. The **yellow** lines indicate the standard deviation of the part exit temperatures from its mean. The model predictive controller is turned on immediately after the first part exits the furnace. The variations in the total enthalpy change of the first five parts are due to the model predictive controller varying the set points of the feedback controllers to drive the minimum part temperatures to their target. The model predictive controller keeps part exit temperatures relatively stationary once the target is reached.

Finally, we plot the heat input to the 20th part and the parameters of the part temperature distribution with respect to processing time in Figure 7. Note that the residence time of a part is roughly 4 h. Therefore, the time spent within the furnace also corresponds to the zone in which the part is getting heated. As expected, the amount of heat transferred to a part decreases with time since, as the part becomes hotter, the temperature difference between the part and the burners becomes smaller. The maximum temperature of a part is at its boundary/exterior. Intuitively, the minimum temperature occurs at the interior (which is heated only via conduction), and hence the corresponding temperature gradually raises to its target value as the parts exit the furnace.

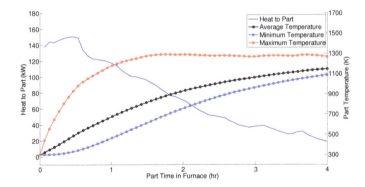

Figure 7. Heat input to the 20th part and its temperature distribution details as a function of its time (and thus position in the furnace) of processing.

5. Energy Efficiency Comparison

In Table 2, we compare the furnace operation under regulatory control with heuristic zone temperature set points reported in Heng et al. [24] and under model predictive control. In heuristic operation mode, the minimum temperature of parts at exit, 1126 K, is higher than the desired value of 1088 K. This overheating of parts results in the furnace consuming additional fuel. Furthermore, overheating of parts results in austenite grain size growth, which adversely affects the toughness of the quenched product. However, under the two layer hierarchical control operating mode, the part exit temperature is maintained at its desired value of 1088 K. The energy metric we compare is the total energy input to the furnace per part processed. We see that the furnace operation under model predictive control requires 5.3% less energy than that under a heuristic operation scenario. The energy efficiency gain is mainly due to the lowered fuel use. Moreover, additional gains can be a consequence of different nonlinear surface-to-surface radiation interactions due to changing zone temperature set points. The standard deviation of part temperatures is similar in both of these operation modes. This means that the model predictive controller has maintained the minimum temperature of part at exit at its desired value without compromising the uniformity in heating. The distribution of energy input to the furnace to parts, exhaust, nitrogen and insulation are comparable for both of these operation modes.

Table 2. Total energy input to the furnace and part temperature distribution at the exit of the furnace under heuristic operation mode of Heng et al. [24] and two-level hierarchical control. We also show the energy distribution of the heat input to process a batch of 40 parts.

Heat Sources and Sinks	Heuristic Set Points	Model Predictive Control
Total Energy Input per Part (GJ)	3.76 GJ	3.56 GJ
Part Minimum Temperature (K)	1126 K	1088 K
Temperature Standard Deviation (K)	52 K	46 K
Energy to Parts (%)	54.2%	54.3%
Energy Lost with the Exhaust (%)	42.7%	42.5%
Energy to Flowing Nitrogen (%)	0.5%	0.5%
Energy Through Insulation (%)	2.6%	2.7%

6. Conclusions

In this work, a two-dimensional radiation-based model of the furnace developed in Heng et al. [24] is used to simulate an industrial radiant tube roller hearth heat treating furnace for a batch of 40 parts. The model computes the energy consumption of the furnace by solving energy conservation equations and evaluates the temperature distribution of parts as a function of time and position within the furnace using the Crank–Nicolson finite difference method. For control purposes, the furnace is divided into four zones. The zone temperature is controlled by a proportional-integral controller that simultaneously manipulates the fuel to all the burners of the respective zones.

Model predictive control is then implemented as a supervisory control to limit the part temperature at exit by varying the zone temperature set points of the regulatoryl temperature tracking controller. We first develop a step-response model to predict the future evolution of the output variables. The time interval of the model predictive control is longer than that of the regulatory control. A comparison in terms of energy consumption is made between the furnace operation under the two-level hierarchical control and under constant heuristic temperature set points reported in Heng et al. [24]. We obtain an energy efficiency gain of 5.3% under model predictive control by preventing the parts from overheating.

Acknowledgments: The material presented in this paper is based upon work supported by the Department of Energy under Award Number DE-EE0005763.

Author Contributions: Michael Baldea and Thomas F. Edgar formulated and directed the research. Hari S. Ganesh implemented the model predictive control and performed the furnace simulations. Hari S. Ganesh, Thomas F. Edgar and Michael Baldea analyzed the results and wrote the paper.

Nomenclature

Symbol	Description	Units
A_i	Area of surface i	m^2
ϵ_i	Emissivity for surface i	-
$\hat{E}$	Predicted error vector between the target and the model predictions	K
$F_{i,j}$	View factor from surface i to j	-
h_{air}	Ambient air heat transfer coefficient	$W/(m^2 \cdot K)$
h_{furn}	Furnace heat transfer coefficient	$W/(m^2 \cdot K)$
h_{part}	Part heat transfer coefficient	$W/(m^2 \cdot K)$
J_i	Radiosity of surface i	W/m^2
k	Current sampling instant	-
k_{ins}	Thermal conductivity of insulating material	$W/(m \cdot K)$
k_{part}	Thermal conductivity of part	$W/(m \cdot K)$
M	Control horizon	-
$\vec{n}_i$	Inward unit normal to part surface i	m
N	Number of step response coefficients for each input	-
N_s	Total number of surfaces for furnace	-
P	Prediction horizon	-
Q	Output weighting matrix	-
$Q_{convection,i}$	Heat transfer through convection to surface i	W
$Q_{net,i}$	Total heat transfer to surface i	W
$Q_{radiation,i}$	Heat transfer through radiation to surface i	W
R	Input weighting matrix	-
$S_{\psi,i}$	Step response coefficient of ψth input at i^{th} time step	-
σ	Stefan–Boltzmann constant	$W/(m^2 \cdot K^4)$
ψ	Control zone index	-
T_{air}	Temperature of ambient air	K
T_i	Temperature of surface i	K
$T_{ins,out,i}$	Temperature of outer surface of insulating wall i	K
T_{min}	Part minimum temperature at exit of furnace	K
$T_{min,ss}$	Steady state part minimum temperature at exit of furnace	K
$T_{sp,\psi}$	Temperature set point of zone ψ	K
$T_{sp,\psi,ss}$	Steady state temperature set point of zone ψ	K
T_w^∞	Temperature of gas in control volume w	K
Δt_{MPC}	Control time interval of model predictive controller	s
u_{diff}	Enforced set points temperature difference	K
u_{max}	Upper bound of temperature set points	K
u_{min}	Lower bound of temperature set points	K
u_ψ	Deviation variable of temperature set point of zone ψ	K
ΔU	Vector of control actions	K
$\vec{x}_i$	Inward unit normal to insulating surface i	m
y	Deviation variable of part minimum temperature at furnace exit	K

References

1. Fawcett, A.A.; Iyer, G.C.; Clarke, L.E.; Edmonds, J.A.; Hultman, N.E.; McJeon, H.C.; Rogelj, J.; Schuler, R.; Alsalam, J.; Asrar, G.R.; et al. Can Paris pledges avert severe climate change? *Science* **2015**, *350*, 1168–1169.

2. Moya, J.A.; Pardo, N. The potential for improvements in energy efficiency and CO_2 emissions in the EU27 iron and steel industry under different payback periods. *J. Clean. Prod.* **2013**, *52*, 71–83.

3. Morrow, W.R.; Hasanbeigi, A.; Sathaye, J.; Xu, T. Assessment of energy efficiency improvement and CO_2 emission reduction potentials in India's cement and iron & steel industries. *J. Clean. Prod.* **2014**, *65*, 131–141.

4. Worrell, E.; Price, L.; Martin, N. Energy efficiency and carbon dioxide emissions reduction opportunities in the US iron and steel sector. *Energy* **2001**, *26*, 513–536.

5. Hasanbeigi, A.; Morrow, W.; Sathaye, J.; Masanet, E.; Xu, T. A bottom-up model to estimate the energy efficiency improvement and CO_2 emission reduction potentials in the Chinese iron and steel industry. *Energy* **2013**, *50*, 315–325.

6. Kintisch, E. After Paris: The rocky road ahead. *Science* **2015**, *350*, 1018–1019.

7. Hoffert, M.I.; Caldeira, K.; Benford, G.; Criswell, D.R.; Green, C.; Herzog, H.; Jain, A.K.; Kheshgi, H.S.; Lackner, K.S.; Lewis, J.S.; et al. Advanced technology paths to global climate stability: Energy for a greenhouse planet. *Science* **2002**, *298*, 981–987.

8. Carrasco, J.M.; Franquelo, L.G.; Bialasiewicz, J.T.; Galván, E.; Guisado, R.C.P.; Prats, M.Á.M.; León, J.I.; Moreno-Alfonso, N. Power-electronic systems for the grid integration of renewable energy sources: A survey. *IEEE Trans. Ind. Electr.* **2006**, *53*, 1002–1016.

9. Powell, K.M.; Edgar, T.F. Modeling and control of a solar thermal power plant with thermal energy storage. *Chem. Eng. Sci.* **2012**, *71*, 138–145.

10. Kim, J.S.; Edgar, T.F. Optimal scheduling of combined heat and power plants using mixed-integer nonlinear programming. *Energy* **2014**, *77*, 675–690.

11. Powell, K.M.; Hedengren, J.D.; Edgar, T.F. Dynamic optimization of a hybrid solar thermal and fossil fuel system. *Solar Energy* **2014**, *108*, 210–218.

12. Kapoor, K.; Powell, K.M.; Cole, W.J.; Kim, J.S.; Edgar, T.F. Improved large-scale process cooling operation through energy optimization. *Processes* **2013**, *1*, 312–329.

13. Demailly, D.; Quirion, P. European Emission Trading Scheme and competitiveness: A case study on the iron and steel industry. *Energy Econ.* **2008**, *30*, 2009–2027.

14. Pardo, N.; Moya, J.A. Prospective scenarios on energy efficiency and CO_2 emissions in the European iron & steel industry. *Energy* **2013**, *54*, 113–128.

15. World Steel Association (WSA). Steel Statistical Yearbook. 2014. Available online: http://www.worldsteel.org/statistics/ (accessed on 3 June 2016).

16. United States Energy Information Administration. Monthly Energy Review November 2014. Available online: http://www.eia.gov/totalenergy/data/monthly/ (accessed on 15 December 2014).

17. Stones, E.; Ferland, K.; Noack, M. *Industrial Efficiency*; Technical Report; NPC Global Oil and Gas Study, 2007. Available online: http://www.npc.org/study_topic_papers/5-dtg-industrial-efficiency.pdf (accessed on 8 December 2016)

18. Viswanathan, V.; Davies, R.; Holbery, J. *Opportunity Analysis for Recovering Energy from Industrial Waste Heat and Emissions*; Pacific Northwest National Laboratory: Richland, WA, USA, 2005.

19. Pellegrino, J.; Margolis, N.; Justiniano, M.; Miller, M.; Thekdi, A. *Energy Use, Loss and Opportunities Analysis*; Technical Report, Energetics, Incorporated, Columbia, USA and E3M, Incorporated: North Potomac, MD, USA, 2004.

20. Thekdi, A. *Energy Efficiency Improvement Opportunities in Process Heating for the Forging Industry*; E3M: Canton, NY, USA, 2010.

21. Richalet, J.; Rault, A.; Testud, J.; Papon, J. Model predictive heuristic control: Applications to industrial processes. *Automatica* **1978**, *14*, 413–428.

22. Cutler, C.R.; Ramaker, B.L. Dynamic matrix control? A computer control algorithm. *Jt. Autom. Control Conf.* **1980**, *17*, 72, doi:10.1109/JACC.1980.4232009

23. Qin, S.J.; Badgwell, T.A. A survey of industrial model predictive control technology. *Control Eng. Pract.* **2003**, *11*, 733–764.

24. Heng, V.R.; Ganesh, H.S.; Dulaney, A.R.; Kurzawski, A.; Baldea, M.; Ezekoye, O.A.; Edgar, T.F. Energy-Oriented Modeling and Optimization of a Heat Treating Furnace. *J. Dyn. Syst. Meas. Control* **2017**, in press.

25. Callister, W.D.; Rethwisch, D.G. *Materials Science and Engineering: An Introduction*; Wiley: New York, NY, USA; 2007; Volume 7.

26. Gupta, S.P. *Solid State Phase Transformations*; Allied Publishers: New Delhi, India, 2002.

27. Thelning, K.E. *Steel and Its Heat Treatment*; Butterworth-Heinemann: Oxford, UK, 2013.

28. Totten, G.E. *Steel Heat Treatment: Metallurgy and Technologies*; CRC Press: Boca Raton, FL, USA, 2006.

29. Grossmann, M.A.; Bain, E.C. *Principles of Heat Treatment*; American Society for Metals: Cleveland, OH, USA, 1964.
30. Roberts, C. Effect of carbon on the volume fractions and lattice parameters of retained austenite and martensite. *Trans. AIME* **1953**, *197*, 203–204.
31. Krauss, G. Principles of heat treatment of steel. *Am. Soc. Met.* **1980**, *1980*, 291.
32. Hollomon, J.; Jaffe, L. Time-temperature relations in tempering steel. *Trans. AIME* **1945**, *162*, 223–249.
33. Speich, G.; Leslie, W. Tempering of steel. *Metall. Trans.* **1972**, *3*, 1043–1054.
34. Kruger, S.E.; Damm, E.B. Monitoring austenite decomposition by ultrasonic velocity. *Mater. Sci. Eng. A* **2006**, *425*, 238–243.
35. Wadley, H.; Norton, S.; Mauer, F.; Droney, B.; Ash, E.; Sayers, C. Ultrasonic Measurement of Internal Temperature Distribution [and Discussion]. *Philos. Trans. R. Soc. Lond. A Math. Phys. Eng. Sci.* **1986**, *320*, 341–361.
36. Scruby, C.; Moss, B. Non-contact ultrasonic measurements on steel at elevated temperatures. *NDT & E Int.* **1993**, *26*, 177–188.
37. Holcroft, A. Conveyor Furnaces: Continuous Conveyor Thermal Treatment System. 2014. Available online: http://www.afc-holcroft.com/userfiles/file/pdf/ConveyorFurnace_Brochure.pdf (accessed on 9 April 2015).
38. Incropera, F. *Fundamentals of Heat and Mass Transfer*; John Wiley & Sons: Hoboken, NJ, USA, 2011.
39. Derrick, G. A three-dimensional analogue of the Hottel string construction for radiation transfer. *J. Mod. Opt.* **1985**, *32*, 39–60.
40. Seborg, D.E.; Mellichamp, D.A.; Edgar, T.F.; Doyle, F.J., III. *Process Dynamics and Control*; John Wiley & Sons: Hoboken, NJ, USA, 2010.

MDPI AG

St. Alban-Anlage 66

4052 Basel, Switzerland

Tel. +41 61 683 77 34

Fax +41 61 302 89 18

http://www.mdpi.com

Processes Editorial Office

E-mail: processes@mdpi.com

http://www.mdpi.com/journal/processes

www.ingramcontent.com/pod-product-compliance
Lightning Source LLC
LaVergne TN
LVHW071357070326
832902LV00028B/4633